The War of the Worlds
A Critical Text

Books by Leon Stover

Anthropology and History

The Cultural Ecology of Chinese Civilization
China: An Anthropological Perspective
(with Takeko K. Stover)
Stonehenge and the Origins of Western Culture

Fiction

Stonehenge (with Harry Harrison)
Stonehenge: Where Atlantis Died
(the above revised and expanded)
The Shaving of Karl Marx

Criticism

La Science Fiction Américaine
Robert A. Heinlein
Harry Harrison
The Prophetic Soul: A Reading of
H.G. Wells's "Things to Come" (McFarland, 1987)

The Annotated H.G. Wells

Volume 1. *The Time Machine* (McFarland, 1996)
Volume 2. *The Island of Doctor Moreau* (McFarland, 1996)
Volume 3. *The Invisible Man* (McFarland, 1998)
Volume 4. *The War of the Worlds* (McFarland, 2001)
Volume 5. *When the Sleeper Wakes* (McFarland, 2000)
Volume 6. *The First Men in the Moon* (McFarland, 1998)
Volume 7. *The Sea Lady* (McFarland, 2001)

Anthologies

Apeman, Spaceman (with Harry Harrison)
Above the Human Landscape (with Willis McNelly)

The War of the Worlds

A Critical Text of the 1898
London First Edition, with an
Introduction, Illustrations and Appendices

H. G. Wells

edited by
Leon Stover

THE ANNOTATED H.G. WELLS, 4

McFarland & Company, Inc., Publishers
Jefferson, North Carolina

Facing the title page: "The angel of socialism interrupts the capitalist vampire." Cartoon by Walter Crane, early 1890s.

Library of Congress Cataloguing-in-Publication Data

Wells, H.G. (Herbert George), 1866–1946.
   The war of the worlds : a critical text of the 1898 London
first edition, with an introduction, illustrations, and appendices /
H.G. Wells ; edited by Leon Stover.
      p.   cm. — (The annotated H.G. Wells ; 4)
   Includes bibliographical references and index.
   ISBN 0-7864-0780-8 (library binding : 50# alkaline paper) ∞
   1. Imaginary wars and battles — Fiction.   2. Space warfare —
Fiction.   I. Stover, Leon E.   II. Title.   [III. Series: Wells, H.G.
(Herbert George), 1866–1946. Annotated H.G. Wells ; 4.]
PR5774.W3   2001
823'.912 — dc21   00-68377

Manufactured in the United States of America

McFarland & Company, Inc., Publishers
   Box 611, Jefferson, North Carolina 28640
   www.mcfarlandpub.com

For
cousin Peggy,
with whom in our childhood
I first discussed the scientific romances

The past is merely a mistake.

    — Ernest Renan, *The Future of Science* (1891:461)

Destruam et aedificabo

    — Pierre-Joseph Proudhon (motto)

Preface

Some years ago, before I retired, my chairman in his annual faculty report to the dean listed me as an expert on H.G. Welles [*sic*]. It is a familiar mistake I have seen made by many a journliast and not a few experts on popular culture. This conflates the author of *The War of the Worlds* with Orson Welles who produced "Invasion from Mars," the legendary CBS radio broadcast based on the novel, which aired on 30 October 1938. The memorable panic spooking the nation with that Halloween show has forever after melded Wells with Welles (see text of the radio play in Koch 1970 and in Welles 1949).

Worse, the panic broadcast reduced its source, for one influential critic, to the basest sort of pulp magazine science fiction: "the Martians and their strange irresistible weapons ... are used to arouse wonder, terror, and excitement, rather than for any allegorical or satirical end" (Amis 1961:39). The novel, however, is no empty fantasy. More sophisticated critics take it as an attack on racism and imperialism.

But Wells did not waste his art on prefiguring the banalities of today's political correctness. The two cosmic worlds at war are those "two fundamental opposites in human affairs as we know them — creation and tradition ... a conflict between past claims and future achievement" (1932:20f). His progressive Martians are his allies in "The War with Tradition" (1931: chapter 11, title). With Renan (see my epigraph), he sees the past as a mistake to be rectified by war and revolution; with Proudhon he can say, "I will destroy and rebuild."

Leon Stover, Ph.D., Litt.D.
Professor of Anthropology Emeritus
Illinois Institute of Technology

Chicago, Summer 2000

Table of Contents

Introduction

1. The Text

As usual, Wells would serialize his early novels and then revise them for book publication. *The War of the Worlds* (1898; hereafter *Worlds*) first appeared in *Pearson's Magazine*, April–December 1897 (photo-reprint in Russell 1978:1–103). The same text and layout appeared the same months in *The Cosmopolitan.*

The serialization lacked both the book's key chapter, "The Man on Putney Hill" (a subject of intense interest to be developed in textual note 158), and its Epilogue. The book then came out in both London (1898) and New York (1898a), with the latter unaccountably missing the Epilogue added to the former (Lake 1988:10). Thereafter the text was revised for the authorized version in the Atlantic Edition (1926–1927, vol. 3), only to be passed through the Essex Edition (1926–1927, vol. 13) and then further fiddled with when collected in *The Scientific Romances* (1933a).

Hughes (1962:49–85) has analyzed all the extensive verbal refinements done for the authorized Atlantic Edition and finds them making for greater precision and "scientific" exactitude. Still I prefer the more youthful poetic vigor of the original, and so use the London first edition as my copy text. Besides, it is fixed prejudice to mistrust revisions done by a different man 26 years older at age 58.

However, I urge that students of *Worlds* consult Hughes and Geduld (1993), whose outstanding critical edition based on the Atlantic text and its variants, is nothing if not an essential companion to mine.* Among the many

---

*A critical edition, *sensu stricto*, is one in which the editor redacts all variants of a given text to create a synthetic text he believes to be definitive; and which is accompanied by a scholarly introduction, textual notes, and relevant appendices. In the present series, the term is used more liberally. My critical apparatus is the same, but I do not manufacture a text, believing that the first editions, with typos corrected, are the definitive ones. It was these, after all, that made Wells's reputation as the world's most famous author.

1

virtues of its apparatus is an exhaustive glossary of place names, which are exceedingly numerous. Geography in the novel serves to establish for contemporary readers an overpowering sense of photojournalistic immediacy — it is *their* London and suburbs being devastated by the Martians — a sense impossible to recapture. I therefore in my commentaries tend to slight place names except when they have some particular interpretive significance (but I do provide in fig. 11 of the plates a map of the narrator's itinerary). Hughes and Geduld also offer a veritable encyclopedia of all important commentaries on *Worlds* ever made, citing critics I often disagree with (but never when they offer complementary readings at, say, the level of biographical criticism*). To contest the contestable at every turn would retard forward movement in the on-going critical debate, open-ended as it has to be given the essential ambiguities of genuine art.† So it is best to make uncluttered way for those fresh insights into Wellsian ideas already identified in previous volumes with "Stoverism" (Sherborne 1996; Parrinder 1998): a doctrine that reverses polarity in the general scheme of interpretation from humanistic to antihumanistic, liberal to illiberal.

As it happens, *Worlds* is the one scientific romance to have a sequel. It is *When the Sleeper Wakes* (1899), hereafter *Sleeper*, whose future, set in 2100, follows upon the Martian invasion about a century earlier. My critical edition (Stover 1999) presents that future as utopian, not dystopian as invariably taken in established opinion.‡ It were tedious, then, to rehash what is argued there against every inherited cliché. The most profitable use to which the present edition of *Worlds* may be put is to integrate it with the Hughes and Geduld edition and with the Stover edition of *Sleeper*.

I also highly recommend the York Notes on *Worlds* done by Parrinder (1981), the British version of the American Cliffs Notes.

*A number of reviewers faulted my earlier volumes for *not* reading the author's life into his work, blaming this lack on ignorance. Biographical criticism applied to the scientific romances is a standard fixture I studiously avoid, in the belief that the immortality of these classics depends not in the least on knowledge of their personal allusions. For example, I see no reason to dwell on Wells's dyspepsia as the focus of Martian biology absent digestive organs when there are more cosmic issues at stake.

†No conclusion can be final because Wells in his Victorian youth was just as much the artist as the didact. This exquisite balance tilted in later novels when he became increasingly preachy. With *Anticipations* (1901) he turned more and more to social prophecy, expressly vatic in both his fiction and nonfiction. The latter, at least, has the virtue of allowing us to recover the didactic elements dissolved in the wonderful fabulation of the early scientific romances. Near the end of his life he said, "My rôle has always been that of a propagandist, direct or indirect, of world socialism" (1944:56). *My* role is to make the indirect direct, while retaining appreciation for Wells's artistic facility to novelize his ideas. This includes a talent for subtle characterization widely overlooked.

‡ Although *Worlds* is number 4 in the seven-volume series on the scientific romances, it was undertaken after doing *Sleeper* (number 5). It therefore looked back on that volume as it was prepared.

Thereby some advance is possible in the on-going study of *Worlds* as a monumental classic of *Weltliteratur*. Here it is appraised as a prophecy of startling originality foreseeing the coming of totalitarianism in the 20th century. In retrospect we may see its evil portended by the Martians, but who are by no means monstrous in the eyes of their creator. They are rather agents of his "Religion of Progress" (1927:32) in his vindictive "War with Tradition."

I should like to see Wells credited for the great artist and propagandist he is, while yet recognizing him to be a great errorist. His influential view of progress is now largely repudiated by the collapse of the Soviet Union in 1991. All the same, his is a monument to a powerful concept in the history of ideas that cannot be dismissed, in reckoning the most horrible of centuries. Progress for Wells meant a radical "ethical reconstruction" (1901:311) that shall displace "Individualistic Humanitarianism" (1904:25), otherwise "individualistic liberalism" (1933:82), with "inhuman humanitarianism." It is a policy of "cruel rationality" (345), "pitilessly benevolent" (346) in its mission to reform human nature. It means to burn out man's "animal individualism" (334), to war upon his "natural animal-like acceptance of the established thing" (270), and so to have "socialized [him] against his natural disposition" (428). The end product is "the coming man" (426), not unlike New Soviet Man, who shall find egoless happiness in his duty to the collective well-being of a world state embracing the entire species. In *The Outline of History* (1920:Chapter XLI) that organic world-state is the Modern State belonging to "the next stage of history."* Its "aggressive order of religiously devoted men and women [the Modern State Society not unlike the Communist Party] will ... impose a new pattern of living upon our race" (1933:431): a new moral world absent private property and competitive capitalism: a Martianized world.

2. The Frontispiece

Walter Crane's cartoon (*ca.* 1892) facing the title page is captioned, "The angel of socialism interrupts the capitalist vampire feeding on labour." The point is to illustrate how Wells, quite typically, would take a statement by somebody else and then respond with his opposite idea (see Reed 1979).

The picture of capital as a vampire comes directly from Karl Marx. In *Das Kapital* (1887, first English translation) he wrote, "Capital is dead labour

---

*Elsewhere it is the New Republic (1901, 1904), Modern Utopia (1905), or else the Great State (1912). But the Modern State is most often reiterated (1933, 1936a, 1939 and other places).

that, vampire-like, only lives by sucking living labour, and lives the more, the more labour it sucks." He then compares the English factory system to the lord-peasant relationship typified by that "Wallachian Boyard," Vlad Dracula (in Frayling 1991:84). This is the first metaphorical reference to Dracula in the English language (he who also inspired the Bram Stoker novel *Dracula* of 1897); hence the memorable image in leftist locution of capitalists as "blood suckers."

Walter Crane (*d.* 1915) devoted his art to the Socialist League founded by William Morris in 1884, and his cartoons appeared in Morris's periodical, *Commonweal: A Journal of Revolutionary Socialism*. It was in this journal that Morris published *News from Nowhere* (1890), his utopian novel dramatizing Marx's communitarian shape of things to come, "when mastery has changed into fellowship" (Chapter 18). He wrote it in response to *Looking Backward* (1888) by the American Edward Bellamy. This novelizes his utopia of industrial mastery, which incited an antilaborite movement known as Bellamyism (see Lipow 1982). Bellamyism, however, turns out to be a restatement of a doctrine originated by the French savant, Henri Saint-Simon (*d.* 1825). One of his disciples actually coined the term *socialisme* for what his master had called *industrialisme*. Let us call it Old Testament socialism. Marx in response redefined the evocative term *socialismus* (in German) to mean a fellowship of communards who shall in time replace the hierophants of industrial society itself: New Testament socialism (Stover 1992).

If Wells gathered his anti–Marxist ammunition from Saint-Simonian doctrine, which originally had no rival socialism to attack, Marx made himself that rival by first turning against same. The history of socialism is replete with opposite ideas reacting to each other in a battlefield of doctrinal warfare, carried over into the literary fights of utopian literature — which extended to planet Mars itself (see section 4 of this Introduction). In that game Wells excelled, and today *Worlds* can be read for its majestic artistry without reference to forgotten disputes. But it will be helpful to review some of them.

To start with: William Morris, a name still remembered. In 1884 he had been cofounder of the Social Democratic Federation (SDF), one of the many Marxist-inspired SD parties throughout western and eastern Europe and in Russia (Salvadori 1975:8). But Morris deemed SDF not radical enough, and so started up his own Socialist League with the help of Eleanor Marx, the bearded guru's daughter. The same year saw the founding of the counter–Marxist Fabian Society, which later became a think tank for the newly emergent Labour Party (1893, with its first MPs by 1900). But the Fabians were far from acting as agents for the sectarian interests of the working class; they rather worked for what became a bureaucratic welfare state given to the taming and subordination of labor. In this they were stimulated by Edward Bellamy's *Look-*

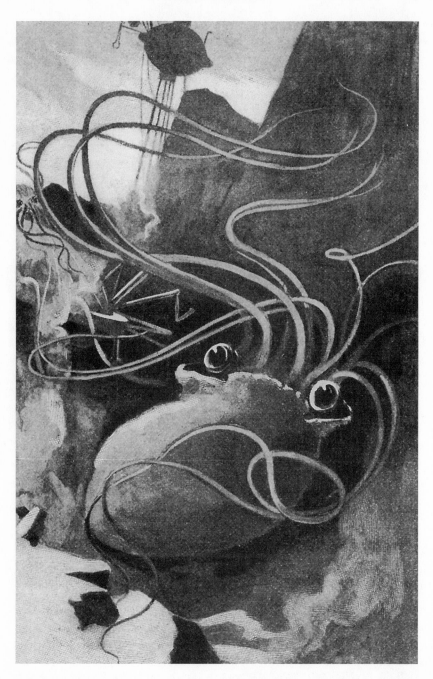

Figure 1. A Martian fallen from its fighting machine. In the 1897 serialized version of *Worlds.*

ing Backward (1888), a novel that attacked the American labor movement (Lipow 1982:15). The Fabian Society's position was nowhere better expressed than in a hostile review of *News from Nowhere* (1890), itself a rebuttal by Morris of Bellamy. Morris's novel gave socialism a bad name with its false utopian benefits of proletarian revolution (see in Faulkner 1973:315–317, item 55).

The year 1884 also saw Wells entering the Normal School of Science, where he first encountered Marxism, only to conclude that his red-tie wearing fellow students were mistaken (Stover 1992:30, 33 *n*29). Above all, that year marked the beginning of the age of ideology, a new departure in world history, with the buzzword socialism its contested field.

Wells very early caught the drift, and had the astounding insight to name ideology for what it is, a "political religion" (1917:96). His own pre–Marxist variety he formulated so soon as he took the negative in a college debate on "Democratic Socialism" (1886). Thereafter he established himself as a world-class fighter in the partisan war of words over the meaning of socialism.

To further explain Wells's position, it must be remembered that Bellamy, his forerunner, was aware of the SD parties formed in response to Marx's *Communist Manifesto* (1848), as of course the Moses of Old Testament socialism himself was not. Saint-Simon wrote before the advent of the labor movement; his *industrialisme* was a doctrinalization of industrial capitalism. It is this doctrine that the patriarch of New Testament socialism repudiated, when Marx captured the term *socialisme* for his anticapitalist "spector" about to haunt Europe. Himself responding to that communist spector in America, Bellamy redefined Saint-Simonism as an anti–working-class collectivist ideology. If I tag Wells as an allegiant of Old Testament socialism, it is by virtue of his *post hoc* use (like Bellamy) of Saint-Simon as a weapon against Marx: something unforeseen by the master himself. In his day there was not yet any labor movement.

My English friends in the H.G. Wells Society often chide me at their London meetings for claiming that it was a Saint-Simonian who originated the term socialism. They credit it to Robert Owen, their favorite socialist after Wells, attracted as they are to the magnetic word cooperation. I am told that Owen coined the term socialism, for the spirit of Wellsism, in his *Co-Operative Magazine* in 1827. But the word there is rather *socialist*, with no -ism attached, a word kicking around in the language from 1833 for a believer in the community of goods (*Oxford English Dictionary*), not unlike those portrayed in the Acts of the Apostles. It was only after one H. Joncièrs, the disciple of Saint-Simon who doctrinalized socialism as a synonym for his master's *industrialisme* that the -ism gained currency: this in the Saint-Simonian journal *Le Globe* for 2 February 1832 (Hayek 1979:282 *n*54). Owen did not adopt the -ism until ten years later in *The Book of the New Moral World*

(1842). But, like Marx's communes, his cooperatives are based on a weak principle of organization that for Wells is lacking in scientific design; for him, *cooperation* is the very opposite of *coordination*, the real thing in organizational planning. See Wells 1904a on this verbal distinction, reprinted as Appendix II in Stover 1998b, which illuminates what is idealized in *The First Men in the Moon.* Here the cerebral Grand Lunar *coordinates* the function of every Selenite subserving his purposive integration. He fantastically glorifies the organicist principle of Saint-Simon's authoritarian socialism, with its coercive division of labor managed by a single command-and-control brain center. Again, *cooperation* is far too voluntary and self-serving to provide socialism a meaningful basis. It is little removed from the spontaneous social order created by a democratic, free market economy, scorned by Wells as but "the chance occasional co-operations of self-indulgent men" (1905:172). His "economic world republic" (1926:770) will not come about of itself, not without a Grand Earthly the likes of Oswald Cabal, President of the World Council of Direction in *Things to Come*, he who sees to the "co-ordinating of the species in a common general end" (1908c:131).

Owen had said in his 1827 article that his cooperative principle would "merge all individualism in the social," and would do so by abolishing "useless private property." The result would be "new habits and new feelings" in a new moral world, exactly the Marxist notion. Saint-Simon believed in the same moral sacrifice of *la personalité* (= individualism) to *socialisme* (Hayek 1979:282 *n*54), but with this difference. For him the abolition of private property meant the surrender of ownership to governmental administration and its guiding principle: *"respect for production and producers* is infinitely more fruitful than respect for property and property owners" (in Taylor 1975:167). Lenin enacted this prescription on deceptive Marxist grounds when in 1918 he had all property deeds destroyed (see document 31 in Pipes 1996:60f). There can be little doubt that Saint-Simonian theory influenced Lenin, as it did Mussolini and Hitler (Radel 1975). In the latter two cases, however, private property was not so much confiscated as directed and controlled by the State. These two options opened up by Saint-Simon are respectively now deemed leftist (communism) and rightist (fascism), but actually both belong to the socialist left. The left/right thing is an artifact of early European parliaments, following the French Revolution, in which radicals sat to the left of the president and their opponents to the right. The basic contest thereafter was between attacks on private property and its defense (Bethell 1988). Because the fascists in Fascist Italy and Nazi Germany married big business with government they were tagged as right-wing reactionaries (the term fascism in lower case is generic, applied to a wide range of authoritarian regimes at the time; Fascism in upper case is Mussolini's coinage as

Figure 2. John Cabal's octopus head gas helmet. From Stover 1987: plate 18.

is the word totalitarian), whereas Lenin's outright confiscation was tagged left-wing for the purity of his assault on property. But it is a difference without much of a distinction. As Schoenbaum (1980) points out, in Hitler's Germany there was in fact no private enterprise or private initiative, only the vestigial language and labels of a free economic system to differentiate fascism from the Russian system.

Curiously, the late Soviet Union, despite its Marxist cover story, is now so generally assumed to have been no less totalitarian than the fascist regimes (Gleason 1995)* that Marxism itself is mistakenly taken as a statist credo. "The dictatorship of the proletariat [Marx] envisioned implies some kind of collective self-management, not bureaucratic power at all" (Kornai 1993:55 *n*10). Wells had this correct perception of New Testament socialism in mind when he opposed its Russian perversion with his Old Testament critique, in which a bureaucratic class of "expert officials" comprising "a new class" is "*the* power of the future" (1911:213). That new class of rulers who manage public property for the collective good is featured in *Sleeper*: a remarkable anticipation of the communist system as analyzed by Milovan Djilas in his classic study, *The New Class* (1957) — whose title echoes Wells's naming of it half a century earlier.

During his college days at the Normal School of Science (1884–1887), Wells had attended political debates in Morris's home; finding them wanting, he went over to hear those conducted by the Fabian Society, which he joined 1903–1908 before rejecting its gradualist reforms within the existing order as not radical enough (Cole 1961:117–124). His guide on these political tours was Cosmo Rowe, a friend and room-renting neighbor who became one of his earliest illustrators (Eshleman 1940:331–335). At the time Rowe ran the bookstall in Morris's establishment, decorated with Walter Crane posters. These and his work in *Commonweal* he called "cartoons for the cause" (*Encyclopædia Britannica*, 11th edition, 7:367).

As a piece of socialist art for the wrong cause, Wells could not have missed the cartoon reproduced in my frontispiece, especially since it so picturesquely concentrates the essence of Marxist doctrine he came to loathe. I therefore take it as a stimulus prompting *Worlds*, insofar as the novel's thesis is just the reverse: The true vampire is labor bleeding capital to death with its demands, and the avenging angel is the *other* socialism. Indeed, the Martians

---

*By the time of the Anti-Fascist Popular Front from about 1935, promoted by Soviet Russia in seeking western allies against Hitler, Wells dropped his likening of the Nazi Party and the Communist Party as both equally good exemplars of a needed corrective to the "under-governed and under-organized" democracies (1927:26). By then he adopted "totalitarianism" as a term of opprobrium applying only to fascist regimes (1939b:Chapter 16), which helped to cloud the distinction still unmarked in left-wing rhetoric. No amount of comparativist scholarship, like Gleason's (1995), has been able to fully discredit the Popular Front's formula: not to be anti-anticommunist is to be a wicked fascist. It is Wells's later stance on this issue that identifies him for the critics as a like-minded liberal and saves him from his earlier illiberalism. His Martians, therefore, cannot be anticipatory agents of totalitarian or collectivist things to come, right or left; they must rather be monsters indicting the evils of British colonialism and such like iniquities of capitalistic imperialism.

who represent that celestial savior are themselves vampires, but the blood they suck is drained from the traditional body politic (see Appendix II in the present work).

The scientific romances covered in the present series have been aptly described as "ideological fables" (Parrinder 1977:18). Wells himself in his autobiography said they "discuss sociology in fable," making "a general criticism of the socialism of the opening century," and so "novelize my reactions to the assumptions and limitations of the Socialist [=labor] movement" (1934:558). "Marxist pretences and sentimentalities" were his avowed target, to which he opposed "my conception of a scientifically organized class-less society" (69). *Contra* Marx, he proposes "not to exalt the labour class but to abolish it" (1928:78), that is, to abolish trade unions because they represent a sectarian class interest that goes against organic state unity. The benefit is a docile, strike-free, subjected labor force, one that Lenin appreciated in stamping out unionism in his first act as head of state, a model for the fascist regimes (facing the same problem) that followed in Italy and Germany.

But how can this represent a "class-less society," if the odious Marx proposed same? The difference is, in Saint-Simon's technocratic order, all members of society are equally functional industrial workers (*industriels*) contributing to production, be they worker workers or brain workers in planning and management. All are unified in that collective purpose by means of industry's organizational principle: a scientific division of labor under the leadership of a center — the very opposite of Marx's egalitarian principle, the tearing down of just such a division of labor between the physical and the mental. Or as Wells has it, "civilization is based on the organized subdivision of labour" (1904:109).

That Wells held this other view of classlessness in projecting his own utopian future is incontestable; he acknowledges Auguste Comte (*d.* 1857), Saint-Simon's number one disciple and synthesizer of the master's voluminous work, as having the "sort of priority he had in sketching the modern outlook" (1934:562).* "Sort of" is telling, since he knew only too well how useful was the master's doctrine in contesting thoroughly unmodern Marx;

*The basic source Wells consulted must be Comte (1877), translated from the French. Selected translations of Saint-Simon himself are in Ionescue (1976) and Taylor (1975). But it would be surprising if Wells, who knew French like a second language (1926a:20), did not look into some of these original texts during his voracious library readings in college days (Smith 1986:39–42). He also knew enough German for the study of scientific literature (essential in those days for anybody seeking a career in science, including biology, when the Germans dominated all fields), which must account for his familiarity with *Auf zwei Planeten* by Kurd Lasswitz (1897) (see textual note 158). Besides, Wells as a competitive scientific romancer kept up to date with all rivals in this field, including the still-living Jules Verne.

and so he did not grudge to recycle it in the name of "Wellsism" (1984:172). In Bellamy's case, the -ism attached to his name was not self-applied.

At all events, the Martians are nothing if not a pure embodiment of Wellsism, in which, after Saint-Simon, "politics is the *science of production*" (in Taylor 1975:168). In this inhumane managerial theory what is most important is "the proper allocation of service duties, not the rights of man" (Manuel 1956:320). This is the "ethical reconstruction" (1901:311) of Wells's New Republic, in which "social efficiency" (34) is the measure of the new division-of-labor morality.

In time, Wells came to prefer the term collectivism over socialism for this idea (1921:186). He certainly was in tune with a shifting vocabulary that now embraced all three of the major totalitarian movements in Russia, Italy, and Germany. William Henry Chamberlin saw all of them converging in his comparative analysis, *Collectivism: A False Utopia* (1936). Until then, "collectivism" had been used in France from 1869 as a term opposing "state socialism" (Williams 1963:69); it served as a handy synonym for Marxian communalism, reacting to Saint-Simonism. Only collectivism was the true blue socialism. Somehow, the term got turned around, as indicated in Chamberlin's 1936 title. The drift is traced in Gray (1946:495f), in which the organized (collective) production of wealth is now opposed to its egalitarian (collective) distribution. By then, state socialism was operational in the big-three totalitarian regimes, and Hayek (1935) could edit a book titled *Collectivist Economic Planning*, which made democratic collectivism seem obsolete and distinctly unmodern to its statist enemies. Wells ran with the new terminology until the advent of the Popular Front, when for obvious reasons he took fascism out of the picture. All the same, his Martians are a true prophecy of the entire collectivist era.

Returning now to Walter Crane's cartoon, the Martians (in Wells's reversal) represent not alone the angel of Socialism but also the Capitalist vampire the angel saves labor from. This logic is altogether clear when its terms are looked at in a Wellsian light. There are (1) two socialisms, (2) two capitalisms, and (3) two concepts of labor. First of all, at (1), democratic socialism plays against authoritarian socialism; Marxism and Saint-Simonism are incompatible with state capitalism (= state socialism = Saint Simonian technocracy, Wellsism, Bellamyism, etc.). In the cartoon, the vampire's head says Capitalism, and its two supportive wings read Religious Hypocrisy and Party Politics. There is none of that nonsense in Wells's "autocratic state capitalism" (1931:60), a command economy that is wholly rational: no churches and no voting booths. Finally, at (3), labor (the prostrate workingman the vampire feeds upon) may be seen as a victim in a different way. Under democratic capitalism, labor is at a disadvantage, as a voting block, given the power of private-profit capitalism to manipulate religious and democratic institutions in its favor — a precarious minority that will be put in its place by a proletarian majority come the angelic advent of laborite socialism. For Wells, however, this would only let loose "a chaotic labour communism" (1933:124). For the salvation of the State, and for the saving of labor from suicidal Marxism, the only solution is to "abolish" the labor class itself (1928:78). As a divisive and sectarian class interest within the body politic, it must be relegated to its place in the organic unity of all *industriels* under state capitalism: scientific planners and industrial managers at the top, manual workers at the bottom: a just hierarchy in which all will be happy to contribute their share to the glories of collectivist production. Then "Humanity will be one labour organisation and the only capitalist in the world" (letter of 1921 in West 1930:216).

This is quite in accord with Comtian doctrine (after Saint-Simon), which in its new division-of-labor ethic "throughout substitutes duties for rights" (Comte 1877:326). But not all duties are equal, as Wells acknowledges. Essential to business as to big-business government "is an intricate system of specialization and subordination of functions and great freedom of action for the executives" (1927:19). Yet all are equal, in his sophistry, because all are equally functional cogs in "a single world economic machine" (1931a: 373), Saint-Simon's World Republic of United Interests. Purposeful integration makes equal partners of every unequal part, high and low: "a scientifically organized class-less society" (1934:69): the perfect "machine age ideology" (Jordan 1994:title). It was the genius of Saint-Simon to conceive it at the very outset of the industrial revolution, even as the French Revolution proclaimed egalitarian rights. In time, the two revolutions conflated in fascism and communism, collectivist doctrines that could stamp out the rights of labor in the name of—*egalité*.

In light of these twentieth-century developments, Wells's Martianized reversal of Walter Crane's paradigm is all the more prophetic. To summarize:

	Walter Crane	**Opposite Idea**
Angel	class-war socialism	state capitalism
Vampire	private-profit capitalism	
Labor	saved by angel's trumpet-call to unionize	absorbed into body politic

The vampire state is now the avenging angel, serving industrial society from self-destruction by the divisive labor movement.

Figure 3. Cabal's helmet with visor down. From Stover 1987: plate 19.

3. Benevolent Catastrophe

While the Martian invasion is indeed catastrophic, it is all to the good as shock therapy. The narrator in the Epilogue concludes, "it has done much to promote the conception of the commonweal of mankind." Likewise in

"The Star" (1897, in 1927a:716–729), the devastating effects of a passing comet are responsible for a "new brotherhood that grew presently among men" (728). Martian astronomers, however, observe that the fiery missile merely caused some shrinkage of the polar ice caps. "Which only shows how small the vastest of human catastrophes may seem, at a distance of a few million miles" (729).

The element of Martian detachment is a key metaphor, as in the opening paragraph of *Worlds*, in which the Martians are said to have "intellects vast and cool and unsympathetic." Theirs is Wells's detachment in calculating the necessary human costs of his destruction/reconstruction dialectic, encapsulated in the ominous title of his big socialist manifesto, *New Worlds for Old* (1980). As a "World Revolutionary Socialist" (1940:31), nothing will do for him but "a vast tragic clearance for a new order" (25).

In the usual scenario of war and revolution leading on to the Wellsian utopia (1905, 1914a, 1923), a shattering world conflict, mooted in *Anticipations* (1901), is the inevitable prelude to rebuilding. From the perspective of "our present world state," the narrator of *The War in the Air* (1908b:345) says this outcome was not possible "until every organized government was as shattered and broken as a heap of china beaten with a stick" (355). The *summa* of Wells's "dialectic of human destiny" (1933:20) is his film *Things to Come* (1936), done at age 70. Its opening scenes are crucial to appreciating the famous first paragraph in *Worlds* (see textual note 3).

Its film treatment, *Whither Mankind?* (1934),* offers a template in

---

*This title Wells intended for the film until its producer, Alexander Korda, changed it to *Things to Come*. The original title copies, without the interrogative, *Whither Mankind* (1929) by the American historian Charles Beard, who pondered the irrelevance of democratic values in a technocratic future. Writing as he did at the high point of a short-lived (1911–1939) movement for social engineering, Beard thought its triumph immanent (see Jordan 1994:217).

In Wells's *Whither Mankind?* the question mark is addressed by John Cabal in a speech to an assembly of "rebel savants," the partymen of the Modern State Revolution.

> We have let ancient and outworn traditions, old hates and ape-like cunning, wreck the world.
>   It has been *our* fault. We have not *insisted* that scientific methods could be applied to all human relations, to law and government — as well as to material things....
>   But now we insist —
>   Let our watchwords be:
>   RESEARCH, INVENTION, WORLD PLANNING — AND SCIENTIFIC CONTROL.
>   Freedom from the dead past....
>   Let the Makers rule! Let us who know, take power!
>   [1934:149f]

which the Martian invasion may be fitted. Here Wells divides the story line into four main parts, with musical signatures as follows:

1. Present Conditions (*Pastoral*)
2. The World Smashed (*Marche Funèbre*)
3. Reconstruction — a rush series
4. The world in 2054 [2036 in the release script of 1936]
    (*Chorale*)

In *Worlds*, the pastoral conditions of merrie olde England prevail, with no sense of the impending catastrophe when Martians fall out of the sky. Then comes "the cleansing disillusionment" (1933:214). And there the novel ends, with a funeral march for the traditional order, now shaken to its foundations. No reconstruction and no utopian *Chorale* is indicated. That follows in *Sleeper*.

The future historian in *The Shape of Things to Come*, from which the film derives, says "The millennium arrived in anything but millennial fashion" (1933:344)— utopia arrives by means far from utopian. The problem is, how to get from war in *Worlds* to revolution in *Sleeper*, a gap of some 200 years.

This after a prolonged World War II reduces the combatant nation-states to still-fighting ministates, when John Cabal emerges as the heroic Air Dictator who imposes a new world order under his *pax aeronautica*. His Airmen are "men of steel, men of knowledge, men of power" (*ibid.*:140), fully capable of rectifying the mistakes and crimes of history committed up until their advent saves mankind from its benighted past. Cabal vows to rededicate "all those giant possibilities of science that have been squandered hitherto upon war and senseless competition" (film shot 725 in 1936).

Not that Beard's *Whither Mankind* suggested scientific government to Wells, only that its title resonated with his prophetic vision from *Anticipations* (1901) onwards. Beard's influential work lay behind the promotion of that apotheosis of the technocratic movement, the 1933 Chicago World's Fair, whose motto was, "Science Finds — Industry Applies — Man Conforms" (Jordan 1944:283). Similarly, the official guidebook of the 1939 New York World's Fair claimed that its World of Tomorrow exhibits were meant to educate the public in the need "to apply the scientific method to social problems" (282). It was a view glowingly endorsed by H.G. Wells in a special edition of the *New York Times* devoted to them (1939a:5). As it happens, the New York World's Fair was the last gasp of American technocracy (Akin 1977), with 1939 being the last year of peace before the outbreak of World War II — the benevolent catastrophe that in *Things to Come/Whither Mankind?* finally educates the world to its predestined tomorrow.

Wells's technocratic dream, however, goes back to Saint-Simon. When John Cabal, in the above speech, enjoins his partymen to keep the watchwords "research, invention, world planning — and scientific control," he utters the basic Saint-Simonian premise. Scientific research and engineering development, today's R & D, must be applied to non-military ends, with innovative technology for the conquest of nature, not of other men, if society itself in that peaceful mission is to be run collectively as a worldwide production factory. Long before Henry Ford's pioneering assembly-line plant for the mass production of automobiles, with its exquisite division of labor on the shop floor, Saint-Simon had predicted as much for the future of industrialism, and calculated that it would serve as a principle of government (see Stover 1988b: 20 note). The same premise is Bellamy's in his *Looking Backward* of 1888.

Figure 4.   G·R·H

Figure 5.

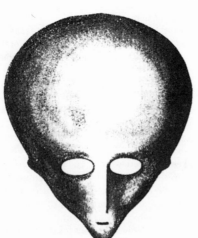

Figure 6.

Top: Punch cartoon satirizing Wells's "Man of the Year Million." See Appendix I. *Above:* Wells's drawing of a Martian in a presentation copy of *Worlds. Left:* Visiting Martian in *If Tomorrow Comes* (Reitmeister 1934).

The protagonist of *Sleeper* is a Marxist named Graham, who wakes up disappointed to a Saint-Simonian future, in which authoritarian socialism has triumphed: a big-business government ruling a capitalist world-state. (Bellamy's sleeper awakens to same only to rejoice in it.) What made it possible was a financial revolution that actually occurred at the turn of the century (for a contemporary account of it see Appendix VI in Stover 1999), enabling the money-credit system to achieve unprecedented freedom, independent of any national economy. Now the finance capital of the whole world is integrated, with all the major cartels or trusts in every field brought together within one interlocking directorate. Graham falls asleep in 1897 (the year of Queen Victoria's diamond jubilee, the high tide of monarchy), and the invasion comes soon after, putting finish to the traditional order, with the blasting of Windsor Castle among other targets of the Martian Heat-Ray. But already friends of Graham have set up a trust fund for the preservation of his comatose body, which revives in 2100. He discovers a world governed by a Council of Trustees descended from those who administered the original fund. Eventually it merges with other cartels and the Council becomes the supreme trust of trusts. Horrified to find himself the nominal owner of more than half the world's accumulated wealth, he attempts to raise a proletarian mob against the regime in accord with his egalitarian ideals. He fails and with his death, in a personal contest with Ostrog, the Council's CEO, dies the last gasp of democratic socialism.

The world of *Sleeper* seems to be a peaceful outcome of what Wells dubbed "Clissoldism" in *The World of William Clissold* (1926; see Stover 1999). William Clissold is a big businessman who philosophizes that transnational corporations like his (and like many today) will in time assume political control of a global economy in trade, money, and investment. Wells (1920:title) himself called it an "open conspiracy" to subvert national governments and replace them with a world government founded upon his ideals of "autocratic state capitalism" (1931:63), the system that finally prevails in *Sleeper*. This comes about when the question, "Has the Money-credit System a Mind?" (1928a) is answered with a yes. Evidently the Martian invasion stimulated business leaders into awareness that the instrument of the financial revolution in their hands could serve a consciously higher purpose, as if it were endowed with a central nervous system capable of functioning like a collective mind or "world brain" (1938:title; see Mayne 1944 for commentary). That collective mind does indeed emerge in *Sleeper*, with the resolve of Graham's legatees to unify all planetary affairs under their direction. Heretofore the traditional order prone to belligerent patriotism and economic warfare had "achieved a hypertrophy of bone, muscle and stomach, without any corresponding enlargement of its nervous controls" (1933:32).

The brainy Martians who rule their home planet with mental unity provide a ganglionic model for a terrestrial World Brain.

Another benefit is, "the gifts to human science it has brought are enormous."* The technology of the Martian fighting machines and the science behind them are instructive. Most important are their flying machines, with which they intended to "go round the world" (II:7), distributing poison gas ("Black Smoke") everywhere, as they had in London, in the course of world conquest. In *Sleeper*, passenger and cargo planes derived from these warplanes are the vital transportation links of the novel's global economy, imagined well in advance of the first Wright flyer of 1903, developed for military use. Only after World War I were airplanes developed for commercial use.

---

*This must be the ultimate source of today's UFO cult. Its mythomaniacs base everything on the reputed crash of a flying disc in the desert sands of New Mexico near Roswell in 1947, which then became the secret of a government cover-up. The fullest account is given by Col. Philip J. Corso in *The Day After Roswell* (1997), actually a well crafted science-fiction novel that works his own professional experience into it. Colonel Corso had been head of the Foreign Technology Desk at the U.S. Army's Research & Development Department, which he claims was the official cover for harvesting alien technology from the Roswell crash; his job was to feed its relics to defense contractors for back-engineering. Among the resulting products were fiber optics, microprocessors, lasers, night visors, brain-wave navigational systems, supertenacity fibers, molecular alignment metallic alloys, particle-beam weapons, and stealth technology.

The reason for the cover-up, Corso says, was to prevent a worse panic than the one following the Orson Welles panic broadcast of 1938. The public had to be shielded from knowledge of a very real invasion by hostile aliens their government was powerless to protect them from. Meanwhile, secret work went on to develop counter-measures that finally drove the aliens away, or at least fought them to a standoff, using their own technology against them. Corso's heroic plan to save the planet is not unlike that proposed by the artilleryman in *Worlds* (II:7), for whom the Martians are at once enemy and model: Learn from them to defeat them.

In the event, the Martians die of bacterial infection, and the artilleryman's plan is mooted. Their alien technology is back-engineered, as the narrator reports in the Epilogue, for civilian products making for the material progress advanced in *Sleeper*. All the same, Colonel Corso is not unfamiliar with *Worlds*, a title he actually cites, and with the German novel that feeds into the chapter regarding the artilleryman. This is *Auf zwei Planeten* by Kurd Lasswitz (1897; see textual note 158), who has Martians establishing a base at the North Pole. German scientists discover the base, raid it, steal their technology, and drive the invaders away. Corso claims to have discovered a similar base there and to have set up the dewline array of tracking radar units in the Arctic (distant early warning system) to monitor the aliens, then to harvest the Roswell crash for the means to combat them. These included elements of the Strategic Development Initiative (SDI), principally the anti–ballistic missile (ABM) that Colonel Corso developed as a weapon of the Cold War; but SDI, the Star Wars of popular locution, really *was* a case of Star Wars in fighting a secret war against the extraterrestrials. Although the aliens remained more advanced with their spaceships driven by some unmatchable electro-gravitic device, the same used by Lasswitz's Martians, the American military was able to stand off the flying saucers, bringing some of them down not only with ABMs but with radar pulses that jammed their propulsion system.

Figure 7. Plan of Jules Verne's space cannon in *From the Earth to the Moon* (1865).

In *Things to Come*, the *pax aeronautica* of John Cabal's Air Dictatorship is imposed with a fleet of bombers which drop a "Gas of Peace" (film shot 627 in 1936) on the last combatant states to deploy military aircraft. Significantly, the letter-numeral designations of these bombers are prefixed with WT for World Trade (Stover 1987:73). In making war for peace, the Airmen make the world safe for civil aviation and for its utility in uniting the Modern State. John Cabal clears the way for his grandson Oswald Cabal who,

as President of the World Council of Direction, presides over the accomplished utopia of Wells's autocratic state capitalism. Further, Oswald Cabal institutes a space program, designed to save mankind from earth's cosmic fate, just as had the Martians in escaping from their older planet. Scientific planning in the Modern State is nothing if not long term.

In *Sleeper*, the trust in charge of civil aviation (the Aeronautical Society) is staffed with a subset of space enthusiasts called "vernies," after Jules Verne (Stover 1999: textual note 106). So, like Oswald Cabal in the 1936 film, Ostrog the world dictator in the 1899 novel is planning ahead for the exploration of outer space and the search for a new planet to inhabit when that distant need is felt. The scientific vernies who research this project are an allusion to *From the Earth to the Moon* (1865), in which their namesake imagines a space cannon for the title journey and then speculates, "Will this means of locomotion allow us to visit those suns which swarm in the firmament?"

That Wells in *Things to Come* ignores rocketry — already established in science fiction after the work of Robert H. Goddard, the German Rocket Society, and the Nazi weapons program (Ley 1945) — is pointed symbolism. In Verne's novel, all the artillery pieces of the American Civil War are melted down to cast the space cannon, for which an international subscription has been raised, and astronomers from all around the world join in tracking and reporting on the space capsule's flight. Like Wells after him, Verne was a doctrinal writer allegiant to Saint-Simonism. His moon shot is a trope for the utopian object of Old Testament socialism: the conquest of nature as a collective human venture to extract its scarce and obdurate resources for the peaceful production of wealth-in-common. In Verne, the space project is a glorification of that ideal, directed by retired artillery officers and associated mathematicians forming the Baltimore Gun Club — a distinct echo of Saint-Simon's Council of Newton. The scriptural source is the words of the disciple Bazard. Technology "has been represented in the past by the actions of both war and industry but in the future will be represented by industry alone, for the exploitation of man by man will have been replaced by the harmonious action of man on nature" (in Iggers, tr. 1958:29). Comte (1877:4: 99) put it in the maxim, "Science and Industry are destined to replace Theology and War."

The Wellsian space gun, whose mission is directed by a World Council under the leadership of Oswald Cabal, is oddly decorated with a vestigial gunsight, suggesting a similar conversion of military technology to civilian industry in the Modern State. That colonists from the Red Planet shoot themselves

Opposite: Figure 8. Wells's Verne-modeled space gun in *Things to Come*. From Stover 1987: plate 44.

from Mars by means of a Vernian space cannon further suggests the same conversion. The Martians, in their history, must also have evolved toward the peaceful Wellsian world-state they presage here on earth. That they bring war machines with them is no contradiction, since these are meant to fight against human aggression from lower beings, whose few brave artillerymen have the temerity to attempt resistance. Nothing can withstand a superior technology and the superior (socialist) moral idea behind it.

The same scenario is replayed in "The Land Ironclads" (1903a, in 1927a:131–157). Makers of the world-state attack a backward and stupidly traditional country for its "bawling patriotisms," using advanced killing machines — futuristic tanks. The defenders on foot and horse are such "unimaginative men" (152) they fail to see any connection between technological and political progress. For after all, utopian products of technical prowess are "the outward and visible sign of an inward and spiritual grace" (1905:172). The defenders of an obsolete national identity, therefore, are redefined as the aggressors; their resistance to a new world order is at fault in sparking the war. This is Martian logic. So is John Cabal's in *Things to Come*; his Airmen, flying warplanes against cavalrymen, extinguish the last pathetic vestige of regressive nationalism. It is also a remarkable anticipation of Bolshevik logic, which justified armed conflict with primitive-minded capitalist countries. As a Soviet policy document of 1968 put it,

> A worldwide Socialist system is the decisive factor for the political and economic development of the world. The balance of power has shifted in favour of Socialism, but nothing can happen by itself and victory can only be achieved through struggle. Aggressive forces are raising a tremendous resistance to the growth of Socialist power — growth-resistance [in Myagkov 1976:169].

What the Martians fight is exactly that, growth-resistance.

In the event, the Martians fail to recreate the socialist world-state of their home planet on earth for their own benefit, but they do succeed in passing on the concept to humans in need of it. Their interplanetary adventure is far from a lost cause. From it humans learn (in *Sleeper*) how to defy tradition and build for world unity; at the same time they learn the necessity of planning ahead for escape to other worlds when their own planet wears out: man's immortality will outlast entropic heat death in this part of the universe. "Growth" is what the Martians end up stimulating.

The first order of business in the Modern State, then, is "conquest of the social order" (1942:64). Without that prelude, there can be no planetary unity focused on the conquest of space. In *The Time Machine* (1895), humans fail to get their act together, and so are unprepared for cosmic doom when earth at last dies. In *Worlds*, the Martians are at once enemy and model in recalling humanity to its survival needs in a universe indifferent to them. As the narrator says in the Epilogue, "the invasion has robbed us of that serene confidence in the future which is the most fruitful source of decadence" — exactly the cautionary point made in *The Time Machine* (Stover 1996a:15). Man must make his own future without the protection of divine providence, as the "scientific aetheists" (1917:69) of the Modern State Revolution are wise enough to know in replacing theology with the religion of the future. Not for them the erroneous "belief in some underlying benevolence in uncontrolled events" (1933:30) — "the great disillusionment" to which the opening paragraph of *Worlds* refers.

In *Sleeper*, the invasion is a stimulus to this new realistic view of the universe. Progress on all fronts is now guaranteed. Tradition is cleared away, the social order conquered, and a world state comes into being, facilitated by the back-engineering of Martian high tech, above all in the deterministic field of aviation. That takes a little time to evolve, but among the first artifacts of alien technology to be developed, in getting from *Worlds* to *Sleeper*, are the robotic Handling Machines in II:2.*

---

*The science of comparative anatomy is also advanced so soon as Martian corpses are dissected. Here is the basis for that most sensational of UFO hoaxes, *The Alien Autopsy* (Frakes 1995), a film in which the title operation is done on the body of one of the Extraterrestrial Biological Entities (EBEs) recovered from the 1947 Roswell Crash. Corso (1997) affirms this from medical records he studied, claiming that the EBEs are humanoid in appearance, with bigger brains but with no internal digestive organs, suspiciously similar to the condition of Wells's octopoid Martians. Corso, however, draws upon a later work in the history of science fiction for his general description: rather atrophied bodies topped with a lightbulb-shaped head with large almond eyes and a small slit for a mouth — the very image of alien faces promoted by the UFO mystery mongers from the start, and which figure as "the greys" in all hysterical accounts of alien abductions. The illustration (see the plates in the present work, fig. 6) in *If Tomorrow Comes* (1934) by Louis Aaron Reitmeister is the origin of that now ubiquitous visage, belonging to a castaway from a wrecked spaceship, who represents an older and more advanced world, none other than Mars (Arno Press 1974:10). Reitmeister in his turn draws upon Wells and his 1893 essay, "The Man of the Year Million," in which the future of humanity is predicted to evolve along the lines already taken by his exemplary Martians (see Appendix I in the present work).

By the way, Colonel Corso has coined the term EBEs for his aliens because they are not in fact true organisms, only "entities" created and programmed by their unknown masters. They are rather living robots or "androids," products of biotechnical engineering energized electronically, which accounts for their lack of digestive organs as with Wells's Martians. While the latter are not androids, they *are* artificial creatures, self-created. Mars had once been populated by a race of humanoids, whose vivisectionists transformed a portion of them into octopoids, all brains and hands (tentacles), the very essence of unemotional, Kantian rationality: no organs but for thinking and making. The remaining humanoids provide them with an energizing blood supply for their vampiric existence. Such relics are brought along by the advanced Martians to sustain themselves during their space voyage to earth; once landed, they draw upon human blood, injected directly into their veins. The history of Mars tells the story of a successful Doctor Moreau, whose experiments in artificial evolution finally triumph (see section 5 of this Introduction).

Figure 9. Martians tearing up tracks of the London & Southwestern Railroad. In the illustrated magazine serial of *Worlds.*

But for all the Martian-stimulated science and invention that takes place in *Sleeper*, labor-saving machines are not allowed to altogether replace toil. Nor are they ever in any Wellsian future. It might be supposed they could, since Wells insists that "the Modern Utopia must not be static but kinetic, must shape not as a permanent state but as a hopeful stage, leading to a long ascent of stages" (1905:5). Yet even in its most far-reaching stage, its future historian reports that state slavery remains intact because "compulsory public service ... is an integral part of our education" (1933:425). Pedagogical violence is the only way "to develop a service mentality in place of a proprietary mentality" (322), given that man must be "socialized entirely against his natural disposition" (428). That is the only way to Martianize men, to remake them on that perfect model set by they who "[i]n twenty-four hours [do] twenty-four hours of work" (II:2), and who selflessly live for nothing else. This is very much the Saint-Simonian principle that to organize for work in the name of peaceful production is the be-all of socialism.

In the pre-utopian past, nations were driven to gain wealth by making economic raids one against the other, in destructive wars unending. Saint-Simon laid it down that permanent additions to wealth are possible only by constructive means. The choice for the world in future is "either to *steal* or *produce*; that is, it must be *military* or *industrial*; otherwise it will be nothing but a *bastard association*, if it does not declare itself openly for one of these two ends" (in Ionescue 1976:123). That bastard association is in Wells called a "capitalist military civilization" (1914c:60), which reminds of today's reference to the military-industrial complex. Nothing is more vital than it be overthrown if civilization itself is to be saved from a final war catastrophe.

As it happens, a new *dégringolade* always occurs on the road to utopia in Wells. In *Things to Come*, John Cabal's League of the Airmen, recruited from the German enemy as well as from England, add to the general destruction of World War II, only to end it just short of a *fin de monde* outcome: enough ruination to kill off the old order while leaving sufficient on which to rebuild the new. This reflects on one of the most original passages in Saint-Simon, in which he is the first to define utopia not as a restoration of some legendary past but as an achievement of the future; socialism for him breaks with tradition and preserves little from the past.

> The Golden Age of mankind does not lie behind us, but before us; it lies in the perfection of the social order. Our forefathers did not see it; one day our children will see it. It is for us to clear the way [in Ionescue 1976:120].

To clear the way: That is what the Airmen do, in "kick[ing] the past to pieces" (1905:359). The Air Dictatorship they found needs no apology for its autocratic rule, for its "Tyranny was in essence a liberation" (1933:363) representing "freedom from the past" (1905:9). The epigraph to the present work, "The past is merely a mistake," is Renan's epigram encapsulating the futuristic idea in six words. The Martian invasion clears the way. Again, it is a trope for Wells's ideological war with tradition. And the Martians themselves, all head and hands and no stomach (the latter equating with appetite, greed, selfishness, possessiveness) are the very embodiment of the selfless Saint-Simonian work ethic.

4. Socialist Mars

In 1971, Mariner 9 orbited Mars and took photographs of the planet's entire surface, from which a topographic map was made. Among its features is a crater in the south polar region named, for obvious reasons, after (H.G.) Wells. Nearby, and just as significant, is one named after (Charles) Darwin (U.S. Geological Survey 1976). Wells's Martians are nothing if not a demonstration of Darwinian theory.*

At latitude 49° S. and longitude 80° W. is a larger crater named after (Percival) Lowell, the American astronomer whose observations of Mars were not in the least confirmed by Mariner (itself given a crater on the map): no canals and no Martian civilization. Mars is a dead planet as crater-pocked as the moon. Wells, of course, could not know this when he drew upon Lowellian Mars for his invaders. But no matter. *Worlds* is a philosophical novel with a long tradition, and it will long survive astronomical truth.

From the middle of the eighteenth century there arose a debate, continued to this day, concerning the plurality of worlds. Is life on earth a singularity, or does it also exist elsewhere (Hefferman 1981)? That is the very question addressed by Wells in his historically-minded epigraph (see textual note 1). Moreover he drew upon nineteenth-century astronomical theory that held the outer planets of the solar system to be older than ones closer to the sun. In metaphysical speculation this meant that life on the older planets must be wiser, with a lesson to teach us greener earthlings. Such is the assumption in the opening paragraph, which speaks to "the older worlds of space," which geocentric humans (the ignorant public insofar as it thought on the matter) considered inferior worlds no less "ready to welcome a mis-

---

*Curiously, Levine (1988) in his book on the impact of Darwinism on Victorian novelists has not a single reference to Wells: a case of belletristic snobbery. The literati still refuse to recognize Wellsian science fiction as literature. Morton (1989) on the same subject devotes almost a quarter of his book to Wells and makes much of *Worlds*. As a historian of science, Morton correctly sees in Wells a literary imagination inspired by Darwin far beyond the capacity of any other novelist to understand.

sionary enterprise" than darkest Africa. In the event, it is the Martians who do the missionizing, "the great disillusionment" of the opening paragraph.

Lowell was the first astronomer to attempt to validate the plurality-of-worlds thesis. That his pre-observational bias influenced what he thought he saw is everything. He sought to prove that the Red Planet is red in more than one way, as an examplar of socialism we humans must adopt if we are to progress.

A socialist Mars long has been current in speculative literature. Perhaps the first is *A Cityless and Countryless World* by Henry Olerich (1883:see Arno Press 1961:9). It is a Marxist world, not unlike that envisioned for the terrestrial future by William Morris in his utopian classic, *News from Nowhere* (1890). Also in 1883 Ismar Thiusen published *The Diothas; or A Far Look Ahead* (Arno Press 1961:11). This time the global culture of Mars is highly urbanized, a capitalist world-state founded on Bellamyism five years before Bellamy himself wrote *Looking Backward* (1888).* Here, the *other* socialism (originated by Saint-Simon) has the author's endorsement as an attack on Marxism. Thiusen may be the source of Lowell's preconception of Mars.

Another definite source, to which Wells had to react negatively, is Percy Greg's two volume anti-utopian novel *Across the Zodiac* (1880), which finds the Bellamyism of Thiusen's novel a sinister example that is imperative to warn against. The particular evils of Mars in Greg are noted examples of what must follow from the general principles of "Comtian positivism": the progressive idea that society ought to be scientifically organized along the technocratic lines laid down and carried forward by Edward Bellamy. That Lowell from the start decided on a counter–Marxist Mars may have been reinforced by his reading of Greg's *Across the Zodiac* as a libel on the positivism advanced by Ismar Thiusen in *his* thesis novel on Mars. It is impossible to believe Lowell ignorant of such political literature any more than it can be believed of Wells.†

---

*Olerich evidently was familiar with Bellamy's articles and pamphlets written prior to the novelization of his ideas (see Lipow 1982:289f). In the battle of the books over the two socialisms, Morris on his part, with *News from Nowhere*, took arms against the Saint-Simonian thesis of Bellamy's *Looking Backward*: a rebuttal endorsed by Eleanor Marx, the bearded guru's daughter. Wells then targeted Morris in *The Time Machine*, with a *fin de globe* scenario that must follow should chaotic Marxism prevail over orderly Saint-Simonism (Stover 1996a).

†Lowell did not become interested in planetology until his trip to Japan in 1892 in pursuit of Far Eastern religious studies he had been writing about from 1886. From a Japanese astronomer (among other savants including priests he consulted) he learned about Schiaparelli's 1877 observations of Martian *canali*, or channels (Hetherington 1981)— natural formations that soon became engineered canals in Lowell's positivist cult devoted to them at his observatory founded near Flagstaff, Arizona, in 1893. In Comte (1877:title) positivism is designated the new "Religion of Humanity," and in Mars Lowell saw it prefigured.

Figure 10. Wells's favored illustrator, the Belgian artist Johan Briandé, in a 1916 drawing for *Worlds*.

Lowell's books, articles and letters often refer to "socialism" as his credo (Hoyt 1976:index), although he never specified which brand. He had no need to. As heir to the Lowell textile fortune made in Lowell, Massachusetts, which enabled him to build his Mars observatory in Arizona, he cannot have been a Marxist — not unless he were a precocious limousine liberal. Besides, at the turn of the century Marxism was little known outside the Social Democratic Party in various European countries and in Russia. The name of Karl Marx did not become generally known until the Russian Revolution of 1917, even more so after Stalin named "Marxism-Leninism" the Soviet regime's official doctrine. Before then, nobody had any idea that the democratic socialism to the left of the hyphen would ever become a cover story for the authoritarian socialism represented on its right. Indeed, Wells was the only Soviet apologist to see through this rhetorical sham; he claimed that the cause of Communism and its proposed world revolution were better advanced without duplicity, if only Leninism (=Saint-Simonism) were served up plain, without the hyphen (see Stover 1992). In Lowell's time the name Henri Saint-Simon had not yet been forgotten, much less obliterated by later Soviet propaganda declaring Marxism the one and only socialism that ever existed or can exist*; and so he just assumed his readers would take "socialism" to mean Saint-Simonian doctrine.

Wells, too, saw it there, after Lowell's first book of 1895 on the subject, and through the same literary lens focused on the two rival schools of socialist thought. Greg's *Across the Zodiac* (1880) is another example of a work prompting Wells to assert the opposite idea: Everything bad Greg has to say about Mars he finds good. One trivial example: Greg's wicked Martians use the duodecimal system (as do Thiusen's good ones), a presumed evil reflecting that horror of the French Revolution, its antitraditionalist adoption of the superrationalistic metric system. Yet duodecimal accounting is happily endorsed as a utopian feature in *A Modern Utopia* as in *Sleeper*. Another trivial example, the futuristic device for house construction to replace bricklaying "that will squeeze out wall as one squeezes paint from a tube," in *Anticipations* (1901:*n*99), also derives from Greg (I:193). More significantly, his "coldly wise" (II:136) Martians are those "intellects vast and cool and unsympathetic" in Wells's opening paragraph. In Greg the natives of Mars are called Martials, a term Wells toyed with (Hughes 1962:336 *n*47) and for good reason. The term suggests an authoritarian stance traceable to the Saint-Simonian "cult of authority" that Iggers (1958:title) finds the taproot of the modern dictatorships under Fascism, National Socialism, and Communism alike (confirmed by Radel 1975). Above all, the Martials are the same aggressive missionaries (Greg II:119f), in the cause of "positive polity" (Comte 1877:title), that the Martians most certainly are in *Worlds*.

*The die-hard authors of a recent book on the history of socialism still are wedded to this doctrinal orthodoxy when they write, "socialism here means ... the opposition to capitalism as an alternative conception of society" (Hardarch *et al.* 1979:vii); they consciously erase from the record the *state* capitalism (=state socialism) of Saint-Simon's formulation. Small wonder, with such examples of revisionist history in circulation, that hostile reviewers of the present series "The Annotated H.G. Wells" have attacked me for

Lowell's first book on the Red Planet was *Mars* (1895), published in London. A year later there was the American edition cited here (because it is a holding of my 20,000 volume library, from which all the bibliographies in the present series are drawn). But given the unexpected success of the London first edition, Lowell's next books on the subject (1896a, 1908, 1909), came under the imprint of New York's biggest publisher, Macmillan; they recognized in him a worldwide celebrity and best selling author, then the most famous American alive.

Mars quickly became an international sensation, with Lowell elevated as the patron saint of the intelligent-life-on-Mars cult. In magnitude it was as big as the hysterical cults devoted to some late 20th century celebrities though sustained much longer as the public followed his latest findings and ever-more detailed maps of the Martian canals in book after book. Wells

---

blasphemy. Is not Wells the avowed allegiant of "socialism," the sacred -ism, which can only mean Marxism? How dare I discredit this good, liberally-minded social democrat by linking his name with that of Saint-Simon? His brand of authoritarian socialism (say critics) is not a socialism at all, it is fascism, state slavery. Yet this is exactly what is prophesied as a normative prediction in *Sleeper* (Stover 1999).

It has long puzzled me why my friends in the H.G. Wells Society promote their man not as a socialist (evidently the term is too highly charged and perhaps even discredited on the horrific Soviet example) but as a liberal democrat. Then I chanced to reread Harold J. Laski's classic treatise on the subject, *The Rise of European Liberalism*. Its rise out of the feudal past featured a number of new ideas Wells agrees with, others not. In the liberal age, the bourgeoisie and their interests triumph (bad, especially bourgeois respectability). In law, contracts replace the rights and privileges of classes (good; also bad insofar as contracts legalize private property). Wealth is derived from trade and manufacture rather than from land (good, the landed aristocracy is irrelevant). The divine right of kings gives way to the idea of natural rights (good to weaken monarchy, bad to stress rights). Established religion gives way to tolerance for many denominations (good, so far as there is liberty for Wellsism to prevail, which it does when the Airmen impose their "Act of Uniformity" [1933:332]). A belief in progress replaces nostalgia for a golden age (good). Material benefits in this work replace hope for a better life in the hereafter (good). Reason replaces faith; science and experimentation replace superstition and tradition (altogether good). So, Wells passes as a good *liberal* on some key points, but that he is not a *democrat* is passed over. It is enough to be a saint of atheistic progressivism if other aspects of the illiberal past are repudiated.

But not only is it my Wellsian colleagues in their single-author society who take this view, it is general. When I submitted my entry on "H.G. Wells" for *Contemporary Authors* (Stover 1987a), the editor made a significant change. In the standard format where "politics" is to be indicated, I inserted "statist," which was changed to "liberal democrat." This reflects a long trend in the history of ideas, from the late eighteenth century (Age of Enlightenment) when the secular intellectual, the likes of Voltaire and Rousseau, replaced the declining cleric as moral mentor and critic of mankind (see Johnson 1988). In Wells, intellectuals finally get "the whip hand," in the Airmen's Act of Uniformity, to "erase" all "misleading doctrines" (1933:351) other than theirs. Wells, it seems, has more in common with dogmatic statists than with liberal democrats.

captured that wild enthusiasm, to his own more lasting glory, in *Worlds*: a work of *Weltlitertur* that leaves its inspirational faddist nearly forgotten, except for a memorial crater on the canal-less planet mapped by Mariner 9.

The immediate context making for Lowell's huge success was a canal-building mania right here on earth. Men of his generation had completed the Suez Canal in 1869, an engineering marvel that directly connected the Mediterranean, via the Red Sea, to the Indian Ocean: a plus for world trade. And, at the very time the Panama Canal was being dug, to connect the Atlantic and Pacific oceans, daily press reports of its progress ran parallel to excited discussion of the Lowellian canals (Hoyt 1976:205). Startling news it was even to hear of plans for the Panamanian project, for it had been attempted once before by the same French engineers who built the Suez Canal, and whose mastermind was none other than Ferdinand de Lesseps — the most active disciple of Saint-Simon's romantic globalism.*

Lowell's familiar thesis reduces to ridiculous caricature. Mars is a desiccated planet older than ours. Its inhabitants bring water from the polar ice caps to irrigate the desert waste lands, ruddy-colored from oxidation of elemental iron in the sand. The canal system is planet-wide, therefore no rivalrous nation-states on Mars; its hydraulic works are the product of a unified world-state. Where the canals intersect, with geometrical regularity, there are located great urban centers. The canals themselves are not visible, but the zone of green vegetation alongside them is. Conclusion: the socialist world-state on the red planet shows the peaceful direction of terrestrial progress toward utopia.

In *Worlds*, that progressive movement is hastened along by the bringing of Lowellian Martians to earth, which they mean to colonize and unify in the image of their home planet. The rationale for this adventure across the gulf of space is that Mars, having aged beyond the saving utility of its irrigation canals to fight off desertification, must needs be replaced with a new homeland closer to the sun, younger and greener. For humans, however, it is an act of war; the martial Martians are first of all aggressors before they are appreciated as exemplars in the enemy-model dialectic.

This dialectic is grounded in yet another historical context, antedating the Mars mania set off by Lowell in 1895 by 25 years. *War of the Worlds* belongs to (however superior to) that new genre of future war stories initiated by Lt.-Col. Sir George T. Chesney in *The Battle of Dorking* (1871). As

---

*Significantly, it was de Lesseps who inducted Jules Verne into the French Legion of Honor. This in recognition of his being a socialist writer in the Saint-Simonian tradition. So too was Wells after him, although critical opinion mistakenly holds these two fathers of science fiction to be in no way alike (see Stover 1998b: Introduction and Appendix IV).

the cautionary tale of a retired artillery officer, that book warns that the prowess of the Prussian war machine demonstrated in the Franco-Prussian War (1870) might next be turned against unprepared England. In *Worlds*, however, England is but the beachhead of a planetary invasion, carried out by Martians with the same military superiority and with the same political objective. Or rather the reverse. The Martians, already unified, prompt unity in the enemy.

Before the War, Germany was not the empire it became under its first chancellor, Otto von Bismarck, who had contrived French aggression in order to gain that end. Until then, Germania was a loose confederation of four kingdoms, six grand-duchies, five duchies, seven principalities, and three freetowns. With Prussia, the most powerful kingdom, in the lead, Bismarck got the rest to cooperate in the invasion of France, resulting in the crowning of King Wilhelm I as Kaiser in the very outskirts of Paris, even as the city was under siege; he was now emperor of what in retrospect is dominated by the Second Reich.* Victory had been assured by the Prussians' advanced military science that quickly felled the French army in mass carnage. They had rapid-firing, breech-loading cannon of *Kruppstahl*, accurate at long range, against bronze muzzle-loaders. To the same degree were their rifles modernized (Howard 1960).

In *Worlds*, the "strange irresistible weapons" of the Martians (Amis, *loc. cit.*) are no empty fantasy. Their laser-like Heat-Ray and Black Smoke are extensions of the Prussian advantage; or as the artilleryman says, "It's bows and arrows against the lightning" (I:12). But human military defeat is not political defeat. After the Martians die of natural causes,† their legacy, as the narrator concludes, is "the conception of the commonweal of mankind," verified in *Sleeper* the sequel.

Wells (1908a) acknowledges that his invaders come from Lowellian Mars; but they come not to dig more canals. These gigantic projects of hydraulic engineering are but emblematic of what Martian technology can do by way of planetary unification in the building of a world-socialist state. To be sure, Lowell had in mind the Suez Canal accomplished by de Lesseps, and the Panama Canal he attempted; yet behind these projects, designed to facilitate world trade, lie the grander Saint-Simonian plan to conquer nature as the unified purpose of all mankind. What the Martian canals point to, insofar as they are exemplary, is this larger vision destined to guide human affairs.

---

*Hitler's Third Reich traces through this one of Bismarck's invention to the Holy Roman Empire, the supposed first one.

†The fate of the Martians is foreshadowed in the very first sentence of the opening paragraph, where the narrator says they are "as mortal" as mankind.

Figure 11. Costume of the German Youth Movement or *Wandervögel*, to which the artilleryman harks back in note 166.

The key passage in Saint-Simonian scripture is the words of the disciple Bazard. To repeat them in a different translation:

> The exploitation of man by man — that is the state of human relations in the past. The exploitation of nature by man in association with man — that is the picture the future offers [in Durkheim 1958:211].

In the past, men were divided by two different but related forms of exploitation: a downward class war within and interstate warfare without. If new wealth is to be created, then men must rather make war on nature, not on each other, in a collective enterprise to exploit natural resources for industrial productivity. To that end "Society must become a vast production company" (in Durkheim 1958:134).

Thus would be constituted a World Republic of United Interests.* "There will never be permanent public peace until the most important industrialists are in charge of the administration of public wealth" (in Taylor 1958: 261). From this derives the Wellsian prophecy that "The future belongs to big-scale business" (1916:22) in a "world-wide industrial civilization without nationalism, warfare and economic selfishness" (1925:346).

Wells's world-state, predicted as "the next stage in history" (1920:599–608), is nothing if not Saint-Simon's visionary World Republic of United Interests. It is most forcefully dramatized in *Things to Come* (1936), "a propagandist film [for] Wellsism" (1984: 73, 172). In a speech to the Airmen, their leader John Cabal addresses future prospects now they have nearly defeated the last vestiges of belligerent nationalism following a protracted World War II — a benevolent catastrophe that allows them to rebuild anew on the ashes of the old order. He says,

> Do you realize the immense task we shall undertake, when we set ourselves to an active and aggressive peace, when we direct our energies to tear out the wealth of this planet, and exploit all these giant possibilities of science that have been squandered hitherto upon war and senseless competition.† We shall excavate the eternal hills. We shall make such use of the treasures of sky and sea and earth as men have never dreamt of hitherto [film shot 725 in 1936; in Stover 1987:261f].

Oswald Cabal, John's grandson, fulfills that speech. By the year 2036 he comes on as President of the World Council of Direction (located in London), which exactly corresponds to the Council of Newton (in Paris) proposed by Saint-Simon. For Saint-Simon, Newton was *the* scientific genius,

---

*The phrase was coined in a satirical novel by a French contemporary of Saint-Simon (Stover 1987:60, 102 *n* 20); but the reactionary critic is dead on. No one locution in Saint-Simon's own writings better intimates his utopian vision.

†Note that Wells equates bloody war with the "senseless competition" of private-profit capitalism. All that will end under a moralized state capitalism given to harmony and purposeful integration.

as Einstein is in our day; and he transferred that éclat to the name of his Council, in which science was to be the new spiritual power guiding temporal power. Standing above his hierarchs is the "Council-in-Chief" (Taylor 1975:80), a philosopher-king whose lofty state-idea is incarnated by the Council of Newton. Ranked by function, its members form the Estate of Direction directing the Estate of Labor.

Saint-Simon's table of organization is outlined below together with its parallel in the Wells film.*

Saint-Simon	Things to Come	
Council-in-Chief	Oswald Cabal	
Council of Newton	World Council	
Direction	Direction	*functions*
1. savants	1. poietics	1. command
2. managers	2. kinetics	2. administration
Labor	Labor	
3. proletariat	3. dull & base	3. obedience

In Saint-Simon, the Estate of Direction comprises two ranks: (1) the savants are scientific planners, (2) the managers are production engineers who execute the plan. (3) the proletariat, of Saint-Simon's coinage, is given only to obey orders in a collective cause from which it is expected to benefit.†

So too in *Things to Come*. The Council-in-Chief appears as Oswald Cabal, who presides over a neo–Newtonian Council of World Direction. Since Wells elsewhere has named Saint-Simon's two estates, of Direction and of Labor, as basic to his world formula (1916:100), they are givens in the film. As for the three Saint-Simonian castes — the savants and managers of Direction,

---

*Drawn from Stover (1992:30), where a further comparison to the former Soviet Union is made, and then to Plato's *Republic* (34). Saint-Simon industrialized and globalized his little city-state, while retaining the platonic notion of state guardianship (ranked by the same two functions) over a citizenry too unwise and selfish to appreciate the state-idea of organic unity.

†When Marx borrowed the term proletariat, he signified a force antagonistic to the collaboration between capital and labor proposed by Saint-Simon. He rather advocated a proletarian revolution against the capitalist establishment. But as soon as Marxism-Leninism became the official credo of the Soviet Union, its propaganda advertising a workers' state was able to have it both ways. Saint-Simon had said that all three castes in his doctrinialized industrialism were functionally equal workers: (1) the *industriels* of science, (2) the *industriels* of management, (3) the *industriels* of manual labor. His World State of United Interests did indeed envision a workers' state of all working *industriels*. But in Marxism-Leninism, the term worker is ambiguous. To the left of the hyphen is the democratic cover story, *industriels* as only function 3, engaged in collective self-management. To the right is the authoritarian, even despotic reality, putting function 3 in its place.

and the proletarians of Labor — these are the temperamental types defined in *A Modern Utopia* (1905), in which a world party-state is run by a "directive elite" (1934:215) called Samurai, after the ruling nobility of Tokugawa-era Japan. The film's imagery directly alludes to this novel in the dress worn by members of the World Council: Their upper garments are modeled after the wide-shouldered court costume of the Samurai, *kata-ginu* in Japanese (Stover 1987:plates 36–38). Wells's samurai are of two temperamental types. First the Poietic or creative type (=Saint-Simon's savants of function 1), and next the kinetic or managerial type (=Saint-Simon's function 2). Together the poietics and kinetics dominate the common run of men, whom Wells tags as intellectually Dull and morally Base types: too dull to understand the state-idea or too base to wish to understand it (1905: Chapter 9; see also 1934:562f).

Oswald Cabal also corresponds to the big-brained Grand Lunar in *The First Men in the Moon* (1901a). Under his ganglionic mastery every Selenite "is a perfect unit in a world machine" (Stover 1998b:239 *n*211). The Grand Lunar is dismayed to learn that on earth there is yet no Grand Earthly to administer its disunified planet, as does he the moon's inner world: a complete universe in microcosm. That terrestrial savior has come in Oswald Cabal, he who is destined to rule "a single world economic machine" (1931a: 373) in the "coming age of scientific management" (1925:129), which amounts to "an economic world republic and a single world civilization" (1926:770).

But before Wells novelized that Saint-Simonian prospect in his lunar utopia, it was expounded in the Martian utopia of Greg's *Across the Zodiac* (1880). The story's Martials are just as critical of ill-run earthly affairs. On Mars, it has been

> assumed as a matter of course ... that when everyone was forced to work there would be enough for all; that public spirit, and if necessary coercion, would prove as effectual stimulants to exertion and industry as interest and necessity had done under the system of private ownership [Greg, I:126].

Exactly the same assumption was made by Lenin's corevolutionary in Bolshevik Russia, the pretentious theorizer Trotsky.

> "In a country where the sole employer is the state, opposition means death by starvation," he said. And he was candid enough to add: "The old principle, 'Who does not work shall not eat,' has been replaced by a new one: 'Who does not obey shall not eat'" [Bethell 1998:179].

Why Trotsky should so closely echo the words of Greg the science fiction writer has only one answer: 20th century revolutionaries were far more influenced by 19th century utopian literature than by the doctrinal texts informing it (Carson 1990:67–71). In this case, the original is the text of Saint-Simon's first commandment:

All men will work; they will regard themselves as laborers attached to one work-shop.... The Supreme Council of Newton will direct their works.... Anybody who does not obey the orders will be treated by the others as a quadruped* [in Hayek 1979:223f].

Lenin himself, however, knew the source material as his colleague Trotsky perhaps did not. In *State and Revolution* (1917:93), written on the eve of his bid for power, he wrote, "The whole of society will have become a single office and a single factory." Then, "Unquestioning Subordination to a single will is absolutely necessary for the success of processes on the pattern of large-scale machine industry" (Lenin in Tucker 1975:455). This means that "factory discipline will extend to the whole of society" (Lenin 1917:92f), the techno-cratic idea in a nutshell as proposed by Saint-Simon in his own *summa summarum*: "Society must become a vast production company" (in Durkheim 1958:134). So too in Wells. His Modern State is a global version of the U.S.S.R., Inc., under Stalin. Building on Lenin's legacy, he articulated a policy rejoiced in by Wells when he said of it that the Soviet Union was now to become "one great departmentalized business, a single rationalized system ... of which there will be one owner, one single capitalist — the State — and everyone else will be an employee ... or a prisoner of that supreme power" (1932:181f).

Lenin's plan for a Soviet world-state (see Goodman 1960) designed that earth become a planetary workshop — as on Lowellian Mars. Its technocrats get here from there, like Quaker Puffed Wheat, shot from guns. These recall Verne's gigantic space cannon, the *Columbiad* (fig. 7 of the plates in the present work), a Saint-Simonian triumph exalting the "united interests" of capital and labor. The space gun in *Things to Come* (fig. 8) has the identical symbolic meaning.

The artillery shells, or "cylinders," that arrive from Mars in *Worlds* likewise carry passengers. But they are far from human.

5. Vampire State

Lowell had written that his Martians were "not men in trousers" (Appendix VI in the present work). Wells, however, allows that some of them might be: those humanoid sources of blood for the vampiric others: octopus-like monsters the size of bears.†

---

*That is, as an antisocial animal. In Wells they are disposed of in "islands of exile" (1905:147) anticipating *The Gulag Archipelago* (Solzhenitsyn 1974:title), the Soviet regime's "sewage disposal system" (24), its means of "hygienic purging" (28). This cloacal metaphor may derive from Wells's "excretary organs of the state" in *Sleeper* (Stover 1999: textual note 195).

†Actual octopusses of large size and equal intelligence are the subject of "The Sea

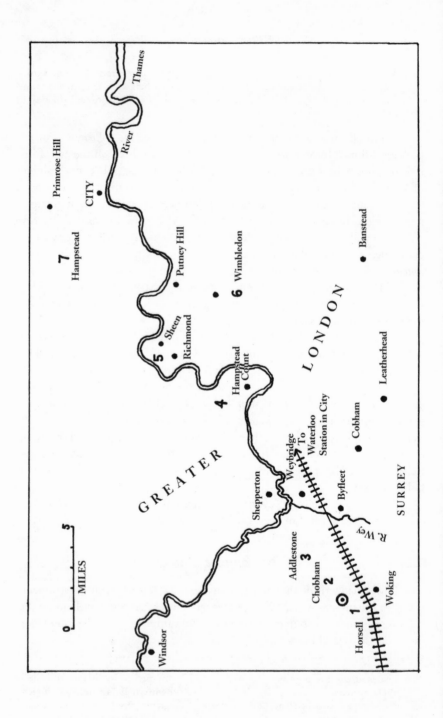

MILES

0 5

River Thames

Primrose Hill

CITY

7
Hampstead

Putney Hill

Sheen
Richmond

5

Hampstead
Court

4

6
Wimbledon

Banstead

GREATER

LONDON

Leatherhead

Shepperton

Weybridge

To
Waterloo
Station in City

Cobham

Byfleet

R. Wey

SURREY

Windsor

Addlestone

3
Chobham

2

1
Horsell

Woking

They are gutless wonders, which is why their intellects are so "vast and cool." They lack the emotions that arise from troublesome digestive and sexual organs. They are all brain and "hands" (tentacles): creative organs of thinking and making only.* They are in fact a composite of all three functions of Saint-Simon's *industriels*, from the theoretical and directive ones to the physical operatives.

How they got that way is through artificial evolution, a process by which they transformed themselves from lower to higher beings. Somewhere in their past is a successful Doctor Moreau. The "Beast Men" he creates out of animals are surrogates for the "man beast" that is the half-way condition of human evolution toward "Beyond-Man"/"After-Man" (see Stover 1996b:32). Since in Darwinian theory *Homo sapiens* like any other evolving species is a child of the past and a parent to the future, the good doctor's experiments in vivisection aim to produce that future now: a "rational man" in his own precocious image.†

How the Martians did this to themselves is suggested by the work of the Russian-French bacteriologist Élie Metchnikoff‡ (*d.* 1916). He already was famous in the technical literature and in the popular press by the time he arrived at the Pasteur Institute (Paris) in 1888 where he applied his theories to the problem of health and disease, for which he won the Nobel Prize in Medicine in 1908. His most notable book, *The Nature of Man* (1903), Wells reviewed with fellow-feeling for a like-minded Darwinist (Appendix III in the present work). The book argues that man at this present moment in his continuing evolution is incomplete, that medical intervention is possible to improve the human condition.

The problem is, nature has designed *Homo sapiens* badly, with too much long intestine; the colon harbors undigested food that putrifies only to poison the mind with disorderly emotions and to shorten life. To alter the

---

Raiders" (1896c: in 1927a:471–482). The dooming of common humanity is their prospect as with the Martians. But they are strictly metaphorical, since the brainy-looking head of the octopus is but a food sac. The trope in Wells is, big stomach needs to be traded for a larger ganglion, in a change from animal appetite to selfless intelligence.

*C.S. Lewis in *That Hideous Strength* (1945) identifies H.G. Wells (Horace Jules in the novel) as a sinister influence promoting a Martianized, post–Christian rationality that has led to totalitarianism. In *The Abolition of Man* (1947) he made that thesis explicit.

†In *The Shape of Things to Come*, a Supreme Council plans for "the directed evolution of life upon the planet" (1933:391). In *Across the Zodiac*, the equivalent Academy on Mars is headed by a titular "Vivisector-General" (Greg 1880: II:186). His good work ensures a check on old age and disease, so as to ensure longevity (I:139).

‡ The Frenchified version of Ilya Ilich Mechnikov.

Opposite: Figure 12. 1–7 are landing sites of the Martian cylinders. ⊙ signifies sand pits. ┼┼┼┼ is the London and south-western Railway. ---- is the narrator's journey to Primrose Hill. Returns to Leatherhead.

species he recommended the ingestion of good bacteria in the form of cur-
dled milk to counteract bad bacteria. Thus began the yogurt fad with us to
this day. No longer current, though, are the colectomies practiced by fashionable French physicians: procedure called Metchnikoffing. Why not cut
out the problem at its source? The complete therapy entails first the removal
of the large intestine, harborer of bad bacteria, and then ingestion of good
bacteria into the remaining small intestine, all that is really needed (Tauber
and Chernyak 1991: Introduction).

The Martians, then, have been Metchnikoffed; but they are not yogurt
eaters, being completely gutless. The premise of this condition, as Doctor
Moreau has it, is that acquired traits might be inherited, thus ending the
disharmony of mind and body. As for the Martians' braininess, that too has
a surgical procedure behind it. Wells conceives "of delaying the closing-up
of the sutures of the human skull and so permitting the grey matter of the
brain a longer period of expansion, with a consequent prolongation of mental development" (1942:70). He looks to "the removal of the human brain-
case as a possible undertaking to release the human will and intelligence to
ampler achievements" (1928b:320). Thus is manufactured "The Man of the
Year Million" (1893:title), who will "have a larger brain, and a slightly smaller
body than at present" (Appendix I and see fig. 4 of the plates in the present
work). In *Worlds*, at textual note 137, the narrator agrees with the author of
that article, in which he had prophesied a future condition of mankind not
unlike that of the Martian invaders. They show the way.*

---

*In a curious anticipation of John Cabal's octopus-head helmet, Wells in the following
extract alludes to both Metchnikoff and the pioneer French aviator, Louis Blériot, first
to fly across the English Channel in 1909, from Calais to Dover. This epochal event in
the history of aviation was reported by Wells in "The Coming of Blériot" (1909a). Later,
in "Some Possible Discoveries" (1914:397–407), he writes, "by knife and physical treatment ... we could correct and develop ourselves in the most extraordinary way." That
essay goes on to say,

> We have already had some very astonishing suggestions in this direction from
> Doctor Metchnikoff. He regards the human stomach and large intestine as not only
> vestigial and superfluous in the human economy, but as positively dangerous on
> account of the harbour they afford for those bacteria that accelerate the decay of
> age. He proposes that these viscera should be removed. To a layman like myself
> this is an altogether astounding and horrifying idea, but Doctor Metchnikoff is a
> man of the very greatest scientific reputation, and it does not give him any qualm
> or horror or absurdity to advance it. I am quite sure that if a gentleman called upon
> me "done up" in the way I am dimly suggesting, with most of the contents of his
> abdomen excavated, his lungs and heart probably enlarged and improved, parts of
> his brain removed to eliminate harmful tendencies and make room for the expan-
> sion of the remainder, his mind and sensibilities increased, and his liability to
> fatigue and the need of sleep abolished, I should conceal with the utmost difficulty
> my inexpressible disgust and terror. But, then, if M. Blériot, with his flying

Once landed on earth, the Martians capture humans and inject their blood into their own veins. Being gutless, they have not digestive organs, just like real-life vampires. There are numerous species of insects and some fewer vampire bats that alike extract the predigested juices of their host. The insects prey on other insects, the bats on other mammals, South American cattle especially (which, since their introduction there, have replaced mice as the bats' habitual prey). In all cases there is the bite that poisons and paralyzes, and then dissolves and liquefies the inner tissues for sucking up.

The first Martian cylinder to strike the earth sticks into its skin "like a poisoned dart" (I:8). There follows paralysis of the social body and then its "liquefaction" (I:16). The venom dissolves the old order and makes ready for the new.

That new order, in *The Shape of Things to Come*, is "the Modern State octopus" (1933:292), "a vast business octopus" (289). In the derivative film (1936), John Cabal wears a gas helmet shaped like the cranial dome of an octopus (fig. 2 of the plates in the present work), but when the visor is dropped (fig. 3) his head and shoulders "are suggestive of a Buddha against a circular halo" (1935:56) (and see these figures from Stover 1987: plates 18, 19). With his Airmen, Cabal makes war for peace, gassing the last of the nationalist brigands, then establishes his Air Dictatorship leading on to the Modern World-State headed by his grandson Oswald. John is, in turn, destroyer and saintly salvationist (the Buddha image in plate 19). The Martian example, first enemy then model, is realized not alone in *Things to Come*. The film's destruction/reconstruction dialectic clearly harks back to the invasion from Mars in *Worlds*, which indirectly leads on to the same global business octopus that emerges in *Sleeper*. In both cases the world ends up being run as a single production factory *à la* Saint-Simon. That utopian result is for Wells "autocratic state socialism" (1931:60), for which state socialism and technocracy are syno-nyms.

Eventually he came to prefer the term "collectivism" (1921:186), in deference to common usage during the totalitarian era. The big-three dictatorships of the time all claimed to exemplify a collectivist state acting as the

---

machine, ear-flaps and goggles, had soared down in the year 54 B.C., let us say, upon my woad-adorned ancestors — every family man in Britain was my ancestor in those days — at Dover, they would have had entirely similar emotions. And at present I am not discussing what is beautiful in humanity, but what is possible — and what, being possible is likely to be attempted [1914:402f].

In other words, had Blériot with his exotic headgear landed in Dover in 54 B.C., it could not have been more astonishing than Cabal's presence in *Things to Come*. Landing as he does among the primitive ancestors of "the coming man," he presages "a new species" (1933:426) of socialist man.

supreme arbiter of labor and capital — whether private capital, as in Germany and Italy, or state capital as in the Soviet Union.* The free-world press pictured it as "the octopus state" (Chamberlin 1936:69); as illustrated in cartoons, its liberty-crushing tentacles reached into all aspects of life. John Cabal's gas helmet certainly resonates with this commonplace image, but it cannot account for the octopoidal Martians.

Their frightfulness for readers of *Worlds* may be traced to a similar trope just as monstrous.

> Gaslight and the railway were often compared in the nineteenth century. These two industrial innovations came into the world at the same time, with similar technologies. "A gas-work, like a railway, must be viewed as one entire and indivisible machine; the mains in one case being analogous to the rails in the other."† To contemporaries it seemed that industries were expanding, sending out tentacles, *octopus-like*, into every house. Being connected to them as consumers made people uneasy. They clearly felt a loss of personal freedom [Schivelbusch 1988:29, emphasis added].

In the London area, a proliferation of private companies delivered gas for all purposes in a patchwork of competitive services that survived well into the 1940s (Jones 1989:83). The early efforts of the Fabian Society to municipalize these undertakings were long delayed. But even then, it proposed only to substitute municipal gas works for the private ones, just as localized.

During the first year of Wells's membership in the Fabian Society (1903–1908), he addressed himself to this very problem with a paper titled, "The Question of Scientific Administrative Areas in Relation to Municipal Undertakings" (Hammond 1977:78). Soon after Wells resigned because he found it impossible to convert Fabian thinking away from its focus on particular reforms within the existing social fabric; he had more holistic designs (Bergonzi 1971:8; on Fabian policy see Funderburck and Thobaben 1994:85f; on "The Episode of Mr. Wells," see Cole 1961:117–124).

Wells published his Fabian paper with the title shortened to "On Administrative Areas," in *Mankind in the Making* (1904:371–392). It is reprinted in the present work as Appendix II, from which I draw the language that identifies the Modern State Octopus as, quite literally, a vampire state.

The problem is, the political geography of England had not changed since the time of the Norman Conquest, with its introduction of shires (=counties) and every little governing body within them: parish and vestry councils, boroughs and municipalities, rural and urban district boards. The narrator of *Tono-Bungay*, Wells's epic novel of social criticism, says, "I have

---

Sleeper is a prophecy of the former two examples (Stover 1999); whereas *Things to Come* is a critique of the latter, with its communism-minus-Marx thesis (Stover 1992).
    †The author's quote is from a mid-nineteenth century technical journal.

written of England as a feudal scheme overtaken by fatty degeneration" (1909:488). He was, in fact, not far wrong (see entry under "counties" in *Encyclopædia Britannica* 11th edition, 7:316f). The same local entities took on gas supply, as they did the no more coordinated supply of electricity, its competitor. "By 1919, in the London area alone there were fifty supply companies, using twenty-four voltages and ten different frequencies" (Jones 1989:89; more in Stover 1996a:23–4 *n*4).

For Wells, the proper area for the scientific administration of London is the entire metropolitan region that feeds commuter trains into the city from dormitory towns, all those now under feudalistic boroughs and municipalities. What is wanted is a "mammoth municipality" to provide them with public services of every sort by a "delocalized class" of administrators that *"sucks the ebbing life from your old communities into the veins of the new"* (see Appendix II in the present work; emphasis added).

Significantly, the first group of Martian cyclinders land near the terminus of the London & Southwestern Railway, the next in the city itself. With the poisonous bite of the Martians, all communities along the railway line (itself torn up; see fig. 9 of the plates in the present work) are dissolved, are liquefied, made ready to be insufflated into the body of the state octopus, the vampiric state monster. For in the larger scheme, greater metropolitan London is but one economic unit in a "new world order" (1940a:title), the same "new order" (1936: film shot 482 in 1936) the octopus-headed John Cabal brings to the war ruins of the traditional order he and his Airmen conclusively smashed. "So the world which had once been divided among territorial Great Powers became divided among functional Great Powers" (1933: 355). The nation-states are now obliterated under a globalized big-business government, whose bureaucratic controls administer this or that industry wherever on the planet they are located. This is the future in *Sleeper* (see Stover 1999: Introduction, section 6), subsequent to the Martian invasion, as it is in *Things to Come*.

In *Worlds*, the Martians are for people "ugly *brutes*" (I:5). But the people don't know how lucky they are to have them to save them from a mistaken past. Elsewhere they are "quite nice monsters" (1937:971), and indeed, Wells's drawing of a Martian is as cute as a Walt Disney octopus (fig. 5 in the present work).* These beatific monsters are from *Star-Begotten*, in which they send out telepathic signals to selective humans receptive to Wellsism, who then, getting "Martianized," will form that emergent elite ready to lead the Modern State Revolution. One who gets the message confides in another,

---

*From an inscribed copy in the Wells Archive, University of Illinois, Urbana (also reprinted in West 1930:107).

the Martians "are not so much invading as acting as a sort of inter-planetary tutor" (*ibid.*:98).

In *Worlds*, the artilleryman views them in the same light. He proposes to learn from the Martians and then, with a band of like-minded followers, defeat them and take over their mission. He fails. But in the end, as the narrator concludes, their tutorial example models the coming commonwealth of mankind.

*   *   *

The last word goes to Bismarck the Iron Chancellor, the true father of the Martians. As Hayek (1979:353) points out, Saint-Simonism was known as the Prussian Idea, not the least of all because it had become the religion of the Young German Movement antedating the Nazi Movement (Butler 1926).

Prussianism itself is a byword for that arrogance and overbearing method associated with the Prussian military machine and governmental attitudes going back to the days of Frederick the Great (*d.* 1786), surviving until World War I and then to be revived by the Nazis. "It is the spirit of an army carried over into a bureaucracy and into society itself.... It is discipline — and servility, Standardized" (Evans 1994:869). Wells characterized it as "collective submission" to "German order and discipline" (1908b:202, 197), in his admiring portrait of a Prussian officer leading a German airfleet in *The War in the Air*. He may as well be "the great John Cabal" (film shot 837 in 1936), Air Dictator.

Wells no doubt gets his Prussianism from Comte (1877). He asserts, as Hayek (1979:355f) reports, "that in the future society the 'immoral' concept of individual rights will disappear and then will there be only duties." That is exactly the servitude of labor in the Modern State, in which "impossible 'rights'" (1933:107) are no longer possible. This clears the way for a militarized labor force whose only choice is obedience. Once the blood suckers of private capitalism are replaced by the managers of "autocratic state capitalism" (1931:60) devoted to integral purpose, the antagonism between labor and capital is dissolved in a unity of interests. Even with a "labour conscription" (1912a:22) to enforce it, "most [men] will toil very cheerfully in subordination if they feel that the collective interest is a fine thing and a great thing" (60). In Saint-Simon it is that "joyous partnership in a great experience" (Talmon 1967:65), shared by a confraternity of believers in the world as industrial workshop. Those not so cheerful go to the gulag, the fate of Saint-Simon's antisocial "quadrupeds."

The master had conceived of a "labor army," in Bellamy's phrase, the same adopted by Trotsky (Rossi 1989:446) as Lenin's partner in the Russian

Revolution of 1917. Both he and Lenin also learned from the practical experience of German "War socialism," the nation's total mobilization during World War I. This led to Lenin's notion of "universal labor service" on the analogy of military conscription (Johnson 1983:90f). Eventually the Soviet Union rationalized this barbaric practice on the grounds that it formed a New Soviet Man happy and willing to serve as one of many "cogs in the wheel" (Heller 1988:title). The resulting prison state was exalted as an advance in the evolution of human consciousness from individualism to a collective mentality. (What difference, after all, between the forced labor of quadrupeds in the gulag camps and state employees on the outside, when a supreme power controls both?) Wells upheld that policy as evidence of the nonfixity of human nature; the collectivist state makes sure that "man becomes a different animal" (1928c: Chapter I, title). His "congenital traditionalism" (1932:137) can be modified only by "forcible conformities" (1901:281) that shape a new species, "the coming man" (1933:426). His coming lies in the future, the prevision of which militates against the past in a war of the worlds, ideas old and new.

But Wells, perhaps, put too much faith in the Prussian Idea which, after all, is fit only for Prussians, and not always for them. This returns us to Bismarck. The Prussian virtues he represents are readiness to serve, discipline, hard work, punctuality, cleanliness, self-control and selflessness, and acceptance of responsibility, among others. But some of these easily turn to vices, when obedience yields blind obedience, conscious of duty abject servility. MacDonogh (1994: chapter III) has written of this in his book *Prussia: The Perversion of an Idea*. What could be more perverse than a sound work ethic subverted to state slavery, personality to total self-abnegation? It can never happen, yet it has been tried. Human nature is not plastic, attempts to recast it are futile and tragic.

The Prussian Idea exalts authority, duty, hierarchy over the liberal slogans of the French Revolution: liberty, equality, fraternity: ideals hateful to Saint-Simon and his "totalitarian technocracy" (Talmon 1960:30). Outside Prussia, however, his world formula never did make for a good marching song, and so it cannot avoid being a coercive ideology. What is good for universal welfare is not understood by the common run of men, so they must be forced to be happy in their work, or at least to submit to it. Ideally, new habits of subjected labor will in time so remold human nature that duty and discipline, in the cause of industrial productivity and purposeful state-integration, must become second nature. The Modern State Octopus proposes as much. "Within its far-flung tentacles it embraced and sought to permeate with its own nature, with the concepts and methods of a commonweal of mutual service, a mass of some thousands and a half million human beings,

still carried on by inertias established during thousands of generations"
(1933:293). Forcibly squeezed by the octopus tentacles of the state monster,
the masses of mankind are *permeated* by its *concepts and methods*, becoming
believers in their own subjection. They are so indoctrinated (=concept) and
coerced (=method) under a police-and-propaganda regime that they partake
of the metaphorical monster's *own nature*, all head and hands eviscerated of
selfish stomach motives. Martianized man breaks with the *inertias* of tradition, putting the world's work on a new socialist basis, its toilers the willing
hands of the willful head.

To play on the title of Wells's big socialist manifesto, *New Worlds for
Old* (1908), the Martians in a complex way carry out his war with tradition.
They arrive as enemies from an older (and wiser) world to conquer a newer
one (in need of wisdom). In turn, after their demise, they serve as a model
for earthlings in *their* conquest of a new world: the future created out of the
destruction of a mistaken past. Just as the progressive empire-building Prussians had rallied all the obsolete German states of feudal heritage in a national
war, so too with the Bismarckian Martians. Their effect is to rally the obsolete nation-states of earth to form a planetary imperium: the big-business
octopus that is the world of autocratic state capitalism in *Sleeper*: Martian
technocracy reincarnated.

That it is totalitarian by design Wells does not deny. In the Modern State
there is "no real distinction between political, social, and economic control
… they are inseparable in a rational order" (1939:353). But while the all-swal-
lowing new Leviathan, the Coming Beast, is indeed a fearful state monster,
it is withal a nice monster because it is rational. Nothing could be nicer and
more beatific than disposing of prescientific history in that "Ultimate Revolution" (1933b:subtitle; 1933:374), making for central planning and collectivist labor, in the final war of the worlds between visionary future and
misbegotten past.

As in heaven (the red planet Mars), so shall be the kingdom on earth,
God's promise. "Red he is and Red he always has been" (1941:70), as Wells
the voice ordains of human destiny.

H. G. Wells

The War of the Worlds

text of the first London
edition, 1898, with annotations

The

War of the Worlds

By

H. G. Wells

Author of ' The Time Machine,' ' The Island of Doctor Moreau,'
'The Invisible Man,' etc.

' But who shall dwell in these Worlds if they be inhabited?
. . . Are we or they Lords of the World? . . . And
how are all things made for man?'
KEPLER (quoted in *The Anatomy of Melancholy*)

London
William Heinemann
1898

TO

MY BROTHER
FRANK WELLS,
THIS RENDERING OF HIS IDEA.[2]

---

1. Epigraph on title page. Johannes Kepler (*d.* 1630) laid the foundation of modern astronomy with his calculation of planetary motions, as immortalized in Kepler's Laws. His words, from a letter to Galileo, are quoted by Robert Burton in *The Anatomy of Melancholy* (1621). Wells has abridged them slightly, the better to punctuate the novel's general thesis.

Astronomy as a new optical science (Galileo's contribution) had confirmed the Copernican model and displaced the geocentric Ptolemaic one. The prescientific universe of medieval theology held the entire macrocosm divinely ordained for the benefit of man, its embodied microcosm. Kepler's "the World" (capital "W") is that macrocosm, which in its other planetary worlds might also harbor intelligent life; so that man of the *Minor Mundus*, in whom all creation supposedly had centered a rational being, may not be so exclusive after all. There could be other "Lords of the World" out there (see Adams 1938:66–68). Wells's Martians affirm Kepler's speculation, at the same time they prove to be more rational than the earthly lords they war upon.

Man, as presently constituted, is not all he could be. The fall of humanity the Martian invasion portends relates only to the species *Homo sapiens* in its transitional stage of evolution, its unprogressive majority deserving of massacre; "I hate common humanity" (1937:201). The invasion stimulates upward movement toward a new Martianized, star-begotten species, "*Homo sideralis*" (152), whose destiny is to be the true Lord of the sidereal universe.

2. Wells explains this dedication to elder brother Frank in a document reprinted as Appendix IV of the present work.

CONTENTS

---

*[Publisher's note: page references are to the present annotated edition.]

Book I.—The Coming
of the Martians.

I

THE EVE OF THE WAR.

No one would have believed, in the last years of the nineteenth century, that human affairs were being watched keenly and closely by intelligences greater than man's and yet as mortal as his own; that as men busied themselves about their affairs they were scrutinized and studied, perhaps almost as narrowly as a man with a microscope might scrutinize the transient creatures that swarm and multiply in a drop of water. With infinite complacency men went to and fro over this globe about their little affairs, serene in their assurance of their empire over matter. It is possible that the infusoria under the microscope do the same. No one gave a thought to the older worlds of space as sources of human danger, or thought of them only to dismiss the idea of life upon them as impossible or improbable. It is curious to recall some of the mental habits of those departed days. At most, terrestrial men fancied there might be other men upon Mars, perhaps inferior to themselves and ready to welcome a missionary enterprise. Yet, across the gulf of space,[3] minds that are to our minds as ours are to those of the beasts that perish, intellects vast and cool and unsympathetic, regarded this earth with envious eyes, and slowly and surely drew their plans against us. And early in the twentieth century came the great disillusionment.[4]

---

3. The phrase "across the gulf of space" is from Lowell (1896:129), describing the deeps through which he peers. Here it is used for Martian astronomers peering at earth with telescopes as a man looks through a microscope at lowly infusoria, the distance between microorganisms, men, and Martians being of the same hyperbolic magnitude.
4. This opening paragraph is justly famous for its magnificent poetic dic-

The planet Mars, I scarcely need remind the reader, revolves about the sun at a mean distance of 140,000,000 miles, and the light and heat it receives from the sun is barely half of that received by this world. It must be, if the nebular hypothesis has any truth, older than our world,

---

tion. Its meaning resonates in the opening scenes of *Things to Come*. On the eve of World War II, on Xmas Eve, Londoners demonstrate their holiday revelry serenely unaware that war and revolution are about to overtake and transform their lives. Their "self-complacent ignorance" (1941:150) is tagged "everydayism" (1928:93), a term of contempt for the "false securities and fatuous satisfactions of the everyday life" (1934:154) (see more in Stover 1987:27–37).

In "The Past and the Great State" (1912a), everydayism comprehends the whole of the Normal Social Life as received by tradition: a mistaken past erased and corrected by the Great State, the utopian future realized in *Sleeper* subsequent to the Martian invasion (Stover 1999). Meanwhile, "our political, our economic, our social lives have still to become illuminated and directed by the scientific spirit — are still sick and feeble with congenital traditionalism" (1932:137).

The "great disillusionment" (last sentence) is a "cleansing disillusionment [that effects] the liquidation of a bankrupt civilization preparatory to a drastic reconstruction" (1933:214). The Martians massacre the diseased carriers of everydayism and the Normal Social Life is demodeled, then remodeled with its terrorized survivors. In *Anticipations*, Wells foresees just such a necessary clearance. "It has become apparent that whole masses of human population are, as a whole, inferior in their claim upon the future" (1901:314). He said the same 43 years later: "The *average* contemporary man is *en masse* a degenerate creature." What is wanted for transforming humanity are "exceptional types" who look forward and not back, "an emergent elite" (1944:192). One such is the artilleryman, who attempts to learn from the Martians how to fulfill their progressive mission for the human cause, with the aid of a band of exceptional types loyal to his grand ambition (II:7). In this he anticipates the cephalopodic John Cabal and his Air League, which devastates what remains of the old order, and rebuilds the Modern State Octopus on its postwar ruin fields.

That state monster is the "Coming Beast" (1891:253; see Stover 1987: 50–65), that "higher organism ... of the coming years" (1901:189). It is a "new social Leviathan" (1926:589), the "Hobbesian monster as a completely unified social organism" (1942:36), in which "converge all lives upon a common existence" (12). It is a *new* social Leviathan in that Hobbes's corporative state is universalized and industrialized. It is Wells's "world economic machine" (1931a: 373) under scientific management, in which all lives converge in selfless production. The "non-effective masses" (1901:93) are remolded for "social efficiency" (340) by means of "forcible conformities" (281). This is the managerial terror exerted by a new "aristocracy of organizers" (1899a, Appendix I in

and long before this earth ceased to be molten, life upon its surface must have begun its course. The fact that it is scarcely one-seventh of the volume of the earth must have accelerated its cooling to the temperature at which life could begin. It has air and water, and all that is necessary for the support of animated existence.

Yet so vain is man, and so blinded by his vanity, that no writer, up to the very end of the nineteenth century, expressed any idea that intelligent life might have developed there far, or indeed at all, beyond its earthly level.[5] Nor was it generally understood that since Mars is older

---

Stover 1999) that reforms human nature and makes it compliant to economic slavery. In "The Extinction of Man" (1898b), Wells writes that "Even now ... the coming terror may be crouching for its spring and the fall of humanity be at hand," but the extinction so prophesied is that of the existing species before its remaking as the "Coming Man" (179). If Wells can say, "I hate common humanity" (1909:249), he can welcome a Martianized change.

The phrase, "the coming terror," is the title of a book by a certified reactionary who fears that socialist revolutionaries will base "the salvation of the State on the destruction of the individual" (Buchanan 1891:9). Once again (see the Introduction to the present work, section 2), Wells in response goes for the opposite idea: "The Modern State [is] the whole duty of man" (1933:398), under which "Man's soul is no longer his own" (1931:28). What the noted poet Robert Buchanan feared, out of his egotistical concern for artistic self-expression, is what is coming.

Thus does the calculated frightfulness of John Cabal's octopus-headed helmet (see the plates in the present work, fig. 2) have its saving grace. With visor down (fig. 3), he is a saint, come to elevate a degenerate species. It "squirmed in the pitilessly benevolent grip of the Air Dictatorship," all the while protesting its "harshly rational schooling of human motives" (1933:346). But at last emerged "the coming man from the man of the past" (426).

5. "No writer," that is, except the narrator himself. His empty boast is meant to be obvious, because all readers of the time were expected to see the colonists' homeland is the Mars of Percival Lowell (1895; 1896 with first American edition). To that Wells had added his own speculation, "Intelligence on Mars" (1896a). In II:2 the narrator postures as just such a writer, crediting to himself the insight of Wells's essay, "The Man of the Year Million" (1893:Appendix I), in which perfectable human beings are seen in future to evolve toward the improved Martian condition. But although the narrator is identified with this Wellsian idea, he is not a spokesman for the author; he rather comes across as a know-it-all. At note 71 he is pegged as a lightweight intellectual associated with Voltaire's Dr. Pangloss. Not everything he says is reliable, however authoritative he pretends to be.

than our earth, with scarcely a quarter of the superficial area, and remoter from the sun, it necessarily follows that it is not only more distant from life's beginning but nearer its end.

The secular cooling that must some day overtake our planet has already gone far indeed with our neighbour. Its physical condition is still largely a mystery, but we know now that even in its equatorial region the mid-day temperature barely approaches that of our coldest winter. Its air is much more attenuated than ours, its oceans have shrunk until they cover but a third of its surface, and as its slow seasons change huge snowcaps gather and melt about either pole, and periodically inundate its temperate zones. That last stage of exhaustion, which to us is still incredibly remote, has become a present-day problem for the inhabitants of Mars. The immediate pressure of necessity has brightened their intellects, enlarged their powers, and hardened their hearts. And looking across space, with instruments and intelligences such as we have scarcely dreamt of, they see, at its nearest distance, only 35,000,000 of miles sunward of them, a morning star of hope, our own warmer planet, green with vegetation and gray with water, with a cloudy atmosphere eloquent of fertility, with glimpses through its drifting cloud-wisps of broad stretches of populous country and narrow navy-crowded seas.

And we men, the creatures who inhabit this earth, must be to them at least as alien and lowly as are the monkeys and lemurs to us. The intellectual side of man already admits that life is an incessant struggle for existence, and it would seem that this too is the belief of the minds upon Mars. Their world is far gone in its cooling, and this world is still crowded with life, but crowded only with what they regard as inferior animals. To carry warfare sunward is indeed their only escape from the destruction that generation after generation creeps upon them.

And before we judge of them too harshly, we must remember what ruthless and utter destruction our own species has wrought, not only upon animals, such as the vanished bison and the dodo, but upon its own inferior races. The Tasmanians, in spite of their human likeness, were entirely swept out of existence in a war of extermination waged by European immigrants, in the space of fifty years. Are we such apostles of mercy as to complain if the Martians warred in the same spirit?[6]

---

6. The racially Australoid natives of Tasmania survived until 1876 in a state of upper paleolithic culture. To the island's Dutch and later British colonists,

The Martians seem to have calculated their descent with amazing subtlety—their mathematical learning is evidently far in excess of ours—and to have carried out their preparations with a well-nigh perfect unanimity. Had our instruments permitted it, we might have seen the gathering trouble far back in the nineteenth century. Men like

---

they were so many subhumans hunted down for dog meat. The vampirish colonists from Mars hunt down humans for their blood, and the above comparison is made. Whence the inherited cliché that *Worlds* is a liberal-minded, antiracist tract. Beckson (1992) in a chapter titled "Empire Builders and Destroyers" finds it exceptional, on the London literary scene in the 1890s, for its attack on the cheerleaders of British imperialism. This can hardly be the case if Wells in *Anticipations* (1901: Chapter 7) looks to English as the language of his world state.

In *A Short History of the World* he evinces little sympathy for the Tasmanians, describing them as "a race of human beings at a lower level of physical and intellectual development than any other of [the] earliest races of mankind" (1922:59). But while the Tasmanians are thankfully eliminated, there remain other inferior types low on the evolutionary scale that are not fit raw material for remaking as productive citizens of the Modern State. Or as Wells poses the problem for his earlier New Republicans, what are they to do with

> Those swarms of black, and brown, and dirty-white, and yellow people, who do not come into the new needs of efficiency?
> Well, the world is a world, not a charitable institution, and I take it they will have to go [1901:342].

More than thirty years later he asks the same question: "What are we going to do with all the swarming multitude of unsuitable people who constitute the great majority of mankind? (1942a:55). In *Things to Come*, war and revolution conveniently "killed more than half the human race" (film shot 366 in 1936), the debased half, as a cleansing prelude to rebuilding a "new order" (film shot 482 in 1936) on the ashes of the old. This answers the issue raised in *The Science of Life*: "The dead weight of inferior population may overpower the constructive few" (1931b:1474).

It is hard to overlook the genocidal bent of utopism, not alone in Wells. Thoroughly known to him (Stover 1987:88) is the decisive classic of post–Christian rationalism, *The Future of Science* by Ernest Renan, who took the inferiority of the nonwhite races as proven, and thus as a problem to be dealt with in the coming scientific order. But even the animality of the best stock falls short of what could be, excepting a few select men of science in the vanguard. "The State is neither a charity bureau nor a hospital. It is a machine for making progress." Its prophylactic watchword is, "Of these beasts let us make men" (Renan 1891:317, 359). It is Doctor Moreau's as well (Stover 1995b:142f, *n*114).

Schiaparelli[7] watched the red planet—it is odd, by-the-by, that for countless centuries Mars has been the star of war—but failed to interpret the fluctuating appearances of the markings they mapped so well. All that time the Martians must have been getting ready.

During the opposition of 1894 a great light was seen on the illuminated part of the disc, first at the Lick Observatory, then by Perrotin of Nice, and then by other observers. English readers heard of it first in the issue of *Nature* dated August 2.[8] I am inclined to think that the

---

7. Giovanni Virginio Schiaparelli (*d.* 1910), whose mapping of Mars during the opposition of 1877 provided names for some extensive surface features still in use today (U.S. Geological Survey, 1976). His linear *canali*, however, are not among them, unless he observed the huge canyon later mapped by Mariner 9, *Valles Marineris*, and imagined more of the same. It was Lowell after him who took his *canali*, natural channels, as artificial waterways.

8. This is a genuine reference to the said 1894 article in *Nature*, "A Strange Light on Mars" (reprinted as Appendix VI in Hughes and Geduld 1993). The light may have been that of a fiery meteor crash, or else the glint of sunlight on the planet's horizon. In the novel, that flash is taken as the casting of a gigantic space gun, as molten metal from burning furnaces is poured into a deep pit: exactly the fabricating scene in Verne's novel. Six years later new flashes are of its firing of missiles earthward, which would date their landing to 1900 (last year of the nineteenth century, per the opening line). They land very shortly after the observed flashes, meaning that they travel with supernal speed. The astronomer who reports these flaming outbursts in the next paragraph is one Lavelle of Java. His name recalls the Lavelle of Nice (working under the observatory's director, Perrotin) whose *Nature* article was a sensation. Given the specificity of that reference, so well impressed on the public mind, the reader is led to suspect that the narrator is unreliable, that he often distorts or makes up references to suit his know-it-all pretensions (note 5). At the same time, beyond reflecting on the narrator's dubious character, the author himself indulges in a departure from the empirical: The speedy missiles are meant to be mythic, befitting a planet home to the Roman god of war.

Hughes and Geduld (1993:200, *n*27) blame Wells for a goofy miscalculation in not waiting upon the next opposition of 1907. Human astronomers may need the closer approach of Mars to observe it, but the mighty Martians care not for ballistic convenience. So soon as their space gun is cast they invade. This may in fact be the point, calculated to show that the Martians are such master conquerors of nature they are able to go anywhere in the solar system anytime they please. Indeed, the text mentions their shooting shells at Venus as well, another inner and younger planet to earth's sunside.

The narrator, in his last words following note 10, speaks of "that unerring

appearance may have been the casting of the huge gun, the vast pit sunk into their planet, from which their shots were fired at us. Peculiar markings, as yet unexplained, were seen near the site of that outbreak during the next two oppositions.

The storm burst upon us six years ago now. As Mars approached opposition, Lavelle of Java set the wires of the astronomical exchange palpitating with the amazing intelligence of a huge outbreak of incandescent gas upon the planet. It had occurred towards midnight of the 12th, and the spectroscope, to which he had at once resorted, indicated a mass of flaming gas, chiefly hydrogen, moving with an enormous velocity towards this earth. This jet of fire had become invisible about a quarter past twelve. He compared it to a colossal puff of flame, suddenly and violently squirted out of the planet, "as flaming gas rushes out of a gun."

A singularly appropriate phrase it proved. Yet the next day there was nothing of this in the papers, except a little note in the *Daily Telegraph,* and the world went in ignorance of one of the gravest dangers that ever threatened the human race. I might not have heard of the eruption at all had I not met Ogilvy,[9] the well-known astronomer, at Ottershaw.

---

missile" he senses coming so soon as he sees the first flash on Mars (witnessed from a local observatory manned by his friend Ogilvy). Charles Darwin's younger brother, Sir George the eminent astronomer, has a comment on this in his book *The Tides.* "In his interesting romance, 'The War of the Worlds,' Mr. Wells imagines the Martians to be able to shoot their bombs from Mars with such precision as to hit a particular spot on earth. It was not necessary for Mr. Wells to consider the difficulties of the problem his wonderful Martians solved, but I doubt if we poor terrestrials will be able to solve it ten thousand years from now" (1911:421). These ballistic difficulties, however, did not prevent Wells from using a Martian-like space cannon for the conquest of space in *Things to Come.* Yet by 1969, American astronauts of the Apollo 11 mission, using rockets, were able to hit and land upon a particular spot on the moon. Wells's deliberate avoidance of rocketry, however, is entirely symbolic (see plates, figs. 7 and 8).

Interesting to note, Wells himself references the work of "the younger Darwin" on tidal drag in *The Time Machine* (Stover 1996a:99, *n*133).

Sir George repays the compliment some years later.

9. A fictitious astronomer named after the Ogilvy in "The Star" (1897a, in 1927a:716–729), who observes the cataclysmic coming of the title's cometary body. He senses the inevitable *fin de globe* as the Ogilvy of *Worlds* does not. The author reinvents this character for his own purpose, which is to show the narrator an intellect superior (as he thinks) to the experts'.

He was immensely excited at the news, and in the excess of his feelings invited me up to take a turn with him that night in a scrutiny of the red planet.

In spite of all that has happened since, I still remember that vigil very distinctly: the black and silent observatory, the shadowed lantern throwing a feeble glow upon the floor in the corner, the steady ticking of the clockwork of the telescope, the little slit in the roof—an oblong profundity with the star dust streaked across it. Ogilvy moved about, invisible but audible. Looking through the telescope, one saw a circle of deep blue, and the little round planet swimming in the field. It seemed such a little thing, so bright and small and still, faintly marked with transverse stripes, and slightly flattened from the perfect round. But so little it was, so silvery warm, a pin's head of light! It was as if it quivered a little, but really this was the telescope vibrating with the activity of the clockwork that kept the planet in view.

As I watched, the little star seemed to grow larger and smaller, and to advance and recede, but that was simply that my eye was tired. Forty millions of miles it was from us—more than 40,000,000 miles of void. Few people realize the immensity of vacancy in which the dust of the material universe swims.

Near it in the field, I remember, were three little points of light, three telescopic stars infinitely remote, and all around it was the unfathomable darkness of empty space. You know how that blackness looks on a frosty starlight night. In a telescope it seems far profounder. And invisible to me, because it was so remote and small, flying swiftly and steadily towards me across that incredible distance, drawing nearer every minute by so many thousands of miles, came the Thing they were sending us, the Thing[10] that was to bring so much struggle and

---

10. Star-gazing is a frequent motif in Wells, who identifies the stars with human aspiration; those few who do the gazing have the power of dispassionate observation to see how lowly is man's estate, how short it falls from higher prospects (Reed 1982:44). The Martians who come from out there are at once a threat to human complacency and a stimulus to betterment. They are that ominous "Thing" bringing death and calamity. The story "In the Avu Observatory" (1894, in 1927a:241–249) has a Borneo-based astronomer confront a hideous "Thing" that drops through the slit of the dome. No doubt it is no more than a bat or flying lemur, but the Avu astronomer is badly shaken, having imagined something just arrived from a planetary body he has just observed. His fright, however, is not mistaken; it intuits that some invading Thing *is* possible. Ogilvy, by contrast, is not in the least attuned to that sensitivity.

calamity and death to the earth. I never dreamt of it then as I watched; no one on earth dreamt of that unerring missile.

That night, too, there was another jetting out of gas from the distant planet. I saw it. A reddish flash at the edge, the slightest projection of the outline, just as the chronometer struck midnight, and at that I told Ogilvy, and he took my place. The night was warm and I was thirsty, and I went, stretching my legs clumsily, and feeling my way in the darkness, to the little table where the siphon stood, while Ogilvy exclaimed at the streamer of gas that came out towards us.

That night another invisible missile started on its way to earth from Mars, just a second or so under twenty-four hours after the first one. I remember how I sat on the table there in the blackness, with patches of green and crimson swimming before my eyes. I wished I had a light to smoke by, little suspecting the meaning of the minute gleam I had seen, and all that it would presently bring me. Ogilvy watched till one, and then gave it up, and we lit the lantern and walked over to his house. Down below in the darkness were Ottershaw and Chertsey,[11] and all their hundreds of people, sleeping in peace.

He was full of speculation that night about the condition of Mars, and scoffed at the vulgar idea of its having inhabitants who were signalling us.[12] His idea was that meteorites might be falling in a heavy shower upon the planet, or that a huge volcanic explosion was in progress. He pointed out to me how unlikely it was that organic evolution had taken the same direction in the two adjacent planets.[13]

---

11. These are two small villages, now "sleeping in peace," a few miles northwest of Woking where Ogilvy's observatory is located. Woking is also the narrator's home and where, nearby, the first Martian cylinder falls.

12. A reference to the signalling mania of the day. From 1869 there had been a series of "Letters to Mars" proposals for interplanetary communication by way of inscribing arithmetic and geometric theorems in the sands of the Sahara, for instance — letters to astronomers on Venus, the moon, and Mars alike (Ley 1945:38–40). Francis Galton, Darwin's polymathic cousin, brought the mania to its peak with his article, "Intelligible Signals Between Neighboring Stars" (1896; see more in Stover 1998b:141f, *n*114). Ogilvy in his matter-of-face everydayism dismisses all this.

13. The self-inflated philosophic narrator feels oppressed by Ogilvy's matter of fact discourse (with that ticking of the clock against his metronome voice), very much like the poet in Walt Whitman's "When I Heard the Learned Astronomer":

When I heard the learned astronomer,
When the proofs, the figures, were ranged in columns before me,

"The chances against anything man-like on Mars are a million to one," he said.

Hundreds of observers saw the flame that night and the night after, about midnight, and again the night after, and so for ten nights, a flame each night. Why the shots ceased after the tenth no one on earth has attempted to explain. It may be the gases of the firing caused the Martians inconvenience. Dense clouds of smoke or dust, visible through a powerful telescope on earth as little gray, fluctuating patches, spread through the clearness of the planet's atmosphere, and obscured its more familiar features.

Even the daily papers woke up to the disturbances at last, and popular notes appeared here, there, and everywhere concerning the volcanoes upon Mars. The serio-comic periodical *Punch*, I remember, made a happy use of it in the political cartoon. And, all unsuspected, those missiles the Martians had fired at us drew earthward, rushing now at a pace of many miles a second through the empty gulf of space, hour by hour and day by day, nearer and nearer. It seems to me now almost incredibly wonderful that, with the swift fate hanging over us, men could go about their petty concerns as they did. I remember how jubilant Markham was at securing a new photograph of the planet for

---

When I was shown the charts and diagrams, to add, divide, and measure them,
When I sitting heard the astronomer where he lectured with much applause in the
    lecture-room,
How soon unaccountable I became tired and sick,
Till rising and gliding out I wandered off by myself,
In the mystical moist night-air, and from time to time,
Looked up in perfect silence at the stars.

To be sure, Wells looks to science as the religion of the future, but not all scientists are equal. Some are reactionary, others progressive. A distinction is made, for example, between the orthodox Dr. Kemp in *The Invisible Man* (1897) and its title figure. Dr. Kemp is busy writing a paper disproving the idea of invisibility when Griffin (the invisible man) comes upon him: he who exemplifies the truly miraculous power of science (Stover 1998a). Another example is Doctor Moreau, whose experiments in the possibilities of vivisection go against both orthodoxy and law.

Ogilvy is one of the bad guys, lacking the imagination of the Avu astronomer (note 10). The narrator walks out on him, into the night, under the starry stillness, to look upon the sleeping hamlets outside (note 11) he knows will be disturbed by a falling Thing. Significantly, Ogilvy is the first victim of the Martians' death ray when he goes to investigate the initial landing near Woking at Horsell Commons.

the illustrated paper he edited in those days. People in these latter times scarcely realize the abundance and enterprise of our nineteenth-century papers.[14] For my own part, I was much occupied in learning to ride the bicycle, and busy upon a series of papers discussing the probable developments of moral ideas as civilization progressed.[15]

---

14. The suggestion is that, "in these latter days" after the invasion, there is less reckless journalism (of which the fictive Markham is a god-awful example). In future, the press will be a monopoly of the divinized state, whose "Act of Uniformity" shall enforce a scientific world-view. Its truth establishes "that there can be only one right way of looking at the world ... and that all others must be wrong and misleading and involve destructive distortions of conduct" (1933:332f).

Otherwise, the narrator remarks, "men [would not have gone] about their petty concerns as they did ... with that swift fate hanging over [them]." Everydayism (note 4) is just that sort of self-defeating behavior, oblivious to "the triviality of men" in the face of world-historical forces greater than themselves (1922a: 1). But the narrator himself turns out to be the most petty of men, unchallenged by the great events he reports.

15. As it happens, Wells himself was just learning to ride the bicycle whilst living in Woking. "I wheeled about the district marking down suitable places and people for destruction by my Martians" (1934:458). Apart from railway trains, the bicycle then was the fastest thing on wheels in the transition from horse-drawn carriages to automobiles. The first models were in fact no more than four-wheeled bicycles with a Daimler engine, further developed for London's first motor-car exhibition by 1895 (Greg 1967:383). By 1903 two bicycle mechanics, the Wright brothers, flew the first airplane, exactly the line of development Wells foresaw in his *Anticipations* of 1901. Elaborating, he went on to speculate that aviation, making national borders obsolete, would unify the globe in a world-state. And so we have his Airmen, in *Things to Come*, accomplishing just that — but only after they bomb obstructive nationalists out of existence. The Martians, with their futuristic warplanes, attempt to do same in their plan to conquer earth and impose on it the politics of Mars. Wells on his new bicycle, touring Woking, marks down suitable locality-minded targets.

The coming of mechanism thus makes for moral progress, because motorized transport is destined to create a global village, that modern cliché, by obliterating all local patriotisms. This is the subject of an article the narrator says he was writing at the time of the invasion. It alludes to Wells's own "Morals and Civilization" (1897b: reprinted as Appendix V in Stover 1996b). But, as at note 5, the narrator is not to be mistaken for the author. The two share some ideas but Wells makes it clear that his narrator is a shallower version of himself, a Panglossian simpleton.

One night (the first missile then could scarcely have been 10,000,000 miles away) I went for a walk with my wife. It was starlight, and I explained the Signs of the Zodiac to her, and pointed out Mars, a bright dot of light creeping zenithward, towards which so many telescopes were pointed. It was a warm night. Coming home, a party of excursionists from Chertsey or Isleworth passed us singing and playing music. There were lights in the upper windows of the houses as the people went to bed. From the railway-station in the distance came the sound of shunting trains, ringing and rumbling, softened almost into melody by the distance. My wife pointed out to me the brightness of the red, green and yellow signal lights, hanging in a framework against the sky. It seemed so safe and tranquil.[16]

16. Having returned home after his visit to Ogilvy's private observatory, the narrator tells his wife what they saw from there, now general news confirmed in more distant reports. Excursionists from Chertsey (note 11) and further-away Isleworth (a London suburb) are also returning home after a gala trip as if to no more than a pleasing fireworks display. The narrator himself is not in a singing mood, and his wife reassures him by referencing the homely signal lights of Woking railway station against the night sky. Everydayism again, "safe and tranquil." Significantly, it is the dissolution of the railway system (1:16) that first reveals the poison-dart effect of the vampiric Martians. At end of story, it is to his wife the narrator returns to tell all, making of it, somehow, just a domestic episode: she safe, he returned to her. For all his philosophic reflections, he remains an everydayist: a contradiction resolved in the final textual note (183).

II

THE FALLING STAR.

THEN came the night of the first falling star. It was seen early in the morning rushing over Winchester eastward, a line of flame, high in the atmosphere. Hundreds must have seen it, and taken it for an ordinary falling star. Albin described it as leaving a greenish streak behind it that glowed for some seconds. Denning, our greatest authority on meteorites,[17] stated that the height of its first appearance was about ninety or one hundred miles. It seemed to him that it fell to earth about one hundred miles east of him.

I was at home at that hour and writing in my study, and although my French windows face towards Ottershaw and the blind was up (for I loved in those days to look up at the night sky), I saw nothing of it. Yet this strangest of all things that ever came to earth from outer space must have fallen while I was sitting there, visible to me had I only looked up as it passed. Some of those who saw its flight say it travelled with a hissing sound. I myself heard nothing of that. Many people in Berkshire, Surrey, and Middlesex must have seen the fall of it, and, at most, have thought that another meteorite had descended. No one seems to have troubled to look for the fallen mass that night.

But very early in the morning poor Ogilvy, who had seen the shooting star, and who was persuaded that a meteorite lay somewhere on

---

17. William Frederick Denning (*d*. 1931), an amateur astronomer living in Bristol, was indeed a recognized authority on meteorites (Hughes and Geduld 1993:202, *n*3 under I:2). Albin is another fictive name like Ogilvy's. But Denning is real enough, mixed in with the others. The narrator's pretense is to be familiar with scientific men in all fields, as if he was as *au courant* as the author himself, which he is not. He is but a pale imitation, if not a parody of Wells the true intellectual writer on the philosophy of science. Ogilvy, however, is the author's own necessary invention.

the common between Horsell, Ottershaw and Woking, rose early with the idea of finding it. Find it he did, soon after dawn, and not far from the sand-pits. An enormous hole had been made by the impact of the projectile, and the sand and gravel had been flung violently in every direction over the heath and heather, forming heaps visible a mile and a half away.[18] The heather was on fire eastward, and a thin blue smoke rose against the dawn.

The Thing itself lay almost entirely buried in sand, amidst the scattered splinters of a fir-tree it had shivered to fragments in its descent. The uncovered part had the appearance of a huge cylinder, caked over, and its outline softened by a thick, scaly, dun-coloured incrustation. It had a diameter of about thirty yards. He approached the mass, surprised at the size and more so at the shape, since most meteorites are rounded more or less completely. It was, however, still so hot from its flight through the air as to forbid his near approach. A stirring noise within its cylinder he ascribed to the unequal cooling of its surface; for at that time it had not occurred to him that it might be hollow.

He remained standing at the edge of the pit that the thing had made for itself, staring at its strange appearance, astonished chiefly at its unusual shape and colour, and dimly perceiving even then some evidence of design in its arrival.[19] The early morning was wonderfully still, and the sun, just clearing the pine-trees towards Weybridge, was already warm. He did not remember hearing any birds that morning, there was certainly no breeze stirring, and the only sounds were the faint movements from within the cindery cylinder. He was all alone on the common.

---

18. The first cylinder lands in Horsell Common (I:3), a recreational area near Woking. There today one may see fir trees picturesquely standing about pits from which material had been excavated for material used in Victorian times for making concrete. They look like immense impact-craters and as I in 1988 gazed on the hugest I could sense Wells's imagination racing to the question: What can I do with *that* spectacular site? First the evocative crater, then the Martian invasion.

19. Too late, "poor Ogilvy" realizes that the alien "Thing" anticipated by the narrator (note 10) is not a natural object after all, and so he meets his doom. The narrator reports it as if he were an eye-witness, the author's usual vantage. That Wells departs from it here is no great matter, since as a Victorian novelist, unlike the modernists, he did not strive for utter consistency in auctorial point of view. He does, however, consciously shift in Book II for his brother's account of events in London.

Then suddenly he noticed with a start that some of the gray clinker, the ashy incrustation that covered the meteorite, was falling off the circular edge of the end. It was dropping off in flakes and raining down upon the sand. A large piece suddenly came off and fell with a sharp noise that brought his heart into his mouth.

For a minute he scarcely realized what this meant, and, although the heat was excessive, he clambered down into the pit close to the bulk to see the thing more clearly. He fancied even then that the cooling of the body might account for this, but what disturbed that idea was the fact that the ash was falling only from the end of the cylinder.

And then he perceived that, very slowly, the circular top of the cylinder was rotating on its body. It was such a gradual movement that he discovered it only through noticing that a black mark that had been near him five minutes ago was now at the other side of the circumference. Even then he scarcely understood what this indicated, until he heard a muffled grating sound and saw the black mark jerk forward an inch or so. Then the thing came upon him in a flash. The cylinder was artificial—hollow—with an end that screwed out! Something within the cylinder was unscrewing the top!

"Good heavens!" said Ogilvy. "There's a man in it—men in it! Half roasted to death! Trying to escape!"

At once, with a quick mental leap, he linked the thing with the flash upon Mars.

The thought of the confined creature was so dreadful to him that he forgot the heat, and went forward to the cylinder to help turn. But luckily the dull radiation arrested him before he could burn his hands on the still glowing metal. At that he stood irresolute for a moment, then turned, scrambled out of the pit, and set off running wildly into Woking. The time then must have been somewhere about six o'clock. He met a waggoner and tried to make him understand, but the tale he told, and his appearance, were so wild—his hat had fallen off in the pit—that the man simply drove on. He was equally unsuccessful with the potman who was just unlocking the doors of the public-house by Horsell Bridge. The fellow thought he was a lunatic at large, and made an unsuccessful attempt to shut him into the tap-room. That sobered him a little, and when he saw Henderson, the London journalist, in his garden, he called over the palings and made himself understood.

"Henderson," he called, "you saw that shooting star last night?"

"Well?" said Henderson.

"It's out on Horsell Common now."

"Good Lord!" said Henderson. "Fallen meteorite! That's good."

"But it's something more than a meteorite. It's a cylinder—an artificial cylinder, man! And there's something inside."

Henderson stood up with his spade in his hand.

"What's that?" he said. He is deaf in one ear.

Ogilvy told him all that he had seen. Henderson was a minute or so taking it in. Then he dropped his spade, snatched at his jacket, and came out into the road. The two men hurried back at once to the common, and found the cylinder still lying in the same position. But now the sounds inside had ceased, and a thin circle of bright metal showed between the top and the body of the cylinder. Air was either entering or escaping at the rim with a thin, sizzling sound.

They listened, rapped on the scale with a stick, and, meeting with no response, they both concluded the man or men inside must be insensible or dead.

Of course the two were quite unable to do anything. They shouted consolation and promises, and went off back to the town again to get help. One can imagine them, covered with sand, excited and disordered, running up the little street in the bright sunlight, just as the shop folks were taking down their shutters and people were opening their bedroom windows. Henderson went into the railway-station at once, in order to telegraph the news to London. The newspaper articles had prepared men's minds for the reception of the idea.

By eight o'clock a number of boys and unemployed men had already started for the common to see the "dead men from Mars." That was the form the story took. I heard of it first from my newspaper boy, about a quarter to nine, when I went out to get my *Daily Chronicle*. I was naturally startled, and lost no time in going out and across the Ottershaw bridge to the sand-pits.[20]

---

20. The sand pits (note 18) are indubitably there, a marked feature of the locale adding topographic realism. The first cylinder just happened to blast out a bigger one.

III

ON HORSELL COMMON.

I FOUND a little crowd of perhaps twenty people surrounding the huge hole in which the cylinder lay. I have already described the appearance of that colossal bulk, imbedded in the ground. The turf and gravel about it seemed charred as if by a sudden explosion. No doubt its impact had caused a flash of fire. Henderson and Ogilvy were not there. I think they perceived that nothing was to be done for the present, and had gone away to breakfast at Henderson's house.

There were four or five boys sitting on the edge of the pit, with their feet dangling, and amusing themselves—until I stopped them—by throwing stones at the giant mass. After I had spoken to them about it, they began playing at "touch" in and out of the group of bystanders.

Among these were a couple of cyclists, a jobbing gardener I employed sometimes, a girl carrying a baby, Gregg the butcher and his little boy, and two or three loafers and golf caddies who were accustomed to hang about the railway-station. There was very little talking. Few of the common people in England had anything but the vaguest astronomical ideas in those days.[21] Most of them were staring quietly at the big table-like end of the cylinder, which was still as Ogilvy and Henderson had left it. I fancy the popular expectation of a heap of charred corpses was disappointed at this inanimate bulk. Some went away while I was there, and other people came. I clambered into the pit and fancied I heard a faint movement under my feet. The top had certainly ceased to rotate.

---

21. That is, back in 1900 (note 8), the time of the invasion in the narrator's retrospect. Now of course, the world's outlook is more in line with his, considerably chastened as he thinks it ought to be. But he himself remains unreconstructed, the novel's final irony (note 183).

It was only then when I got thus close to it that the strangeness of this object was at all evident to me. At the first glance it was really no more exciting than an overturned carriage or a tree blown across the road. Not so much so, indeed. It looked like a rusty gas-float[22] half buried, more than anything else in the world. It required a certain amount of scientific education to perceive that the gray scale of the thing was no common oxide, that the yellowish-white metal that gleamed in the crack between the lid and the cylinder had an unfamiliar hue. "Extra-terrestrial" had no meaning for most of the onlookers.

At that time it was quite clear in my own mind that the Thing had come from the planet Mars, but I judged it improbable that it contained any living creature. I thought the unscrewing might be automatic. In spite of Ogilvy, I still believed that there were men in Mars. My mind ran fancifully on the possibilities of its containing manuscript, on the difficulties in translation that might arise, whether we should find coins and models in it, and so forth.[23] Yet it was a little too

---

22. A "gas float" is a harbor beacon erected on a floating hull containing bottled gas to fuel it. The trope suggests that the Martian cylinders are beacons to light mankind's new direction.

23. The narrator refers to his "paper on the probable development of Moral ideas with the development of the civilising process" (at note 15), as an example of his "abstract investigations." Far from empirical, his interest in the progressive development of civilization is metaphysical: wooly-minded in the worst way. By his time, about 60 years after the French Revolution, Progress had come to mean industrial expansion, mammon + raw materials = improvement. But Wells retained Saint-Simon's passion for organic state unity in and through *industrialisme*, his doctrinalized version of industry's coercive division-of-labor morality applicable society-wide. In this light does Wells address "ethical reconstruction" (1901:311) as the object of his Modern State revolutionaries given to "the obliteration of out-of-date moral values" (1933:360). In Saint-Simonist terms, the progress of industrialism is "the progress of the moral conception by which man becomes conscious of a social destiny" (Iggers, tr. 1958:28). The Martians gift humanity with that lofty conception, arriving as they do from their Saint-Simonist planet of unified interests.

That phrase, "ethical reconstruction," is from *Anticipations*, which is a vatic statement (per subtitle) on "the Reaction of Mechanical and Scientific Progress upon Human Life and Thought." In a letter confiding its purpose he said, "'Anticipations' is designed to undermine and destroy the monarch, monogamy, faith in God & respectability & the British Empire, all under the guise of a speculation about motor cars & electrical heating" (in Smith 1998, I:379). The

large for assurance on this idea. I felt an impatience to see it opened. About eleven, as nothing seemed happening, I walked back, full of such thoughts, to my home in Maybury. But I found it difficult to get to work upon my abstract investigations.[24]

In the afternoon the appearance of the common had altered very much. The early editions of the evening papers had startled London with enormous headlines:

"A MESSAGE RECEIVED FROM MARS,"

"REMARKABLE STORY FROM WOKING,"

and so forth. In addition, Ogilvy's wire to the Astronomical Exchange had roused every observatory in the three kingdoms.[25]

There were half a dozen flys or more from the Woking station standing in the road by the sand-pits, a basket chaise from Chobham, and a rather lordly carriage. Besides that, there was quite a heap of bicycles. In addition, a large number of people must have walked, in spite of the heat of the day, from Woking and Chertsey, so that there was altogether quite a considerable crowd—one or two gaily dressed ladies among the others.

It was glaringly hot, not a cloud in the sky, nor a breath of wind, and the only shadow was that of the few scattered pine-trees. The burning heather had been extinguished, but the level ground towards Ottershaw was blackened as far as one could see, and still giving off vertical streamers of smoke. An enterprising sweetstuff dealer in the Chobham Road[26] had sent up his son with a barrow-load of green apples and ginger-beer.

Going to the edge of the pit, I found it occupied by a group of about

---

artilleryman (in II:7) speaks the same language when he proposes to take over Martian technology and resume the same attack on the culture of bourgeois civilization.

24. Echoes of Percy Gregg's *Across the Zodiac* (see the Introduction to the present work, section 4) in which a "meteorite" from Mars contains within a manuscript detailing its civilization. The sensational headline below raises the same expectation.

25. Of Great Britain.

26. The road leading to Chobham, a market town not far from Woking to the northwest. Rural England had its busy commercial traffic, and Chobham Road passes nearby Horsell Common. The gawkers, then, were readily supplied with refreshments at the landing site, lending it a falsely festive atmosphere. Everydayism again.

half a dozen men—Henderson, Ogilvy, and a tall fair-haired man that I afterwards learnt was Stent, the Astronomer Royal,[27] with several workmen wielding spades and pickaxes. Stent was giving directions in a clear, high-pitched voice. He was standing on the cylinder, which was now evidently much cooler; his face was crimson and streaming with perspiration, and something seemed to have irritated him.

A large portion of the cylinder had been uncovered, though its lower end was still embedded. As soon as Ogilvy saw me among the staring crowd on the edge of the pit, he called to me to come down, and asked me if I would mind going over to see Lord Hilton, the lord of the manor.

The growing crowd, he said, was becoming a serious impediment to their excavations, especially the boys. They wanted a light railing put up, and help to keep the people back. He told me that a faint stirring was occasionally still audible within the case, but that the workmen had failed to unscrew the top, as it afforded no grip to them. The case appeared to be enormously thick, and it was possible that the faint sounds we heard represented a noisy tumult in the interior.

I was very glad to do as he asked, and so become one of the privileged spectators within the contemplated enclosure. I failed to find Lord Hilton at his house, but I was told he was expected from London by the six o'clock train from Waterloo; and as it was then about a quarter past five, I went home, had some tea, and walked up to the station to waylay him.[28]

---

27. The Astronomer Royal was director of the Royal Greenwich Observatory, but "Stent" is not recorded as one of them (another example of the narrator's unreliability). The post itself is rather indicated, he who keeps Greenwich Mean Time — now to become planetary time on the Martian clock.

28. Lord Hilton is not the real name of the Lord of Horsell Manor. It were impolitic of the author to say he is Lord Onslow (see Hughes and Geduld 1993:203, *n*13 under I:13), since Wells casts him as a useless dignitary in the gathering crisis. The misnomer in this case is not the narrator's typical slip-shod reference; it is rather the author's cautiousness. So too with Stent, whatever the Royal representative from Greenwich on the scene. Nothing can allay the swift unfolding of the inevitable catastrophe. The old order is dead at this very moment.

IV

THE CYLINDER UNSCREWS.

WHEN I returned to the common the sun was setting. Scattered groups were hurrying from the direction of Woking, and one or two persons were returning. The crowd about the pit had increased, and stood out black against the lemon-yellow of the sky—a couple of hundred people, perhaps. There were a number of voices raised, and some sort of struggle appeared to be going on about the pit. Strange imaginings passed through my mind. As I drew nearer I heard Stent's voice:

"Keep back! Keep back!"

A boy came running towards me.

"It's a-movin'," he said to me as he passed—'a-screwin' and a-screwin' out. I don't like it. I'm a-goin' 'ome, I am."

I went on to the crowd. There were really, I should think, two or three hundred people elbowing and jostling one another, the one or two ladies there being by no means the least active.

"He's fallen in the pit!" cried someone.

"Keep back!" said several.

The crowd swayed a little, and I elbowed my way through. Everyone seemed greatly excited. I heard a peculiar humming sound from the pit.

"I say!" said Ogilvy, "help keep those idiots back. We don't know what's in the confounded thing, you know!"

I saw a young man, a shop assistant in Woking I believe he was, standing on the cylinder and trying to scramble out of the hole again. The crowd had pushed him in.

The end of the cylinder was being screwed out from within. Nearly two feet of shining screw projected. Somebody blundered against me, and I narrowly missed being pitched on to the top of the screw. I turned, and as I did so the screw must have come out, and the lid of the cylinder fell upon the gravel with a ringing concussion. I stuck my elbow into the person behind me, and turned my head towards the Thing again. For a moment that circular cavity seemed perfectly black. I had the sunset in my eyes.

I think everyone expected to see a man emerge—possibly something a little unlike us terrestrial men, but in all essentials a man. I know I did.[29] But, looking, I presently saw something stirring within the shadow—grayish billowy movements, one above another, and then two luminous discs like eyes. Then something resembling a little gray snake, about the thickness of a walking-stick, coiled up out of the writhing middle, and wriggled in the air towards me—and then another.

A sudden chill came over me. There was a loud shriek from a woman behind. I half turned, keeping my eyes fixed upon the cylinder still, from which other tentacles were now projecting, and began pushing my way back from the edge of the pit. I saw astonishment giving place to horror on the faces of the people about me. I heard inarticulate exclamations on all sides. There was a general movement backward. I saw the shopman struggling still on the edge of the pit. I found myself alone, and saw the people on the other side of the pit running off, Stent among them. I looked again at the cylinder, and ungovernable terror gripped me. I stood petrified and staring.

A big grayish, rounded bulk, the size, perhaps, of a bear, was rising slowly and painfully out of the cylinder. As it bulged up and caught the light, it glistened like wet leather. Two large dark-coloured eyes were regarding me steadfastly. It was rounded, and had, one might say, a face. There was a mouth under the eyes, the lipless brim of which quivered and panted, and dropped saliva. The body heaved and pulsated

---

29. Lowell (1896) says of intelligent life on Mars that we should not imagine "men in trousers." But this is exactly what is expected to emerge from the opening cylinder even by the narrator. This belies his later claim to have always known better. Since he also prides himself on being the only writer (note 5) ever to invoke the plurality-of-worlds thesis, a fixture of astronomical thought from Kepler onward, the reader quickly twigs to the narrator as a hugely conceited ass. Like the archetypical Dr. Pangloss, he is a pseudointellectual whose word often is to be mistrusted, even as he reports actual facts on the battlefield. The author sets him up as a foil to his own wiser perspective on the war. By means of artistic contrast, the author distances himself from his unreliable narrator and allows the reader to judge the true meaning of these epic events without having to directly state the ideological message he drives home.

convulsively. A lank tentacular appendage gripped the edge of the cylinder, another swayed in the air.

Those who have never seen a living Martian can scarcely imagine the strange horror of their appearance. The peculiar V-shaped mouth with its pointed upper lip, the absence of brow ridges, the absence of a chin beneath the wedge-like lower lip, the incessant quivering of this mouth, the Gorgon groups of tentacles, the tumultuous breathing of the lungs in a strange atmosphere, the evident heaviness and painfulness of movement, due to the greater gravitational energy of the earth—above all, the extraordinary intensity of the immense eyes— culminated in an effect akin to nausea. There was something fungoid in the oily brown skin, something in the clumsy deliberation of their tedious movements unspeakably terrible. Even at this first encounter, this first glimpse, I was overcome with disgust and dread.[30]

Suddenly the monster vanished. It had toppled over the brim of the cylinder and fallen into the pit, with a thud like the fall of a great mass of leather. I heard it give a peculiar thick cry, and forthwith another of these creatures appeared darkly in the deep shadow of the aperture.

At that my rigour of terror passed away. I turned and, running madly, made for the first group of trees, perhaps a hundred yards away; but I ran slantingly and stumbling, for I could not avert my face from these things.[31]

---

30. Kingsley Amis (1960) quotes this paragraph as the first one in his book on science fiction, treating the Martian monsters as the genre's archetype of things dreadful and terrifying, serving no purpose other than to excite cheap thrills. This is true in epigonal magazine science-fiction after Wells, in which invariably tentacled monsters of every sort, not always octopoidal, invade earth for the purpose of wreaking havoc, eating all the men and raping all the women (strange exobiology that).

The phrase "Gorgon groups of tentacles" alludes to those brass-clawed monsters of Greek myth whose head hair of writhing snakes was death to look upon. The gazing narrator is not turned to stone (or incinerated by the Martian Heat-Ray); he alone is elected to comprehend what the Martians mean for the benefit of human destiny. Or so he interprets his escape, while inflating the self-importance of his perceptiveness.

31. The Gorgons (note 30) irresistibly attract human attention with doom-laden results. But the narrator is exceptional; he can look, fascinated, upon the horror and not die. He concludes that maybe the monsters are not so horrible after all; that maybe the horrific exists only in the sight of the terrified beholder. Determined now not to be transfixed, the narrator undertakes to report on the war as just another invasion-of-England story so commonly fantasied after Ches-

There, among some young pine-trees and furze bushes, I stopped, panting, and waited further developments. The common round the sand-pits was dotted with people, standing, like myself, in a half-fascinated terror, staring at these creatures, or, rather, at the heaped gravel at the edge of the pit in which they lay. And then, with a renewed horror, I saw a round, black object bobbing up and down on the edge of the pit. It was the head of the shopman who had fallen in, but showing as a little black object against the hot western sky. Now he got his shoulder and knee up, and again he seemed to slip back until only his head was visible. Suddenly he vanished, and I could have fancied a faint shriek had reached me. I had a momentary impulse to go back and help him that my fears overruled.

Everything was then quite invisible, hidden by the deep pit and the heap of sand that the fall of the cylinder had made. Anyone coming along the road from Chobham or Woking would have been amazed at the sight—a dwindling multitude of perhaps a hundred people or more standing in a great irregular circle, in ditches, behind bushes, behind gates and hedges, saying little to one another, and that in short, excited shouts, and staring, staring hard at a few heaps of sand. The barrow of ginger-beer stood, a queer derelict, black against the burning sky, and in the sand-pits was a row of deserted vehicles with their horses feeding out of nose-bags or pawing the ground.

---

ney's *Battle of Dorking*. But it is much more than that. When all is over, the narrator returns home, satisfied that his England has been saved for his personal benefit. Little does he sense that his happy little island and the comforts of his everydayism are about to end. In *Sleeper*, the sequel, a Martian-inspired Great State overtakes the Normal Social Life and finishes forever his trivial, bourgeois way of life.

V

THE HEAT-RAY.

AFTER the glimpse I had had of the Martians emerging from the cylinder in which they had come to the earth from their planet, a kind of fascination paralyzed my actions. I remained standing knee-deep in the heather, staring at the mound that hid them. I was a battleground of fear and curiosity.

I did not dare to go back toward the pit, but I felt a passionate longing to peer into it. I began walking, therefore, in a big curve, seeking some point of vantage, and continually looking at the sand-heaps that hid these new-comers to our earth. Once a leash of thin black whips, like the arms of an octopus, flashed across the sunset and was immediately withdrawn, and afterwards a thin rod rose up, joint by joint, bearing at its apex a circular disc that spun with a wobbling motion. What could be going on there?

Most of the spectators had gathered in one or two groups—one a little crowd towards Woking, the other a knot of people in the direction of Chobham. Evidently they shared my mental conflict. There were few near me. One man I approached—he was, I perceived, a neighbour of mine, though I did not know his name—and accosted. But it was scarcely a time for articulate conversation.

"What ugly *brutes!*" he said. "Good God! what ugly brutes!" He repeated this over and over again.[32]

"Did you see a man in the pit?" I said; but he made me no answer to that. We became silent, and stood watching for a time side by side, deriving, I fancy, a certain comfort in one another's company. Then I

---

32. "Ugly brutes" is the general perception, contrasted with Wells's "nice monsters" in *Star-Begotten* (1937). The narrator, however, but dimly perceives how nice they really are.

shifted my position to a little knoll that gave me the advantage of a yard or more of elevation, and when I looked for him presently he was walking towards Woking.

The sunset faded to twilight before anything further happened. The crowd far away on the left, towards Woking, seemed to grow, and I heard now a faint murmur from it. The little knot of people towards Chobham dispersed. There was scarcely an intimation of movement from the pit.

It was this, as much as anything, that gave people courage, and I suppose the new arrivals from Woking also helped to restore confidence. At any rate, as the dusk came on, a slow, intermittent movement upon the sand-pits began, a movement that seemed to gather force as the stillness of the evening about the cylinder remained unbroken. Vertical black figures in twos and threes would advance, stop, watch, and advance again, spreading out as they did so in a thin irregular crescent that promised to enclose the pit in its attenuated horns. I, too, on my side began to move towards the pit.

Then I saw some cabmen and others had walked boldly into the sand-pits, and heard the clatter of hoofs and the gride of wheels. I saw a lad trundling off the barrow of apples. And then, within thirty yards of the pit, advancing from the direction of Horsell, I noted a little black knot of men, the foremost of whom was waving a white flag.

This was the Deputation. There had been a hasty consultation, and, since the Martians were evidently, in spite of their repulsive forms, intelligent creatures, it had been resolved to show them, by approaching them with signals, that we too, were intelligent.

Flutter, flutter, went the flag, first to the right, then to the left. It was too far for me to recognise anyone there, but afterwards I learnt that Ogilvy, Stent, and Henderson were with others in this attempt at communication.[33] This little group had in its advance dragged inward, so

---

33. The illustration of this scene in the serialized version shows the flag to be the white flag of surrender, as if, stupid assumption, the Martians would understand human color symbolism in "this attempt at communication" with beings of fellow intelligence. But the Martians are *more* intelligent and do not wish to communicate with their lessers, only to dominate them; just as Wells's Modern Octopus State lords over the mass of common humanity, for its own good, without bothering to consult popular opinion.

> It is no good asking people what they want.... That is the error of democracy. You have first to think out what they ought to want if society is to be saved. Then you have to tell them what they want and see that they get it [1933:254].

to speak, the circumference of the now almost complete circle of people, and a number of dim black figures followed it at discreet distances.

Suddenly there was a flash of light, and a quantity of luminous greenish smoke came out of the pit[34] in three distinct puffs, which drove up, one after the other, straight into the still air.

This smoke (or flame, perhaps, would be the better word for it) was so bright that the deep blue sky overhead, and the hazy stretches of brown common towards Chertsey, set with black pine-trees, seemed to darken abruptly as these puffs arose, and to remain the darker after their dispersal. At the same time a faint hissing sound became audible.

Beyond the pit stood the little wedge of people, with the white flag at its apex, arrested by these phenomena, a little knot of small vertical black shapes upon the black ground. As the green smoke rose, their faces flashed out pallid green, and faded again as it vanished.

Then slowly the hissing passed into a humming, into a long, loud, droning noise. Slowly a humped shape rose out of the pit, and the ghost of a beam of light seemed to flicker out from it.

Forthwith flashes of actual flame, a bright glare leaping from one to another, sprang from the scattered group of men. It was as if some invisible jet impinged upon them and flashed into white flame. It was as if each man were suddenly and momentarily turned to fire.

Then, by the light of their own destruction, I saw them staggering and falling, and their supporters turning to run.

I stood staring, not as yet realizing that this was death leaping from man to man in that little distant crowd. All I felt was that it was some-

---

In plain words, first you hijack control, then make them like it: the strong-arm code of gangsterdom. That fascist formula is what Wells's ideal, autocratic state capitalism amounts to, as novelized so prophetically in *Sleeper*, the sequel to *Worlds*.

34. Allusion to Revelation 9:2, "and there arose a smoke out of the pit...." Wells always is full of biblical allusions, nowhere more than in *Worlds*. Gibbons (1984) has traced some of these, but not all of them. The curate with whom the narrator first meets in I:13 is of course in character when he cites scripture, with relish, affirming that the Martian invasion is God's judgment on a sinful mankind. In II:4 his hellfire sermonizing so wearies the narrator that he kills him, and all critics rightly agree this murderous act expresses Wells's hateful anti-clericalism. But the curate's apocalyptic rantings are so out of proportion as a target of that animus that we must reconsider it. Does not the narrator himself, from a secular point of view, relish the same damnation of degenerate humanity? And does he not, in this instance, reflect the auctorial point of view?

thing strange. An almost noiseless and blinding flash of light, and a man fell headlong and lay still, and as the unseen shaft of heat passed over them, pine-trees burst into fire, and every dry furze-bush became with one dull thud a mass of flames. And far away towards Knaphill I saw the flashes of trees and hedges and wooden buildings suddenly set alight.[35]

It was sweeping round swiftly and steadily, this flaming death, this invisible, inevitable sword of heat. I perceived it coming towards me by the flashing bushes it touched, and was too astounded and stupefied to stir. I heard the crackle of fire in the sand-pits and the sudden squeal of a horse that was as suddenly stilled. Then it was as if an invisible yet intensely heated finger was drawn through the heather between me and the Martians, and all along a curving line beyond the sand-pits the dark ground smoked and crackled. Something fell with a crash, far away to the left where the road from Woking Station opens out on the common. Forthwith the hissing and humming ceased, and the black, dome-like object sank slowly out of sight into the pit.

All this had happened with such swiftness that I had stood motionless, dumfounded and dazzled by the flashes of light. Had that death swept through a full circle, it must inevitably have slain me in my surprise. But it passed and spared me, and left the night about me suddenly dark and unfamiliar.

The undulating common seemed now dark almost to blackness, except where its roadways lay gray and pale under the deep-blue sky of the early night. It was dark, and suddenly void of men. Overhead the stars were mustering, and in the west the sky was still a pale, bright, almost greenish blue. The tops of the pine-trees and the roofs of Horsell came out sharp and black against the western after-glow. The Martians and their appliances were altogether invisible, save for that thin mast upon which their restless mirror wobbled.[36] Patches of bush and isolated trees here and there smoked and glowed still, and

---

35. Knaphill is about three miles from Horsell Common. The "sword of heat" (*infra*) has a long reach, setting on fire trees and houses at that distance after blasting the Deputation bearing a white flag at note 33.

36. At this point the Heat-Ray is reflected from a periscopic mirror raised from the Horsell Commons pit, spraying "flaming death" in all directions. Later the Martians mount their rayguns on tripodal fighting machines, which direct their fire on specific targets. The narrator is providentially spared from this general sweep because its circle was not complete.

the houses towards Woking Station were sending up spires of flame into the stillness of the evening air.

Nothing was changed save for that and a terrible astonishment. The little group of black specks with the flag of white had been swept out of existence, and the stillness of the evening, so it seemed to me, had scarcely been broken.

It came to me that I was upon this dark common, helpless, unprotected and alone. Suddenly like a thing falling upon me from without came—Fear.

With an effort I turned and began a stumbling run through the heather.

The fear I felt was no rational fear but a panic terror, not only of the Martians, but of the dusk and stillness all about me. Such an extraordinary effect in unmanning me it had that I ran weeping silently as a child might do. Once I had turned, I did not dare to look back.

I remember I felt an extraordinary persuasion that I was being played with, that presently, when I was upon the very verge of safety, this mysterious death—as swift as the passage of light—would leap after me from the pit about the cylinder, and strike me down.

VI

THE HEAT-RAY IN THE CHOBHAM ROAD.

IT is still a matter of wonder how the Martians are able to slay men so swiftly and so silently. Many think that in some way they are able to generate an intense heat in a chamber of practically absolute non-conductivity. This intense heat they project in a parallel beam against any object they choose by means of a polished parabolic mirror of unknown composition—much as the parabolic mirror of a lighthouse projects a beam of light.[37] But no one has absolutely proved these details. However it is done, it is certain that a beam of heat is the essence of the matter. Heat, and invisible, instead of visible light. Whatever is combustible flashes into flame at its touch, lead runs like water, it softens iron, cracks and melts glass, and when it falls upon water incontinently that explodes into steam.

That night nearly forty people lay under the starlight about the pit, charred and distorted beyond recognition, and all night long the common from Horsell to Maybury was deserted, and brightly ablaze.

---

37. The Heat-Ray is often taken as a prophecy of beam-focused lasers, but this is to miss the photographic metaphor Wells uses: "the camera that fired the Heat-Ray (I:12), "the camera-like generator of the Heat-Ray" (I:17). The Martians' rayguns are in fact cameras in reverse, emitting light not receiving it, and they are in fact mounted on tripods as were the heavy old cameras of the day. What they see they zap.

More, the photo-journalistic realism of the invasion recounted by the narrator recalls that of Roger Fenton, whose coverage of the Crimean War in 1855 is the first instance of a war photographer on the scene of action. His pictures were accompanied by sensational stories done by the famed William Howard Russell of the London *Times*, the first war correspondent in the modern sense (Gascoigne 1993:228, 561). The narrator's account is modeled after both precedents, visually and journalistically.

The news of the massacre probably reached Chobham, Woking, and Ottershaw about the same time. In Woking the shops had closed when the tragedy happened, and a number of people, shop-people and so forth, attracted by the stories they had heard, were walking over Horsell Bridge and along the road between the hedges that run out at last upon the common. You may imagine the young people brushed up after the labours of the day, and making this novelty, as they would make any novelty, the excuse for walking together and enjoying a trivial flirtation. You may figure to yourself the hum of voices along the road in the gloaming....

As yet, of course, few people in Woking even knew that the cylinder had opened, though poor Henderson had sent a messenger on a bicycle to the post-office with a special wire to an evening paper.

As these folks came out by twos and threes upon the open they found little knots of people talking excitedly, and peering at the spinning mirror over the sand-pits, and the new-comers were, no doubt, soon infected by the excitement of the occasion.

By half-past eight, when the Deputation was destroyed, there may have been a crowd of 300 people or more at this place, besides those who had left the road to approach the Martians nearer. There were three policemen, too, one of whom was mounted, doing their best, under instructions from Stent, to keep the people back and deter them from approaching the cylinder. There was some booing from those more thoughtless and excitable souls to whom a crowd is always an occasion for noise and horse-play.

Stent and Ogilvy, anticipating some possibilities of a collision, had telegraphed from Horsell to the barracks as soon as the Martians emerged, for the help of a company of soldiers to protect these strange creatures from violence. After that they returned to lead that ill-fated advance. The description of their death, as it was seen by the crowd, tallies very closely with my own impressions: the three puffs of green smoke, the deep humming note, and the flashes of flame.

But that crowd of people had a far narrower escape than mine. Only the fact that a hummock of heathery sand intercepted the lower part of the Heat-Ray saved them. Had the elevation of the parabolic mirror been a few yards higher, none could have lived to tell the tale. They saw the flashes, and the men falling, and an invisible hand, as it were, lit the bushes as it hurried towards them through the twilight. Then, with a whistling note that rose above the droning of the pit, the beam swung close over their heads, lighting the tops of the beech-trees that line the road, and splitting the bricks, smashing the windows, firing the window-frames, and bringing down in crumbling ruin a portion of the gable of the house nearest the corner.

In the sudden thud, hiss and glare of the igniting trees, the panic-stricken crowd seems to have swayed hesitatingly for some moments.

Sparks and burning twigs began to fall into the road, and single leaves like puffs of flame. Hats and dresses caught fire. Then came a crying from the common.

There were shrieks and shouts, and suddenly a mounted policeman came galloping through the confusion with his hands clasped over his head, screaming.

"They're coming!" a woman shrieked, and incontinently everyone was turning and pushing at those behind, in order to clear their way to Woking again. They must have bolted as blindly as a flock of sheep. Where the road grows narrow and black between the high banks the crowd jammed and a desperate struggle occurred. All that crowd did not escape; three persons at least, two women and a little boy, were crushed and trampled there and left to die amidst the terror and the darkness.

VII

HOW I REACHED HOME.

FOR my own part, I remember nothing of my flight except the stress of blundering against trees and stumbling through the heather. All about me gathered the invisible terrors of the Martians; that pitiless sword of heat seemed whirling to and fro, flourishing overhead before it descended and smote me out of life. I came into the road between the cross-roads and Horsell, and ran along this to the cross-roads.

At last I could go no further; I was exhausted with the violence of my emotion and of my flight, and I staggered and fell by the wayside. That was near the bridge that crosses the canal by the gasworks. I fell and lay still.

I must have remained there some time.

I sat up, strangely perplexed. For a moment, perhaps, I could not clearly understand how I came there. My terror had fallen from me like a garment. My hat had gone, and my collar had burst away from its stud. A few minutes before there had only been three real things before me—the immensity of the night and space and nature, my own feebleness and anguish, and the near approach of death. Now it was as if something turned over, and the point of view altered abruptly. There was no sensible transition from one state of mind to the other. I was immediately the self of every day again, a decent ordinary citizen. The silent common, the impulse of my flight, the starting flames, were as if it were a dream. I asked myself had these latter things indeed happened. I could not credit it.

I rose and walked unsteadily up the steep incline of the bridge. My mind was blank wonder. My muscles and nerves seemed drained of their strength. I dare say I staggered drunkenly. A head rose over the arch, and the figure of a workman carrying a basket appeared. Beside him ran a little boy. He passed me, wishing me good-night. I was minded to speak to him, and did not. I answered his greeting with a meaningless mumble and went on over the bridge.

Over the Maybury arch a train, a billowing tumult of white, firelit smoke, and a long caterpillar of lighted windows, went flying south: clatter, clatter, clap, rap, and it had gone. A dim group of people talked in the gate of one of the houses in the pretty little row of gables that was called Oriental Terrace. It was all so real and so familiar. And that behind me! It was frantic, fantastic! Such things, I told myself, could not be.

Perhaps I am a man of exceptional moods. I do not know how far my experience is common. At times I suffer from the strangest sense of detachment from myself and the world about me; I seem to watch it all from the outside, from somewhere inconceivably remote, out of time, out of space, out of the stress and tragedy of it all. This feeling was very strong upon me that night. Here was another side to my dream.

But the trouble was the blank incongruity of this serenity and the swift death flying yonder, not two miles away. There was a noise of business from the gasworks, and the electric lamps were all alight. I stopped at the group of people.

"What news from the common?" said I.

There were two men and a woman at the gate.

"Eh?" said one of the men, turning.

"What news from the common?" I said.

"Ain't yer just *been* there?" asked the men.

"People seem fair silly about the commons," said the woman over the gate. "What's it all abart?"

"Haven't you heard of the men from Mars?" said I. "The creatures from Mars?"

"Quite enough," said the woman over the gate. "Thenks;" and all three of them laughed.

I felt foolish and angry. I tried and found I could not tell them what I had seen. They laughed again at my broken sentences.

"You'll hear more yet," I said, and went on to my home.

I startled my wife at the doorway, so haggard was I. I went into the dining-room, sat down, drank some wine, and so soon as I could collect myself sufficiently told her the things I had seen. The dinner, which was a cold one, had already been served, and remained neglected on the table while I told my story.

"There is one thing," I said to allay the fears I had aroused. "They are the most sluggish things I ever saw crawl. They may keep the pit

and kill people who come near them, but they cannot get out of it....
But the horror of them!"

"Don't, dear!" said my wife, knitting her brows and putting her
hand on mine.

"Poor Ogilvy!" I said. "To think he may be lying dead there!"

My wife at least did not find my experience incredible. When I saw
how deadly white her face was, I ceased abruptly.

"They may come here," she said again and again.

I pressed her to take wine, and tried to reassure her.

"They can scarcely move," I said.

I began to comfort her and myself by repeating all that Ogilvy had
told me of the impossibility of the Martians establishing themselves
on the earth. In particular I laid stress on the gravitational difficulty.
On the surface of the earth the force of gravity is three times what it
is on the surface of Mars. A Martian, therefore, would weigh three
times more than on Mars, albeit his muscular strength would be the
same. His own body would be a cope of lead to him, therefore. That
indeed was the general opinion. Both the *Times* and the *Daily Telegraph*,
for instance, insisted on it the next morning, and both overlooked, just
as I did, two obvious modifying influences.

The atmosphere of the earth, we now know, contains far more oxygen or far less argon[38] (whichever way one likes to put it) than does

---

38. Up to date in his discussion of the Martian atmosphere, Wells brings
in the recently discovered element Argon (number 18 on the Periodic Table), a
newsworthy event he himself had reported on (1895a). But the specifics of Mars
have a general application to planetology. In I:1 (4th paragraph), the cooling of
our own planet is foredestined in the fate of our neighbor's. "That last stage of
exhaustion, which to us is still incredibly remote, has become a present-day
problem for the inhabitants of Mars. The immediate pressure of necessity has
brightened their intellects, enlarged their powers, and hardened their hearts."
And so (in the next paragraph) follows their decision to carry the Darwinian
war of nature sunward, for the conquest of a fresh planet crowded "with what
they regard as inferior animals." If "The intellectual side of man already admits
that life is an incessant struggle for existence, and it would seem this too is the
belief of the minds upon Mars."

Yet the same belief of our best scientific minds has not been acted on.
There remains a complacent faith in a "humanitarian philanthropic type of liberalism" that accords equality to the inferior masses, whose "fecundity" threat-
ens to swamp society. Despite "wide vistas opened by geological and astronomical discovery" (1901:314), the lessons of natural selection, on Mars as on
earth, have not been learned; democracy offers no Malthusian checks to the

Mars'. The invigorating influences of this excess of oxygen upon the Martians indisputably did much to counterbalance the increased weight of their bodies. And, in the second place, we all overlooked the fact that such mechanical intelligence as the Martian possessed was quite able to dispense with muscular exertion at a pinch.

But I did not consider these points at the time, and so my reasoning was dead against the chances of the invaders. With wine and food, the confidence of my own table, and the necessity of reassuring my wife, I grew, by insensible degrees, courageous and secure.

"They have done a foolish thing," said I, fingering my wineglass. "They are dangerous, because no doubt they are mad with terror. Perhaps they expected to find no living things—certainly no intelligent living things. A shell in the pit," said I, "if the worst comes to the worst, will kill them all."

The intense excitement of the events had no doubt left my perceptive

---

breeding of degenerates. Enter Wells's salvationists, the New Republicans (the Modern State Revolutionaries of later denomination), who deal honestly "with the primary, inexorable logic of natural laws"; they come on "with all the inevitableness and patience of a natural force" (108). Theirs is the Martianized policy of "inhuman humanitarianism" (1933:345), a patient course of applied natural history looking to the distant good of the species in its revocation of a disabling "Individualistic Humanitarianism" (1904:25).

The nineteenth century's organicist bias, of which Wells is such a complete expression, was obsessed with the holistic notion that society ought to form a systematic whole, with each part performing some useful operation. Its philosophers idealized a social order that functioned like a machine or a living organism, or both — as in Saint-Simon's prompting model, his industrialized World Republic of United Interests, "a veritable organic machine whose every part contributes in a different manner to the movement of the whole" (in Durkheim 1958:99). Hence the post-liberal twentieth century corporatism of the fascists and the collectivism of the communists. The same applied globally is Wells's universal production company, his "single world economic machine" (1931a:373), served by "economically functional people" (1928:74) comprising scientific managers and their minions. The organic side of the metaphor comes in with his Modern State Octopus (in 1933), a state monster that militates against every humanistic principle of the classical liberals, whose "adherents recognized the dangers of insisting that individuals have significance only if they are part of a larger whole" (Herman 1997:451). The free and autonomous individual, that liberal product of the Western humanist tradition, is the enemy of Wellsian holism. "All lives have to be made political lives. We can't run about *loose* any more" (1918:566). Such might be the Martian motto.

powers in a state of erethism. I remember that dinner-table with extra-ordinary vividness even now. My dear wife's sweet, anxious face peering at me from under the pink lamp-shade, the white cloth with its silver and glass table furniture—for in those days even philosophical writers had many little luxuries—the crimson-purple wine in my glass, are photographically distinct. At the end of it I sat, tempering nuts with a cigarette, regretting Ogilvy's rashness, and denouncing the short-sighted timidity of the Martians.

So some respectable dodo in the Mauritius might have lorded it in his nest, and discussed the arrival of that shipful of pitiless sailors in want of animal food. "We will peck them to death to-morrow, my dear."

I did not know it, but that was the last civilized dinner I was to eat for very many strange and terrible days.[39]

---

39. The whole point of this chapter is to give depth to the narrator's inner struggle to find a philosophical meaning in the Martian invasion, and to portray him as despicable naïf who does not live up to his writings; while they echo Wellsian prophecies, he is *not* Wells but his inauthentic counterpart. He is at once "the self of everyday" and one who suffers "from the strangest sense of detachment from myself and the world about me." He pretends to reassure people, including his wife, that nothing really significant has happened. Yet he cannot help feeling that men are about to go the way of the dodo wiped out by a hungry crew of "pitiless sailors" in the Mauritius Islands *ca.* 1680; later the very existence of such a stupid, self-complacent species of bird was doubted until fossils were discovered in the late twentieth century.

What turns out to be his "last civilized dinner" is for the gleeful artilleryman at note 166 a good sign that bourgeois culture is now as extinct as the dodo (referenced earlier just before the Tasmanians at note 6); and that a new order is about to begin under his leadership, as he plans to steal the invaders' fighting equipment and use it against them, then to continue the Martian mission on human terms. The artilleryman's design for a world-state is more in line with Wells's than with anything dreamed of by the narrator, who in the end returns home to his old everydayist self. But unknown to him, the seeds of a new world order on the Martian model have indeed been planted, and they come to fruit in *Sleeper.*

VIII

FRIDAY NIGHT.

THE most extraordinary thing to my mind, of all the strange and wonderful things that happened upon that Friday, was the dovetailing of the commonplace habits of our social order with the first beginnings of the series of events that was to topple that social order headlong. If on Friday night you had taken a pair of compasses and drawn a circle with a radius of five miles round the Woking sand-pits, I doubt if you would have had one human being outside it, unless it was some relation of Stent or of the three or four cyclists or London people who lay dead on the common, whose emotions or habits were at all affected by the new-comers. Many people had heard of the cylinder, of course, and talked about it in their leisure, but it certainly did not make the sensation an ultimatum to Germany would have done.

In London that night poor Henderson's telegram describing the gradual unscrewing of the shot was judged to be a canard, and his evening paper, after wiring for authentication from him and receiving no reply—the man was killed—decided not to print a special edition.

Within the five-mile circle even the great majority of people were inert. I have already described the behaviour of the men and women to whom I spoke. All over the district people were dining and supping; working-men were gardening after the labours of the day, children were being put to bed, young people were wandering through the lanes love-making, students sat over their books.

Maybe there was a murmur in the village streets, a novel and dominant topic in the public-houses, and here and there a messenger, or even an eye-witness of the later occurrences, caused a whirl of excitement, a shouting and a running to and fro; but for the most part the daily routine of working, eating, drinking, sleeping, went on as it had done for countless years—as though no planet Mars existed in the sky.[40] Even at Woking Station and Horsell and Chobham that was the case.

---

40. Here Wells makes a biblical judgment on the state of Sin before the Advent (see note 34 on the curate). "As were the days of Noah, so will be the coming of the Son of Man. For in those days before the flood they were eating and drinking, marrying and giving in marriage" (Matthew 24:37f). Such is everydayism (note 4), "the commonplace habits of our social order" (first paragraph above). Nobody sensed that, "with the swift fate hanging over us, men could go about their petty concerns as they did" (I:1, next to last paragraph). It is all pointless iteration, "vain repetitions" of the Normal Social Life, "this comic *crambe repetita*" (1904:17). The Latin phrase used by Wells is from the *Satires* of Juvenal: cold cabbage warmed over. It echoes the Greek proverb, cabbage boiled twice is death, referring to the endless repetitiousness of a grammar teacher's task (Morwood 1998:37). It is all so futile and animal-like. "All that they feel has been felt, all that they do has been done before" (1922b:155f).

Time now for a collective purpose, "of living lives for remote and mighty ends" (1927:30). Time now for the cosmic Human Adventure, "knowing oneself for Man on his planet, flying swiftly to unmeasured destinies through the starry stillnesses of space" (1914:415). The "great disillusionment" at note 4 is the shattering realization that human life is nothing more than deathly warmed over cabbage; the Martians, from another part of the cosmos, bring that great spiritual awakening, whatever the mortal cost of those slow to learn the lesson. Something has to shake mankind out of "The 'Cyclic' Delusion" (1894b) if it is to get moving toward a higher destiny. Sunrise and sunset, regular seasons, birth and death, generational regularity — all these natural cycles falsely validate the tradition-bound recooking of the same old cabbage dish on this "little fretful midge of life spinning on its axis [in] a gyrating solar system." How stale and unprofitable; there must be something more to it. Out there, in the deeps of space and time, the wider "universe flows past us and onward." Yet human history, ever repetitious, ignores this cosmic reality; we are hapless captives of a localized eddy in that mighty current, deluded by our backwater existence. "But the main course is forward, from things that are past and done with for ever to things that are altogether new" (506). The Martians, cosmic outsiders, teach that lesson: Go with the flow or die the death of a species doomed to extinction. While they themselves threaten human extinction, they set a new example and show that it is within human power to out–Martian the Martians. Such is the catastrophic invasion's benevolent legacy. The countereffect is to immortalize the human race in its response: a forward-looking, open-ended utopian world-state destined to conquer the entire universe.

In *Things to Come*, whose Modern State Octopus is cognate with the Great State in *Sleeper* the sequel to *Worlds*, mankind is at last readied to take advantage of its star-begotten Martian heritage.

In Woking Junction, until a late hour, trains were stopping and going on, others were shunting on the sidings, passengers were alighting and waiting, and everything was proceeding in the most ordinary way. A boy from town, trenching on Smith's monopoly,[41] was selling papers with the afternoon's news. The ringing and impact of trucks, the sharp whistle of the engines from the junction, mingled with his shouts of "Men from Mars!" Excited men came into the station with incredible tidings about nine o'clock, and caused no more disturbance than drunkards might have done. People rattling Londonwards peered into the darkness outside the carriage windows and saw only a rare, flickering, vanishing spark dance up from the direction of Horsell, a red glow and a thin veil of smoke driving across the stars, and thought that nothing more serious than a heath fire was happening. It was only round the edge of the common that any disturbance was perceptible. There were half a dozen villas burning on the Woking border. There were lights in all the houses on the common side of the three villages, and the people there kept awake till dawn.

A curious crowd lingered restlessly, people coming and going but the crowd remaining, both on the Chobham and Horsell bridges. One or two adventurous souls, it was afterwards found, went into the darkness and crawled quite near the Martians; but they never returned, for now and again a light-ray, like the beam of a warship's searchlight, swept the common, and the Heat-Ray was ready to follow. Save for such, that big area of common was silent and desolate, and the charred

---

Rest enough for the individual man. Too much and too soon, and we call it death. But for Man no rest and no ending. He must go on. Conquest beyond conquest.

First this little planet with its winds and waves. And all the laws of mind and matter that restrain him. Then the planets about him. And at last out across immensity to the stars [film shots 1044–45 in 1936].

The Martian service to mankind is the story of *Worlds*, conveyed by the narrator but only implicitly. For all his fatuous philosophizing, he is the last to fully apprehend what he has reported. When the time comes for others to act on these great events, he will be counted as but one more trivial obstruction in the path of progress.

41. Reference to W.H. Smith, whose chain of stationery stores to this day has the exclusive rights to sell newspapers, books, and magazines in British railway stations. When at note 103 the railway system begins to dissolve thanks to the "poisoned dart" effect (note 42), so too must the entire basis of civilized society go into dissolution, since its flow of information, exclusively in the medium of print in pre-electronic times, is distributed by that system.

bodies lay about on it all night under the stars, and all the next day. A noise of hammering from the pit was heard by many people.

So you have the state of things on Friday night. In the centre, sticking into the skin of our old planet Earth like a poisoned dart, was this cylinder. But the poison was scarcely working yet.[42] Around it was a patch of silent common, smouldering in places, and with a few dark, dimly-seen objects lying in contorted attitudes here and there. Here and there was a burning bush or tree. Beyond was a fringe of excitement, and further than that fringe the inflammation had not crept as yet. In the rest of the world the stream of life still flowed as it had flowed for immemorial years. The fever of war that would presently clog vein and artery, deaden nerve and destroy brain, had still to develop.

All night long the Martians were hammering and stirring, sleepless, indefatigable, at work upon the machines they were making ready, and ever and again a puff of greenish-white smoke whirled up to the starlit sky.

About eleven a company of soldiers came through Horsell, and deployed along the edge of the common to form a cordon. Later a second company marched through Chobham to deploy on the north side of the common. Several officers from the Inkerman barracks had been on the common earlier in the day, and one, Major Eden, was reported to be missing. The Colonel of the regiment came to the Chobham bridge, and was busy questioning the crowd at midnight. The military authorities were certainly alive to the seriousness of the business. About eleven, the next morning's papers were able to say, a squadron of hussars, two Maxims,[43] and about 400 men of the Cardigan regiment, started from Aldershot.

A few seconds after midnight the crowd in the Chertsey road, Woking, saw a star fall from heaven into the pine-woods to the northwest. It fell with a greenish light, causing a flash of light like summer lightning. This was the second cylinder.

---

42. That the Martians are vampires (see the Introduction to the present work, section 5) is here first indicated. The "poisoned dart" that is the initial cylinder to stick into the planet's skin has yet to work its effect. When it does, tissues dissolve, as in the dramatic metaphor opening I:16 —"that swift liquefaction of the social body." So begins the destruction/reconstruction dialectic.

43. The Maxim Gun, Hiram Maxim's patent of 1884, was an early form of the machine-gun devastating to native peoples under British colonial rule; but it is hopeless against superior Martian weaponry, whose targets are proportionally inferior.

IX

THE FIGHTING BEGINS.

SATURDAY lives in my memory as a day of suspense. It was a day of lassitude too, hot and close, with, I am told, a rapidly fluctuating barometer. I had slept but little, though my wife had succeeded in sleeping, and I rose early. I went into my garden before breakfast, and stood listening, but towards the common there was nothing stirring but a lark.

The milkman came as usual. I heard the rattle of his chariot, and I went round to the side-gate to ask the latest news. He told me that during the night the Martians had been surrounded by troops, and that guns were expected. Then, a familiar reassuring note, I heard a train running towards Woking.

"They aren't to be killed,' said the milkman, "if that can possibly be avoided."

I saw my neighbour gardening, chatted with him for a time, and then strolled in to breakfast. It was a most unexceptional morning. My neighbour was of opinion that the troops would be able to capture or to destroy the Martians during the day.

"It's a pity they make themselves so unapproachable," he said. "It would be curious to learn how they live on another planet; we might learn a thing or two."

He came up to the fence and extended a handful of strawberries, for his gardening was as generous as it was enthusiastic. At the same time he told me of the burning of the pine-woods about the Byfleet Golf Links.

"They say," said he, "that there's another of those blessed things fallen there—number two. But one's enough, surely. This lot 'll cost the insurance people a pretty penny before everything's settled."[44] He

44. The narrator's neighbor in Woking assumes, with a touching faith in bourgeois property values, that "the insurance people" will settle for damages

laughed with an air of the greatest good-humour as he said this. The woods, he said, were still burning, and pointed out a haze of smoke to me. "They will be hot under foot for days on account of the thick soil of pine-needles and turf," he said, and then grew serious over "poor Ogilvy."

After breakfast, instead of working, I decided to walk down towards the common. Under the railway bridge I found a group of soldiers— sappers, I think, men in small round caps, dirty red jackets unbuttoned, and showing their blue shirts, dark trousers, and boots coming to the calf. They told me no one was allowed over the canal, and, looking along the road towards the bridge, I saw one of the Cardigan men standing sentinel there. I talked with these soldiers for a time; I told them of my sight of the Martians on the previous evening. None of them had seen the Martians, and they had but the vaguest ideas of them, so that they plied me with questions. They said that they did not know who had authorized the movement of the troops; their idea was that a dispute had arisen at the Horse Guards. The ordinary sapper is a great deal better educated than the common soldier, and they discussed the peculiar conditions of the possible fight with some acuteness.[45] I described the Heat-Ray to them, and they began to argue among themselves.

---

once the Martians are defeated. In II:7, the artilleryman mocks the smug everydayism of this insurance mentally, knowing that it is doomed. In a letter of 1901 to his friend Sidney Dark, Wells says he is fond of *Worlds* "because of its spirited destruction of property" (Dark 1922:46). With the artilleryman, he relishes the disillusionment of bourgeois respectability, that basis of the Normal Social Life destined for overthrow with the coming of the tradition-smashing Great State (1912: Chapter 1), elsewhere the Modern State Octopus (1933). As Renan says in the epigraph to the present work, "The past is merely a mistake," a record of human stupidity to be rectified only by a scientific government on the Martian model Wells projects onto his corporative Great State.

45. Sappers are military engineers trained in the construction of fortifications, trenches, or tunnels that approach or undermine enemy positions. Given their technical skills, the ones talking with the narrator discuss their task with "some acuteness." They are discontented, however, by a seeming dispute that has arisen among the Royal Horse Guards as to the tactical movement of troops. These are the ornamental cavalrymen stationed opposite Whitehall in central London, guardians of the English Household, whose parading is today a tourist attraction; but even then they were more for ceremonial display than for deployment in battle. Not surprisingly, the "ordinary sapper thinks these elite troopers out of touch with the local situation." In II:7, the artilleryman is just

"Crawl up under cover and rush 'em, say I," said one.

"Get aht!" said another. "What's Cover against this 'ere 'eat? Sticks to cook yer! What we got to do is to go as near as the ground 'll let us, and then drive a trench."

"Blow yer trenches! You always want trenches; you ought to ha' been born a rabbit, Snippy."

"Ain't they got any necks, then?" said a third abruptly—a little, contemplative, dark man, smoking a pipe.

I repeated my description.

"Octopuses," said he, "that's what I calls 'em. Talk about fishers of men—fighters of fish it is this time!"[46]

"It ain't no murder killing beasts like that," said the first speaker.

"Why not shell the darned things strite off and finish 'em?" said the little dark man. "You carn tell what they might do."

"Where's your shells?" said the first speaker. "There ain't no time. Do it in a rush, that's my tip, and do it at once."

So they discussed it. After a while I left them, and went on to the railway-station to get as many morning papers as I could.

But I will not weary the reader with a description of that long morning and of the longer afternoon. I did not succeed in getting a glimpse of the common, for even Horsell and Chobham church towers were in the hands of the military authorities. The soldiers I addressed didn't know anything; the officers were mysterious as well as busy. I found

---

such a realist, like the sappers, who with professional pride says he is "not an ornamental soldier."

46. In Matthew 4:19 Jesus says to his disciples, "Follow me, and I will make you fishers of men." Confronted by "octopuses," one of the sappers jokes, "fighters of fish it is this time!" Little does he realize that the monsters he is about to fight are themselves bringers of salvation. The artilleryman alone senses that truth, when he sees in the Martians both enemy and model: Once driven off they are to be emulated (II:7). In their wake, mankind will no longer need them to help clear the way for a socialist world-state. The Martian ideal is borne by John Cabal the Air Dictator, whose octopus-headed helmet is both monstrous and redemptive. When closed (fig. 2 of the plates in the present work) it is a mask protecting him from the all-subduing gas he drops from on high, as do the Martians from *their* airplanes; when open (fig. 3), with visor down, he is a haloed icon of benignity, whose terrorist war for peace rescues humanity from the sins of its evil past. Indeed, the pious Airmen (as partymen of the Modern State Revolution) profess nothing less than a "rule of the new saints" (1933:359).

people in the town quite secure again in the presence of the military, and I heard for the first time from Marshall, the tobacconist, that his son was among the dead on the common. The soldiers had made the people on the outskirts of Horsell lock up and leave their houses.

I got back to lunch about two, very tired, for, as I have said, the day was extremely hot and dull, and in order to refresh myself I took a cold bath in the afternoon. About half-past four I went up to the railway-station to get an evening paper, for the morning papers had contained only a very inaccurate description of the killing of Stent, Henderson, Ogilvy, and the others. But there was little I didn't know. The Martians did not show an inch of themselves. They seemed busy in their pit, and there was a sound of hammering and an almost continuous streamer of smoke. Apparently, they were busy getting ready for a struggle. "Fresh attempts have been made to signal, but without success," was the stereotyped formula of the papers. A sapper told me it was done by a man in a ditch with a flag on a long pole. The Martians took as much notice of such advances as we should of the lowing of a cow.

I must confess the sight of all this armament, all this preparation, greatly excited me. My imagination became belligerent, and defeated the invaders in a dozen striking ways; something of my schoolboy dreams of battle and heroism came back.[47] It hardly seemed a fair fight to me at that time. They seemed very helpless in this pit of theirs.

About three o'clock there began the thud of a gun at measured intervals from Chertsey or Addlestone. I learnt that the smouldering pine-wood into which the second cylinder had fallen was being shelled, in the hope of destroying that object before it opened. It was only about five, however, that a field-gun reached Chobham for use against the first body of Martians.

About six in the evening, as I sat at tea with my wife in the sum-mer-house talking vigorously about the battle that was lowering upon us, I heard a muffled detonation from the common, and immediately after a gust of firing. Close on the heels of that came a violent, rattling crash, quite close to us, that shook the ground; and, starting out upon the lawn, I saw the tops of the trees about the Oriental College burst into smoky red flame, and the tower of the little church beside it slide down into ruin. The pinnacle of the mosque[48] had vanished, and the

---

47. This provides the motivation for the narrator to leave home and wife in order to play at being a sightseeing war correspondent.

48. The Martians are equal-opportunity enemies of religion, Islam and Christianity alike, as the most conservative bearers of out-dated tradition. The

roof-line of the college itself looked as if a hundred-ton gun had been at work upon it. One of our chimneys cracked as if a shot had hit it, flew, and the piece of it came clattering down the tiles and made a heap of broken red fragments upon the flower-bed by my study window.

I and my wife stood amazed. Then I realized that the crest of Maybury Hill must be within range of the Martians' Heat-Ray now that the college was cleared out of the way.

At that I gripped my wife's arm, and without ceremony ran her out into the road. Then I fetched out the servant, telling her I would go upstairs myself for the box she was clamouring for.

"We can't possibly stay here," I said; and as I spoke the firing re-opened for a moment upon the common.

"But where are we to go?" said my wife in terror.

I thought, perplexed. Then I remembered her cousins at Leatherhead.[49]

"Leatherhead!" I shouted above the sudden noise.

She looked away from me downhill. The people were coming out of their houses astonished.

"How are we to get to Leatherhead?" she said.

Down the hill I saw a bevy of hussars ride under the railway-bridge; three galloped through the open gates of the Oriental College; two others dismounted, and began running from house to house. The sun, shining through the smoke that drove up from the tops of the trees, seemed blood-red, and threw an unfamiliar lurid light upon everything.

"Stop here," said I; "you are safe here;" and I started off at once for the Spotted Dog, for I knew the landlord had a horse and dogcart. I ran, for I perceived that in a moment everyone upon this side of the hill would be moving. I found him in his bar, quite unaware of what was going on behind his house. A man stood with his back to me, talking to him.

"I must have a pound," said the landlord, "and I've no one to drive it."

---

mosque was built for Muslim students at the Oriental College, a center for distinguished Indian visitors from the British Raj. As I myself have seen, the mosque still stands as an exotic feature of the Woking landscape, undestroyed by the Martians or by recent real estate developments that swept away the College.

49. The narrator means his *own* cousins, living about 12 miles east of Woking in Leatherhead, as given in 1:10 and elsewhere. That he confused his kinship relations perhaps indicates that he is not quite the family man he professes to be, having now embarked on the dangers of amateur war reporting (note 50).

"I'll give you two," said I, over the stranger's shoulder.

"What for?"

"And I'll bring it back by midnight," I said.

"Lord!" said the landlord, "what's the hurry? I'm selling my bit of a pig. Two pounds, and you bring it back? What's going on now?"[50]

I explained hastily that I had to leave my home, and so secured the dogcart. At the time it did not seem to me nearly so urgent that the landlord should leave his. I took care to have the cart there and then, drove it off down the road, and, leaving it in charge of my wife and servant, rushed into my house and packed a few valuables, such plate as we had, and so forth. The beech-trees below the house were burning while I did this, and the palings up the road glowed red. While I was occupied in this way, one of the dismounted hussars came running up. He was going from house to house, warning people to leave. He was going on as I came out of my front-door, lugging my treasures, done up in a table-cloth. I shouted after him:

"What news?"

He turned, stared, bawled something about "crawling out in a thing like a dish cover," and ran on to the gate of the house at the crest. A sudden whirl of black smoke driving across the road hid him for a moment. I ran to my neighbour's door, and rapped to satisfy myself, what I already knew, that his wife had gone to London with him, and had locked up their house. I went in again according to my promise to get my servant's box, lugged it out, clapped it beside her on the tail of the dogcart, and then caught the reins and jumped up into the driver's seat beside my wife. In another moment we were clear of the smoke and noise, and spanking down the opposite slope of Maybury Hill towards Old Woking.

In front was a quiet sunny landscape, a wheat-field ahead on either

---

50. The landlord is puzzled by the narrator's haste to pay two pounds for his "bit of pig" (=his valuable piece of property) coupled with a strong promise to return it. What the landlord fails to grasp is that the narrator wants his dogcart (a light, two-wheeled, horse-drawn vehicle that originally had a box under the rear seat for the family dog) for the escape of his (the narrator's) wife from an immediate danger the landlord has yet to appreciate. When the narrator returns to Woking on foot (after having crashed the dogcart in the gathering war storm), he finds on passing by the inn its keeper a victim of the havoc he had saved his wife from. But he himself recklessly follows the trail of destruction in a family-disregarding "war-fever" (I:10). The innkeeper thus has been deprived of *his* means of escape, which the selfish narrator does not bother to agonize over.

side of the road, and the Maybury Inn with its swinging sign. I saw the doctor's cart ahead of me. At the bottom of the hill I turned my head to look at the hillside I was leaving. Thick streamers of black smoke shot with threads of red fire were driving up into the still air, and throwing dark shadows upon the green tree-tops eastward. The smoke already extended far away to the east and west—to the Byfleet pine-woods eastward, and to Woking on the west. The road was dotted with people running towards us. And very faint now, but very distinct through the hot, quiet air, one heard the whirr of a machine-gun that was presently stilled, and an intermittent cracking of rifles. Apparently, the Martians were setting fire to everything within range of their Heat-Ray.

I am not an expert driver, and I had immediately to turn my attention to the horse. When I looked back again the second hill had hidden the black smoke. I slashed the horse with the whip, and gave him a loose rein until Woking and Send lay between us and that quivering tumult. I overtook and passed the doctor between Woking and Send.

X

IN THE STORM.

LEATHERHEAD is about twelve miles from Maybury Hill. The scent of hay was in the air through the lush meadows beyond Pyrford, and the hedges on either side were sweet and gay with multitudes of dog-roses. The heavy firing that had broken out while we were driving down Maybury Hill ceased as abruptly as it began, leaving the evening very peaceful and still. We got to Leatherhead without misadventure about nine o'clock, and the horse had an hour's rest while I took supper with my cousins and commended my wife to their care.

My wife was curiously silent throughout the drive, and seemed oppressed with forebodings of evil. I talked to her reassuringly, pointing out that the Martians were tied to the pit by sheer heaviness, and, at the utmost, could but crawl a little out of it, but she answered only in monosyllables. Had it not been for my promise to the innkeeper, she would, I think, have urged me to stay in Leatherhead that night. Would that I had! Her face, I remember, was very white as we parted.

For my own part, I had been feverishly excited all day. Something very like the war-fever, that occasionally runs through a civilized community, had got into my blood, and in my heart I was not so very sorry that I had to return to Maybury that night. I was even afraid that last fusillade I had heard might mean the extermination of our invaders from Mars. I can best express my state of mind by saying that I wanted to be in at the death.[51]

It was nearly eleven when I started to return. The night was unexpectedly dark; to me, walking out of the lighted passage of my cousins'

---

51. The same evening the narrator's brother had thought of coming down from London "to see the Things before they were killed" (1:14). But in the end he flees northward and out to the sea, when the unkillable Things approach London itself.

house, it seemed indeed black, and it was as hot and close as the day. Overhead the clouds were driving fast, albeit not a breath stirred the shrubs about us. My cousins' man lit both lamps. Happily, I knew the road intimately. My wife stood in the light of the doorway, and watched me until I jumped up into the dogcart. Then abruptly she turned and went in, leaving my cousins side by side wishing me good hap.

I was a little depressed at first with the contagion of my wife's fears, but very soon my thoughts reverted to the Martians. At that time I was absolutely in the dark as to the course of the evening's fighting. I did not know even the circumstances that had precipitated the conflict. As I came through Ockham (for that was the way I returned, and not through Send and Old Woking) I saw along the western horizon a blood-red glow, which, as I drew nearer, crept slowly up the sky. The driving clouds of the gathering thunderstorm mingled there with masses of black and red smoke.

Ripley Street was deserted, and except for a lighted window or so the village showed not a sign of life; but I narrowly escaped an accident at the corner of the road to Pyrford, where a knot of people stood with their backs to me. They said nothing to me as I passed. I do not know what they knew of the things happening beyond the hill, nor do I know if the silent houses I passed on my way were sleeping securely, or deserted and empty, or harassed and watching against the terror of the night.

From Ripley until I came through Pyrford I was in the valley of the Wey, and the red glare was hidden from me. As I ascended the little hill beyond Pyrford Church the glare came into view again, and the trees about me shivered with the first intimation of the storm that was upon me. Then I heard midnight pealing out from Pyrford Church behind me, and then came the silhouette of Maybury Hill, with its tree-tops and roofs black and sharp against the red.

Even as I beheld this a lurid green glare lit the road about me, and showed the distant woods towards Addlestone. I felt a tug at the reins. I saw that the driving clouds had been pierced as it were by a thread of green fire, suddenly lighting their confusion and falling into the fields to my left. It was the Third Falling Star!

Close on its apparition, and blindingly violet by contrast, danced out the first lightning of the gathering storm, and the thunder burst like a rocket overhead. The horse took the bit between his teeth and bolted.

A moderate incline runs down towards the foot of Maybury Hill, and down this we clattered. Once the lightning had begun, it went on in as rapid a succession of flashes as I have ever seen. The thunderclaps, treading one on the heels of another and with a strange crackling accompaniment, sounded more like the working of a gigantic electric machine than the usual detonating reverberations.[52] The flickering light was blinding and confusing, and a thin hail smote gustily at my face as I drove down the slope.

At first I regarded little but the road before me, and then abruptly

---

52. The detonations of the electrical storm sound to the narrator like those of some "gigantic electric machine," an allusion to the Wimshurst electrostatic induction generator invented in 1880 by James Wimshurst (Grun 1982:439, column f). A much bigger version was developed by the American physicist Robert Van de Graaff in 1931, made famous when displayed for years thereafter at the Massachusetts Institute of Technology. It looks like two dumbbells standing on end, whose two metal globes give rise between them to spectacular, high-voltage bolts of "man-made lightning." But unlike the Wimshurst machine, the Van de Graaff generator was designed as a research tool, specifically in the new field of nuclear physics. From the start, Ernest Lawrence used it as a high voltage source for accelerator tubes in the "cyclotron" he developed and so named (Asimov 1972:1024, 1019f).

The seven-foot tall Wimshurst device was displayed in London's Science Museum from 1884, which Wells surely would have seen in action whilst a student at the nearby Normal School of Science. At the time it was a mere curiosity, serving only to demonstrate the power of electricity, itself then a novelty. Indeed, electric lighting was so retarded by conservative politics in London that it lagged far behind cities like Chicago and Berlin where great power grids already had expanded into surrounding communities (T.P. Hughes 1983). The narrator's suburban Woking is without it, while the metropolis itself was only spottily electrified. Moreover, electricity supply undertakings in London were divided, gridless, among numerous rival private companies, with only a few of them under municipal authority, notably in Hamstead from 1894 (Pope 1989:89, map 4.16)—still a progressive exemplar of unrealized socialism, as late as 1904, for all of greater metropolitan London in Wells's critique of that year (see Appendix II in the present work).

Significantly, suburban Hamstead is an enemy camp, from which the Martians have devastated largely gaslit London, and which in II:7 the artilleryman points out to the narrator as a model of modernity. "Of a night, all over there, Hampstead way, the sky is alive with their lights. It's like a great city, and in the glare you can just see them moving." The Martians themselves seem to be electrically powered, as indicated by the Wimshurst-like detonating sound heard when the Heat-Ray is turned on.

my attention was arrested by something that was moving rapidly down the opposite slops of Maybury Hill. At first I took it for the wet roof of a house, but one flash following another showed it to be in swift rolling movement. It was an elusive vision—a moment bewildering darkness, and then in a flash like daylight, the red masses of the Orphanage[53] near the crest of the hill, the green tops of the pine-trees, and this problematical object came out clear and sharp and bright.

And this thing I saw! How can I describe it? A monstrous tripod, higher than many houses, striding over the young pine-trees, and smashing them aside in its career; a walking engine of glittering metal, striding now across the heather; articulate ropes of steel dangling from it, and the clattering tumult of its passage mingling with the riot of the thunder. A flash, and it came out vividly, heeling over one way with two feet in the air, to vanish and reappear almost instantly as it seemed, with the next flash, a hundred yards nearer.[54] Can you imagine a milking stool tilted and bowled violently along the ground? That was the impression those instant flashes gave. But instead of a milking-stool imagine it a great body of machinery on a tripod stand.

Then suddenly the trees in the pine-wood ahead of me were parted, as brittle reeds are parted by a man thrusting through them; they were snapped off and driven headlong, and a second huge tripod appeared, rushing, as it seemed, headlong towards me. And I was galloping hard to meet it! At the sight of the second monster my nerve went altogether. Not stopping to look again, I wrenched the horse's head hard round to the right, and in another moment the dogcart had heeled

---

53. Hughes and Geduld (1993:208, *n7*) believe they have caught Wells in a stupid mistake. The orphanage on the crest of Maybury Hill was not built until 1909; in its place at the time there stood St. Peter's Memorial Home for the aged. Maybury itself is a section of Woking, the location of the narrator's house and also of Wells's during the writing of *Worlds*. I myself have visited that house and scouted the locale, and am convinced that Wells knew it with mistake-free accuracy. If he imagines an orphanage in place of the old-age home, he takes a conspicuous liberty only for effect: the locals are now orphans of a war storm who will never live long enough to enter even the ruins of St. Peter's.

54. Wells's powers of visualization always are acute. Here the narrator observes the movement of a Martian machine at flashing intervals of lightning, as in a stroboscopic effect not seen until modern movies showed realistically-filmed battle scenes. A like stop-motion snapshot is visualized in *The War in the Air*, in which a warplane against an explosive background is caught "in the light of the flash as a thing altogether motionless" (1908b:213).

over upon the horse; the shafts smashed noisily, and I was flung sideways and fell heavily into a shallow pool of water.

I crawled out almost immediately, and crouched, my feet still in the water, under a clump of furze. The horse lay motionless (his neck was broken, poor brute!), and by the lightning flashes I saw the black bulk of the overturned dogcart, and the silhouette of the wheel still spinning slowly. In another moment the colossal mechanism went striding by me, and passed uphill towards Pyrford.

Seen nearer, the thing was incredibly strange, for it was no mere insensate machine driving on its way. Machine it was, with a ringing metallic pace, and long flexible glittering tentacles (one of which gripped a young pine-tree) swinging and rattling about its strange body. It picked its road as it went striding along, and the brazen hood that surmounted it moved to and fro with the inevitable suggestion of a head looking about it. Behind the main body was a huge thing of white metal like a gigantic fisherman's basket, and puffs of green smoke squirted out from the joints of the limbs as the monster swept by me.[55] And in an instant it was gone.

---

55. The "fisherman's basket" mounted on the machine is later shown to be a repository for captured humans, whose blood is drained for injection into Martian veins (II:2). Fishers of men they are indeed (note 46), these vampires! For manipulation each machine is fitted with prehensile cables, mechanical extensions of bodily tentacles. The tripodal legs on which the Martians ambulate, however, are no such extension of organic function, as three-limbed creatures do not occur in nature. The four-limbed humanoids, from which the Martian body has been modified by multiples of two for octopodal tentacles, do not in the least suggest a basis for artificial tripod legs. All the same the legs, like the cables, are actuated by electric-powered mechanical musculature (II:2). The narrator observes "green smoke" squirting from their joints, like steam from the pistons of a locomotive. Steam, electrically heated, is in fact used to hose down residues of the Black Smoke after poison-gas attacks on London (II:15).

Green also is the color of a blazing cylinder falling through the atmosphere, "a green meteor" (I:16). Like Verne's space capsule, the Martian vehicles are made of aluminum, and its making here on earth is lit by a "green fire" (II:3). But there is no possible chemical reaction with that metal (least of all in the tripod legs from contact with superheated steam) that would emit a green color. Here again is a calculated departure from realism, as with the missiles arriving only days after being fired (note 9). So green must be a signature of something alien, entirely symbolic, as indeed it is in science-fictional tradition. Now green is a *good* color in its normal place — grass, pastures, tree leaves, forested mountains — and when a fellow anthropologist friend of mine helped to design a lunar habi-

So much I saw then, all vaguely for the flickering of the lightning, in blinding high lights and dense black shadows.

As it passed it set up an exultant deafening howl that drowned the thunder, "Aloo! aloo!" and in another minute it was with its companion, and half a mile away, stooping over something in the field. I have no doubt this thing in the field was the third of the ten cylinders they had fired at us from Mars.

For some minutes I lay there in the rain and darkness watching, by the intermittent light, these monstrous beings of metal moving about

---

tat, he insisted that greenery be planted within, so as to meet an almost instinctive need by humans to associate the color with terrestrial security. When out of place, however, it is weird and scary — the green steam *etc.* associated with the Martians.

In the classic science fiction film *This Island Earth* (1955, Universal), an alien spacecraft (inevitably a flying saucer) lifts up an airplane into its gigantic bowels with a sinister green ray. In *The Tommyknockers* (1987) by Stephen King, whom I know to be saturated in the older literature from H.G. Wells onward, a spaceship (another disc) buried for millions of years is dug up, its metal radiating a green glow. Its effect on people nearby is to meld them into a group mind and to induce them to produce gadgets of technological brilliance that likewise glow green — the prelude to world takeover until stopped by the novel's hero. The made-for-television movie based on it adds to these enchanted people the radiance of those green-eyed monsters and demons ever seen in cheapo horror films. I need scarcely add that, in the George Pal production of *The War of the Worlds* (1953, Paramount), light from inside a Martian fighting machine is — green. The sinister greenness of things Martian must relate to this tradition arising from Wells himself (perhaps even those gremlin-like, trouble-making "little green men from Mars" owe to him). In *Worlds*, however, the aliens are anything but evil, yet what has been made of them in later science fiction makes it difficult to see them otherwise. Now that fascist corporatism has been defeated in World War II and communism self-destructed during the Cold War, it is hard to believe the Martian mission benevolent in bringing a discredited group-minded collectivism to our planet, for the saving of mankind from itself. Yet Wells has it "that damnation is really over-individuation and that salvation is escape from self into the larger being of life" (1917:76).

There is, of course, one other possible association. *In the Days of the Comet* (1906a) has a passing cometary body give off "green vapours" that puts humanity to sleep, then to awaken in peace and harmony: instant utopia. However strange and menacing Martian vapors may seem to humans, even the Black Smoke, it is all for their own good — those who survive, at any rate. More at note 143.

in the distance over the hedge-tops. A thin hail was now beginning, and as it came and went, their figures grew misty and then flashed into clearness again. Now and then came a gap in the lightning, and the night swallowed them up.

I was soaked with hail above and puddle-water below. It was some time before my blank astonishment would let me struggle up the bank to a drier position, or think at all of my imminent peril.

Not far from me was a little one-roomed squatter's hut of wood, surrounded by a patch of potato-garden. I struggled to my feet at last, and, crouching and making use of every chance of cover, I made a run for this. I hammered at the door, but I could not make the people hear (if there were any people inside), and after a time I desisted, and, availing myself of a ditch for the greater part of the way, succeeded in crawling, unobserved by these monstrous machines, into the pine-wood towards Maybury.

Under cover of this I pushed on, wet and shivering now, towards my own house. I walked among the trees trying to find the footpath. It was very dark indeed in the wood, for the lightning was now becoming infrequent, and the hail, which was pouring down in a torrent, fell in columns through the gaps in the heavy foliage.

If I had fully realized the meaning of all the things I had seen I should have immediately worked my way round through Byfleet to Street Cobham, and so gone back to rejoin my wife at Leatherhead. But that night the strangeness of things about me, and my physical wretchedness, prevented me, for I was bruised, weary, wet to the skin, deafened and blinded by the storm.

I had a vague idea of going on to my own house, and that was as much motive as I had. I staggered through the trees, fell into a ditch and bruised my knees against a plank, and finally splashed out into the lane that ran down from the College Arms.[56] I say splashed, for the storm water was sweeping the sand down the hill in a muddy torrent. There in the darkness a man blundered into me and sent me reeling back.

---

56. The narrator three times within five paragraphs mentions the name of this local pub, which actually existed at the time and still does. The only two other pubs named College Arms are located in academic environs (Dunkling and Wright 1987:57), but Woking is no such place. The Oriental College at note 48 is a mosque devoid of any heraldic device. Wells allows the narrator to stress the pretentious naming of the College Arms as one more indictment of a society deserving destruction.

He gave a cry of terror, sprung sideways, and rushed on before I could gather my wits sufficiently to speak to him. So heavy was the stress of the storm just at this place that I had the hardest task to win my way up the hill. I went close up to the fence on the left and worked my way along its palings.

Near the top I stumbled upon something soft, and, by a flash of lightning, saw between my feet a heap of black broadcloth and a pair of boots. Before I could distinguish clearly how the man lay, the flicker of light had passed. I stood over him waiting for the next flash. When it came, I saw that he was a sturdy man, cheaply but not shabbily dressed; his head was bent under his body, and he lay crumpled up close to the fence, as though he had been flung violently against it.

Overcoming the repugnance natural to one who had never before touched a dead body, I stooped and turned him over to feel for his heart. He was quite dead. Apparently his neck had been broken. The lightning flashed for a third time, and his face leapt upon me. I sprang to my feet. It was the landlord of the Spotted Dog, whose conveyance I had taken.[57]

I stepped over him gingerly and pushed on up the hill. I made my way by the police-station and the College Arms towards my own house. Nothing was burning on the hillside, though from the common there still came a red glare and a rolling tumult of ruddy smoke beating up against the drenching hail. So far as I could see by the flashes, the houses about me were mostly uninjured. By the College Arms a dark heap lay in the road.

Down the road towards Maybury Bridge there were voices and the sound of feet, but I had not the courage to shout or to go to them. I let myself in with my latch-key, closed, locked and bolted the door, staggered to the foot of the staircase and sat down. My imagination was full of those striding metallic monsters, and of the dead body smashed against the fence.

I crouched at the foot of the staircase with my back to the wall, shivering violently.

---

57. The transaction at note 50, falsely promising return of the dogcart, is the proximate cause of the landlord's death, for which the narrator in his war fever feels no remorse.

XI

AT THE WINDOW.

I HAVE said already that my storms of emotion have a trick of exhausting themselves. After a time I discovered that I was cold and wet, and with little pools of water about me on the stair-carpet. I got up almost mechanically, went into the dining-room and drank some whisky, and then I was moved to change my clothes.

After I had done that I went upstairs to my study, but why I did so I do not know. The window of my study looks over the trees and the railway towards Horsell Common. In the hurry of our departure this window had been left open. The passage was dark, and, by contrast with the picture the window-frame enclosed, that side of the room seemed impenetrably dark. I stopped short in the doorway.

The thunderstorm had passed. The towers of the Oriental College and the pine-trees about it had gone, and very far away, lit by a vivid red glare, the common about the sand-pits was visible. Across the light, huge black shapes, grotesque and strange, moved busily to and fro.

It seemed, indeed, as if the whole country in that direction was on fire—a broad hillside set with minute tongues of flame, swaying and writhing with the gusts of the dying storm, and throwing a red reflection upon the cloud scud above. Every now and then a haze of smoke from some nearer conflagration drove across the window and hid the Martian shapes. I could not see what they were doing, nor the clear form of them, nor recognise the black objects they were busied upon. Neither could I see the nearer fire, though the reflections of it danced on the wall and ceiling of the study. A sharp, resinous twang of burning was in the air.

I closed the door noiselessly and crept towards the window. As I did so, the view opened out until, on the one hand, it reached to the houses about Woking Station, and on the other to the charred and blackened pine-woods of Byfleet. There was a light down below the hill, on the railway, near the arch, and several of the houses along the Maybury road and the streets near the station were glowing ruins. The light upon the railway puzzled me at first; there was a black heap and a vivid glare, and to the right of that a row of yellow oblongs. Then I perceived this was a wrecked train, the fore part smashed and on fire, the hinder carriages still upon the rails.

Between these three main centres of light, the houses, the train, and the burning country towards Chobham, stretched irregular patches of dark country, broken here and there by intervals of dimly glowing and smoking ground. It was the strangest spectacle, that black expanse set with fire. It reminded me, more than anything else, of the Potteries seen at night. People at first I could distinguish none, though I peered intently for them. Later I saw against the light of Woking Station a number of black figures hurrying one after the other across the line.

And this was the little world in which I had been living securely for years, this fiery chaos![58] What had happened in the last seven hours I still did not know, nor did I know, though I was beginning to guess, the relation between these mechanical colossi and the sluggish lumps I had seen disgorged from the cylinder. With a queer feeling of impersonal interest I turned my desk-chair to the window, sat down, and stared at the blackened country, and particularly at the three gigantic black things that were going to and fro in the glare about the sand-pits.

They seemed amazingly busy. I began to ask myself what they could be. Were they intelligent mechanisms? Such a thing I felt was impossible. Or did a Martian sit within each, ruling, directing, using, much as a man's brain sits and rules in his body?[59] I began to compare the things to human machines, to ask myself for the first time in my life how an ironclad or a steam-engine would seem to an intelligent lower animal.

The storm had left the sky clear, and over the smoke of the burning land the little fading pin-point of Mars was dropping into the west,

---

58. Revelation 20:9, "and fire came down from God out of heaven, and devoured them." The narrator leads on to this hellish vision by referencing above "the Potteries seen at night," evoking a vivid image of furnace glare and smoke in the pottery-making region of Staffordshire.

59. Some critics, overly eager to credit Wells with fathering the most far-out prophecies of modern science fiction, see in this passage evidence of a mind-machine symbiosis called the cyborg (short for cybernetic organism). But this is stretching it, given the exposition of Martian technology in II:2.

when the soldier came into my garden. I heard a slight scraping at the fence, and rousing myself from the lethargy that had fallen upon me, I looked down and saw him dimly, clambering over the palings. At the sight of another human being my torpor passed, and I leant out of the window eagerly.

"Hist!" said I in a whisper.

He stopped astride of the fence in doubt. Then he came over and across the lawn to the corner of the house. He bent down and stepped softly.

"Who's there?" he said, also whispering, standing under the window and peering up.

"Where are you going?" I asked.

"God knows."

"Are you trying to hide?"

"That's it."

"Come into the house," I said.

I went down, unfastened the door and let him in, and locked the door again. I could not see his face. He was hatless, and his coat was unbuttoned.

"My God!" he said as I drew him in.

"What has happened?" I asked.

"What hasn't?" In the obscurity I could see he made a gesture of despair. "They wiped us out—simply wiped us out," he repeated again and again.

He followed me, almost mechanically, into the dining-room.

"Take some whisky," I said, pouring out a stiff dose.

He drank it. Then abruptly he sat down before the table, put his head on his arms, and began to sob and weep like a little boy, in a perfect passion of emotion, while I, with a curious forgetfulness of my own recent despair, stood beside him wondering.

It was a long time before he could steady his nerves to answer my questions, and then he answered perplexingly and brokenly. He was a driver in the artillery, and had only come into action about seven. At that time firing was going on across the common, and it was said the first party of Martians were crawling slowly towards their second cylinder under cover of a metal shield.

Later this shield staggered up on tripod legs, and became the first of the fighting machines I had seen. The gun he drove had been unlimbered near Horsell, in order to command the sand-pits, and its arrival had precipitated the action. As the limber gunners went to the rear, his horse trod in a rabbit-hole and came down, throwing him into a depression of the ground. At the same moment the gun exploded behind him, the ammunition blew up, there was fire all about him, and he found himself lying under a heap of charred dead men and dead horses.

"I lay still," he said, "scared out of my wits, with the fore-quarter of a horse atop of me. We'd been wiped out. And the smell—good God! Like burnt meat! I was hurt across the back by the fall of the horse, and there I had to lie until I felt better. Just like parade it had been a minute before—then stumble, bang, swish!

"Wiped out!" he said.

He had hid under the dead horse for a long time, peeping out furtively across the common. The Cardigan men[60] had tried a rush, in skirmishing order, at the pit, simply to be swept out of existence. Then the monster had risen to its feet, and had begun to walk leisurely to and fro across the common, among the few fugitives, with its head-like hood turning about exactly like the head of a cowled human being. A kind of arm carried a complicated metallic case, about which green flashes scintillated, and out of the funnel of this there smote the Heat-Ray.

In a few minutes there was, so far as the soldier could see, not a living thing left upon the common, and every bush and tree upon it that was not already a blackened skeleton was burning. The hussars had been on the road beyond the curvature of the ground, and he saw nothing of them. He heard the Maxims rattle for a time, and then become still. The giant saved Woking Station and its cluster of houses until last; then in a moment the Heat-Ray was brought to bear, and the town became a heap of fiery ruins. Then the thing shut off the Heat-Ray, and, turning its back upon the artilleryman, began to waddle away towards the smouldering pine-woods that sheltered the second cylinder. As it did so, a second glittering Titan built himself up out of the pit.

The second monster followed the first, and at that the artilleryman began to crawl very cautiously across the hot heather ash towards Horsell. He managed to get alive into the ditch along by the side of the road, and so escaped to Woking. There his story became ejaculatory. The place was impassable. It seems there were a few people alive there, frantic for the most part, and many burnt and scalded. He was turned aside by the fire, and hid among some almost scorching heaps

---

60. The 400 men of the Cardigan regiment at note 43 equipped with two Maxim guns.

of broken wall as one of the Martian giants returned. He saw this one pursue a man, catch him up in one of its steely tentacles, and knock his head against the trunk of a pine-tree. At last, after nightfall, the artilleryman made a rush for it and got over the railway embankment.

Since then he had been skulking along towards Maybury, in the hope of getting out of danger Londonward. People were hiding in trenches and cellars, and many of the survivors had made off towards Woking Village and Send. He had been consumed with thirst until he found one of the water mains near the railway arch smashed, and the water bubbling out like a spring upon the road.

That was the story I got from him bit by bit. He grew calmer telling me and trying to make me see the things he had seen. He had eaten no food since mid-day, he told me early in his narrative, and I found some mutton and bread in the pantry and brought it into the room. We lit no lamp, for fear of attracting the Martians, and ever and again our hands would touch upon bread or meat. As he talked, things about us came darkly out of the darkness, and the trampled bushes and broken rose-trees outside the window grew distinct. It would seem that a number of men or animals had rushed across the lawn. I began to see his face, blackened and haggard, as no doubt mine was also.

When we had finished eating we went softly upstairs to my study, and I looked again out of the open window. In one night the valley had become a valley of ashes. The fires had dwindled now. Where flames had been there were now streamers of smoke; but the countless ruins of shattered and gutted houses and blasted and blackened trees that the night had hidden stood out now gaunt and terrible in the pitiless light of dawn. Yet here and there some object had had the luck to escape—a white railway signal here, the end of a greenhouse there, white and fresh amidst the wreckage. Never before in the history of warfare had destruction been so indiscriminate and so universal.[61] And, shining with the growing light of the east, three of the

---

61. This grim prospect of World War I and its universal havoc is meant to be just that. In his first work of social prophecy, *Anticipations* (1901), Wells predicts global warfare as the inevitable consequence of industrialized military technology, to be followed by technocratic reconstruction. The same scenario is novelized in *The War in the Air*, in which "every organised government in the world was as shattered and broken as a heap of china beaten with a stick" (1908b:355). Out of this "furnace of war," says the narrator, came "our present world state, orderly, scientific, and secured" (345). In the same year, Wells wrote his big socialist manifesto, ominously titled *New Worlds for Old* (1908).

metallic giants stood about the pit, their cowls rotating as though they were surveying the desolation they had made.

It seemed to me that the pit had been enlarged, and ever and again puffs of vivid green vapour streamed up out of it towards the brightening dawn—streamed up, whirled, broke, and vanished.

Beyond were the pillars of fire about Chobham. They became pillars of bloodshot smoke at the first touch of day.

Wells, however, is not unique in predicating a great battle to come. Others had done so ever since the Franco-Prussian War of 1870 (see Clarke 1995 for reprints of such tales, with his excursus on them in Clarke 1992). But Wells did it most memorably of them all.

XII

WHAT I SAW OF THE DESTRUCTION OF
WEYBRIDGE AND SHEPPERTON.

As the dawn grew brighter we withdrew ourselves from the window from which we had watched the Martians, and went very quietly downstairs.

The artilleryman agreed with me that the house was no place to stay in. He proposed, he said, to make his way Londonward, and thence rejoin his battery—No. 12, of the Horse Artillery. My plan was to return at once to Leatherhead, and so greatly had the strength of the Martians impressed me that I had determined to take my wife to Newhaven, and go with her out of the country forthwith. For I already perceived clearly that the country about London must inevitably be the scene of a disastrous struggle before such creatures as these could be destroyed.[62]

---

62. Exodus 13:21–22, "And the Lord went before them by day in a pillar of cloud to lead them along the way, and by night in a pillar of fire to give them light, that they might travel by day and night; the pillar of cloud by day and the pillar of fire by night did not depart from before the people." As the Lord guided the Israelites through the Sinai desert, so the Martians lead humanity through a wasteland of suffering. Ahead, leaving the old order behind, is the promise of world unity. As in the heavenly world-state on Mars, so shall it be on earth. But the road to utopia is not peaceful: "The millennium arrived in anything but millennial fashion" (1933:344).

Admixed with the "pillars of bloodshot smoke" are "puffs of vivid green vapour," the mysterious signature of advanced Martian technology (note 55), itself the means and model of human advancement.

Later in the story the narrator's unmarried brother flees London by taking ship from a port on the North Sea. The narrator himself, however, is less careful of his wife now ensconced in Leatherhead just south of London. In Chesney's *The Battle of Dorking* (1871), his imagined extension of the Franco-Prus-

Between us and Leatherhead, however, lay the third cylinder, with its guarding giants. Had I been alone, I think I should have taken my chance and struck across country. But the artilleryman dissuaded me: "It's no kindness to the right sort of wife," he said, "to make her a widow;" and in the end I agreed to go with him, under cover of the woods, northward as far as Street Cobham before I parted with him. Thence I would make a big détour by Epsom to reach Leatherhead.

I should have started at once, but my companion had been in active service, and he knew better than that. He made me ransack the house for a flask, which he filled with whiskey; and we lined every available pocket with packets of biscuits and slices of meat. Then we crept out of the house, and ran as quickly as we could down the ill-made road by which I had come overnight. The houses seemed deserted. In the road lay a group of three charred bodies close together, struck dead by the Heat-Ray; and here and there were things that the people had dropped—a clock, a slipper, a silver spoon, and the like poor valuables. At the corner turning up towards the post-office a little cart, filled with boxes and furniture, and horseless, heeled over on a broken wheel. A cash-box had been hastily smashed open, and thrown under the débris.

Except the lodge at the Orphanage, which was still on fire, none of the houses had suffered very greatly here. The Heat-Ray had shaved the chimney-tops and passed. Yet, save ourselves, there did not seem to be a living soul on Maybury Hill. The majority of the inhabitants

---

sian War of 1870 to Britain brings the Prussian army northward close to Leatherhead after its beaching on the Channel coast (see reprint in Clarke 1995:41), a topographic fact Wells surely had in mind, since the narrator foresees that London soon will be the scene of Martian action, which then must move southward directly through Leatherhead. Yet, in his war fever, he is unconcerned. He says that he had planned to take his wife to Newhaven, a Channel port, "and go with her out of the country forthwith." But he does not. Rather, falling in with the artilleryman, he decides to investigate all that is happening. In the event (II:7), he falls out with the artilleryman, when he proposes to fight back and then usurp the Martian mission. Although the narrator agrees with Wells the writer of philosophical tracts, one of which speculates on a future humanity not unlike the Martian condition (II:2), he has not the guts to follow through with the artilleryman's plan to realize its incipiency. The narrator is a complex character, at once Wells and anti–Wells. The latter aspect is especially marked at the end when he returns, complacently, to the world of everydayism: embracing wife and family after having abandoned all such domestic virtues: the very essence of *crambe repetita* (note 40).

had escaped, I suppose, by way of the Old Woking road—the road I had taken when I drove to Leatherhead—or they had hidden.

We went down the lane, by the body of the man in black, sodden now from the overnight hail, and broke into the woods at the foot of the hill. We pushed through these towards the railway, without meeting a soul. The woods across the line were but the scarred and blackened ruins of woods; for the most part the trees had fallen, but a certain proportion still stood, dismal gray stems, with dark-brown foliage instead of green.

On our side the fire had done no more than scorch the nearer trees; it had failed to secure its footing. In one place the woodmen had been at work on Saturday; trees, felled and freshly trimmed, lay in a clearing, with heaps of sawdust, by the sawing machine and its engine. Hard by was a temporary hut, deserted. There was not a breath of wind this morning, and everything was strangely still. Even the birds were hushed, and as we hurried along, I and the artilleryman talked in whispers, and looked now and again over our shoulders. Once or twice we stopped to listen.

After a time we drew near the road, and as we did so we heard the clatter of hoofs, and saw through the tree-stems three cavalry soldiers riding slowly towards Woking. We hailed them, and they halted while we hurried towards them. It was a lieutenant and a couple of privates of the 8th Hussars, with a stand like a theodolite, which the artilleryman told me was a heliograph.

"You are the first men I've seen coming this way this morning," said the lieutenant. "What's brewing?"

His voice and face were eager. The men behind him stared curiously. The artilleryman jumped down the bank into the road and saluted.

"Gun destroyed last night, sir. Have been hiding. Trying to rejoin battery, sir. You'll come in sight of the Martians, I expect, about half a mile along this road."

"What the dickens are they like?" asked the lieutenant.

"Giants in armour, sir. Hundred feet high. Three legs and a body like 'luminium,[63] with a mighty great head in a hood, sir."

---

63. Aluminium (aluminum in American diction). This metal, in II:3, is given out as the supreme product of futuristic Martian industry.

The Weybridge of the chapter title is a town about four miles northeast of Woking. At first, the distances are pedestrian; then the action quickly expands to include the greater metropolitan London area, and would have embraced the entire world had not the Martians died a natural death from the dirty germs of

"Get out!" said the lieutenant. "What confounded nonsense!"

"You'll see, sir. They carry a kind of box, sir, that shoots fire and strikes you dead!"

"What d'ye mean—a gun?"

"No, sir," and the artilleryman began a vivid account of the Heat-Ray. Halfway through the lieutenant interrupted him and looked up at me. I was still standing on the bank by the side of the road.

"Did you see it?" said the lieutenant.

"It's perfectly true," I said.

"Well," said the lieutenant, "I suppose it's my business to see it too. Look here"—to the artilleryman—"we're detailed here clearing people out of their houses. You'd better go along and report yourself to Brigadier-General Marvin, and tell him all you know. He's at Weybridge. Know the way?"

"I do," I said; and he turned his horse southward again.

"Half a mile, you say?" said he.

"At most," I answered, and pointed over the tree-tops southward. He thanked me and rode on, and we saw them no more.

Further along we came upon a group of three women and two children in the road, busy clearing out a labourer's cottage. They had got hold of a little hand-truck, and were piling it up with unclean-looking bundles and shabby furniture. They were all too assiduously engaged to talk to us as we passed.

By Byfleet Station we emerged from the pine-trees, and found the country calm and peaceful under the morning sunlight. We were far beyond the range of the Heat-Ray there, and had it not been for the silent desertion of some of the houses, the stirring movement of packing in others, and the knot of soldiers standing on the bridge over the railway and staring down the line towards Woking, the day would have seemed very like any other Sunday.

Several farm waggons and carts were moving creakily along the road to Addlestone, and suddenly through the gate of a field we saw, across a stretch of flat meadow, six twelve-pounders, standing neatly at equal distances and pointing towards Woking. The gunners stood

---

earth, against which they had no immunity. Coming from a sanitary civilization on Mars, they did not expect that microorganisms, as lowly as the humans they meant to vanquish, from their point of view (note 3), could undo them. Yet filthy London, the world's greatest city for all that, prevailed. In the aftermath, in *Sleeper*, it becomes the cleaned-up metropolitan center of a world-state on the Martian model.

by the guns waiting, and the ammunition waggons were at a business-like distance. The men stood almost as if under inspection.

"That's good!" said I. "They will get one fair shot, at any rate."

The artilleryman hesitated at the gate.

"I shall go on," he said.

Further on towards Weybridge, just over the bridge, there were a number of men in white fatigue jackets throwing up a long rampart, and more guns behind.

"It's bows and arrows against the lightning,[64] anyhow," said the artilleryman. "They 'aven't seen that fire-beam yet."

The officers who were not actively engaged stood and stared over the tree-tops southwestward, and the men digging would stop every now and then to stare in the same direction.

Byfleet was in a tumult, people packing, and a score of hussars, some of them dismounted, some on horseback, were hunting them about. Three or four black Government waggons, with crosses in white circles, and an old omnibus, among other vehicles, were being loaded in the village street. There were scores of people, most of them sufficiently Sabbatical to have assumed their best clothes. The soldiers were having the greatest difficulty in making them realize the gravity of their position. We saw one shrivelled old fellow with a huge box and a score or more of flower-pots containing orchids, angrily expostulating with the corporal who would leave them behind. I stopped and gripped his arm.

"Do you know what's over there?" I said, pointing at the pine-tops that hid the Martians.

"Eh?" said he, turning. "I was explainin' these is vallyble."

"Death!" I shouted. "Death is coming! Death!"[65] and, leaving him to digest that if he could, I hurried on after the artilleryman. At the corner I looked back. The soldier had left him, and he was still standing by his box with the pots of orchids on the lid of it, and staring vaguely over the trees.

No one in Weybridge could tell us where the headquarters were established; the whole place was in such confusion as I had never seen

---

64. Here the artilleryman sums up the odds: "bows and arrows against the lightning." It is the inequality of combat, magnified, between French and German forces in the Franco-Prussian War (see the Introduction to the present work, section 4).

65. Revelation 6:8, "And I saw, and behold, a pale horse, and its rider's name was Death."

in any town before. Carts, carriages everywhere, the most astonishing miscellany of conveyances and horseflesh. The respectable inhabitants of the place, men in golf and boating costumes, wives prettily dressed, were packing, riverside loafers energetically helping, children excited, and, for the most part, highly delighted at this astonishing variation of their Sunday experiences. In the midst of it all the worthy vicar was very pluckily holding an early celebration, and his bell was jangling out above the excitement.

I and the artilleryman, seated on the step of the drinking-fountain, made a very passable meal upon what we had brought with us. Patrols of soldiers—here no longer hussars, but grenadiers in white—were warning people to move now or to take refuge in their cellars as soon as the firing began. We saw as we crossed the railway bridge that a growing crowd of people had assembled in and about the railway-station, and the swarming platform was piled with boxes and packages. The ordinary traffic had been stopped, I believe, in order to allow of the passage of troops and guns to Chertsey, and I have heard since that a savage struggle occurred for places in the special trains that were put on at a later hour.

We remained at Weybridge until mid-day, and at that hour we found ourselves at the place near Shepperton Lock where the Wey and Thames join. Part of the time we spent helping two old women to pack a little cart. The Wey has a treble mouth, and at this point boats are to be hired, and there was a ferry across the river. On the Shepperton side was an inn, with a lawn, and beyond that the tower of Shepperton Church—it has been replaced by a spire[66]—rose above the trees.

---

66. The square-topped tower of Shepperton Church is replaced "by a spire," *i.e.*, by the Martian tripod that destroyed it. This imposing cathedral, the Church of St. Nicolas, is a notable landmark of venerable tradition whose west tower was built in 1710 (Hughes 1962: 291, *n*56). The new spire is the steeple of a new religion, but it is not a Christian one. It is rather the "religion of the future" (1917:76), science, which the Martians confess. But they also are as martial as the heathen god naming them. In Wells's equation, their "Religion of Progress" (1927:32) = "War with Tradition" (1931:65). Such was the twentieth century's errorist faith in Collectivism, the belief that the state can improve on the spontaneous tendencies of civil society and democratic capitalism, which for Wells always threatened a "loosening of bonds and general disintegration" (1927:15). Its extreme manifestations were in Communism and Fascism, beginning with the exemplary Russian Revolution of 1917. Led by Lenin, Wells had by the next to last year of the First World War learned the totalitarian formula: "If the state can organize society for war, why not for peace?" (Skidelsky 1995:

Here we[67] found an excited and noisy crowd of fugitives. As yet the flight had not grown to a panic, but there were already far more people than all the boats going to and fro could enable to cross. People came panting along under heavy burdens; one husband and wife were even carrying a small outhouse door between them, with some of their household goods piled thereon. One man told us he meant to try to get away from Shepperton Station.

There was a lot of shouting, and one man was even jesting. The idea people seemed to have here was that the Martians were simply formidable human beings, who might attack and sack the town, to be certainly destroyed in the end. Every now and then people would glance nervously across the Wey, at the meadows towards Chertsey, but everything over there was still.

Across the Thames, except just where the boats landed, everything was quiet, in vivid contrast with the Surrey side. The people who landed there from the boats went tramping off down the lane. The big ferry-boat had just made a journey. Three or four soldiers stood on the lawn of the inn, staring and jesting at the fugitives, without offering to help. The inn was closed, as it was now within prohibited hours.

"What's that!" cried a boatman, and "Shut up, you fool!" said a man

---

47). Anticipating that great War of the Nations and the total mobilization it everywhere would entail, he wrote,

> I think that the phase of universal military service we seem to be approaching is one through which the mass of mankind may have to pass, learning something that can be learnt in no other way, that the uniforms and flags, the conceptions of order and discipline, the tradition of service and devotion, of physical fitness, unstinted exertion and universal responsibility, will remain a permanent acquisition, though the last ammunition has been used ages since in the pyrotechnic display that welcomed the coming of the ultimate Peace [1908c:226f].

Today war, tomorrow revolution. But first, war's "vast tragic clearance for a new order" (1940:25). Such is the scenario of *Things to Come* (1936), in which John Cabal the octopus-headed leader of the Airmen establishes his Dictatorship following that general clearance effected by World War II. But it was first mooted in *Anticipations*, whose New Republicans rebuild a war-devastated world using civilian conscription, and its "forcible conformities" (1901:281), to ensure ultimate Peace. In *Worlds* the Martians destroy, in the sequel *Sleeper* human technocrats reconstruct.

67. This is last time "we" includes the artilleryman. Thereafter he silently vanishes in the ensuing confusion, to reappear with climactic effect as "The Man on Putney Hill" in II:7.

near me to a yelping dog. Then the sound came again, this time from the direction of Chertsey, a muffled thud—the sound of a gun.

The fighting was beginning. Almost immediately unseen batteries across the river to our right, unseen because of the trees, took up the chorus, firing heavily one after the other. A woman screamed. Everyone stood arrested by the sudden stir of battle, near us and yet invisible to us. Nothing was to be seen save flat meadows, cows feeding unconcernedly for the most part, and silvery pollard willows motionless in the warm sunlight.

"The sojers 'll stop 'em," said a woman beside me doubtfully. A haziness rose over the tree-tops.

Then suddenly we saw a rush of smoke far away up the river, a puff of smoke that jerked up into the air, and hung, and forthwith the ground heaved under foot and a heavy explosion shook the air, smashing two or three windows in the houses near, and leaving us astonished.

"Here they are!" shouted a man in a blue jersey. "Yonder! D'yer see them? Yonder!"

Quickly, one after the other, one, two, three, four of the armoured Martians appeared, far away over the little trees, across the flat meadows that stretch towards Chertsey, and striding hurriedly towards the river. Little cowled figures they seemed at first, going with a rolling motion and as fast as flying birds.[68]

Then, advancing obliquely towards us, came a fifth. Their armoured bodies glittered in the sun, as they swept swiftly forward upon the guns, growing rapidly larger as they drew nearer. One on the extreme left, the remotest, that is, flourished a huge case high in the air, and the ghostly terrible Heat-Ray I had already seen on Friday night smote towards Chertsey, and struck the town.

At sight of these strange, swift, and terrible creatures, the crowd along by the water's edge seemed to me to be for a moment horror-struck. There was no screaming or shouting, but a silence. Then a hoarse murmur and a movement of feet—a splashing from the water. A man, too frightened to drop the portmanteau he carried on his shoulder, swung round and sent me staggering with a blow from the cor-

---

68. That the Martian fighting machines march "as fast as flying birds" evokes the almost magical speed with which the astonished French regarded the swift mobility of Prussian guns (Howard 1961:24). See the Introduction to the present work, section 4, on the Martians as a military force of Bismarckian superiority.

ner of his burden. A woman thrust at me with her hand and rushed past me. I turned, too, with the rush of the people, but I was not too terrified for thought. The terrible Heat-Ray was in my mind. To get under water! That was it!

"Get under water!" I shouted unheeded.

I faced about again, and rushed towards the approaching Martian—rushed right down the gravelly beach and headlong into the water. Others did the same. A boatload of people putting back came leaping out as I rushed past. The stones under my feet were muddy and slippery, and the river was so low that I ran perhaps twenty feet scarcely waist-deep. Then, as the Martian towered overhead scarcely a couple of hundred yards away, I flung myself forward under the surface. The splashes of the people in the boats leaping into the river sounded like thunderclaps in my ears. People were landing hastily on both sides of the river.

But the Martian machine took no more notice for the moment of the people running this way and that than a man would of the confusion of ants in a nest against which his foot has kicked. When, half suffocated, I raised my head above the water the Martian's hood pointed at the batteries that were still firing across the river, and as it advanced it swung loose what must have been the generator of the Heat-Ray.

In another moment it was on the bank, and in a stride wading halfway across. The knees of its foremost legs bent at the further bank, and in another moment it had raised itself to its full height again, close to the village of Shepperton. Forthwith the six guns, which, unknown to anyone on the right bank, had been hidden behind the outskirts of that village, fired simultaneously. The sudden near concussions, the last close upon the first, made my heart jump. The monster was already raising the case generating the Heat-Ray, as the first shell burst six yards above the hood.

I gave a cry of astonishment. I saw and thought nothing of the other four Martian monsters: my attention was riveted upon the nearer incident. Simultaneously two other shells burst in the air near the body as the hood twisted round in time to receive, but not in time to dodge, the fourth shell.

The shell burst clean in the face of the thing. The hood bulged, flashed, was whirled off in a dozen tattered fragments of red flesh and glittering metal.[69]

---

69. The first and next to last time any Martian fighting machine is damaged by human shellfire: a pathetic victory.

"Hit!" shouted I, with something between a scream and a cheer.

I heard answering shouts from the people in the water about me. I could have leapt out of the water with that momentary exultation.

The decapitated colossus reeled like a drunken giant; but it did not fall over. It recovered its balance by a miracle, and, no longer heeding its steps, and with the camera that fired the Heat-Ray now rigidly upheld, it reeled swiftly upon Shepperton. The living intelligence, the Martian within the hood, was slain and splashed to the four winds of heaven,[70] and the thing was now but a mere intricate device of metal whirling to destruction. It drove along in a straight line, incapable of guidance. It struck the tower of Shepperton Church, smashing it down as the impact of a battering ram might have done, swerved aside, blundered on, and collapsed with a tremendous impact into the river out of my sight.

A violent explosion shook the air, and a spout of water, steam, mud, and shattered metal, shot far up into the sky. As the camera of the Heat-Ray hit the water, the latter had incontinently flashed into steam. In another moment a huge wave, like a muddy tidal bore, but almost scaldingly hot, came sweeping round the bend up-stream. I saw people struggling shorewards, and heard their screaming and shouting faintly above the seething and roar of the Martian's collapse.

For the moment I heeded nothing of the heat, forgot the patent need of self-preservation. I splashed through the tumultuous water, pushing aside a man in black to do so, until I could see round the bend. Half a dozen deserted boats pitched aimlessly upon the confusion of the waves. The fallen Martian came into sight down-stream, lying across the river, and for the most part submerged.

Thick clouds of steam were pouring off the wreckage, and through the tumultuously whirling wisps I could see, intermittently and vaguely, the gigantic limbs churning the water and flinging a splash and spray of mud and froth into the air. The tentacles swayed and struck like living arms, and, save for the helpless purposelessness of these movements, it was as if some wounded thing struggled for life amidst the waves. Enormous quantities of a ruddy brown fluid were spurting up in noisy jets out of the machine.

My attention was diverted from this sight by a furious yelling, like that of the thing called a siren in our manufacturing towns. A man, knee-deep near the towing-path, shouted inaudibly to me and pointed.

---

70. Daniel 7:2, "Daniel said, 'I saw in my vision by night, and behold, the four winds were stirring up the great sea.'"

Looking back, I saw the other Martians advancing with gigantic strides down the river-bank from the direction of Chertsey. The Shepperton guns spoke this time unavailingly.

At that I ducked at once under water, and, holding my breath until movement was an agony, blundered painfully along under the surface as long as I could. The water was in a tumult about me, and rapidly growing hotter.

When for a moment I raised my head to take breath, and throw the hair and water from my eyes, the steam was rising in a whirling white fog that at first hid the Martians together. The noise was deafening. Then I saw them dimly, colossal figures of gray, magnified by the mist. They had passed by me, and two were stooping over the frothing tumultuous ruins of their comrade.

The third and fourth stood beside him in the water, one perhaps 200 yards from me, the other towards Laleham. The generators of the Heat-Rays waved high, and the hissing beams smote down this way and that.

The air was full of sound, a deafening and confusing conflict of noises, the clangorous din of the Martians, the crash of falling houses, the thud of trees, fences, sheds, flashing into flame, and the crackling and roaring of fire. Dense black smoke was leaping up to mingle with the steam from the river, and as the Heat-Ray went to and fro over Weybridge, its impact was marked by flashes of incandescent white, that gave place at once to a smoky dance of lurid flames. The nearer houses still stood intact, awaiting their fate, shadowy, faint and pallid in the steam, with the fire behind them going to and fro.

For a moment, perhaps, I stood there, breast-high in the almost boiling water, dumfounded at my position, hopeless of escape. Through the reek I could see the people who had been with me in the river scrambling out of the water through the reeds, like little frogs hurrying through grass from the advance of a man, or running to and fro in utter dismay on the towing-path.

Then suddenly the white flashes of the Heat-Ray came leaping towards me. The houses caved in as they dissolved at its touch, and darted out flames; the trees changed to fire with a roar. It flickered up and down the towing-path, licking off the people who ran this way and that, and came down to the water's edge not fifty yards from where I stood. It swept across the river to Shepperton, and the water in its track rose in a boiling wheal crested with steam. I turned shoreward.

In another moment the huge wave, well-nigh at the boiling-point, had rushed upon me. I screamed aloud, and scalded, half blinded, agonized, I staggered through the leaping, hissing water towards the shore. Had my foot stumbled, it would have been the end. I fell help-lessly, in full sight of the Martians, upon the broad, bare gravelly spit that runs down to mark the angle of the Wey and Thames. I expected nothing but death.

I have a dim memory of the foot of a Martian coming down within a score of yards of my head, driving straight into the loose gravel, whirling it this way and that, and lifting again; of a long suspense, and then of the four carrying the débris of their comrade between them, now clear, and then presently faint, through a veil of smoke, receding interminably, as it seemed to me, across a vast space of river and meadow. And then, very slowly, I realized that by a miracle I had escaped.

XIII

HOW I FELL IN WITH THE CURATE.

AFTER giving this sudden lesson in the power of terrestrial weapons, the Martians retreated to their original position upon Horsell Common, and in their haste, and encumbered with the débris of their smashed companion, they no doubt overlooked many such a stray and unnecessary victim as myself. Had they left their comrade, and pushed on forthwith, there was nothing at that time between them and London but batteries of twelve-pounder guns, and they would certainly have reached the capital in advance of the tidings of their approach; as sudden, dreadful and destructive their advent would have been as the earthquake that destroyed Lisbon a century ago.[71]

---

71. The great Lisbon earthquake occurred in 1775, "a century ago." If the Martian invasion happened in 1900, the narrator is off by 25 years. Wells cannot be that ignorant; from student days he kept notebooks on historical chronology (and other matters of polymathic interest fed by rapacious reading) that led on to *The Outline of History* (1920). So the narrator is unreliable on this point, which hints at a characterological flaw. For all his pretentious philosophical writings on themes taken up by Wells himself, he lacks understanding and after the horrors of the Lisbon-like trauma induced by the Martians he simply returns, unaffected, to a life of everydayist bourgeois respectability. For others, the devastating earthquake in Portugal remained a challenge to soteriology in Christian doctrine. In *Candide*, Voltaire dramatizes the clash between ideas and reality; the ideas are those of the philosopher Leibniz, whose smug theology explained away evil, and reality is represented by the Lisbon earthquake and other sufferings endured by the titular hero and his cheerful tutor, Dr. Pangloss — the very epithet of a conceited pedant.

Allusion to the dreadful Portuguese case leads into a contrast of character between the curate (embodiment of institutionalized religion) and the Panglossian narrator. For thinkers of the Enlightenment, the Lisbon earthquake

But they were in no hurry. Cylinder followed cylinder in its interplanetary flight; every twenty-four hours brought them reinforcement.[72] And meanwhile the military and naval authorities, now fully alive to the tremendous power of their antagonists, worked with furious energy. Every minute a fresh gun came into position, until, before twilight, every copse, every row of suburban villas on the hilly slopes about Kingston and Richmond, masked an expectant black muzzle. And through the charred and desolated area—perhaps twenty square miles altogether—that encircled the Martian encampment on Horsell Common, through charred and ruined villages among the green trees, through the blackened and smoking arcades that had been but a day ago pine spinneys, crawled the devoted scouts with the heliographs that were presently to warn the gunners of the Martian approach. But the Martians now understood our command of artillery and the danger of human proximity, and not a man ventured within a mile of either cylinder, save at the price of his life.

It would seem these giants spent the earlier part of the afternoon in going to and fro, transferring everything from the second and third

---

smashed the optimistic theology codified by Leibniz, just as Wells smashes the curate's theology-as-insurance-policy: if only we pray to God for deliverance of our sins, we shall be delivered from the Martians. To that, the narrator (who realizes they butcher humans like so many lowly cattle, not as divine creatures turned disobedient) retorts, "Do you think God had exempted Weybridge? He is not an insurance agent" (see note 44). Yet the narrator himself is not untinged with a view of the Martians as avenging angels when he speaks of their Heat-Ray as "flaming death" cut by a biblical "sword of heat" (just after note 35). But in the end nothing for him is avenged, everyday life is restored, and it is for more perceptive minds to profit from the catastrophe and, in *Sleeper* the sequel, to build a world-state. As with Lisbon, the Martian shake-up heralds a new and greater "great disillusionment" (note 4) that leads on to a dismissal of God-centered theology and a secular reordering of global affairs. All the same, the invasion proves to be Providential, shocking non–Panglossian types into the reality missed by the narrator.

72. With supernal speed, they arrive only days after the missiles are fired from Mars, a magic that belies the photojournalistic realism elsewise pervasive. In a way this contrasts Leibnizian idealism with Panglossian everydayism (note 71). The Martian cylinders are agents of swift God-like vengeance, but at the same time bring a realistic sense of Providence that reorients humanity away from the false notion of theological salvation. Man makes himself, and if the Martians help to stimulate that insight, all to the good.

cylinders—the second in Addlestone Golf Links, and the third at Pyr-ford—to their original pit on Horsell Common. Over that, above the blackened heather and ruined buildings that stretched far and wide, stood one as sentinel, while the rest abandoned their vast fighting-machines and descended into the pit. They were hard at work there far into the night, and the towering pillar of dense green smoke[73] that rose therefrom could be seen from the hills about Merrow, and even, it is said, from Banstead and Epsom Downs.

And while the Martians behind me were thus preparing for their next sally, and in front of me Humanity gathered for the battle, I made my way, with infinite pains and labour, from the fire and smoke of burning Weybridge towards London.

I saw an abandoned boat, very small and remote, drifting down-stream, and, throwing off the most of my sodden clothes, I went after it, gained it, and so escaped out of that destruction. There were no oars in the boat, but I contrived to paddle, as much as my parboiled hands would allow, down the river towards Halliford and Walton, going very tediously, and continually looking behind me, as you may well understand. I followed the river because I considered the water gave me my best chance of escape, should these giants return.

The hot water from the Martian's overthrow drifted down-stream with me, so that for the best part of a mile I could see little of either bank. Once, however, I made out a string of black figures hurrying across the meadows from the direction of Weybridge. Halliford, it seemed, was quite deserted, and several of the houses facing the river were on fire. It was strange to see the place quite tranquil, quite des-olate under the hot blue sky, with the smoke and little threads of flame going straight up into the heat of the afternoon. Never before had I seen houses burning without the accompaniment of an inconvenient crowd. A little further on the dry reeds up the bank were smoking and glowing, and a line of fire inland was marching steadily across a late field of hay.

For a long time I drifted, so painful and weary was I after the vio-lence I had been through,[74] and so intense the heat upon the water. Then my fears got the better of me again, and I resumed my paddling.

---

73. The Martians' sinister hallmark of alienage (see note 55).

74. After a sample of Martian violence, the narrator's war fever is cooled and he wants out. Now, washing ashore by chance on the north bank of the Thames, he begins his overland adventure toward London, drawn there by who knows what. And there he is witness to the natural death of the last Martian.

The sun scorched my bare back. At last, as the bridge at Walton was coming into sight round the bend, my fever and faintness overcame my fears, and I landed on the Middlesex bank, and lay down, deadly sick, amidst the long grass. I suppose the time was then about four or five o'clock. I got up presently, walked perhaps half a mile without meeting a soul, and then lay down again in the shadow of a hedge. I seem to remember talking wanderingly to myself during that last spurt. I was also very thirsty, and bitterly regretful I had drunk no more water. It is a curious thing that I felt angry with my wife; I cannot account for it, but my impotent desire to reach Leatherhead worried me excessively.

I do not clearly remember the arrival of the curate, so that I probably dozed. I became aware of him as a seated figure in soot-smudged shirtsleeves, and with his upturned clean-shaven face staring at a faint flickering that danced over the sky. The sky was what is called a mackerel sky, rows and rows of faint down-plumes of cloud, just tinted with the midsummer sunset.

I sat up, and at the rustle of my motion he looked at me quickly.

"Have you any water?" I asked abruptly.

He shook his head.

"You have been asking for water for the last hour," he said.

For a moment we were silent, taking stock of one another. I dare say he found me a strange enough figure, naked save for my water-soaked trousers and socks, scalded, and my face and shoulders blackened from the smoke. His face was a fair weakness, his chin retreated, and his hair lay in crisp, almost flaxen curls on his low forehead; his eyes were rather large, pale blue, and blankly staring. He spoke abruptly, looking vacantly away from me.

"What does it mean?" he said. "What do these things mean?"

I stared at him and made no answer.

He extended a thin white hand and spoke in almost a complaining tone.

"Why are these things permitted? What sins have we done? The morning service was over, I was walking through the roads to clear my brain for the afternoon, and then—fire, earthquake, death! As if it were Sodom and Gomorrah![75] All our work undone, all the work ... What are these Martians?"

---

75. The twin cities of sin and corruption in Genesis 18–19, destroyed by a wrathful God. Now the curate's church in Weybridge, and the whole town and his ministry there has been undone by "fire, earthquake, death! As if it were

"What are we?" I answered, clearing my throat.

He gripped his knees and turned to look at me again. For half a minute, perhaps, he stared silently.

"I was walking through the roads to clear my brains," he said. "And suddenly fire, earthquake, death!"

He relapsed into silence, with his chin now sunken almost to his knees.

Presently he began waving his hand:

"All the work—all the Sunday-schools. What have we done—what has Weybridge done? Everything gone—everything destroyed. The church! We rebuilt it only three years ago. Gone!—swept out of existence! Why?"

Another pause, and he broke out again like one demented.

"The smoke of her burning goeth up for ever and ever!" he shouted.[76]

His eyes flamed, and he pointed a lean finger in the direction of Weybridge.

By this time I was beginning to take his measure. The tremendous tragedy in which he had been involved—it was evident he was a fugitive from Weybridge—had driven him to the very verge of his reason.

"Are we far from Sunbury?" I said in a matter-of-fact tone.

"What are we to do?" he asked. "Are these creatures everywhere? Has the earth been given over to them?"

"Are we far from Sunbury?"

"Only this morning I officiated at early celebration...."

Sodom and Gomorrah!" What happened to Lisbon (note 71), a great cathedral city, has taken down his own parish with no justification whatsoever. The self-centered curate is personally offended — "What are these Martians?" to have done that to *him* and *his* good work. The narrator replies, "What are we?" as if to say, maybe we humans are in no way objects of divine retribution: We make our own fate and deserve what we get if guided by false doctrine.

That much he shares with Voltaire in his theology-smashing judgment on Lisbon, a case for rational thinking about unexpected tragedy. But the narrator is more emotional; it is with glee that he relishes that disillusionment of belief in God as an insurance agent (note 79) held by the likes of the whining, weak-kneed curate. Yet he comes to despise the artilleryman as well, who in II:7 actually proposes to do something about the new state of affairs. In the end the narrator is no less a weakling than the curate for his shrinking from any action implied by his own man-makes-himself thesis. He is a philosophical fraud.

76. Revelation 19:3, "Hallelujah! The smoke from her goes up for ever and ever." "Her" is the great harlot of Babylon = Rome.

"Things have changed," I said quietly. "You must keep your head. There is still hope."

"Hope!"

"Yes; plentiful hope—for all this destruction!"[77]

I began to explain my view of our position. He listened at first, but as I went on the interest in his eyes changed to their former stare, and his regard wandered from me.

"This must be the beginning of the end," he said, interrupting me. "The end! The great and terrible day of the Lord! When men shall call upon the mountains and the rocks to fall upon them and hide them— hide them from the face of Him that sitteth upon the throne!"[78]

I began to understand the position. I ceased my laboured reasoning, struggled to my feet, and, standing over him, laid my hand on his shoulder.

"Be a man," said I. "You are scared out of your wits. What good is religion if it collapses at calamity? Think of what earthquakes and floods, wars and volcanoes, have done before to men. Did you think God had exempted Weybridge?... He is not an insurance agent, man."[79]

For a time he sat in blank silence.

"But how can we escape?" he asked suddenly. "They are invulnerable, they are pitiless...."

"Neither the one nor, perhaps, the other," I answered. "And the mightier they are, the more sane and wary should we be. One of them was killed yonder not three hours ago."

"Killed!" he said, staring about him. "How can God's ministers be killed?"

"I saw it happen," I proceeded to tell him. "We have chanced to come in for the thick of it," said I, "and that is all."

---

77. For the author, the invasion is a case of benevolent catastrophe (see the Introduction to the present work, section 3). But for the narrator the hope he sees "for all this destruction," so utterly dismaying to the curate, is much more limited (note 80).

78. Revelation 6:16.

79. Harks back to the narrator's comment on the insurance business at notes 44 and 71. In II:7, the artilleryman similarly sneers at those little clerks with their "'lives insured and a bit invested for fear of accidents. And on Sunday — fear of the hereafter. As if hell was built for rabbits!'" The petty bourgeoisie think too highly of themselves if they believe hell was designed for infractions of small-minded respectability.

"What is that flicker in the sky?" he asked abruptly.

I told him it was the heliograph signalling—that it was the sign of human help and effort in the sky.[80]

"We are in the midst of it," I said, "quiet as it is. That flicker in the sky tells of the gathering storm. Yonder, I take it, are the Martians, and Londonward, where those hills rise about Richmond and Kingston, and the trees give cover, earthworks are being thrown up and guns are being laid. Presently the Martians will be coming this way again...."

And even as I spoke, he sprang to his feet and stopped me by a gesture.

"Listen!" he said....

From beyond the low hills across the water came the dull resonance of distant guns and a remote, weird crying. Then everything was still. A cockchafer came droning over the hedge and past us. High in the west the crescent moon hung faint and pale, above the smoke of Weybridge and Shepperton and the hot still splendour of the sunset.

"We had better follow this path," I said, "northward."

---

80. The curate's "flicker in the sky" is not the light of the Lord's "terrible day" (at note 78), the narrator tries to reassure him, but that of a military heliograph (a movable mirror that reflects beams of sunlight for signalling). This is his limited hope (note 77) that local troops may yet contain the growing Martian threat. For him, the war still is, and will remain, no more than a feverish episode for his reportage, with no larger meaning than his own safety after it is over. He has no real conception, as does the author, that the war marks the beginning of the end of bourgeois everydayism, per its consequences in the novel's sequel.

XIV

IN LONDON.[81]

My younger brother was in London when the Martians fell at Woking. He was a medical student, working for an imminent examination, and he heard nothing of the arrival until Saturday morning. The morning papers on Saturday contained, in addition to lengthy special articles on the planet Mars, on life in the planets, and so forth, a brief and vaguely-worded telegram, all the more striking for its brevity.

The Martians, alarmed by the approach of a crowd, had killed a number of people with a quick-firing gun, so the story ran. The telegram concluded with the words: "Formidable as they seem to be, the Martians have not moved from the pit into which they have fallen, and, indeed, seem incapable of doing so. Probably this is due to the relative strength of the earth's gravitational energy." On that last text the leader-writers expanded very comfortingly.

Of course, all the students in the crammer's biology class, to which my brother went that day, were intensely interested, but there were no signs of any unusual excitement in the streets. The afternoon papers

---

81. The point of view in this chapter and in 1:16 and 1:17, shifts from that of the narrator to that of his brother in London. Critics are divided as to how clumsy or how effective the shift. The former opinion, I think, underestimates Wells's artistry and complete control of the story-telling. For one thing, the brother's account of the most violent scenes, as recounted by the first-person narrator himself, makes them more convincing, not less. There is also the element of suspense while the reader awaits resumption, from the start of Book II, of eye-witness reporting in the novel's climactic chapters. Further, the brother, a medical student, offers a more empirical point of view unslanted by the primary narrator's war fever which carries him right into the heart of dead London; the brother, at least, had the sanity to get out of there before it was too late.

puffed scraps of news under big headlines. They had nothing to tell beyond the movements of troops about the common, and the burning of the pine-woods between Woking and Weybridge, until eight. Then the *St. James's Gazette*, in an extra special edition, announced the bare fact of the interruption of telegraphic communication. This was thought to be due to the falling of burning pine-trees across the line. Nothing more of the fighting was known that night, the night of my drive to Leatherhead and back.

My brother felt no anxiety about us, as he knew from the description in the papers that the cylinder was a good two miles from my house. He made up his mind to run down that night to me, in order, as he says, to see the things before they were killed. He despatched a telegram, which never reached me, about four o'clock, and spent the evening at a music-hall.

In London, also, on Saturday night there was a thunderstorm, and my brother reached Waterloo in a cab. On the platform from which the midnight train usually starts he learnt, after some waiting, that an accident prevented trains from reaching Woking that night. The nature of the accident he could not ascertain; indeed, the railway authorities did not clearly know at that time. There was very little excitement in the station, as the officials, failing to realize that anything further than a breakdown between Byfleet and Woking Junction had occurred, were running the theatre trains, which usually passed through Woking, round by Virginia Water or Guildford. They were busy making the necessary arrangements to alter the route of the Southampton and Portsmouth Sunday League excursions. A nocturnal newspaper reporter, mistaking my brother for the traffic manager, whom he does to a slight extent resemble, waylaid and tried to interview him. Few people, excepting the railway officials, connected the breakdown with the Martians.

I have read, in another account of these events, that on Sunday morning "all London was electrified by the news from Woking." As a matter of fact, there was nothing to justify that very extravagant phrase. Plenty of people in London did not hear of the Martians until the panic of Monday morning. Those who did took some time to realize all that the hastily-worded telegrams in the Sunday papers conveyed. The majority of people in London do not read Sunday papers.

The habit of personal security, moreover, is so deeply fixed in the Londoner's mind, and startling intelligence so much a matter of course in the papers, that they could read without any personal tremors: "About seven o'clock last night the Martians came out of the cylinder,

and, moving about under an armour of metallic shields, have completely wrecked Woking Station, with the adjacent houses, and mas-
sacred an entire battalion of the Cardigan Regiment. No details are
known. Maxims have been absolutely useless against their armour;
the field-guns have been disabled by them. Flying hussars have been
galloping into Chertsey. The Martians appear to be moving slowly
towards Chertsey or Windsor. Great anxiety prevails in West Surrey,
and earthworks are being thrown up to check the advance Londonwards." That was how the *Sunday Sun* put it, and a clever and remarkably prompt "hand-book" article in the *Referee* compared the affair to
a menagerie suddenly let loose in a village.[82]

No one in London knew positively of the nature of the armoured
Martians, and there was still a fixed idea that these monsters must be
sluggish: "crawling," "creeping painfully"—such expressions occurred
in almost all the earlier reports. None of the telegrams could have been
written by an eye-witness of their advance.[83] The Sunday papers
printed separate editions as further news came to hand, some even in
default of it. But there was practically nothing more to tell people until
late in the afternoon, when the authorities gave the press agencies the
news in their possession. It was stated that the people of Walton and
Weybridge, and all that district, were pouring along the roads Londonward, and that was all.

My brother went to church at the Foundling Hospital[84] in the
morning, still in ignorance of what had happened on the previous
night. There he heard allusions made to the invasion, and a special
prayer for peace. Coming out, he bought a *Referee*. He became alarmed
at the news in this, and went again to Waterloo Station to find out if

82. The *Referee*, as its name indicates, was a London weekly popular for
its focus on sports, always with a humorous twist; hence its account of distant
events experienced directly by the narrator as a runaway "menagerie." Londoners, in their cosmopolitan version of local yokel everydayism, remained super-
sophisticated until the last moment, when panic overtook them.

83. The narrator's reaction to these reports is not expressed but it may be
imagined. He himself had used the same reassuring vocabulary to describe the
Martians to his wife in I:7. But even then he sensed something adventurous
afoot, which is why he lied only to get away from her. When he returns, after
it is all over, his profession of domestic felicity rings hollow.

84. Actually a shelter for illegitimate children whose abusive mothers were
known. But like the misnamed "Orphanage" at note 73, Wells takes a factual
liberty in order to equate foundlings with orphaned children, as now are all
uprooted humans.

communication were restored. The omnibuses, carriages, cyclists, and innumerable people walking in their best clothes, seemed scarcely affected by the strange intelligence that the newsvendors were disseminating. People were interested, or, if alarmed, alarmed only on account of the local residents. At the station he heard for the first time that the Windsor and Chertsey lines were now interrupted. The porters told him that several remarkable telegrams had been received in the morning from Byfleet and Chertsey Stations, but that these had abruptly ceased. My brother could get very little precise detail out of them. "There's fighting going on about Weybridge," was the extent of their information.

The train service was now very much disorganized. Quite a number of people, who had been expecting friends from places on the South-Western network, were standing about the station. One gray-headed old gentleman came and abused the South-Western Company bitterly to my brother. "It wants showing up," he said.

One or two trains came in from Richmond, Putney, and Kingston, containing people who had gone out for a day's boating, and found the locks closed and a feeling of panic in the air. A man in a blue and white blazer addressed my brother, full of strange tidings.

"There's hosts of people driving into Kingston in traps and carts and things, with boxes of valuables and all that," he said. "They come from Molesey and Weybridge and Walton, and they say there's been guns heard at Chertsey, heavy firing, and that mounted soldiers have told them to get off at once because the Martians are coming. We heard guns firing at Hampton Court Station, but we thought it was thunder. What the dickens does it all mean? The Martians can't get out of their pit, can they?"

My brother could not tell him.

Afterwards he found that the vague feeling of alarm had spread to the clients of the underground railway, and that the Sunday excursionists began to return from all the South-Western "lungs"[85]—Barnes, Wimbledon, Richmond Park, Kew, and so forth—at unnaturally early hours; but not a soul had anything but vague hearsay to tell of. Everyone connected with the terminus seemed ill-tempered.

---

85. The so-called "lungs of London" are, strictly speaking, the city's many tree-planted parks offering country-like refuge from metropolitan smoke pollution (Brewer 1894:782). But here the reference is to those open spaces along the South-Western Railway, where authorities are attempting to block the Martian advance. But when they finally arrive at London, they release the worst wort of poisonous pollution — their Black Smoke.

About five o'clock the gathering crowd in the station was immensely excited by the opening of the line of communication, which is almost invariably closed, between the South-Eastern and the South-Western stations, and the passage of carriage-trucks bearing huge guns, and carriages crammed with soldiers. These were the guns that were brought up from Woolwich and Chatham to cover Kingston. There was an exchange of pleasantries: "You'll get eaten!" "We're the beast-tamers!" and so forth. A little while after that a squad of police came into the station, and began to clear the public off the platforms, and my brother went out into the street again.

The church bells were ringing for evensong, and a squad of Salvation Army lasses came singing down Waterloo Road. On the bridge a number of loafers were watching a curious brown scum[86] that came drifting down the stream in patches. The sun was just setting, and the Clock Tower and the Houses of Parliament rose against one of the most peaceful skies it is possible to imagine, a sky of gold, barred with long transverse stripes of reddish-purple cloud. There was talk of a floating body. One of the men there, a reservist he said he was, told my brother he had seen the heliograph flickering in the west.

In Wellington Street my brother met a couple of sturdy roughs, who had just rushed out of Fleet Street with still wet newspapers and staring placards. "Dreadful catastrophe!" they bawled one to the other down Wellington Street. "Fighting at Weybridge! Full description! Repulse of the Martians! London said to be in danger!" He had to give three-pence for a copy of that paper.

Then it was, and then only, that he realized something of the full power and terror of these monsters. He learnt that they were not merely a handful of small sluggish creatures, but that they were minds swaying vast mechanical bodies, and that they could move swiftly and smite with such power that even the mightiest guns could not stand against them.

They were described as "vast spider-like machines, nearly a hundred feet high, capable of the speed of an express train, and able to shoot out a beam of intense heat." Masked batteries, chiefly of field-

---

86. Residue of hosed-down Black Smoke released upstream. That it is "loafers" who idly watch these patches of "brown scum" drift by is a nice touch. They see but do not perceive, even as busy Londoners lack any suspicion of what portends from jockular newspaper reporting. The confident "'beast tamers'" above, however, soon yield below to headlines of "'dreadful catastrophe!'" on "still wet newspapers" (see note 87).

guns, had been planted in the country about Horsell Common, and especially between the Woking district and London. Five of the machines had been seen moving towards the Thames, and one, by a freak of chance, had been destroyed. In the other cases the shells had missed, and the batteries had been at once annihilated by the Heat-Rays. Heavy losses of soldiers were mentioned, but the tone of the despatch was optimistic.

The Martians had been repulsed; they were not invulnerable. They had retreated to their triangle of cylinders again, in the circle about Woking. Signallers with heliographs were pushing forward upon them from all sides. Guns were in rapid transit from Windsor, Portsmouth, Aldershot, Woolwich—even from the north; among others, long wire guns of ninety-five tons from Woolwich. Altogether one hundred and sixteen were in position or being hastily laid, chiefly covering London. Never before in England had there been such a vast or rapid concentration of military material.

Any further cylinders that fell, it was hoped, could be destroyed at once by high explosives, which were being rapidly manufactured and distributed. No doubt, ran the report, the situation was of the strangest and gravest description, but the public was exhorted to avoid and discourage panic. No doubt the Martians were strange and terrible in the extreme, but at the outside there could not be more than twenty of them against our millions.

The authorities had reason to suppose, from the size of the cylinders, that at the outside there could not be more than five in each cylinder—fifteen altogether. And one at least was disposed of—perhaps more. The public would be fairly warned of the approach of danger, and elaborate measures were being taken for the protection of the people in the threatened south-western suburbs. And so, with reiterated assurances of the safety of London, and the confidence of the authorities to cope with the difficulty, this *quasi* proclamation closed.

This was printed in enormous type, so fresh that the paper was still wet,[87] and there had been no time to add a word of comment. It was curious, my brother said, to see how ruthlessly the other contents of the paper had been hacked and taken out to give this place.

All down Wellington Street, people could be seen fluttering out the pink sheets and reading, and the Strand was suddenly noisy with the

---

87. It was no longer true at the time of writing that newsprint was dampened in order to take a good impression, then dried (Hughes and Geduld 1993: 213, *n*18). But Wells keeps up the practice for the sake of unprecedented urgency.

voices of an army of hawkers following these pioneers. Men came scrambling off buses to secure copies. Certainly this news excited people intensely, whatever their previous apathy. The shutters of a map-shop in the Strand were being taken down, my brother said, and a man in his Sunday raiment, lemon-yellow gloves even,[88] was visible inside the window, hastily fastening maps of Surrey to the glass.

Going on along the Strand to Trafalgar Square, the paper in his hand, my brother saw some of the fugitives from West Surrey. There was a man driving a cart such as green-grocers use, and his wife and two boys and some articles of furniture. He was driving from the direction of Westminster Bridge, and close behind him came a hay-waggon with five or six respectable-looking people in it, and some boxes and bundles. The faces of these people were haggard, and their entire appearance contrasted conspicuously with the Sabbath-best appearance of the people on the omnibuses. People in fashionable clothing peeped at them out of cabs. They stopped at the Square as if undecided which way to take, and finally turned eastward along the Strand. Some way after these came a man in work-day clothes, riding one of those old-fashioned tricycles with a small front-wheel. He was dirty and white in the face.

My brother turned down towards Victoria, and met a number of such people. He had a vague idea that he might see something of me. He noticed an unusual number of police regulating the traffic. Some of the refugees were exchanging news with the people on the

---

88. Despite the urgency of rushed-out newspapers at note 87, the keeper of a map shop wears "lemon-yellow" gloves while taking down his shutters for the opening of yet another business day — even as map sites on his cartographic wares are being obliterated. The color of his gloves is a typical sign of *fin de siècle* ennui (Hughes 1962:294, *n*60, citing Bergonzi 1961: chapter 1), a symbolic touch that redoubles the "lemon yellow" sunset in the first paragraph of I:4 — a doom-laden, *fin de globe* sunset. For the completest survey of art and society in the 1890s, "an Age of Uncertainty," see Shearer West (1994). The emblematic color in question is replicated by Fraser Harrison (1983) on the cover of *The Yellow Book*, his anthology drawn from the contents of that defining *fin de siècle* quarterly, 1894–1897.

But see Karl Beckson's *London in the 1890s* (1992) for the broader view that the era's cultural life was not all obscene art and declinist angst; there was also a strong force of Empire builders to counter the Empire denigrators (chapter 15). Surely it is this mix that must inform the Martian invasion, which at once destroys the decadent human imperium and inspires the rise of a new world order.

omnibuses. One was professing to have seen the Martians. "Boilers on stilts, I tell you, striding along like men." Most of them were excited and animated by their strange experience.

Beyond Victoria the public-houses were doing a lively trade with these arrivals. At all the street corners groups of people were reading papers, talking excitedly, or staring at these unusual Sunday visitors. They seemed to increase as night drew on, until at last the roads, my brother said, were like the Epsom High Street on a Derby Day. My brother addressed several of these fugitives and got unsatisfactory answers from most.

None of them could tell him any news of Woking except one man, who assured him that Woking had been entirely destroyed on the previous night.

"I come from Byfleet," he said; "a man on a bicycle came through the place in the early morning, and ran from door to door warning us to come away. Then came soldiers. We went out to look, and there were clouds of smoke to the south—nothing but smoke, and not a soul coming that way. Then we heard the guns at Chertsey, and folks coming from Weybridge. So I've locked up my house and come on."

At that time there was a strong feeling in the streets that the authorities were to blame for their incapacity to dispose of the invaders without all this inconvenience.

About eight o'clock, a noise of heavy firing was distinctly audible all over the south of London. My brother could not hear it for the traffic in the main streets, but by striking through the quiet back-streets to the river he was able to distinguish it quite plainly.

He walked back from Westminster to his apartments near Regent's Park about two. He was now very anxious on my account, and disturbed at the evident magnitude of the trouble. His mind was inclined to run, even as mine had run on Saturday, on military details. He thought of all those silent expectant guns, of the suddenly nomadic countryside; he tried to imagine "boilers on stilts" a hundred feet high.[89]

There were one or two cartloads of refugees passing along Oxford Street, and several in the Marylebone Road, but so slowly was the news spreading that Regent Street and Portland Road were full of their

---

89. The brother tries to rationally assess what wildly-imaginative refugees from the scene of action describe as "boilers on stilts." They are of course the walking tripods, with cabins atop them, that the primary narrator knows for what they are.

usual Sunday-night promenaders, albeit they talked in groups, and along the edge of Regent's Park there were as many silent couples "walking out" together under the scattered gas-lamps as ever there had been. The night was warm and still, and a little oppressive, the sound of guns continued intermittently, and after midnight there seemed to be sheet lightning in the south.

He read and re-read the paper, fearing the worst had happened to me. He was restless, and after supper prowled out again aimlessly. He returned and tried to divert his attention by his examination notes in vain. He went to bed a little after midnight, and he was awakened out of some lurid dreams in the small hours of Monday by the sound of door-knockers, feet running in the street, distant drumming, and a clamour of bells. Red reflections danced on the ceiling. For a moment he lay astonished, wondering whether day had come or the world had gone mad. Then he jumped out of bed and ran to the window.

His room was an attic, and as he thrust his head out, up and down the street there were a dozen echoes to the noise of his window-sash, and heads in every kind of night disarray appeared. Inquiries were being shouted. "They are coming!" bawled a policeman, hammering at the door; "the Martians are coming!" and hurried to the next door.

The noise of drumming and trumpeting came from the Albany Street Barracks,[90] and every church within earshot was hard at work killing sleep with a vehement disorderly tocsin. There was a noise of doors opening, and window after window in the houses opposite flashed from darkness into yellow illumination.

Up the street came galloping a closed carriage, bursting abruptly into noise at the corner, rising to a clattering climax under the window, and dying away slowly in the distance. Close on the rear of this came a couple of cabs, the forerunners of a long procession of flying vehicles, going for the most part to Chalk Farm Station, where the North-Western special trains were loading up, instead of coming down the gradient into Euston.

For a long time my brother stared out of the window in blank astonishment, watching the policemen hammering at door after door, and delivering their incomprehensible message. Then the door behind him opened, and the man who lodged across the landing came in, dressed only in shirt, trousers, and slippers, his braces loose about his waist, his hair disordered from his pillow.

---

90. Army barracks in central London. In the event, soldiers quartered there are useless in facing unconventional Martian forces.

"What the devil is it?" he asked. "A fire? What a devil of a row!"

They both craned their heads out of the window, straining to hear what the policemen were shouting. People were coming out of the side-streets, and standing in groups at the corners talking.

"What the devil is it all about?" said my brother's fellow-lodger.

My brother answered him vaguely and began to dress, running with each garment to the window in order to miss nothing of the growing excitement of the streets. And presently men selling unnaturally early newspapers came bawling into the street:

"London in danger of suffocation! The Kingston and Richmond defences forced! Fearful massacres in the Thames Valley!"

And all about him—in the rooms below, in the houses on either side and across the road, and behind in the Park Terraces and in the hundred other streets of that part of Marylebone, and the Westbourne Park district and St. Pancras, and westward and northward in Kilburn and St. John's Wood and Hampstead, and eastward in Shoreditch and Highbury and Haggerston and Hoxton, and, indeed, through all the vastness of London from Ealing to East Ham—people were rubbing their eyes, and opening windows to stare out and ask aimless questions, and dressing hastily as the first breath of the coming storm of Fear blew through the streets. It was the dawn of the great panic. London, which had gone to bed on Sunday night stupid and inert, was awakened in the small hours of Monday morning to a vivid sense of danger.

Unable from his window to learn what was happening, my brother went down and out into the street, just as the sky between the parapets of the houses grew pink with the early dawn. The flying people on foot and in vehicles grew more numerous every moment. "Black Smoke!" he heard people crying, and again "Black Smoke!" The contagion of such a unanimous fear was inevitable. As my brother hesitated on the doorstep, he saw another newsvendor approaching him, and got a copy forthwith. The man was running away with the rest, and selling his papers as he ran for a shilling each—a grotesque mingling of profit and panic.

And from this paper my brother read that catastrophic despatch of the Commander-in-Chief:

> "The Martians are able to discharge enormous clouds of a black and poisonous vapour by means of rockets. They have smothered our batteries, destroyed Richmond, Kingston, and Wimbledon, and are advancing slowly towards London, destroying everything on the way. It is impossible to stop them. There is no safety from the Black Smoke but in instant flight."

That was all, but it was enough. The whole population of the great six-million city was stirring, slipping, running; presently it would be pouring *en masse* northward.[91]

"Black Smoke!" the voices cried. "Fire!"

The bells of the neighbouring church made a jangling tumult, a cart carelessly driven smashed amidst shrieks and curses against the water-trough up the street. Sickly yellow light went to and fro in the houses, and some of the passing cabs flaunted unextinguished lamps. And overhead the dawn was growing brighter, clear and steady and calm.

He heard footsteps running to and fro in the rooms, and up and down stairs behind him. His landlady came to the door, loosely wrapped in dressing-gown and shawl; her husband followed, ejaculating.

As my brother began to realize the import of all these things, he turned hastily to his own room, put all his available money—some ten pounds altogether—into his pockets, and went out again into the streets.

91. Foreshadows the metaphor of societal liquefaction in the opening paragraph of I:16. Over all (*infra*) is cast a "sickly yellow light," end-of-the-world illumination (see note 88). The poison darts that are the Martian cylinders (note 42) now are doing their vampire work.

XV

WHAT HAD HAPPENED IN SURREY.[92]

It was while the curate had sat and talked so wildly to me under the hedge in the flat meadows near Halliford, and while my brother was watching the fugitives stream over Westminster Bridge, that the Martians had resumed the offensive. So far as one can ascertain from the conflicting accounts that have been put forth, the majority of them remained busied with preparations in the Horsell pit until nine that night, hurrying on some operation that disengaged huge volumes of green smoke.

But three certainly came out about eight o'clock, and, advancing slowly and cautiously, made their way through Byfleet and Pyrford towards Ripley and Weybridge, and so came in sight of the expectant

---

92. This chapter resumes the primary narrator's account (A), then shifts back again to his brother's (B) in the final two chapters of Book I. The sequence in the whole Book is 15 A's (establishing shots), then B, A, B, B — very like the jump cuts of mounting excitement in cinematography pioneered by D.W. Griffith in *The Birth of a Nation* (1915) (see Barry 1965). Griffith intercuts action scenes from two different locales that converge in one point, just as powerfully visualized, photojournalistic snapshots taken by A and B lead on to the climactic scenes that play out in Book II.

Wells himself took an early interest in film, with an unsold script fixed up as *An Unconventional Novel* (1929:subtitle). He saw in the new medium, improved by soundtracking, "the Art Form of the Future" (3–14), with the future itself its subject. Realizing this in his personally controlled *Things to Come* (1936), the first film to fully integrate orchestral music with visual flow (Stover 1987), its imagery not surprisingly often evokes that of the cinematic *Worlds*. Note again the embodiment of the Modern Octopus State in the person of John Cabal dressed in his saving octopus-headed helmet (figs. 2–3 of the plates in the present work).

batteries against the setting sun. These Martians did not advance in a body, but in a line, each perhaps a mile and a half from his nearest fellow. They communicated with each other by means of siren-like howls, running up and down the scale from one note to another.[93]

It was this howling and the firing of the guns at Ripley and St. George's Hill that we had heard at Upper Halliford. The Ripley gunners, unseasoned artillery volunteers who ought never to have been placed in such a position, fired one wild, premature, ineffectual volley, and bolted on horse and foot through the deserted village, and the Martian walked over their guns serenely without using his Heat-Ray, stepped gingerly among them, passed in front of them, and so came unexpectedly upon the guns in Painshill Park, which he destroyed.

The St. George's Hill men, however, were better led or of a better mettle. Hidden by a pine-wood as they were, they seem to have been quite unexpected by the Martian nearest to them. They laid their guns as deliberately as if they had been on parade, and fired at about a thousand yards' range.

The shells flashed all round the Martian, and they saw him advance a few paces, stagger, and go down. Everybody yelled together, and the guns were reloaded in frantic haste. The overthrown Martian set up a prolonged ululation,[94] and immediately a second glittering giant, answering him, appeared over the trees to the south. It would seem that a leg of the tripod had been smashed by one of the shells. The whole of the second volley flew wide of the Martian on the ground, and simultaneously both his companions brought their Heat-Rays to bear on the battery. The ammunition blew up, the pine-trees all about the guns flashed into fire, and only one or two of the men who were already running over the crest of the hill escaped.

After this it would seem that the three took counsel together and halted, and the scouts who were watching them report that they remained absolutely stationary for the next half-hour. The Martian

---

93. Not only are Martian weapons superior, so are their field communications in coordinating battle tactics. Again the Prussian military model is evoked (Howard 1961). Nine paragraphs below, Martian strategy for the advance on London, like the Prussian advance on Paris, is described as a "huge crescent," with its two horns trailing behind to cover both flanks.

94. The wail of the first Martian whose machine has been damaged foreshadows the "ulla, ulla" of the last Martian's death wail in II:8. They all die, like so many "speck[s] of blight" (next paragraph). But the blight turns out to be a homeopathic remedy for a society already diseased beyond any other cure.

who had been overthrown crawled tediously out of his hood, a small brown figure, oddly suggestive from that distance of a speck of blight, and apparently engaged in the repair of his support. About nine he had finished, for his cowl was then seen above the trees again.

It was a few minutes past nine that night when these three sentinels were joined by four other Martians, each carrying a thick black tube. A similar tube was handed to each of the three, and the seven proceeded to distribute themselves at equal distances along a curved line between St. George's Hill, Weybridge, and the village of Send, southwest of Ripley.

A dozen rockets sprang out of the hills before them so soon as they began to move, and warned the waiting batteries about Ditton and Esher. At the same time four of their fighting Machines, similarly armed with tubes, crossed the river, and two of them, black against the western sky, came into sight of myself and the curate as we hurried wearily and painfully along the road that runs northward out of Halliford. They moved, as it seemed to us, upon a cloud, for a milky mist covered the fields and rose to a third of their height.

At this sight the curate cried faintly in his throat, and began running; but I knew it was no good running from a Martian, and I turned aside and crawled through dewy nettles and brambles into the broad ditch by the side of the road. He looked back, saw what I was doing, and turned to join me.

The two Martians halted, the nearer to us standing and facing Sunbury, the remoter being a gray indistinctness towards the evening star, away towards Staines.

The occasional howling of the Martians had ceased; they took up their positions in the huge crescent about their cylinders in absolute silence. It was a crescent with twelve miles between its horns. Never since the devising of gunpowder was the beginning of a battle so still. To us and to an observer about Ripley it would have had precisely the same effect—the Martians seemed in solitary possession of the darkling night, lit only as it was by the slender moon, the stars, the afterglow of the daylight, and the ruddy glare from St. George's Hill and the woods of Painshill.

But facing that crescent everywhere, at Staines, Hounslow, Ditton, Esher, Ockham, behind hills and woods south of the river, and across the flat grass meadows to the north of it, wherever a cluster of trees or village houses gave sufficient cover, the guns were waiting. The signal rockets burst and rained their sparks through the night and vanished, and the spirit of all those watching batteries rose to a tense expectation. The Martians had but to advance into the line of fire, and instantly those motionless black forms of men, those guns glittering so darkly in the early night, would explode into a thunderous fury of battle.

No doubt the thought that was uppermost in a thousand of those vigilant minds, even as it was uppermost in mine, was the riddle how much they understood of us. Did they grasp that we in our millions were organized, disciplined, working together? Or did they interpret our spurts of fire, the sudden stinging of our shells, our steady investment of their encampment, as we should the furious unanimity of onslaught in a disturbed hive of bees? Did they dream they might exterminate us? (At that time no one knew what food they needed.)[95] A hundred such questions struggled together in my mind as I watched that vast sentinel shape. And in the back of my mind was the sense of all the huge unknown and hidden forces Londonward. Had they prepared pitfalls? Were the powder-mills at Hounslow ready as a snare? Would the Londoners have the heart and courage to make a greater Moscow of their mighty province of houses?[96]

Then, after an interminable time as it seemed to us, crouching and peering through the hedge, came a sound like the distant concussion of a gun. Another nearer, and then another. And then the Martian beside us raised his tube on high and discharged it gunwise, with a heavy report that made the ground heave. The Martian towards Staines answered him. There was no flash, no smoke, simply that loaded detonation.

I was so excited by these heavy minute-guns following one another that I so far forgot my personal safety and my scalded hands as to clamber up into the hedge and stare towards Sunbury. As I did so a second report followed, and a big projectile hurtled overhead towards Hounslow. I expected at least to see smoke or fire or some such evidence of its work. But all I saw was the deep blue sky above, with one

---

95. Here is a hint of the Martians' vampiric dietary, which answers the narrator's two questions. Are they out to exterminate us? (no). Do they regard us as disorganized for all our "furious unanimity," like a disturbed hive of bees? (yes). Only the Martians can provide a better model of integral purpose. They come to eat us, and in digesting us feed the life of that "higher organism, the world state of the coming years" (1901:190), a collective being possible to come into existence only "through the concussions of war" (189).

96. Would Londoners have the guts to frustrate the Martian objective by setting fire to it, as did Moscovites their city in the face of Napoleon's advance?

solitary star, and the white mist spreading wide and low beneath. And there had been no crash, no answering explosion. The silence was restored; the minute lengthened to three.

"What has happened?" said the curate, standing up beside me.

"Heaven knows!" said I.

A bat flickered by and vanished.[97] A distant tumult of shouting began and ceased. I looked again at the Martian, and saw he was now moving eastward along the river-bank, with a swift rolling motion.

Every moment I expected the fire of some hidden battery to spring upon him; but the evening calm was unbroken. The figure of the Martian grew smaller as he receded, and presently the mist and the gathering night had swallowed him up. By a common impulse we clambered higher. Towards Sunbury was a dark appearance, as though a conical hill had suddenly come into being there, hiding our view of the further country; and then, remoter across the river, over Walton, we saw another such summit. These hill-like forms grew lower and broader even as we stared.

Moved by a sudden thought, I looked northward, and there I perceived a third of these cloudy black kopjes[98] had arisen.

Everything had suddenly become very still. Far away to the southeast, marking the quiet, we heard the Martians hooting to one another, and then the air quivered again with the distant thud of their guns. But the earthly artillery[99] made no reply.

Now, at the time we could not understand these things; but later I was to learn the meaning of these ominous kopjes that gathered in the twilight. Each of the Martians, standing in the great crescent I have described, had discharged at some unknown signal, by means of the

---

97. A diabolical omen. Is not the familiar of Dracula the vampire a bat? Curiously enough, Bram Stoker's *Dracula* was published in 1897, the same year as the serial version of *Worlds*. In Stoker's novel, the Transylvanian Count leads a team of vampires for the conquest of London, in yet another variety of the invasion-of-England genre started with a Prussian invasion in Chesney's *The Battle of Dorking* (1871).

98. Small hills of South African locution made familiar to English readers in accounts of the Boer War, from behind which Boer guerrillas sniped on English troops. Although the war did not officially break out until 1899, the landscape of the coming conflict was reported by Kipling. Here, the "kopjes" are mounds of Black Smoke, covering the Martian advance with moving hillocks of poison gas.

99. The contrast is with the Martians' celestial artillery, against which there can be no effective human "reply."

gun-like tube he carried, a huge canister over whatever hill, copse, cluster of houses, or other possible cover for guns, chanced to be in front of him. Some fired only one of these, some two, as in the case of the one we had seen; the one at Ripley is said to have discharged no fewer than five at that time. These canisters smashed on striking the ground—they did not explode—and incontinently disengaged an enormous volume of a heavy inky vapour, coiling and pouring upwards in a huge and ebony cumulus cloud, a gaseous hill that sank and spread itself slowly over the surrounding country. And the touch of that vapour, the inhaling of its pungent wisps, was death to all that breathes.

It was heavy, this vapour, heavier than the densest smoke, so that, after the first tumultuous uprush and outflow of its impact, it sank down through the air and poured over the ground in a manner rather liquid than gaseous, abandoning the hills, and streaming into the valleys and ditches and water-courses, even as I have heard the carbonic acid gas that pours from volcanic clefts is wont to do.[100] And where it came upon water some chemical action occurred, and the surface would be instantly covered with a powdery scum that sank slowly and made way for more. The scum was absolutely insoluble, and it is a strange thing, seeing the instant effect of the gas, that one could drink the water from which it had been strained without hurt. The vapour did not diffuse as a true gas would do. It hung together in banks, flowing sluggishly down the slope of the land and driving reluctantly before the wind, and very slowly it combined with the mist and moisture of the air, and sank to the earth in the form of dust. Save that an unknown element giving a group of four lines in the blue of the spectrum[101] is concerned, we are still entirely ignorant of the nature of this substance.

---

100. "Carbonic acid gas" = carbon dioxide, a heavier-than-air gas emitted in quantity by erupting volcanoes, and which settles into their low-lying surrounds. So does the Black Smoke settle down with smothering effect. In the Epilogue it is suggested that the Smoke interacts with argon to make it even heavier and blanketing. Argon, in our chemistry, is inert but mysteriously, in Martian chemistry, it has reactive properties. Wells already has referenced argon as a newly discovered element of strange properties at note 38 — the only element known to us that does *not* combine with any other.

101. In the epilogue the unknown element forms "three lines in the green," a match for the color of weirdness at note 88. But so too is blue, taken at note 147 as a variant of green.

Once the tumultuous upheaval of its dispersion was over, the black smoke clung so closely to the ground, even before its precipitation, that, fifty feet up in the air, on the roofs and upper stories of high houses and on great trees, there was a chance of escaping its poison altogether, as was proved even that night at Street Cobham and Ditton.

The man who escaped at the former place tells a wonderful story of the strangeness of its coiling flow, and how he looked down from the church spire and saw the houses of the village rising like ghosts out of its inky nothingness. For a day and a half he remained there, weary, starving, and sun-scorched, the earth under the blue sky and against the prospect of the distant hills a velvet black expanse, with red roofs, green trees, and, later, black-veiled shrubs and gates, barns, outhouses, and walls, rising here and there into the sunlight.

But that was at Street Cobham, where the black vapour was allowed to remain until it sank of its own accord into the ground. As a rule, the Martians, when it had served its purpose, cleared the air of it again by wading into it and directing a jet of steam upon it.

That they did with the vapour-banks near us, and we saw in the starlight from the window of a deserted house at Upper Halliford, whither we had returned. From there we could see the searchlights on Richmond Hill and Kingston Hill going to and fro, and about eleven the window rattled, and we heard the sound of the huge siege guns that had been put in position there. These continued intermittently for the space of a quarter of an hour, sending chance shots at the invisible Martians at Hampton and Ditton, and then the pale beams of the electric light vanished, and were replaced by a bright red glow.

Then the fourth cylinder fell—a brilliant green meteor—as I learnt afterwards, in Bushey Park. Before the guns on the Richmond and Kingston line of hills began, there was a fitful cannonade far away in the southwest, due, I believe, to guns being fired haphazard before the black vapour could overwhelm the gunners.

So, setting about it as methodically as men might smoke out a wasps' nest, the Martians spread this strange stifling vapour over the Londonward country. The horns of the crescent slowly spread apart, until at last they formed a line from Hanwell to Coombe and Malden. All night through their destructive tubes advanced. Never once, after the Martian at St. George's Hill was brought down, did they give the artillery the ghost of a chance against them. Wherever there was a possibility of guns being laid for them unseen, a fresh canister of the black vapour was discharged, and where the guns were openly displayed the Heat-Ray was brought to bear.

By midnight the blazing trees along the slopes of Richmond Park, and the glare of Kingston Hill, threw their light upon a network of black smoke, blotting out the whole Valley of the Thames, and extending as far as the eye could reach. And through this two Martians slowly waded, and turned their hissing steam-jets this way and that.

The Martians were sparing of the Heat-Ray that night, either because they had but a limited supply of material for its production, or because they did not wish to destroy the country, but only to crush and overawe the opposition they had aroused. In the latter aim they certainly succeeded. Sunday night was the end of the organized opposition to their movements. After that no body of men could stand against them, so hopeless was the enterprise. Even the crews of the torpedo boats and destroyers that had brought their quick-firers up the Thames refused to stop, mutinied, and went down again. The only offensive operation men ventured upon after that night was the preparation of mines and pitfalls, and even in that men's energies were frantic and spasmodic.

One has to imagine the fate of those batteries towards Esher, waiting so tensely in the twilight, as well as one may. Survivors there were none. One may picture the orderly expectation, the officers alert and watchful, the gunners ready, the ammunition piled to hand, the limber gunners with their horses and waggons, the groups of civilian spectators standing as near as they were permitted, the evening stillness; the ambulances and hospital tents, with the burnt and wounded from Weybridge; then the dull resonance of the shots the Martians fired, and the clumsy projectiles whirling over the trees and houses, and smashing amidst the neighbouring fields.

One may picture, too, the sudden shifting of the attention, the swiftly spreading coils and bellyings of that blackness advancing headlong, towering heavenward, turning the twilight to a palpable darkness, a strange and horrible antagonist of vapour striding upon its victims, men and horses near it seen dimly, running, shrieking, falling headlong, shouts of dismay, the guns suddenly abandoned, men choking and writhing on the ground, and the swift broadening out of the opaque cone of smoke.[102] And then, night and extinction—nothing but a silent mass of impenetrable vapour hiding its dead.

---

102. A scene repeated in *Things to Come*, when John Cabal gasses the last of the patriotic nationalists who oppose his Air Dictatorship and the beginnings of a world-state (see note 92). In the 1936 film it is "the Gas of Peace," a temporary knockout agent; but in the 1933 novel, "Pacifin" is as deadly as the Black Smoke.

Before dawn the black vapour was pouring through the streets of Richmond, and the disintegrating organism of government was, with a last expiring effort, rousing the population of London to the necessity of flight.

XVI

THE EXODUS FROM LONDON.

So you understand the roaring wave of fear that swept through the greatest city in the world just as Monday was dawning—the stream of flight rising swiftly to a torrent, lashing in a foaming tumult round the railway-stations, banked up into a horrible struggle about the shipping in the Thames, and hurrying by every available channel northward and eastward. By ten o'clock the police organization, and by mid-day even the railway organizations, were losing coherency, losing shape and efficiency, guttering, softening, running at last in that swift liquefaction of the social body.[103]

---

103. The poisonous bite of the Martian vampires, following the first "poisoned dart" at note 42, has at last done its work. As with the prey of real-life vampires (see the Introduction to the present work, section 5), the bitten flesh melts, resolves itself into a bloody stew for insufflation. So too, now, with "that swift liquefaction of the social body." In *Worlds*, as in other Wells novels, catastrophic war effects the "liquidation of a bankrupt civilization preparatory to a drastic reconstruction" (1933:214). Men are reduced to disconnected social atoms, "released from old ties [and made] ready for new associations" (1914a:234). Wells intuitively understood the political theory of mass society that explains the necessary modern conditions making the twentieth-century dictators possible (Kornhauser 1960). Given the breakdown of traditional social forms with radical urbanization, the state can readily move in to fill the vacuum with its agencies of mass mobilization. Wells's Modern State does just that, securing "direct public service" (1916:69) to itself out of the "social magma" (1933:253), to which the volcanic heat of war has subjected a mass society already in meltdown.

In Appendix II, Wells proposes a vampire state to dissolve all localized public services in the greater metropolitan London area, a "mammoth municipality" that "sucks the ebbing life from your old communities into the veins of the new." This is what the Martians do, as they literally liquidate the old order,

All the railway lines north of the Thames and the South-Eastern people at Cannon Street had been warned by midnight on Sunday, and trains were being filled, people were fighting savagely for standing-room in the carriages, even at two o'clock. By three people were being trampled and crushed even in Bishopsgate Street; a couple of hundred yards or more from Liverpool Street Station revolvers were fired, people stabbed, and the policemen who had been sent to direct the traffic, exhausted and infuriated, were breaking the heads of the people they were called out to protect.

And as the day advanced and the engine-drivers and stokers refused to return to London, the pressure of the flight drove the people in an ever-thickening multitude away from the stations and along the north-ward-running roads. By mid-day a Martian had been seen at Barnes, and a cloud of slowly sinking black vapour drove along the Thames and across the flats of Lambeth, cutting off all escape over the bridges in its sluggish advance. Another bank drove over Ealing, and surrounded a little island of survivors on Castle Hill, alive, but unable to escape.

After a fruitless struggle to get aboard a North-Western train at Chalk Farm—the engines of the trains that had loaded in the goods yard there *ploughed* through shrieking people, and a dozen stalwart men fought to keep the crowd from crushing the driver against his furnace—my brother emerged upon the Chalk Farm Road, dodged across through a hurrying swarm of vehicles, and had the luck to be foremost in the sack of a cycle shop. The front tyre of the machine he got was punctured in dragging it through the window, but he got up and off, notwithstanding, with no further injury than a cut wrist. The steep foot of Haverstock Hill was impassable owing to several overturned horses, and my brother struck into Belsize Road.

So he got out of the fury of the panic, and, skirting the Edgware Road, reached Edgware about seven, fasting and wearied, but well ahead of the crowd. Along the road people were standing in the roadway curious, wondering. He was passed by a number of cyclists, some horsemen, and two motor-cars.[104] A mile from Edgware the rim of the

---

preparatory to sucking it up into that "higher organism, the world-state of the coming years" (1901:190). London will be its world-city, the metropolitan brain of a Modern State Octopus — the new Leviathan that digests the entire planet in *Sleeper* the sequel to *Worlds.*

104. Few motor-cars are seen on the road so late as five years after London's first motor exhibition in 1895. Restrictive legislation held the speed of the

wheel broke, and the machine became unrideable. He left it by the roadside and trudged through the village. There were shops half opened in the main street of the place, and people crowded on the pavement and in the doorways and windows, staring astonished at this extraordinary procession of fugitives that was beginning. He succeeded in getting some food at an inn.

For a time he remained in Edgware, not knowing what next to do. The flying people increased in number. Many of them, like my brother, seemed inclined to stop in the place. There was no fresh news of the invaders from Mars.

At that time the road was crowded, but as yet far from congested. Most of the fugitives at that hour were mounted on cycles, but there were soon motor-cars, hansom cabs, and carriages hurrying along, and the dust hung in heavy clouds along the road to St. Albans.

It was perhaps a vague idea of making his way to Chelmsford, where some friends of his lived, that at last induced my brother to strike into a quiet lane running eastward. Presently he came upon a stile, and, crossing it, followed a footpath north-eastward. He passed near several farm-houses and some little places whose names he did not learn. He saw few fugitives until, in a grass lane towards High Barnet, he happened upon the two ladies who became his fellow-travellers. He came upon them just in time to save them.

He heard their screams, and, hurrying round the corner, saw a couple of men struggling to drag them out of the little pony-chaise in which they had been driving, while a third with difficulty held the frightened pony's head. One of the ladies, a short woman dressed in white, was simply screaming; the other, a dark, slender figure, slashed at the man who gripped her arm with a whip she held in her disengaged hand.

My brother immediately grasped the situation, shouted, and hurried towards the struggle. One of the men desisted and turned towards him, and my brother, realizing from his antagonist's face that a fight was unavoidable, and being an expert boxer, went into him forthwith, and sent him down against the wheel of the chaise.

It was no time for pugilistic chivalry, and my brother laid him quiet

---

automobiles to a useless crawl slower than horsedrawn vehicles and bicycles. Not until 1903 was it upped from two miles an hour to twenty (Greg 1967:383f) — three years after the purported invasion. Martian technology looks all the more progressive when contrasted to England's, held back from the advances of every other Western society by reactionary policies. The obtuse case of electrification, at note 52, is definitive.

with a kick, and gripped the collar of the man who pulled at the slender lady's arm. He heard the clatter of hoofs, the whip stung across his face, a third antagonist struck him between the eyes, and the man he held wrenched himself free and made off down the lane in the direction from which he had come.

Partly stunned, he found himself facing the man who had held the horse's head, and became aware of the chaise receding from him down the lane, swaying from side to side and with the women in it looking back. The man before him, a burly rough, tried to close, and he stopped him with a blow in the face. Then, realizing that he was deserted, he dodged round and made off down the lane after the chaise, with the sturdy man close behind him, and the fugitive, who had turned now, following remotely.

Suddenly he stumbled and fell: his immediate pursuer went headlong, and he rose to his feet to find himself with a couple of antagonists again. He would have had little chance against them had not the slender lady very pluckily pulled up and returned to his help. It seems she had a revolver all this time, but it had been under the seat when she and her companion were attacked. She fired at six yards' distance, narrowly missing my brother. The less courageous of the robbers made off, and his companion followed him, cursing his cowardice. They both stopped in sight down the lane, where the third man lay insensible.

"Take this!" said the slender lady, and gave my brother her revolver.

"Go back to the chaise," said my brother, wiping the blood from his split lip.

She turned without a word—they were both panting—and they went back to where the lady in white struggled to hold back the frightened pony.

The robbers had evidently had enough of it. When my brother looked again they were retreating.

"I'll sit here," said my brother, "if I may;" and he got up on the empty front-seat. The lady looked over her shoulder.

"Give me the reins," she said, and laid the whip along the pony's side. In another moment a bend in the road hid the three men from my brother's eyes.

So, quite unexpectedly, my brother found himself, panting, with a cut mouth, a bruised jaw and blood-stained knuckles, driving along an unknown lane with these two women.

He learnt they were the wife and the younger sister of a surgeon living at Stanmore, who had come in the small hours from a dangerous case at Pinner, and heard at some railway-station on his way of the Martian advance. He had hurried home, roused the women—their servant had left them two days before—packed some provisions, put his revolver under the seat—luckily for my brother—and told them to drive on to Edgware, with the idea of getting a train there. He stopped behind to tell the neighbours. He would overtake them, he said, at about half-past four in the morning, and now it was nearly nine and they had seen nothing of him since. They could not stop in Edgware because of the growing traffic through the place, and so they had come into this side-lane.

That was the story they told my brother in fragments when presently they stopped again, nearer to New Barnet. He promised to stay with them at least until they could determine what to do, or until the missing man arrived, and professed to be an expert shot with the revolver—a weapon strange to him—in order to give them confidence.

They made a sort of encampment by the wayside, and the pony became happy in the hedge. He told them of his own escape out of London, and all that he knew of these Martians and their ways. The sun crept higher in the sky, and after a time their talk died out and gave place to an uneasy state of anticipation. Several wayfarers came along the lane, and of these my brother gathered such news as he could. Every broken answer he had deepened his impression of the great disaster that had come on humanity, deepened his persuasion of the immediate necessity for prosecuting this flight. He urged the matter upon them.

"We have money," said the slender woman, and hesitated.

Her eyes met my brother's and her hesitation ended.

"So have I," said my brother.

She explained that they had as much as thirty pounds in gold[105] besides a five-pound note, and suggested that with that they might get upon a train at St. Albans or New Barnet. My brother thought that was hopeless, seeing the fury of the Londoners to crowd upon the trains, and broached his own idea of striking across Essex towards Harwich and thence escaping from the country altogether.

Mrs. Elphinstone[106]—that was the name of the woman in white—

---

105. Gold coins, or sovereigns, worth one English pound each.

106. The self-assertive, revolver-shooting young lady, Mrs. Elphinstone's sister-in-law, is the earliest example of the Wellsian heroine, especially notable in *Ann Veronica* (1909b), a scandalous novel even by Edwardian times. How much more so an independent-minded nonconformist in Victorian literature,

would listen to no reasoning, and kept calling upon "George;" but her sister-in-law was astonishingly quiet and deliberate, and at last agreed to my brother's suggestion. So they went on towards Barnet, designing to cross the Great North Road, my brother leading the pony to save it as much as possible.

As the sun crept up the sky the day became excessively hot, and under foot a thick whitish sand grew burning and blinding, so that they travelled only very slowly. The hedges were gray with dust. And as they advanced towards Barnet, a tumultuous murmuring grew stronger.

They began to meet more people. For the most part these were staring before them, murmuring indistinct questions, jaded, haggard, unclean. One man in evening dress passed them on foot, his eyes on the ground. They heard his voice, and, looking back at him, saw one hand clutched in his hair and the other beating invisible things. His paroxysm of rage over, he went on his way without once looking back.

As my brother's party went on towards the cross-roads to the south of Barnet, they saw a woman approaching the road across some fields on their left, carrying a child and with two other children, and then a man in dirty black, with a thick stick in one hand and a small portmanteau in the other, passed. Then round the corner of the lane, from between the villas that guarded it at its confluence with the highroad, came a little cart drawn by a sweating black pony and driven by a sallow youth in a bowler hat, gray with dust. There were three girls like East End factory girls, and a couple of little children, crowded in the cart.

"This'll tike us rahnd Edgware?" asked the driver, wild-eyed, white-faced; and when my brother told him it would if he turned to the left, he whipped up at once without the formality of thanks.

My brother noticed a pale gray smoke or haze rising among the houses in front of them, and veiling the white façade of a terrace beyond the road that appeared between the backs of the villas. Mrs. Elphinstone suddenly cried out at a number of tongues of smoky red flame leaping up above the houses in front of them against the hot blue sky. The tumultuous noise resolved itself now into the disorderly mingling of many voices, the gride of many wheels, the creaking of wag-

---

this one significantly named after Mountstuart Elphinstone (*d.* 1859), famous for his heroic mission to the dangerous wilds of Afghanistan on behalf of the British Raj (*Encyclopædia Britannica*, 11th edition, 9:298f). His feats would not have been forgotten by the contemporary reader.

gons, and the staccato of hoofs. The lane came round sharply not fifty yards from the cross-roads.

"Good heavens!" cried Mrs. Elphinstone. "What is this you are driving us into?"

My brother stopped.

For the main road was a boiling stream of people, a torrent of human beings rushing northward, one pressing on another. A great bank of dust, white and luminous in the blaze of the sun, made everything within twenty feet of the ground gray and indistinct, and was perpetually renewed by the hurrying feet of a dense crowd of horses and men and women on foot, and by the wheels of vehicles of every description.

"Way!" my brother heard voices crying. "Make way!"

It was like riding into the smoke of a fire to approach the meeting-point of the lane and road; the crowd roared like a fire, and the dust was hot and pungent. And, indeed, a little way up the road a villa was burning and sending rolling masses of black smoke across the road to add to the confusion.

Two men came past them. Then a dirty woman carrying a heavy bundle and weeping. A lost retriever dog with hanging tongue circled dubiously round them, scared and wretched, and fled at my brother's threat.[107]

So much as they could see of the road Londonward between the houses to the right, was a tumultuous stream of dirty, hurrying people pent in between the villas on either side; the black heads, the crowded forms, grew into distinctness and they rushed towards the corner, hurried past, and merged their individuality again in a receding multitude that was swallowed up at last in a cloud of dust.[108]

"Go on! Go on!" cried the voices. "Way! Way!"

---

107. The driven-away dog is associated with "a dirty woman." Pets are unclean, and in *A Modern Utopia*, sanitary and unsentimental to a fault (1905: 231), they are forbidden. Mars, too, is a sanitary utopia and so, unforeseen by them, the Martians are felled by the dirty germs of earth — perhaps undone by man's "dear old doggies" (*ibid.*).

108. Wells's cinematic eye, even before motion-picture cameras were artistically used for modern effects by the likes of D.W. Griffith (note 92), is here most remarkable. His eye pans the length of the tumult into which all individuality is merged, even as it sorts out and selectively focuses on vignettes like the man with the gold coins or the doom-saying hysteric crying "Eter-nity! Eter-nity!"

One man's hands pressed on the back of another. My brother stood at the pony's head. Irresistibly attracted, he advanced slowly, pace by pace, down the lane.

Edgware had been a scene of confusion, Chalk Farm a riotous tumult, but this was a whole population in movement. It is hard to imagine that host. It had no character of its own. The figures poured out past the corner, and receded with their backs to the group in the lane. Along the margin came those who were on foot, threatened by the wheels, stumbling in the ditches, blundering into one another.

The carts and carriages crowded close upon one another, making little way for those swifter and more impatient vehicles that darted forward every now and then when an opportunity showed itself of doing so, sending the people scattering against the fences and gates of the villas.

"Push on!" was the cry. "Push on! they are coming!"

In one cart stood a blind man in the uniform of the Salvation Army, gesticulating with his crooked fingers and bawling, "Eternity! eternity!" His voice was hoarse and very loud, so that my brother could hear him long after he was lost to sight in the southward dust. Some of the people who crowded in the carts whipped stupidly at their horses and quarrelled with other drivers; some sat motionless, staring at nothing with miserable eyes; some gnawed their hands with thirst or lay prostrate in the bottoms of their conveyances. The horses' bits were covered with foam, their eyes bloodshot.

There were cabs, carriages, shop-carts, waggons, beyond counting; a mail-cart, a road-cleaner's cart marked "Vestry of St. Pancras,"[109] a huge timber-waggon crowded with roughs. A brewer's dray rumbled by with its two near wheels splashed with recent blood.

"Clear the way!" cried the voices. "Clear the way!"

"Eter—nity! eter—nity!" came echoing up the road.

There were sad, haggard women tramping by, well dressed, with children that cried and stumbled, their dainty clothes smothered in dust, their weary faces smeared with tears. With many of these came men, sometimes helpful, sometimes lowering and savage. Fighting side by side with them pushed some weary street outcast in faded black

---

109. A public-health committee of that city district responsible for its garbage removal (Hughes and Geduld (1993:214, *n*6)—a task now beyond its capacity as all public services are overwhelmed. It is one more vignette documenting the collapse of civilization (or rather, its liquefaction, note 103) in the world's greatest metropolis.

rags, wide-eyed, loud-voiced, and foul-mouthed. There were sturdy workmen thrusting their way along, wretched unkempt men clothed like clerks or shopmen, struggling spasmodically, a wounded soldier my brother noticed, men dressed in the clothes of railway porters, one wretched creature in a night-shirt with a coat thrown over it.

But, varied as its composition was, certain things all that host had in common. There was fear and pain on their faces, and fear behind them. A tumult up the road, a quarrel for a place in a waggon, sent the whole host of them quickening their pace; even a man so scared and broken that his knees bent under him was galvanized for a moment into renewed activity. The heat and dust had already been at work upon this multitude. Their skins were dry, their lips black and cracked. They were all thirsty, weary, and footsore. And amid the various cries one heard disputes, reproaches, groans of weariness and fatigue; the voices of most of them were hoarse and weak. Through it all ran a refrain:

"Way! way! The Martians are coming!"

Few stopped and came aside from that flood. The lane opened slantingly into the main road with a narrow opening, and had a delusive appearance of coming from the direction of London. Yet a kind of eddy of people drove into its mouth; weaklings elbowed out of the stream, who for the most part rested but a moment before plunging into it again. A little way down the lane, with two friends bending over him, lay a man with a bare leg, wrapped about with bloody rags. He was a lucky man to have friends.

A little old man, with a gray military moustache and a filthy black frock-coat, limped out and sat down beside the trap, removed his boot—his sock was blood-stained—shook out a pebble, and hobbled on again; and then a little girl of eight or nine, all alone, threw herself under the hedge close by my brother, weeping.

"I can't go on! I can't go on!"

My brother woke from his torpor of astonishment, and lifted her up, speaking gently to her, and carried her to Miss Elphinstone. So soon as my brother touched her she became quite still, as if frightened.

"Ellen!" shrieked a woman in the crowd, with tears in her voice. "Ellen!" And the child suddenly darted away from my brother, crying: "Mother!"

"They are coming," said a man on horseback, riding past along the lane.

"Out of the way, there!" bawled a coachman, towering high; and my brother saw a closed carriage turning into the lane.

The people crushed back on one another to avoid the horse. My brother pushed the pony and chaise back into the hedge, and the man drove by and stopped at the turn of the way. It was a carriage, with a pole for a pair of horses, but only one was in the traces.

My brother saw dimly through the dust that two men lifted out something on a white stretcher, and put this gently on the grass beneath the privet hedge.

One of the men came running to my brother.

"Where is there any water?" he said. "He is dying fast, and very thirsty. It is Lord Garrick."

"Lord Garrick!" said my brother, "the Chief Justice?"[110]

"The water?" he said.

"There may be a tap," said my brother, "in some of the houses. We have no water. I dare not leave my people."

The man pushed against the crowd towards the gate of the corner house.

"Go on!" said the people, thrusting at him. "They are coming! Go on!"

Then my brother's attention was distracted by a bearded, eagle-faced man lugging a small hand-bag, which split even as my brother's eyes rested on it, and disgorged a mass of sovereigns that seemed to break up into separate coins as it struck the ground. They rolled hither and thither among the struggling feet of men and horses. The man stopped, and looked stupidly at the heap, and the shaft of a cab struck his shoulder and sent him reeling. He gave a shriek and dodged back, and a cartwheel shaved him narrowly.[111]

"Way!" cried the men all about him. "Make way!"

So soon as the cab had passed, he flung himself, with both hands

---

110. The name is fictive, but the office is not. The Lord Chief Justice of England is equivalent to the Chief Justice of the United States. But even this majestic dignitary is reduced to begging for water.

111. The "eagle-face man" who lost his life in the tumult, grasping his bag of gold coins to the end, is emblematic of greed because he is caricatured as Jewish. Wells's anti–Semitism, endemic to the time, would have gone down better with readers than his progressive feminism at note 106. It is not possible, as do all critics upholding Wells as a paragon of liberalism, to gloss over his anti–Semitic bent. Only Cheyette (1991) has had the courage to face it:

"There is something very ugly about many Jewish faces.... Many Jews are intensely vulgar in dress and bearing, materialistic in thought, and cunning and base in method ... a remnant and legacy of medievalism" that must be overcome if "efficient citizenship" in the New Republic (= the Modern State of later

open, upon the heap of coins, and began clutching handfuls in his pockets. A horse rose close upon him, and in another moment he had half risen, and had been borne down under the horse's hoofs.

"Stop!" screamed my brother, and, pushing a woman out of his way, tried to clutch the bit of the horse.

Before he could get to it, he heard a scream under the wheels, and saw through the dust the rim passing over the poor wretch's back. The driver of the cart slashed his whip at my brother, who ran round behind the cart. The multitudinous shouting confused his ears. The man was writhing in the dust among his scattered money, unable to rise, for the wheel had broken his back, and his lower limbs lay limp and dead. My brother stood up and yelled at the next driver, and a man on a black horse came to his assistance.

"Get him out of the road," said he; and, clutching the man's collar with his free hand, my brother lugged him sideways. But he still clutched after his money, and regarded my brother fiercely, hammering at his arm with a handful of gold. "Go on! Go on!" shouted angry voices behind. "Way! Way!"

There was a smash as the pole of a carriage crashed into the cart that the man on horseback stopped. My brother looked up, and the man with the gold twisted his head round and bit the wrist that held his collar. There was a concussion, and the black horse came staggering sideways, and the cart-horse pushed beside it. A hoof missed my brother's foot by a hair's breadth. He released his grip on the fallen man and jumped back. He saw anger change to terror on the face of the poor wretch on the ground, and in a moment he was hidden and my brother was borne backward and carried past the entrance of the lane, and had to fight hard in the torrent to recover it.

---

locution) is to be realized. Hence the need to "abolish the Jew" for his "dispersed nationality" and "social parasitism" (1901:340f) — ethnocide if not genocide. In *Things to Come* the Polish Jew Wadsky is emblematic of the medieval barbarism into which the world has been thrown back, he who is as ever up to his mercantile tricks, in this case "keeping things back" wanted by the Boss of Everytown for his mistress (film shot 409 in 1936). In the novel on which the film is based there is the following gloss: "One could never tell whether a Jew was being a citizen or whether he was just being a Jew. They married, they traded preferentially" (1933:383) (see more in Stover 1996b:154, *n*139, 157, *n*142).

In *Worlds*, it may be said, the Martians rid the human race of this devitalizing pest, thus clearing the way for the more universalistic commerce of gentiles in a capitalist world-state — that happy upshot in *Sleeper* the sequel.

He saw Miss Elphinstone covering her eyes, and a little child, with all a child's want of sympathetic imagination, staring with dilated eyes at a dusty something that lay black and still, ground and crushed under the rolling wheels. "Let us go back!" he shouted, and began turning the pony round. "We cannot cross this—hell,"[112] he said; and they went back a hundred yards the way they had come, until the fighting crowd was hidden. As they passed the bend in the lane, my brother saw the face of the dying man in the ditch under the privet, deadly white and drawn, and shining with perspiration. The two women sat silent, crouching in their seats and shivering.

Then beyond the bend my brother stopped again. Miss Elphinstone was white and pale, and her sister-in-law sat weeping, too wretched even to call upon "George." My brother was horrified and perplexed. So soon as they had retreated, he realized how urgent and unavoidable it was to attempt this crossing. He turned to Miss Elphinstone suddenly, resolute.

"We must go that way," he said, and led the pony round again.

For the second time that day this girl proved her quality. To force their way into the torrent of people, my brother plunged into the traffic and held back a cab-horse, while she drove the pony across its head. A waggon locked wheels for a moment, and ripped a long splinter from the chaise. In another moment they were caught and swept forward by the stream. My brother, with the cabman's whip-marks red across his face and hands, scrambled into the chaise, and took the reins from her.

"Point the revolver at the man behind," he said, giving it to her, "if he presses us too hard. No!—point it at his horse."

---

112. Parrinder (1981:28) comments, "The fury and violence of this 'exodus from London' are in some ways reminiscent of medieval visions of Hell ... designed to illustrate the traditional 'Deadly Sins' of greed and rage." At note 111, the Jew angered by loss of his gold is their summa. I am not, however, suggesting that Wells shares anything with the later eliminationist anti–Semitism of the Nazis, only that his prejudice was typical of the time. He was in fact more enlightened than his fellow Englishmen, bitterly exclusionist, in that he saw the so-called Jewish problem as the problem of a cultural (not racial) minority — at bottom a problem of delayed modernization on the part of Eastern European immigrants — whose solution was assimilation, principally through intermarriage, already happening (1901:341f). At the same time he exalted the Jewish intellectual tradition as no one else, finding it crucial, if only its bearers would surrender their particularism and help think out the idea of a nonsectarian world state.

Then he began to look out for a chance of edging to the right across the road. But once in the stream, he seemed to lose volition, to become a part of that dusty rout. They swept through Chipping Barnet with the torrent; they were nearly a mile beyond the centre of the town before they had fought across to the opposite side of the way. It was din and confusion indescribable; but in and beyond the town the road forks repeatedly, and this to some extent relieved the stress.

They struck eastward through Hadley, and there on either side of the road, and at another place further on, they came upon a great multitude of people drinking at the stream, some fighting to come at the water. And further on, from a hill near East Barnet, they saw two trains running slowly one after the other without signal or order—trains swarming with people, with men even among the coals behind the engines—going northward along the Great Northern Railway. My brother supposes they must have filled outside London, for at that time the furious terror of the people had rendered the central termini impossible.

Near this place they halted for the rest of the afternoon, for the violence of the day had already utterly exhausted all three of them. They began to suffer the beginnings of hunger, the night was cold, and none of them dared to sleep. And in the evening many people came hurrying along the road near by their stopping-place, fleeing from unknown dangers before them and going in the direction from which my brother had come.

XVII

THE "THUNDER CHILD."

HAD the Martians aimed only at destruction, they might on Monday have annihilated the entire population of London, as it spread itself slowly through the home counties.[113] Not only along the road through Barnet, but also through Edgware and Waltham Abbey, and along the roads eastward to Southend and Shoeburyness, and south of the Thames to Deal and Broadstairs, poured the same frantic rout. If one could have hung that June morning in a balloon in the blazing blue above London, every northward and eastward road running out of the infinite tangle of streets would have seemed stippled black with the streaming fugitives, each dot a human agony of terror and physical distress. I have set forth at length in the last chapter my brother's account of the road through Chipping Barnet, in order that my readers may realize how that swarming of black dots appeared to one of those concerned. Never before in the history of the world had such a mass of human beings moved and suffered together. The legendary hosts of Goths and Huns, the hugest armies Asia has ever seen, would have been but a drop in that current.[114] And this was no disciplined

---

113. The counties nearest London, in this case those to the southwest from which the Martians advance. That they aim not to annihilate and utterly destroy London is here indicated. They will capture its population as a source of human blood for ingestion, those of it who survive the attack. As vampires, the Martians are agents of human transformation. Like Dracula, whose bite makes for more of his kind, the Martians invigorate humanity to form its own vampire state (see the Introduction to the present work, section 5), which sucks up the ebbing life blood of outdated local communities and absorbs it into the larger body of monstrous tentacular control (see Appendix II in the present work)— the Modern State Octopus triumphant.

114. The Goths and Huns and others were the barbarian destroyers of the

march; it was a stampede—a stampede gigantic and terrible—without order and without a goal, six million people, unarmed and unprovisioned, driving headlong. It was the beginning of the rout of civilization, of the massacre of mankind.

Directly below him the balloonist would have seen the network of streets far and wide, houses, churches, squares, crescents, gardens—already derelict—spread out like a huge map, and in the southward *blotted*. Over Ealing, Richmond, Wimbledon, it would have seemed as if some monstrous pen had flung ink upon the chart. Steadily, incessantly, each black splash grew and spread, shooting out ramifications this way and that, now banking itself against rising ground, now pouring swiftly over a crest into a new-found valley, exactly as a gout of ink would spread itself upon blotting paper.

And beyond, over the blue hills that rise southward of the river, the glittering Martians went to and fro, calmly and methodically spreading their poison-cloud over this patch of country, and then over that, laying it again with their stream-jets when it had served its purpose, and taking possession of the conquered country. They do not seem to have aimed at extermination so much as at complete demoralization and the destruction of any opposition. They exploded any stores of powder they came upon, cut every telegraph, and wrecked the railways here and there. They were hamstringing mankind. They seemed in no hurry to extend the field of their operations, and did not come beyond the central part of London all that day. It is possible that a very considerable number of people in London stuck to their houses through Monday morning. Certain it is that many died at home, suffocated by the Black Smoke.

Until about mid-day, the Pool of London was an astonishing scene. Steamboats and shipping of all sorts lay there, tempted by the enormous sums of money offered by fugitives, and it is said that many

---

Roman Empire; but as Wells makes it clear in *The Outline of History* (1920), they fought only for the right to join it. In this process of creative destruction they brought medieval Europe into being and with it the beginnings of modern Europe as a cultural domain along totally new lines, breaking with classical tradition. Now England, a new Rome at the center of a great imperium, is subject to a much more forceful invasion by the Martians, who are destined to stimulate the rise (in *Sleeper*) of a newer and greater world civilization. Cruel as Goths they may be in human eyes, but in their eyes we are less than civilized. We have nothing they wish to share in or join. Yet, inadvertently, their way becomes the human way.

who swam out to these vessels were thrust off with boathooks and drowned. About one o'clock in the afternoon the thinning remnant of a cloud of the black vapour appeared between the arches of Black-friars Bridge. At that the Pool became a scene of mad confusion, fighting and collision, and for some time a multitude of boats and barges jammed in the northern arch of the Tower Bridge, and the sailors and lightermen had to fight savagely against the people who swarmed upon them from the river front. People were actually clambering down the piers of the bridge from above....

When, an hour later, a Martian appeared beyond the Clock Tower and waded down the river, nothing but wreckage floated above Lime-house.

Of the falling of the fifth cylinder I have presently to tell. The sixth star fell at Wimbledon. My brother, keeping watch beside the women sleeping in the chaise in a meadow, saw the green flash of it far beyond the hills. On Tuesday the little party, still set upon getting across the sea, made its way through the swarming country towards Colchester. The news that the Martians were now in possession of the whole of London was confirmed. They had been seen at Highgate, and even, it was said, at Neasdon. But they did not come into my brother's view until the morrow.

That day the scattered multitudes began to realize the urgent need of provisions. As they grew hungry the rights of property ceased to be regarded. Farmers were out to defend their cattle-sheds, granaries, and ripening root crops with arms in their hands. A number of people now, like my brother, had their faces eastward, and there were some desperate souls even going back towards London to get food. These were chiefly people from the northern suburbs, whose knowl-edge of the Black Smoke came by hearsay. He heard that about half the members of the Government had gathered at Birmingham, and that enormous quantities of high explosives were being prepared to be used in automatic mines across the Midland counties.

He was also told that the Midland Railway Company had replaced the desertions of the first day's panic, had resumed traffic, and were running northward trains from St. Albans to relieve the congestion of the home counties. There was also a placard in Chipping Ongar announcing that large stores of flour were available in the northern towns, and that within twenty-four hours bread would be distributed among the starving people in the neighbourhood. But this intelligence did not deter him from the plan of escape he had formed, and the three pressed eastward all day, and saw no more of the bread distribution than this promise. Nor, as a matter of fact, did anyone else see more of it. That night fell the seventh star, falling upon Primrose Hill. It fell while Miss Elphinstone was watching, for she took that duty alternately with my brother. She saw it.

On Wednesday the three fugitives—they had passed the night in a field of unripe wheat—reached Chelmsford, and there a body of the inhabitants, calling itself the Committee of Public Supply,[115] seized the pony as provisions, and would give nothing in exchange for it but the promise of a share in it the next day. Here there were rumours of Martians at Epping, and news of the destruction of Waltham Abbey Powder Mills in a vain attempt to blow up one of the invaders.

People were watching for Martians here from the church towers. My brother, very luckily for him as it chanced, preferred to push on at once to the coast, rather than wait for food, although all three of them were very hungry. By mid-day they passed through Tillingham, which strangely enough seemed to be quite silent and deserted, save for a few furtive plunderers, hunting for food. Near Tillingham they suddenly came in sight of the sea, and the most amazing crowd of shipping of all sorts that it is possible to imagine.

For after the sailors could no longer come up the Thames, they came on to the Essex coast, to Harwich, and Walton, and Clacton, and afterwards to Foulness and Shoebury, to bring off the people. They lay in a huge sickle-shaped curve that vanished into mist at last towards the Naze. Close inshore was a multitude of fishing-smacks, English, Scotch, French, Dutch and Swedish; steam-launches from the Thames, yachts, electric boats; and beyond were ships of larger burthen, a multitude of filthy colliers, trim merchantmen, cattle-ships, passenger-boats, petroleum-tanks, ocean tramps, an old white transport even, neat white and gray liners from Southampton and Hamburg; and along the blue coast across the Blackwater my brother could make out dimly a dense swarm of boats chaffering with the people on the beach, a swarm which also extended up the Blackwater almost to Maldon.

About a couple of miles out lay an ironclad very low in the water, almost, to my brother's perception, like a water-logged ship. This was the ram *Thunder Child*. It was the only warship in sight, but far away

---

115. A vigilante group whose name echoes that of the Committee of Public Safety formed under Robespierre during the French Revolution. But its notorious doings are nothing compared to the ultimate revolutionary vigor prepared by the Martian invasion, when the sternist of statist regimes takes over the whole world in *Sleeper*— a Martianized world of unlimited octopoidal reach.

to the right over the smooth surface of the sea—for that day there was a dead calm—lay a serpent of black smoke to mark the next ironclads of the Channel Fleet, which hovered in an extended line, steam up and ready for action, across the Thames estuary during the course of the Martian conquest, vigilant and yet powerless to prevent it.

At the sight of the sea, Mrs. Elphinstone, in spite of the assurances of her sister-in-law, gave way to panic. She had never been out of England before, she would rather die than trust herself friendless in a foreign country, and so forth. She seemed, poor woman! to imagine that the French and the Martians might prove very similar. She had been growing increasingly hysterical, fearful and depressed, during the two days' journeyings. Her great idea was to return to Stanmore. Things had been always well and safe at Stanmore. They would find George at Stanmore....

It was with the greatest difficulty they could get her down to the beach, where presently my brother succeeded in attracting the attention of some men on a paddle steamer out of the Thames. They sent a boat and drove a bargain for thirty-six pounds for the three. The steamer was going, these men said, to Ostend.

It was about two o'clock when my brother, having paid their fares at the gangway, found himself safely aboard the steamboat with his charges. There was food aboard, albeit at exorbitant prices, and the three of them contrived to eat a meal on one of the seats forward.

There were already a couple of score of passengers aboard, some of whom had expended their last money in securing a passage, but the captain lay off the Blackwater until five in the afternoon, picking up passengers until the seated decks were even dangerously crowded. He would probably have remained longer had it not been for the sound of guns that began about that hour in the south. As if in answer, the ironclad seaward fired a small gun and hoisted a string of flags. A jet of smoke sprang out of her funnels.

Some of the passengers were of opinion that this firing came from Shoeburyness, until it was noticed that it was growing louder. At the same time, far away in the south-east, the masts and upper-works of three ironclads rose one after the other out of the sea, beneath clouds of black smoke. But my brother's attention speedily reverted to the distant firing in the south. He fancied he saw a column of smoke rising out of the distant gray haze.

The little steamer was already flapping her way eastward of the big crescent of shipping, and the low Essex coast was growing blue and hazy, when a Martian appeared, small and faint in the remote distance, advancing along the muddy coast from the direction of Foulness. At that the captain on the bridge swore at the top of his voice with fear and anger at his own delay, and the paddles seemed infected with his terror. Every soul aboard stood at the bulwarks or on the seats of the steamer, and stared at the distant shape, higher than the trees or church towers inland, and advancing with a leisurely parody of a human stride.

It was the first Martian my brother had seen, and he stood, more amazed than terrified, watching this Titan advancing deliberately towards the shipping, wading farther and farther into the water as the coast fell away. Then, far away beyond the Crouch, came another striding over some stunted trees, and then yet another still further off, wading deeply through a shiny mudflat that seemed to hang halfway up between sea and sky. They were all stalking seaward, as if to intercept the escape of the multitudinous vessels that were crowded between Foulness and the Naze. In spite of the throbbing exertions of the engines of the little paddle-boat, and the pouring foam that her wheels flung behind her, she receded with terrifying slowness from this ominous advance.

Glancing north-westward, my brother saw the large crescent of shipping already writhing with the approaching terror; one ship passing behind another, another coming round from broadside to end on, steamships whistling and giving off volumes of steam, sails being let out, launches rushing hither and thither. He was so fascinated by this and by the creeping danger away to the left that he had no eyes for anything seaward. And then a swift movement of the steamboat (she had suddenly come round to avoid being run down) flung him headlong from the seat upon which he was standing. There was a shouting all about him, a trampling of feet, and a cheer that seemed to be answered faintly. The steamboat lurched, and rolled him over upon his hands.

He sprang to his feet and saw to starboard, and not a hundred yards from their heeling, pitching boat, a vast iron bulk like the blade of a plough tearing through the water, tossing it on either side in huge waves of foam that leapt towards the steamer, flinging her paddles helplessly in the air, and then sucking her deck down almost to the water-line.

A douche of spray blinded my brother for a moment. When his eyes were clear again, he saw the monster had passed and was rushing landward. Big iron upper-works rose out of this headlong structure, and from that twin funnels projected, and spat a smoking blast shot with fire into the air. It was the torpedo-ram, *Thunder Child*, steaming headlong, coming to the rescue of the threatened shipping.[116]

Keeping his footing on the heavy deck by clutching the bulwarks, my brother looked past this charging leviathan at the Martians again, and he saw the three of them now close together, and standing so far out to sea that their tripod supports were almost entirely submerged. Thus sunken, and seen in remote perspective, they appeared far less formidable than the huge iron bulk in whose wake the steamer was pitching so helplessly. It would seem they were regarding this new antagonist with astonishment. To their intelligence, it may be, the giant was even such another as themselves. The *Thunder Child* fired no gun, but simply drove full speed towards them. It was probably her not firing that enabled her to get so near the enemy as she did. They did not know what to make of her. One shell, and they would have sent her to the bottom forthwith with the Heat-Ray.

She was steaming at such a pace that in a minute she seemed halfway between the steamboat and the Martians—a diminishing black bulk against the receding horizontal expanse of the Essex coast.

Suddenly the foremost Martian lowered his tube, and discharged a canister of the black gas at the ironclad. It hit her larboard side, and glanced off in an inky jet, that rolled away to seaward, an unfolding torrent of black smoke, from which the ironclad drove clear. To the watchers from the steamer, low in the water and with the sun in their eyes, it seemed as though she was already among the Martians.

They saw the gaunt figures separating and rising out of the water as they retreated shoreward, and one of them raised the camera-like generator of the Heat-Ray. He held it pointing obliquely downward, and a bank of steam sprang from the water at its touch. It must have driven through the iron of the ship's side like a white-hot iron rod through paper.

A flicker of flame went up through the rising steam, and then the Martian reeled and staggered. In another moment he was cut down,

---

116. The fictive *Thunder Child* is an advanced destroyer, the best in the Royal Navy, but it is no match for the Martian fighting machines of Bismarck-ian superiority in every military field. Its pretentious name, which means child of Thor the thunder god, is misprized; its vaunted ramming prow and directed torpedoes are yet another case of "bows and arrows against the lightning" (note 64) — the bolts and thunder of the *real* god of war, Thor's more powerful father, Mars himself. If war today be the essential for tomorrow's revolution, only the Martians are capable of waging it in that cause.

and a great body of water and steam shot high in the air. The guns of the *Thunder Child* sounded through the reek, going off one after the other, and one shot splashed the water high close by the steamer, ricocheted towards the other flying ships to the north, and smashed a smack to matchwood.

But no one heeded that very much. At the sight of the Martian's collapse, the captain on the bridge yelled inarticulately, and all the crowding passengers on the steamer's stern shouted together. And then they yelled again. For, surging out beyond the white tumult drove something long and black, the flames streaming from its middle parts, its ventilators and funnels spouting fire.

She was alive still; the steering gear, it seems, was intact and her engines working. She headed straight for a second Martian, and was within a hundred yards of him when the Heat-Ray came to bear. Then with a violent thud, a blinding flash, her decks, her funnels, leapt upward. The Martian staggered with the violence of her explosion, and in another moment the flaming wreckage, still driving forward with the impetus of its pace, had struck him and crumpled him up like a thing of cardboard. My brother shouted involuntarily. A boiling tumult of steam hid everything again.

"Two!" yelled the captain.

Everyone was shouting; the whole steamer from end to end rang with frantic cheering that was taken up first by one and then by all in the crowding multitude of ships and boats that was driving out to sea.

The steam hung upon the water for many minutes, hiding the third Martian and the coast altogether. And all this time the boat was paddling steadily out to sea and away from the fight; and when at last the confusion cleared, the drifting bank of black vapour intervened, and nothing of the *Thunder Cloud* could be made out, nor could the third Martian be seen. But the ironclads to seaward were now quite close, and standing in towards shore past the steamboat.

The little vessel continued to beat its way seaward, and the ironclads receded slowly towards the coast, which was hidden still by a marbled bank of vapour, part steam, part black gas, eddying and combining in the strangest ways. The fleet of refugees were scattering to the north-east; several smacks were sailing between the ironclads and the steamboat. After a time, and before they reached the sinking cloudbank, the warships turned northwards, and then abruptly went about and passed into the thickening haze of evening southward. The coast grew faint, and at last indistinguishable amidst the low banks of clouds that were gathering about the sinking sun.

Then suddenly out of the golden haze of the sunset came the vibration of guns, and a form of black shadows moving. Everyone struggled to the rail of the steamer and peered into the blinding furnace of the west, but nothing was to be distinguished clearly. A mass of smoke rose slantingly and barred the face of the sun. The steamboat throbbed on its way through an interminable suspense.

The sun sank into gray clouds, the sky flushed and darkened, the evening star trembled into sight. It was deep twilight when the captain cried out and pointed. My brother strained his eyes. Something rushed up into the sky out of the grayness, rushed slantingly upward and very swiftly into the luminous clearness above the clouds in the western sky, something flat and broad and very large, that swept round in a vast curve, grew smaller, sank slowly, and vanished again into the gray mystery of the night. And as it flew it rained down darkness upon the land.[117]

---

117. Martian airplanes, the gas-dropping bombers the artilleryman explains in II:7.

Book II.—The Earth Under the Martians.[118]

I

UNDER FOOT.

IN the first book I have wandered so much from my own adventures to tell of the experiences of my brother, that all through the last two chapters I and the curate have been lurking in the empty house at Halliford, whither we fled to escape the Black Smoke. There I will resume. We stopped there all Sunday night and all the next day—the day of the panic—in a little island of daylight, cut off by the Black Smoke from the rest of the world. We could do nothing but wait, in an aching inactivity, during those two weary days.

My mind was occupied by anxiety for my wife.[119] I figured her at Leatherhead, terrified, in danger, mourning me already as a dead man. I paced the rooms and cried aloud when I thought of how I was cut off from her, of all that might happen to her in my absence. My cousin I knew was brave enough for any emergency, but he was not the sort of man to realize danger quickly, to rise promptly. What was needed

---

118. Some critics complain this heading is misleading, since the Martians never get further than the Thames Valley. No so. The Martian imprint is global, leading on to a *New World Order* (1940a:title) realized in *Sleeper*.

119. The narrator (now resuming after recounting his brother's account) is hypocritical to a degree so flawed that his rotten character is no longer in doubt. He cares only for excitement and to report on it, and to hell with his wife. Only after the adventure is over does he piously embrace hearth and home. While his philosophical speculations align with Wells's, he is *not* Wells. The author takes this opportunity to contrast a hollow man with the fullness of his own ideas and reflective powers. It is the portrait of a pseudointellectual who mistakes self-serving interests for profundity. A searching analysis of just such a vacuous type is expanded in the comically titled *The Bulpington of Blup* (1932a).

now was not bravery, but circumspection. My only consolation was to believe that the Martians were moving Londonward and away from her. Such vague anxieties keep the mind sensitive and painful. I grew very weary and irritable with the curate's perpetual ejaculations, I tired of the sight of his selfish despair. After some ineffectual remonstrance I kept away from him, staying in a room containing globes, forms, and copy-books, that was evidently a children's schoolroom. When at last he followed me thither, I went to a box-room at the top of the house and locked myself in, in order to be alone with my aching miseries.

We were hopelessly hemmed in by the Black Smoke all that day, and the morning of the next. There were signs of people in the next house on Sunday evening—a face at a window and moving lights, and later the slamming of a door. But I do not know who these people were, nor what became of them. We saw nothing of them next day. The Black Smoke drifted slowly riverward all through Monday morning, creeping nearer and nearer to us, driving at last along the roadway outside the house that hid us.

A Martian came across the fields about midday, laying the stuff with a jet of superheated steam that hissed against the walls, smashed all the windows it touched, and scalded the curate's hand as he fled out of the front-room. When at last we crept across the sodden rooms and looked out again, the country northward was as though a black snow-storm had passed over it. Looking towards the river, we were astonished to see an unaccountable redness mingling with the black of the scorched meadows.[120]

For a time we did not see how this change affected our position, save that we were relieved of our fear of the Black Smoke. But later I perceived that we were no longer hemmed in, that now we might get away. So soon as I realized the way of escape was open, my dream of action returned. But the curate was lethargic, unreasonable.

"We are safe here," he repeated—"safe here."

I resolved to leave him—would that I had! Wiser now for the artilleryman's teaching, I sought out food and drink. I had found oil and rags for my burns, and I also took a hat and a flannel shirt that I found in one of the bedrooms. When it was clear to him that I meant to go

---

120. Not bloody corpses floating in the river as the narrator supposes. What he sees is the Red Weed, spawned by botanical spores carried by chance in the Martian cylinders from the home planet. Later, the Red Weed is seen to shrivel up, unadapted to terrestrial ecology, foreshadowing the death of the Martians themselves.

alone, had reconciled myself to going alone, he suddenly roused himself to come. And, all being quiet throughout the afternoon, we started, as I should judge, about five along the blackened road to Sunbury.

In Sunbury, and at intervals along the road, were dead bodies lying in contorted attitudes—horses as well as men—overturned carts and luggage, all covered thickly with black dust. That pall of cindery powder made me think of what I had read of the destruction of Pompeii.[121] We got to Hampton Court without misadventure, our minds full of strange and unfamiliar appearances, and at Hampton Court our eyes were relieved to find a patch of green that had escaped the suffocating drift. We went through Bushey Park, with its deer going to and fro under the chestnuts, and some men and women hurrying in the distance towards Hampton, and so came to Twickenham. These were the first people we saw.

Away across the road the woods beyond Ham and Petersham were still afire. Twickenham was uninjured by either Heat-Ray or Black Smoke, and there were more people about here, though none could give us news. For the most part, they were like ourselves, taking advantage of a lull to shift their quarters. I have an impression that many of the houses here were still occupied by scared inhabitants, too frightened even for flight. Here, too, the evidence of a hasty rout was abundant along the road. I remember most vividly three smashed bicycles in a heap, pounded into the road by the wheels of subsequent carts. We crossed Richmond Bridge about half-past eight. We hurried across the exposed bridge, of course, but I noticed floating down the stream a number of red masses, some many feet across. I did not know what these were—there was no time for scrutiny—and I put a more horrible interpretation on them than they deserved. Here, again, on the Surrey side, was black dust that had once been smoke, and dead bodies—a heap near the approach to the station—and never a sight of the Martians until we were some way toward Barnes.

We saw in the blackened distance a group of three people running down a side-street towards the river, but otherwise it seemed deserted. Up the hill Richmond town was burning briskly; outside the town of Richmond there was no trace of the Black Smoke.

---

121. This great pleasure city of the Roman Empire was buried under volcanic ash, in A.D. 79, by an eruption of Mount Vesuvius which killed all the inhabitants. The narrator thinks of Black Smoke in the same light, but has no idea that it may be suffocating the same useless lives of the sort he himself hangs on to.

Then suddenly, as we approached Kew, came a number of people running, and the upper-works of a Martian Fighting Machine loomed in sight over the housetops, not a hundred yards away from us. We stood aghast at our danger, and had he looked down we must immediately have perished. We were so terrified that we dared not go on, but turned aside and hid in a shed in a garden. There the curate crouched, weeping silently, and refusing to stir again.

But my fixed idea of reaching Leatherhead would not let me rest, and in the twilight I ventured out again. I went through a shrubbery, and along a passage beside a big house standing in its own grounds, and so emerged upon the road towards Kew. The curate I left in the shed, but he came hurrying after me.

That second start was the most foolhardy thing I ever did. For it was manifest the Martians were about us. Scarcely had he overtaken me than we saw either the Fighting Machine we had seen before or another, far away across the meadows in the direction of Kew Lodge. Four or five little black figures hurried before it across the green-gray of the field, and in a moment it was evident this Martian pursued them. In three strides he was among them, and they ran radiating from his feet in all directions. He used no Heat-Ray to destroy them, but picked them up one by one. Apparently he tossed them into the great metallic carrier which projected behind him, much as a workman's basket hangs over his shoulder.

It was the first time I realized the Martians might have any other purpose than destruction with defeated humanity. We stood for a moment petrified, then turned and fled through a gate behind us into a walled garden, fell into rather than found a fortunate ditch, and lay there, scarce daring to whisper to one another until the stars were out.

I suppose it was nearly eleven at night before we gathered courage to start again, no longer venturing into the road, but sneaking along hedgerows and through plantations, and watching keenly through the darkness, he on the right and I on the left, for the Martians, who seemed to be all about us. In one place we blundered upon a scorched and blackened area, now cooling and ashen, and a number of scattered dead bodies of men, burnt horribly about the heads and bodies, but with their legs and boots mostly intact; and of dead horses, fifty feet, perhaps, behind a line of four ripped guns and smashed gun-carriages.

Sheen, it seemed, had escaped destruction, but the place was silent and deserted. Here we happened upon no dead, though the night was too dark for us to see into the side-roads of the place. In Sheen my companion suddenly complained of faintness and thirst, and we decided to try one of the houses.

The first house we entered, after a little difficulty with the window, was a small semi-detached villa,[122] and I found nothing eatable left in the place but some mouldy cheese. There was, however, water to drink, and I took a hatchet, which promised to be useful in our next house-breaking.

We crossed the road to a place where the road turns towards Mortlake. Here there stood a white house within a walled garden, and in the pantry of this we found a store of food—two loaves of bread in a pan, an uncooked steak, and the half of a ham. I give this catalogue so precisely because, as it happened, we were destined to subsist upon this store for the next fortnight. Bottled beer stood under a shelf, and there were two bags of haricot beans and some limp lettuces. This pantry opened into a kind of wash-up kitchen, and in this was firewood, and a cupboard in which we found nearly a dozen of burgundy, tinned soups and salmon, and two tins of biscuits.

We sat in the adjacent kitchen in the dark—for we dared not strike a light—and ate bread and ham and drank beer out of one bottle.[123] The curate, who was still timorous and restless, was now oddly enough for pushing on, and I was urging him to keep up his strength by eating, when the thing that was to imprison us happened.

"It can't be midnight yet," I said, and then came a blinding glare of vivid green light. Everything in the kitchen leapt out, clearly visible in green and black, and then vanished again. And then followed such a concussion as I have never heard before or since. So close on the heels of this as to seem instantaneous, came a thud behind me, a clash of glass, a crash and rattle of falling masonry all about us, and incon-

---

122. A villa, in British diction, is a suburban house maintained by the wealthy either as a permanent dwelling or as a seasonal retreat. The one here is on the outskirts of greater London; in II:2, it is the "Ruined House" of the chapter title. The Martians, in their advance on London, leave behind a trail of blasted villas, in their spirited destruction, not ungenial to the author, of bourgeois real estate.

123. Not unlike the camaraderie enjoyed by the narrator and the artilleryman in I:11 when they first meet; but later (in II:7), they fall out. But this is less aggravative than the narrator's murder of the tiresome curate in II:4. The narrator is too selfish to get along with or tolerate anybody else in his feverish, single-minded purpose to report on the war. It is a characterological flaw the author takes pains to emphasize, distinguishing himself from a man who is Wells-like only in sharing a measure of his philosophical viewpoint (note 119).

tinently the plaster of the ceiling came down upon us, smashing into a multitude of fragments upon our heads. I was knocked headlong across the floor against the oven handle and stunned. I was insensible for a long time, the curate told me, and when I came to we were in darkness again, and he, with a face wet as I found afterwards with blood from a cut forehead, was dabbing water over me.

For some time I could not recollect what had happened. Then things came to me slowly. A bruise on my temple asserted itself.

"Are you better?" asked the curate, in a whisper.

At last I answered him. I sat up.

"Don't move," he said. "The floor is covered with smashed crockery from the dresser. You can't possibly move without making a noise, and I fancy *they* are outside."

We both sat quite silent, so that we could scarcely hear one another breathing. Everything seemed deadly still, though once something near us, some plaster or broken brickword, slid down with a rumbling sound. Outside and very near was an intermittent, metallic rattle.

"That!" said the curate, when presently it happened again.

"Yes," I said. "But what is it?"

"A Martian!" said the curate.

I listened again.

"It was not like the Heat-Ray," I said, and for a time I was inclined to think one of the great Fighting Machines had stumbled against the house, as I had seen one stumble against the tower of Shepperton Church.

Our situation was so strange and incomprehensible that for three or four hours, until the dawn came, we scarcely moved. And then the light filtered in, not through a window, which remained black, but through a triangular aperture between a beam and a heap of broken bricks in the wall behind us. The interior of the kitchen we now saw grayly for the first time.

The window had been burst in by a mass of garden mould, which flowed over the table upon which we had been sitting and lay about our feet. Outside the soil was banked high against the house. At the top of the window-frame we could see an uprooted drain-pipe. The floor was littered with smashed hardware; the end of the kitchen towards the house was broken into, and since the daylight shone in there it was evident the greater part of the house had collapsed. Contrasting vividly with this ruin was the neat dresser, stained in the fashion, pale green, and with a number of copper and tin vessels below it, the wall-paper imitating blue and white tiles, and a couple of coloured supplements fluttering from the walls above the kitchen range.[124]

As the dawn grew clearer, we saw through the gap in the wall the body of a Martian standing sentinel, I suppose, over the still glowing cylinder. At the sight of that we crawled as circumspectly as possible out of the twilight of the kitchen into the darkness of the scullery.

Abruptly the right interpretation of the things dawned upon my mind.

"The fifth cylinder," I whispered, "the fifth shot from Mars, has struck this house and buried us under the ruins!"[125]

---

124. For all the luxury shown by the house, there are, "contrasting vividly," those "coloured supplements fluttering from the walls." These are reproductions of art work or historical scenes included in Sunday newspapers, popular with readers unable to afford framed pictures. They flutter in the breeze admitted by the dwelling's partial ruination. But what is it in this telling sight that contrasts so "vividly"? There is an indictment here of the owner that Wells means to convey, one perhaps too sophisticated for the narrator to formulate.

In a journalistic interview promoting *Sleeper*, Wells explains that the novel bears on his prophecy: "What seems to be inevitable in the future is rule by an aristocracy of organisers, men who manage railroads and similar vast enterprises" (1899a:220). Such is the rule, elsewhere "a vast business octopus" (1933:289), achieved by the novel's capitalist world-state. Its "aristocracy of organisers" at last triumphs over the old landed aristocracy that had for so long retarded industrial progress. "I have written of England as a feudal scheme overtaken by fatty degeneration" (1909:488). What is needed is "a constructive aristocracy" (1911: 398). "We must have an aristocracy — not of privilege — but of understanding and purpose — or mankind will fail" (334). Part and parcel of it, in *Sleeper*, is the formerly middle- and upper-bourgeois, now declassed and assimilated to the directive purposes of big-business government, the Modern State Octopus.

In the ruined villa, the owner's inclinations have gone in the opposite direction, against world-historical trends, towards democratic sentimentality in his favoring of popular taste belonging to the petty bourgeois and other lower classes. He rather belongs to yet another failed elite, deserving of destruction by the Martians, harbingers of a new order.

Are Sunday supplements in the wrong place worth doom-saying? As a habitual crisis-monger, for which only he had medicine strong enough to work as a cure-all, Wells found *everything* in the present filthy order a target of his "destructive criticism" (1925:266). As "the voice of cosmic calamity" (1911:17), he is credentialed to say, "My other name is Noah" (1944:86).

125. Only at this point does the narrator realize that the house has been hit (near miss) by the fifth Martian cylinder, after he and the curate sought

For a space the curate was silent, and then he whispered:
"God have mercy upon us!"
I heard him presently whimpering to himself.
Save for that sound we lay quite still in the scullery. I for my part scarce dared breathe, and sat with my eyes fixed on the faint light of the kitchen door. I could just see the curate's face, a dim oval shape, and his collar and cuffs. Outside there began a metallic hammering, and then a violent hooting, and then, after a quiet interval, a hissing, like the hissing of an engine. These noises, for the most part problematical, continued intermittently, and seemed, if anything, to increase in number as the time wore on. Presently a measured thudding, and a vibration that made everything about us quiver and the vessels in the pantry ring and shift, began and continued. Once the light was eclipsed, and the ghostly kitchen doorway became absolutely

---

refuge in it. Then its damage was no more than a gap where looters had broken in; now it is half buried and further ruinated by the crater thrown up by the cylinder's landing. At first the narrator thinks the concussion was caused by a passing Martian fighting machine banging against the house, one of those laying down Black Smoke from which he and the curate were fleeing. But when he hears the noise of machinery outside, it suddenly sinks in that the midnight concussion, heard in the paragraph following note 123, is more ominous. It is a slow realization, given that the shock was accompanied by a "vivid green light," the same associated with the falling green meteors observed at note 88. All the same, the narrator is now given the opportunity, in the next chapter, to study the Martians close up. His curiosity is stronger than the fear driving the curate hysterical.

The camaraderie of the shared beer bottle at note 123 is now broken. In the event, the narrator who at first had a like fellow-feeling for the artilleryman, in I:11, becomes disaffected with him in II:7, although not to the point of murder. The narrator is nobody's comrade, always pursuing a selfish interest, even if it be admirable scientific curiosity in the next chapter. At first he was in some theological harmony with the curate (the Martians as avenging angels, note 71), only to break with that, then to disagree with the artilleryman's plan to fight the Martians with their own weapons, with a view to a select few human elites working vengeance on the rest of the degenerate lot, to make for a new Martianized order. The narrator is a complex character, whose faults only highlight the Wellsian lesson to be learned from the invasion. Never fully understood by the narrator, a half-baked philosophical version of Wells, he returns home a confirmed everydayist. The adventure over, hearth and home are all that matters, while wiser heads determine the Martian impact and build the Wellsian world-state in *Sleeper*, the novel's sequel.

dark. For many hours we must have crouched there, silent and shivering, until our tired attention failed....

At last I found myself awake and very hungry. I am inclined to believe we must have been the greater portion of a day before that awakening. My hunger was at a stride so insistent that it moved me to action. I told him I was going to seek food, and felt my way towards the pantry. He made me no answer, but so soon as I began eating, the faint noise I made stirred him to action, and I heard him crawling after me.

II

WHAT WE SAW FROM THE RUINED HOUSE.

AFTER eating we crept back to the scullery, and there I must have dozed again, for when presently I stirred I was alone. The thudding vibration continued with wearisome persistence. I whispered for the curate several times, and at last felt my way to the door of the kitchen. It was still daylight, and I perceived him across the room, lying against the triangular hole that looked out upon the Martians. His shoulders were hunched, so that his head was hidden from me.

I could hear a number of noises, almost like those of an engine-shed, and the place rocked with that beating thud. Through the aperture in the wall I could see the top of a tree touched with gold, and the warm blue of a tranquil evening sky. For a minute or so I remained watching the curate, and then I advanced, crouching and stepping with extreme care amidst the broken crockery that littered the floor.

I touched the curate's leg, and he started so violently that a mass of plaster went sliding down outside and fell with a loud impact. I gripped his arm, fearing he might cry out, and for a long time we crouched motionless. Then I turned to see how much of our rampart remained. The detachment of the plaster had left a vertical slit open in the débris, and by raising myself cautiously across a beam I was able to see out of this gap into what had been overnight a quiet suburban roadway. Vast indeed was the change that we beheld.

The fifth cylinder must have fallen right into the midst of the house we had first visited. The building had vanished, completely smashed, pulverized and dispersed by the blow. The cylinder lay now far beneath the original foundations, deep in a hole, already vastly larger than the pit I had looked into at Woking. The earth all round it had splashed under that tremendous impact—"splashed" is the only word—and lay in heaped piles that hid the masses of the adjacent houses. It had behaved exactly like mud under the violent blow of a hammer. Our house had collapsed backwards; the front portion, even on the ground-floor, had been destroyed completely; by a chance, the kitchen and scullery had escaped, and stood buried now under soil and ruins, closed in by tons of earth on every side, save towards the cylinder. Over that aspect we hung now on the very verge of the great circular pit the Martians were engaged in making. The heavy beating sound was evidently just behind us, and ever and again a bright green vapour[126] drove up like a veil across our peephole.

The cylinder was already opened in the centre of the pit, and on the further edge of the pit, amidst the smashed and gravel-heaped shrubbery, one of the great Fighting Machines stood, deserted by its occupant, stiff and tall against the evening sky. At first I scarcely noticed the pit or the cylinder, although it has been convenient to describe them first, on account of the extraordinary glittering mechanism I saw, busy in the excavation, and on account of the strange creatures that were crawling slowly and painfully across the heaped mould near it.

The mechanism it certainly was held my attention first. It was one of those complicated fabrics that have since been called Handling Machines, and the study of which has already given such an enormous impetus to terrestrial invention.[127] As it dawned upon me first it presented a sort of metallic spider with five jointed, agile legs, and with an extraordinary number of jointed levers, bars, and reaching and clutching tentacles about its body. Most of its arms were retracted, but with three long tentacles it was fishing out a number of rods, plates and bars which lined the covering of, and apparently strengthened the walls of, the cylinder. These, as it extracted them, were lifted out and deposited upon a level surface of earth behind it.

Its motion was so swift, complex and perfect that at first I did not see it as a machine, in spite of its metallic glitter. The Fighting Machines were co-ordinated and animated to an extraordinary pitch, but nothing to compare with this. People who have never seen these structures, and have only the ill-imagined efforts of artists or the imperfect

---

126. This "green vapour," as a symbolic color, is hard to ignore if it be more than an incidental detail (note 88).

127. These Handling Machines are robotic, one of those technological advances the narrator in the Epilogue says did much to improve human technology once learned from; although he fails to see how much they would impact the successor world in *Sleeper*— a future he cares nothing for.

descriptions of such eye-witnesses as myself to go upon, scarcely realize that living quality.

I recall particularly the illustration of one of the first pamphlets to give a consecutive account of the war. The artist had evidently made a hasty study of one of the Fighting Machines, and there his knowledge ended. He presented them as tilted, stiff tripods, without either flexibility or subtlety, and with an altogether misleading monotony of effect.[128] The pamphlet containing these renderings had a considerable vogue, and I mention them here simply to warn the reader against the impression they may have created. They were no more like the Martians I saw in action than a Dutch doll is like a human being. To my mind, the pamphlet would have been much better without them.

At first, I say, the Handling Machine did not impress me as a a a machine, but as a crab-like creature with a glittering integument, the controlling Martian, whose delicate tentacles actuated its movements, seeming to be simply the equivalent of the crab's cerebral portion. But then I perceived the resemblance of its gray-brown, shiny, leathery integument to that of the other sprawling bodies beyond, and the true nature of this dexterous workman dawned upon me. With that realization my interest shifted to those other creatures, the real Martians. Already I had had a transient impression of these, and the first nausea no longer obscured my observation. Moreover, I was concealed and motionless, and under no urgency of action.

They were, I now saw, the most unearthly creatures it is possible to conceive. They were huge round bodies—or, rather, heads—about four feet in diameter, each body having in front of it a face. This face had no nostrils—indeed, the Martians do not seem to have had any sense of smell—but it had a pair of very large, dark-coloured eyes, and just beneath this a kind of fleshy beak. In the back of this head or body— I scarcely know how to speak of it—was the single tight tympanic surface, since known to be anatomically an ear, though it must have been almost useless in our denser air. In a group round the mouth were sixteen slender, almost whip-like tentacles, arranged in two bunches of

---

128. The reference here is to the awkward drawings of Warwick Goble in the 1897 serial version of *Worlds*, showing the Martians marching about on tripod legs rigid as erector-set girders. See fig. 9, which probably illustrates a line in I:10, "A monstrous tripod, higher than many houses, striding over the young pinetrees, and smashing them aside in its career." Wells later came to prefer the drawings of the Belgian artist Johan Briedé (dated 1916), which he showcased in a condensation of the novel (1920a) special to their display.

eight each. These bunches have since been named rather aptly, by that distinguished anatomist Professor Howes, the *hands*. Even as I saw these Martians for the first time they seemed to be endeavouring to raise themselves on these hands, but of course, with the increased weight of terrestrial conditions, this was impossible. There is reason to suppose that on Mars they may have progressed upon them with some facility.

The internal anatomy, I may remark here, dissection has since shown,[129] was almost equally simple. The greater part of the structure was the brain, sending enormous nerves to the eyes, ear and tactile tentacles. Besides this were the complex lungs, into which the mouth opened, and the heart and its vessels. The pulmonary distress caused by the denser atmosphere and greater gravitational attraction was only too evident in the convulsive movements of the outer skin.

And this was the sum of the Martian organs. Strange as it may seem to a human being, all the complex apparatus of digestion, which makes up the bulk of our bodies, did not exist in the Martians. They were heads, merely heads. Entrails they had none. They did not eat, much less digest. Instead, they took the fresh living blood of other creatures, and *injected* it into their own veins.[130] I have myself seen this being done, as I shall mention in its place. But, squeamish as I may seem, I cannot bring myself to describe what I could not endure even to continue watching. Let it suffice, blood obtained from a still living animal, in most cases from a human being, was run directly by means of a little pipette into the recipient canal....

The bare idea of this is no doubt horribly repulsive to us, but at the same time I think that we should remember how repulsive our carnivorous habits would seem to an intelligent rabbit.[131]

---

129. The narrator reflects on postmortems done on the Martians (see Epilogue).

130. No digestive organs — the Martians are Metchnikoffed (see the Introduction to the present work, section 5). In place of removed colons for the digestion of solid food, they take blood directly into their veins, vampire style.

131. Here follows a significant passage excised from the serial version.

Let it suffice, blood obtained from a still living animal, was run directly, by means of a little pipette, into the recipient vessel.

The bare idea of this is no doubt horribly repulsive to us, but at the same time I think we should remember how repulsive our carnivorous habits would seem to an intelligent rabbit. I know it is the fashion to write of these Martians as being incredibly cruel, but for my own part I cannot see that we are justified in calling ourselves, as certain flatterers of humanity have called men, their moral superiors.

The physiological advantages of the practice of injection are undeniable, if one thinks of the tremendous waste of human time and
energy occasioned by eating and the digestive process. Our bodies are
half made up of glands and tubes and organs, occupied in turning het-
erogeneous food into blood. The digestive processes and their reaction upon the nervous system sap our strength, colour our minds. Men
go happy or miserable as they have healthy or unhealthy livers, or
sound gastric glands. But the Martians were lifted above all these
organic fluctuations of mood and emotion.

Their undeniable preference for men as their source of nourishment
is partly explained by the nature of the remains of the victims they had
brought with them as provisions from Mars. These creatures, to judge
from the shrivelled remains that have fallen into human hands, were
bipeds, with flimsy siliceous skeletons (almost like those of the
siliceous sponges) and feeble musculature, standing about six feet

---

> The fact that in the pit at Wimbledon (the pit made by the tenth cylinder) the still
> living body of an eminent physician was seen fixed so that he could not move and
> horribly mutilated does not seem to me to carry the point. Let us clear our minds
> of cant. We are not justified in supposing that the Martians had been amusing
> themselves by torturing him. All the circumstances point to the view that they were
> satisfying their curiosity upon some structural point, and that afterward, through
> interruption or inadvertency, they omitted to put him out of his misery [1897c:XXIII:
> 6 (Oct.):610].

The narrator, in defense of the Martians, claims they are not the "incredibly cruel" monsters public opinion makes them out to be. They are rather motivated by high-minded scientific curiosity, in their study of human anatomy,
when cutting up live specimens without benefit of anesthesia (vivisection). The
charge of cruelty is misapplied in the one case where a subject was, by some
"inadvertency," not mercifully "put ... out of his misery" after the dissection
had been completed. This casts a new light on Doctor Moreau, the mad scientist and cruel vivisectionist of critical opinion, who may, after all, not be that
(see Stover 1999b). Indeed, the Martians credit just such a heroic scientist as the
father of their own superior being, transformed out of inferior animal raw material very like humans (see at note 137).

The reason Wells cut this passage from the book version is probably aes-
thetic. He did not wish to give away too much, if he were to keep with the novel's
deepest artistic ambiguity: the sanitary Martians' death from the insanitary planet
they had aimed to remodel along home lines (see note 132). Even the best of
utopias has its uncalculated nemesis. Wells may also have considered the fact
that the narrator's reference to a "tenth cylinder" is three too many. On the other
hand, his miscounting of the seven actual landings would be consistent with his
unreliability on so many other points.

high, and having round erect heads, and large eyes in flinty sockets.[132] Two or three of these seem to have been brought in each cylinder, and all were killed before earth was reached. It was just as well for them, for the mere attempt to stand upright upon our planet would have broken every bone in their bodies.[133]

And while I am engaged in this description, I may add in this place certain further details, which, although they were not all evident to us at the time, will enable the reader who is unacquainted with them to form a clearer picture of these offensive creatures.

In three other points their physiology differed strangely from ours. Their organisms did not sleep, any more than the heart of man sleeps. Since they had no extensive muscular mechanism to recuperate, that periodical extinction was unknown to them. They had little or no sense of fatigue, it would seem. On earth they can never have moved without effort, yet even to the last they kept in action. In twenty-four hours they did twenty-four hours of work, as even on earth is perhaps the case with the ants.[134]

In the next place, wonderful as it seems in a sexual world, the

---

132. These Martian bipeds are like enough to humans for the latter to supply the more evolved octopoidal Martians with their usual vampiric nourishment. This is possible because, as the narrator suggests at note 137, the advanced Martians are descended from humanoid ancestors, not unlike ourselves, by way of artificial evolution. It is the same process Doctor Moreau experimented with in his attempt to make "Beast Men" out of animals, experiments that are paradigmatic for the transformation of the "man beast" into a more rational "Beyond-Man" (Stover 1999b:32). But while the good doctor's work fails it is not lost on Mars, where it succeeds.

133. The fragile "siliceous skeletons" of the Martian humanoids posit "Another Basis of Life" (1894a): not carbon but silicon. The two elements are related to each other on the periodic table, C = no. 6 just above Si = no. 14. Both elements have four valence electrons each, which means in theory they can form similar compounds belonging to organic chemistry. Wells's speculation is that Si may be substituted for C as the chemical basis for living organisms, and supposes this to be the case on Mars — an imaginative idea that has been picked up by modern science-fiction writers in their quest for alien life forms, made all the more alien by their exotic chemistry. But this neat theory has not been demonstrated in the laboratory. Nor has it been confirmed in a study of what appear to be fossilized bacteria in a meteoric rock blasted from Mars (Goldsmith 1998), a sensational discovery of recent years. All the same, Wells prepares the reader for additional weirdness in the Martians' favoring of the green part of the visual spectrum over the yellow in human perception (note 143).

134. In utopian literature, the noble termitary is a recurring model of civic

Martians were absolutely without sex, and therefore without any of the tumultuous emotions that arise from that difference among men. A young Martian, there can now be no dispute, was really born upon earth during the war, and it was found attached to its parent, partially *budded* off, just as young lily bulbs bud off, or the young animals in the fresh-water polyp.[135]

In man, in all the higher terrestrial animals, such a method of increase has disappeared; but even on this earth it was certainly the primitive method. Among the lower animals, up even to those first cousins of the vertebrated animals, the Tunicates,[136] the two processes

---

virtue: the ants as heroes of discipline and untiring work under collective obedience. Wells holds to the same tradition when he says, man as yet "has attained nothing of the frictionless fitting to the needs of association one finds in the bee or the ant" (1912a:7). But it is possible, "I do not regard the organisation of all mankind into one terrestrial ant-hill ... as a Utopian dream, as something that fantastically might be. I regard it as the necessary, the only possible continuation of human history: (1926:549). It's Utopia or oblivion, ant-hill or unending "war and senseless competition" (film shot 725 in 1936). Such is the miniature world-state of the insect-like Selenites in *The First Men in the Moon* (see Stover 1998b:16–23). At all events the ant-like Martians, if not insect-men, are good Saint-Simonian workers: "All men shall work," and do nothing else.

135. That the Martians breed asexually is consistent with their transcendental "suppression of the animal side of the organism by the intelligence"; the lack of reproductive and digestive organs alike allows them to rise untroubled above "the emotional substratum of the human being" (lines within paragraph at note 138). Their method of reproduction, budding, is rather like that of polyps, which live together collectively in colonies (Wells 1892). This harmonious polyp socialism is finally achieved by man, in *The Shape of Things to Come*, "entirely against his natural disposition.... [T]he whole race is now confluent; it is becoming as much a colonial organism as any branching coral or polyp" (1933:428). Man's "animal individualism" (334) is at last suppressed. Such, in a change of metaphor, is the goal of the Modern State Octopus. It began with the Dictatorship of the Airmen with the metaphor at note 134 in mind: "Earth became an ant-hill under their dominion clean and orderly" (360).

136. The Tunicates (discussed in Wells 1891) are Sea Squirts, belonging to the Urchordata, a subphylum of chordata or "vertebrate animals [to which they are] first cousins." The point is, even at this higher stage of evolution, "the two processes [budding and sexual reproduction] occur side by side." Therefore it is conceivable that the octopoidal Martians, descended from vertebrates (the bipedal humanoids) might revert to the asexual method of the *tunicata*. Or such is the scientific patter Wells indulges to justify the observation made at note 134.

occur side by side, but finally the sexual method superseded its competitor altogether. On Mars, however, just the reverse has apparently been the case.

It is worthy of remark that a certain speculative writer of quasi-scientific repute, writing long before the Martian invasion, did forecast for man a final structure not unlike the actual Martian condition. His prophecy, I remember, appeared in November or December, 1893, in a long defunct publication, the *Pall Mall Budget*, and I recall a caricature of it in a pre–Martian periodical called *Punch*.[137] He pointed out— writing in a foolish facetious tone—that the perfection of mechanical appliances must ultimately supersede limbs, the perfection of chemical

---

Darwin, after all had arrived at his theory of natural selection by considering the practice of *artificial* selection, conducted under human agency by design (not chance) for the breeding of barnyard animals, fancy pigeons, and ornamental flowers. No doubt the humanoid Martians transformed themselves the same way, selecting for the dominance of brain and "hands" (tentacles), while leaving in reserve a relict population of ancestors as a source of blood for their new bodies absent less useful digestive organs; not to say absent equally emotion-roiling sex organs.

137. References to "The Man of the Year Million" in a November 1893 issue of the *Pall Mall Budget*, and to a satire on it in *Punch*, both of which are reprinted in Appendix I of the present work. Wells distances himself as author of the former item by having the narrator, who so closely identifies with it, refer to him as a "writer of quasi-scientific repute," far from his own self-estimate. He takes pains to remove the narrator from being a projection of auctorial viewpoint: The narrator is a despicable Panglossian, Wells is not (note 71).

All the same, those fond of biographical criticism like to say that the narrator *is* Wells, especially with reference to the passage at note 47. There the narrator recalls "my schoolboy dreams of battle and heroism" as a rationale for his feverish appetite to go adventuring on a course of war reporting. To be sure, Wells in his autobiography says he had similar boyhood reveries; "I used to fight battles whenever I went for a walk alone" (1934:74). And he went on to fight these in a children's book of imaginative games, *Little Wars* (1913). The first book in the *Kriegspiel* genre, it has become a costly collector's item, far surpassing in value even *Worlds* in the rare book market. But every author draws upon his own life, fractionating it for his various characters, and Wells is no exception. This does not mean, however, that the narrator expresses the all of Wells's persona. The author *uses* the narrator to voice a point of view that stands in ironical contrast to his own more elevated reflection on the novel's events — of more tremendous significance than anything conceived in the narrator's philosophy.

devices, digestion—that such organs as hair, external nose, teeth, ears, chin, were no longer essential parts of the human being, and that the tendency of natural selection would lie in the direction of their steady diminution through the coming ages. The brain alone remained a cardinal necessity. Only one other part of the body had a strong case for survival, and that was the hand, "teacher and agent of the brain." While the rest of the body dwindled, the hands would grow larger.

There is many a true word written in jest, and here in the Martians we have beyond dispute the actual accomplishment of such a suppression of the animal side of the organism by the intelligence. To me it is quite credible that the Martians may be descended from beings not unlike ourselves,[138] by a gradual development of brain and hands (the latter giving rise to the two bunches of delicate tentacles at last) at the expense of the rest of the body. Without the body the brain would of course become a mere selfish intelligence, without any of the emotional substratum of the human being.[139]

---

138. This affirms the narrator's hypothesis, at notes 132 and 134, that the Martians are products of artificial selection, whose raw material for a higher development is not unlike incompletely formed human beings — a terrestrial race not yet living up to its creative potential, not yet Martianized. In the same year *The Island of Doctor Moreau* was published, Wells had an article, "Human Evolution, an Artificial Process" (1896b), in which he explains what the novel's title figure is up to: directed evolution towards perfection of man's more rational faculties (see Stover 1996a).

139. Parrinder (1981:50) suggests that the "selfish intelligence" of the Martians = the narrator's "basic selfishness" and that this equation points up a splendid irony of some indefinable sort. Presumably his war-loving enthusiasm to cover the invasion at the cost of family loyalty is a self-centered match for Martian cruelty, which at note 131 he justifies out of self-serving motives. But while his ethical faults are evident enough, the narrator rather contrasts with the Martians' moral superiority; they are creatures of pure reason, exemplars of Kant's categorical imperative — a more subtle interpretation developed in II:7 at note 145. This chapter is the novel's climax. It accommodates a view held by the Kantian philosopher Kurd Lusswitz, whose own novel of Martian invasion Wells drew upon for this crucial chapter.

Meanwhile, suffice it to say that the phrase "selfish intelligence" is a special usage. Wells, a master of the language, takes the adjective selfish in that unusual way, defined in the *Oxford English Dictionary* as pertaining to or connected with oneself or itself. In this case the "it" is Martian mentality. Their brains, no longer victimized by emotions arising in digestive and sexual organs, are free to exercise Kantian pure reason. They are liberated from the mind/body

The last salient point in which the systems of these creatures differed from ours was in what one might have thought a very trivial particular. Micro-organisms, which cause so much disease and pain on earth, have either never appeared upon Mars, or Martian sanitary science eliminated them ages ago.[140] A hundred diseases, all the fevers and contagions of human life, consumption, cancers, tumours, and such morbidities, never enter the scheme of their life. And speaking of the differences between the life on Mars and terrestrial life, I may allude here to the curious suggestions of the Red Weed.[141]

Apparently the vegetable kingdom in Mars, instead of having green for a dominant colour, is of a vivid blood-red tint. At any rate, the seeds which the Martians (intentionally or accidentally) brought with them gave rise in all cases to red-coloured growths. Only that known popularly as the Red Weed, however, gained any footing in competition with terrestrial forms. The Red Creeper was quite a transitory growth, and few people have seen it growing. For a time, however, the Red Weed grew with astonishing vigour and luxuriance. It spread up the sides of the pit by the third or fourth day of our imprisonment, and its cactus-like branches formed a carmine fringe to the edges of our triangular window. And afterwards I found it broadcast throughout the country, and especially wherever there was a stream of water.[142]

---

dualism that afflicts the fallen estate of sublunary humans. Body evil, mind divine. Separation of the two, in favor of the latter, is the object of Doctor Moreau's experiments in his House of Pain. Always the beast flesh creeps back. "But I will conquer yet. Each time I dip a living creature into the bath of pain, I say, This time I will burn out all the animal, this time I will make a rational creature of my own" (see explication in Stover 1996b:120). Where Doctor Moreau fails, Martian vivisectionists have succeeded. Result: "a suppression of the animal side of the organism by the intelligence" (note 135). *That* is the meaning of their "selfish intelligence," relating only to itself and disconnected from mind-messing-up bodily functions.

140. This remark on "Martian sanitary science" foreshadows the invaders' doom felled by the dirty germs of earth. See more, at note 177, on the ironic implications of their fate.

141. The Red Weed, a river-choking blight spread to earth from spores inadvertently carried in the Martian cylinders, is later observed by the narrator to die out: a premonition of death to come for the Martians themselves. They, too, are ill adapted to terrestrial micro-organisms.

142. The Red Creeper, being "quite a transitory growth," is even more premonitory. These red plants, however, do not derive from the canal-irrigated deserts in Lowell (1896), otherwise a source, but from an earlier book, *Popular*

The Martians had what appears to have been an auditory organ, a single round drum at the back of the head-body, and eyes with a visual range not very different from ours, except that, according to Philips, blue and violet were as black to them.[143] It is commonly supposed that

---

Astronomy, by the very popular French astronomer Camille Flammarion (1894). His chapter on Mars describes the planet's dark areas as oceans and its red areas as vegetation of the same color. That Wells was familiar with Flammarion is evident from his reliance on this source for his idea of industrialized underground lunar life in *The First Men in the Moon* (see Stover 1998b: Appendix V).

143. The name Philips is yet another fiction, giving the narrator a semblance of authority in his all-knowing name dropping. In this he is verily another Dr. Pangloss (note 71), a faker whose own name derives from the Greek for "All-tongue." All the same, his observation on the Martian visual spectrum is meaningful: "blue and violet were as black to them." This returns us to the question of greenness raised at note 55, which now deserves further probing.

Ultraviolet light was discovered by the German chemist Johann Ritter in 1801, when it registered black on photoemulsions, radiation "beyond the violet" invisible to human eyes (Asimov 1972:248f). On this basis Wells makes it clear that the Martian visual range is not shifted with respect to the human visual range, only that it does not include the higher frequency colors (anything beyond green: blue and violet). Otherwise the common frequencies between the two species are perceived as the same colors, as indicated in the table below.

Visual Spectrum

INFRARED— below both Martian and human vision
RED— human and Martian lower limit
ORANGE—
YELLOW— human peak acuity (preferred for artificial illumination)
GREEN— Martian upper limit (peak acuity)
BLUE—
VIOLET— human upper limit
ULTRAVIOLET— above both Martian and human sight

But while humans prefer their mid-range (YELLOW) for their artificial lighting, it seems that Wells allows his Martians to prefer their *lower* range (GREEN) for the same — the only really strange thing about their visual sensitivity. And this may account for green being the signature color of Martian alienage.

There are four different unusual uses of green in *Worlds*. (1) the green ("blue-green" one time) of Martian cylinders falling to earth, (2) green flares deployed by the Martians for area illumination, (3) green smoke resulting from aluminum-making, and (4) green vapor emitted by moving fighting machines and digging mechanisms. Pulling together the relevant quotes we have:

(1)   *Cylinders falling through the atmosphere.*

Then came ... the first falling star ... leaving a greenish streak behind it that glowed for some seconds [I:2].

...a star fell from heaven.... It had a greenish color and caused a silent brightness like summer lightning [I:8].

...a lurid green glare lit the road about me and showed the distant woods toward Addlestone ... the driving clouds had been pierced as it were by a thread of green fire [I:10].

(2)   *Flares.*

Suddenly there was a flash of light, and a quantity of luminous greenish smoke came out of the pit in three distinct puffs.... This smoke (or flame, perhaps, would be the better word for it) was so bright.... As the green smoke arose, their faces flashed out in pallid green, and faded again as it vanished [I:5].

(3)   *Aluminum-making.*

All night long the Martians were hammering and stirring, sleepless, indefatigable, at work upon the machines they were making ready, and ever and again a puff of greenish-white smoke whirled up to the starlit sky [I:8].

They were hard at work there far into the night, and the towering pillar of dense green smoke that rose therefrom could be seen from the hills about Merrow [I:13].

...the pit was illuminated by the flickering green fire that came from the aluminum-making [II:3].

(4)   *Green vapor.*

Seen nearer, the Thing was incredibly strange.... Behind the main body was a huge mass of white metal like a gigantic fisherman's basket, and puffs of green smoke squirted out from the joints of the limbs as the monster swept by me [I:10].

At (1) we have the cylinders, made of aluminum, burning through the atmosphere like green meteors — not a possible color for that metal at any temperature. It is purely symbolic. At (2) we have the Martian flares, more realistic in keeping with the Martian preference for green regarding artificial illumination, however strange that may be. Unlike humans, whose peak visual acuity is in the yellow part of the spectrum, their midrange, the Martians are different in one weird aspect: Their lower limit of visual perception (green) is also their level of peak acuity *and* their basis for artificial illumination. These green flares may account for the narrator's picture of a fighting machine on the move at (4), first quotation. The "white basket" appears as such because the whiteness of its aluminum fabric is not illuminated by a flare as are the steamy plumes of green smoke squirted from its leg joints. But this is at variance with the "green smoke" seen emitted from the digging machines, which are seen in daylight in the second quotation at (4). Further, the green smoke arising from the aluminum-making is not consistent with any manufacturing process known at the time (see note 147).

they communicated by sounds and tentacular gesticulations; this is asserted, for instance, in the able but hastily compiled pamphlet (written evidently by someone not an eye-witness of Martian actions) to which I have already alluded, and which, so far, has been the chief source of information concerning them. Now, no surviving human being saw so much of the Martians in action as I did. I take no credit to myself for an accident, but the fact is so. And I assert that I watched them closely time after time, and that I have seen four, five, and (once) six of them sluggishly performing the most elaborately complicated operations together, without either sound or gesture. Their peculiar hooting invariably preceded feeding; it had no modulation, and was, I believe, in no sense a signal, but merely the expiration of air preparatory to the suctional operation. I have a certain claim to at least an elementary knowledge of psychology, and in this matter I am convinced—as firmly as I am convinced of anything—that the Martians interchanged thoughts without any physical intermediation. And I have been convinced of this in spite of strong preconceptions. Before the Martian invasion, as an occasional reader here or there may remember, I had written, with some little vehemence, against the telepathic theory.[144]

The Martians wore no clothing. Their conceptions of ornament and decorum were necessarily different from ours; and not only were they

---

Conclusion: Wells makes green a symbolic color of Martian strangeness for different reasons. Sometimes it can be justified in science, but not always. What is constant, as insisted at note 55, is his drive to make green emblematic.

The above analysis owes very much to William Drish, a former student in my course on the scientific romances of H.G. Wells nearly thirty years ago. He is now a professional physicist and mathematician; his help on a number of scientific points is hereby gratefully acknowledged.

144. The Martians' supernal ability to organize their fighting machines is yet another reflection of Prussian military competency (see the Introduction to the present work, section 4). In the Franco-Prussian War of 1870, people were amazed at the swift movement and coordination of Prussian troops and artillery. This capacity, however, depended not on spontaneous activity in the field but on meticulous planning at staff headquarters. "Thus the Prussian General Staff acted as a nervous system animating the lumbering body of the army, making possible that articulation and flexibility which alone rendered it an effective military force" (Howard 1961:24). The Martians' telepathic power serves the same purpose. But even as the narrator denies such a possibility, Wells in *The Science of Life* (1931b:1413–1416) affirms telepathy. Here is yet another invidious distinction between the narrator and the auctorial stance.

evidently much less sensible of changes of temperature than we are, but changes of pressure do not seem to have affected their health at all seriously. But if they wore no clothing, yet it was in the other artificial additions to their bodily resources, certainly, that their great superiority over man lay. We men, with our bicycles and road-skates, our Lilienthal soaring-machines, our guns and sticks, and so forth, are just in the beginning of the evolution that the Martians have worked out. They have become practically mere brains, wearing different bodies according to their needs, just as men wear suits of clothes, and take a bicycle in a hurry or an umbrella in the wet.[145] And of their

---

145. In discussing technology as "additions to ... bodily resources," or as the "wearing [of] different bodies" according to need, Wells anticipates with dazzling insight today's anthropological theory of extensions. For example, the first edged tools of the Stone Age are seen as, literally, extensions of canine teeth which in early man (going back to the protohuman ape-men) were too short for tearing flesh as among his pithecoid ancestors, from which the living apes with the huge pointy canines are also descended. The mention of "guns and sticks" is especially interesting. *Sticks* may be taken as wooden clubs extending the arm in physical combat, *guns* as rifles, or fire*arms*, evolved to extend that reach at a distance. But in vernacular English, *sticks* are short for "shooting sticks," pistols: a subtle play on words underlining the point. The "bicycle," pedaled by the feet, extends bipedal locomotion; significantly, the first motor cars were not so much horseless carriages as four-wheeled bicycles, made of the same off-the-shelf parts, save for a gasoline engine. Of all the early aviation pioneers Wells could have cited (in preparation for the surprise appearance of flying machines at note 162), he chooses Otto Lilienthal (*d.* 1896), whose "soaring machines" were very like today's hang gliders (Scott 1995:109–112). The pilot wore his "appliance ... as men wear suits of clothes," and just as intimately directed its flight by throwing his body weight around.

Oddly enough clothing itself, an extension of the skin after all, has no place in Martian culture. "Their conceptions of ornament and decorum were necessarily different from ours." In other words, they were indifferent to a symbolic show of rank and power, a fact consistent with their Kantian ethics, which rise above the petty concerns of public opinion rooted in the psychology of the so-called looking glass self (see note 158). For another thing, they were "much less sensible of changes of temperature," and so needed no clothing on that account. Martian physiology also differed with respect to disease carrying micro-organisms, which "Martian sanitary science [had] eliminated ... ages ago" (see two paragraphs above) — a fateful policy decision. On balance, Martian technology is like ours in being explainable in terms of extension theory, while yet strange in its particulars. Below it is indicated that the wheel never had any place in it,

appliances, perhaps nothing is more wonderful to a man than the curious fact that what is the dominant feature of almost all human devices in mechanism is absent—the *wheel* is absent; amongst all the things they brought to earth there is no trace or suggestion of their use of wheels. One would have at least expected it in locomotion. And in this connection it is curious to remark that even on this earth Nature has never hit upon the wheel, or has preferred other expedients to its development. And not only did the Martians either not know of (which is incredible) or abstain from the wheel, but in their apparatus singularly little use is made of the fixed pivot, or relatively fixed pivot, with circular motions thereabout confined to one plane. Almost all the joints of the machinery present a complicated system of sliding parts moving over small but beautifully curved friction bearings. And while upon this matter of detail, it is remarkable that the long leverages of their machines are in most cases actuated by a sort of sham musculature of discs in an elastic sheath; these discs become polarized and drawn closely and powerfully together when traversed by a current of electricity. In this way the curious parallelism to animal motions, which was so striking and disturbing to the human beholder, was attained. Such quasi-muscles abounded in the crab-like Handling Machine which I watched unpacking the cylinder, on my first peeping out of the slit. It seemed infinitely more alive than the actual Martians lying beyond it in the sunset light, panting, stirring ineffectual tentacles, and moving feebly, after their vast journey across space.

While I was still watching their feeble motions in the sunlight, and noting each strange detail of their form, the curate reminded me of his presence by pulling violently at my arm. I turned to a scowling face, and silent, eloquent lips. He wanted the slit, which permitted only one of us to peep through at a time; and so I had to forego watching them for a time while he enjoyed that privilege.

When I looked again, the busy Handling Machine had already put together several of the pieces of apparatus it had taken out of the cylinder into a shape having an unmistakable likeness to its own; and down on the left a busy little digging mechanism had come into view, emitting jets of green vapour and working its way round the pit, excavat-

nor any pivotal devices around which "circular motions [are] confined to one plane." Instead, Martian mechanism directly extends bodily functions with a system of "sham musculature," whose artificial nerves are "current[s] of electricity"—a very advanced system in light of contemporary England's very retarded development of electrical engineering (note 52).

ing and embanking in a methodical and discriminating manner. This it was had caused the regular beating noise, and the rhythmic shocks that had kept our ruinous refuge quivering. It piped and whistled as it worked. So far as I could see, the thing was without a directing Martian at all.[146]

---

146. The "Handling Machines" are robots, which here make their first appearance in science fiction. The term itself is from Czech *robata*, labor slave, in Karl Capek's play of 1920, *R.U.R.* (Rossum's Universal Robots). The title robots, however, are not mechanical men but creatures of biotechnical engineering, now termed androids in science-fiction jargon. In yet another linguistic switch, androids once *were* mechanical men, the clockwork dolls of eighteenth century amusement (little Mozart, for example, programmed to pen a sheet of music). Wells's robots, in a daring leap of the imagination, are not anthropomorphic (or theriomorphic in the Martian case) but are designed for specialized functions — exactly like those car-welding machines produced by U.S. Robotics. Handling machines are among the first Martian items adapted for the advanced industrial technology that moves the future world of A.D. 2001 in *Sleeper* towards its utopian glory.

III

THE DAYS OF IMPRISONMENT.

THE arrival of a second Fighting Machine drove us from our peep-hole into the scullery, for we feared that from his elevation the Martian might see down upon us behind our barrier. At a later date we began to feel less in danger of their eyes, for to an eye in the dazzle of the sunlight outside our refuge must have seemed a blind of blackness, but at first the slightest suggestion of approach drove us into the scullery in heart throbbing retreat. Yet, terrible as was the danger we incurred, the attraction of peeping was for both of us irresistible. And I recall now with a sort of wonder that, spite of the infinite danger in which we were between starvation and a still more terrible death, we could yet struggle bitterly for that horrible privilege of sight. We would race across the kitchen in a grotesque pace between eagerness and the dread of making a noise, and strike one another, and thrust and kick, within a few inches of exposure.

The fact is that we had absolutely incompatible dispositions and habits of thought and action, and our danger and isolation only accentuated the incompatibility. At Halliford I had already come to hate his trick of helpless exclamation, his stupid rigidity of mind. His endless muttering monologue vitiated every effort I made to think out a line of action, and drove me at times, thus pent up and intensified, almost to the verge of craziness. He was as lacking in restraint as a silly woman. He would weep for hours together, and I verily believe that to the very end this spoilt child of life thought his weak tears in some way efficacious. And I would sit in the darkness unable to keep my mind off him by reason of his importunities. He ate more than I did, and it was in vain I pointed out that our only chance of life was to stop in the house until the Martians had done with their pit, that in the long patience a time might presently come when we should need food.

He ate and drank impulsively in heavy meals at long intervals. He slept little.

As the days wore on, his utter carelessness of any consideration so intensified our distress and danger that I had, much as I loathed doing it, to resort to threats, and at last to blows. That brought him to reason for a time. But he was one of those weak creatures full of a shifty cunning—who face neither God nor man, who face not even themselves, void of pride, timorous, anæmic, hateful souls.

It is disagreeable for me to recall and write these things, but I set them down that my story may lack nothing. Those who have escaped the dark and terrible aspects of life will find my brutality, my flash of rage in our final tragedy, easy enough to blame; for they know what is wrong as well as any, but not what is possible to tortured men. But those who have been under the shadow, who have gone down at last to elemental things, will have a wider charity.

And while within we fought out our dark dim contest of whispers, snatched food and drink and gripping hands and blows, without in the pitiless sunlight of that terrible June was the strange wonder, the unfamiliar routine of the Martians in the pit. Let me return to those first new experiences of mine. After a long time I ventured back to the peephole, to find that the new-comers had been reinforced by the occupants of no less than three of the Fighting Machines. These last had brought with them certain fresh appliances that stood in an orderly manner about the cylinder. The second Handling Machine was now completed, and was busied in serving one of the novel contrivances the big machine had brought. This was a body resembling a milk-can in its general form above which oscillated a pear-shaped receptacle, and from which a stream of white powder flowed into a circular basin below.

The oscillatory motion was imparted to this by one tentacle of the Handling Machine. With two spatulate hands the Handling Machine was digging out and flinging masses of clay into the pear-shaped receptacle above, while with another arm it periodically opened a door and removed rusty and blackened clinkers from the middle part of the machine. Another steely tentacle directed the powder from the basin along a ribbed channel towards some receiver that was hidden from me by the mound of bluish dust. From this unseen receiver a little thread of green smoke rose vertically into the quiet air.[147] As I looked,

---

147. In this passage, and the paragraph above, some mysterious industrial activity is described in deliberate tones of the uncanny; only at note 148 is it

revealed to be the Martians making aluminum — exotic enough for the time. Yet everything about it is realistic, save for the "green smoke," as ever the emblematic color of the Martians' alien presence (note 143).

Elemental aluminum (no. 13 on the period table) was, until 1894, a laboratory curiosity, not yet a commercial produce of mass production. This came about thanks to the Hall Process of electrolysis, named after the American chemist Charles Martin Hall. Theretofore the closest approach to extracting aluminum cheaply from its compounds was demonstrated by the French chemist Saint-Claire Deville in 1855 — still too expensive, however. The big commercial breakthrough came in 1894 with the opening of the world's first production factory on the American side of Niagara Falls, whose rushing waters powered a gigantic hydroelectric facility for the electrolytic reduction of the metal's principal compound, bauxite. Deville had called it "the metal of the future," which it did indeed become, rated only second to structural steel, at the same time making the aviation industry possible. Jules Verne found the epochal Niagara Falls plant of sufficient science-fictional interest to quote Deville as the prophet of his all-aluminum, sea-going city in *The Floating Island* (Verne 1896:53) — even more marvelous than Capt. Nemo's all-steel *Nautilus* in a work of 1872. Wells was just as responsive to the same progressive event in exhibiting his Martians as ultramodern for their turning out huge piles of aluminum ingots, used in fabricating all their machines including airplanes.

To see what Wells has done with the Hall Process, it is best to review what operations it actually entails. The starting point is bauxite, a rich mixture of aluminum minerals which also contains some iron oxide. It is not a "clay" as Wells describes the raw material dug from English soil by the Martians, and therefore is not bauxite, found only in tropical regions. But since aluminum is the most abundant element in the earth's crust after oxygen and silicon, found in many clays, rocks, and minerals, Martian super-science no doubt is able to extract aluminum from any of these, anywhere. All the same, their operations closely follow the Hall Process, outlined below.

Bauxite to Aluminum via the Hall Process

(1) Bauxite is purified by a treatment with a solution of sodium hydroxide, which does not dissolve the iron oxide. The solution is filtered to remove the iron oxide, but it does not come out in "clinker" form as in the Martian process.

(2) The filtered solution is acidified with carbon dioxide, yielding aluminum hydroxide (Al_2O_3) as a precipitate.

(3) The precipitated aluminum hydroxide is dehydrated by ignition (heating to a high temperature), yielding purified aluminum oxide: pure white in color.

(4) Pure aluminum oxide is dissolved in melted cryolite (sodium aluminum

the Handling Machine, with a faint and musical clinking, extended, telescopic fashion, a tentacle that had been a moment before a mere blunt projection, until its end was hidden behind the mound of clay.

---

fluoride). This solution is the electrolyte which conducts current from a series of anodes to a cathode in a tank. Hence the need for a powerful source of electricity.

(5) Molten aluminum is tapped off from the bottom of the tank periodically.

In the Martian process, a "clay" is dug up by one of the robotic Digging Machines. This raw material is passed on to Handling Machines which handle every other step in the process. First the clay is put into the "milk can" for ignition by a "green fire." Out comes a "white powder" (Al_2O_3), which is conveyed by way of a "ribbed channel" into a "pear-shaped receiver" for electrolysis. "Green smoke" is emitted from this receiver, with "blue dust" as a waste product. A foundry process further shapes the molten aluminum, drawn from the rounded bottom of the receiver, into ingots. The following chart is a summary:

Martian Aluminum-Making Process

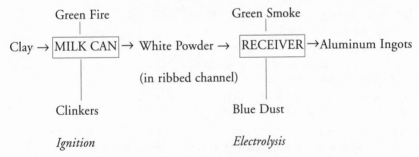

The "white powder" is Al_2O_3 and the "blue dust" is — what? It cannot be rationalized as a waste product of electrolysis (what dry particulate matter can drop from a tank of molten metal?), nor of the foundry process. Nor is "green fire" emitted at the ignition stage or "green smoke" at the stage of electrolysis in the actual Hall Process. It rather signifies a color variant of green, at the same time a huge and growing mound of the dust (also "blue-green") is seen to pile up the more ingots are produced — another dramatic visualization of bulk output. The immense electrical power the Martians require for electrolysis to produce even one bar is assumed. Within their compact capability is all the Niagara Falls plant can generate: progress of stupefying magnitude.

As at note 143 I am indebted to William Drish for his technical help. The above is adapted from his lengthy memo of 28 February 1999, gratefully acknowledged.

In another second it had lifted a bar of white aluminium into sight, untarnished as yet and shining dazzlingly, and deposited it in a growing stack of bars that stood at the side of the pit.[148] Between sunset and starlight this dexterous machine must have made more than a hundred such bars out of the crude clay, and the mound of bluish dust rose steadily until it topped the side of the pit.

The contrast between the swift and complex movements of these contrivances and the inert, panting clumsiness of their masters was acute, and for days I had to tell myself repeatedly that these latter were indeed the living of the two things.

The curate had possession of the slit when the first men were brought into the pit. I was sitting below, crouched together, listening with all my ears. He made a sudden movement backward, and I, fearful that we were observed, crouched in a spasm of terror. He came sliding down the rubbish, and crouched beside me in the darkness, inarticulate, gesticulating, and for a moment I shared his terror. His gesture suggested a resignation of the slit, and after a little while my curiosity gave me the courage, and I rose up, stepped across him, and clambered up to it. At first I could see no reason for his terror. The twilight had now come, the stars were little and faint, but the pit was illuminated by the flickering green fire that came from the aluminium making. The whole picture was a flickering scheme of green gleams and shifting rusty black shadows, strangely trying to the eyes. Over and through it all went the bats, heeding it not at all. The sprawling Martians were no longer to be seen, the mound of blue-green powder had risen to cover them from sight, and a Fighting Machine, with its legs contracted, crumpled and abbreviated, stood across the corner of the pit. And then, amidst the clangour of the machinery, came a drifting suspicion of human voices, that I entertained at first only to dismiss.

---

148. That the Martians are progressive in their aluminum-making is most exemplary. In *The Time Machine*, the Time Traveller comes upon a great ruinous pile of granite, "bound together by masses of aluminum." In the degenerate world of 802,701 he explores, it is the relic of a once progressive, nineteenth century past. Mankind was unable to sustain its forward movement (Stover 1996a:71–72, *n*86). *The Time Machine*, as a cautionary tale published only two years after the Niagara Falls facility opened to worldwide publicity (note 147), points to aluminum as *the* harbinger of a utopian future, providing mankind can hold on to that vision. It takes the Martians to keep humanity on its toes, which they do. Thus invasion is a benevolent catastrophe that moves things onward, in *Sleeper*, toward the Wellsian world state: Lowellian and Saint-Simonian Mars on earth.

I crouched, watching this Fighting Machine closely, satisfying myself now for the first time that the hood did indeed contain a Martian. As the green flames lifted I could see the oily gleam of his integument and the brightness of his eyes. And suddenly I heard a yell, and saw a long tentacle reaching over the shoulder of the machine, to the little cage that hunched upon its back. Then something—something struggling violently—was lifted high against the sky, a black vague enigma against the starlight, and as this black object came down again, I saw by the green brightness that it was a man. For an instant he was clearly visible. He was a stout, ruddy, middle-aged man, well dressed; three days before he must have been walking the world, a man of considerable consequence. I could see his staring eyes and gleams of light on his studs and watch-chain. He vanished behind the mound, and for a moment there was silence. And then began a shrieking and a sustained and cheerful hooting from the Martians....

I slid down the rubbish, struggled to my feet, clapped my hands over my ears, and bolted into the scullery. The curate, who had been crouching silently with his arms over his head, looked up as I passed, cried out quite loudly at my desertion of him, and came running after me....

That night, as we lurked in the scullery, balanced between our horror and the horrible fascination this peeping had, although I felt an urgent need of action, I tried in vain to conceive any plan of escape; but afterwards, during the second day, I was able to consider our position with great clearness. The curate, I found, was quite incapable of discussion; strange terrors had already made him a creature of violent impulses, had robbed him of reason or forethought. Practically he had already sunk to the level of an animal. But, as the saying goes, I gripped myself with both hands. It grew upon my mind, once I could face the facts, that, terrible as our position was, there was as yet no justification for absolute despair. Our chief chance lay in the possibility of the Martians making the pit nothing more than a temporary encampment. Or even if they kept it permanently, they might not consider it necessary to guard it, and a chance of escape might be afforded us. I also weighed very carefully the possibility of our digging a way out in a direction away from the pit, but the chances of our emerging within sight of some sentinel Fighting Machine seemed at first too enormous. And I should have had to have done all the digging myself. The curate would certainly have failed me.

It was on the third day, if my memory serves me right, that I saw the lad killed. It was the only occasion on which I actually saw the Martians feed. After that experience, I avoided the hole in the wall for the better part of a day. I went into the scullery, removed the door, and spent some hours digging with my hatchet as silently as possible; but when I had made a hole about a couple of feet deep the loose earth collapsed noisily, and I did not dare continue. I lost heart, and lay down on the scullery floor for a long time, having no spirit even to move. And after that I abandoned altogether the idea of escaping by excavation.

It says much for the impression the Martians had made upon me, that at first I entertained little or no hope of our escape being brought about by their overthrow through any human effort. But on the fourth or fifth night I heard a sound like heavy guns.

It was very late in the night, and the moon was shining brightly. The Martians had taken away the Excavating Machine, and, save for a Fighting Machine that stood on the remoter bank of the pit, and a Handling Machine that was busied out of my sight in a corner of the pit immediately beneath my peep-hole, the place was deserted by them. Except for the pale glow from the Handling Machine, and the bars and patches of white moonlight, the pit was in darkness, and except for the clinking of the Handling Machine, quite still. That night was a beautiful serenity; save for one planet, the moon seemed to have the sky to herself. I heard a dog howling, and that familiar sound it was made me listen. Then I heard quite distinctly a booming exactly like the sound of great guns. Six distinct reports I counted, and after a long intervals six again. And that was all.

IV

THE DEATH OF THE CURATE.

IT was on the sixth day of our imprisonment that I peeped for the last time, and presently found myself alone. Instead of keeping close to me and trying to oust me from the slit, the curate had gone back into the scullery. I was struck by a sudden thought. I went back quickly and quietly into the scullery. In the darkness I heard the curate drinking. I snatched in the darkness, and my fingers caught a bottle of burgundy.

For a few minutes there was a tussle. The bottle struck the floor and broke, and I desisted and rose. We stood panting, threatening one another. In the end I planted myself between him and the food, and told him of my determination to begin a discipline.[149] I divided the food in the pantry into rations to last us ten days. I would not let him eat any more that day. In the afternoon he made a feeble effort to get at the food. I had been dozing, but in an instant I was awake. All day and all night we sat face to face, I weary but resolute, and he weeping and complaining of his immediate hunger. It was, I know, a night

---

149. The more self-possessed narrator is forced to "begin a discipline" on the curate because he has turned to drink and gluttony, dangerous to them both in that his breakdown leads only to more self-indulgent wailing. The Martians, after all, are just outside the house and can hear what goes on within. To save himself from being eaten by these vampires, he at last kills the curate with a meat cleaver.

In II:7, when the narrator once again falls in with the artilleryman, he too sinks into drink and gluttony for all his grandiose plans to form a self-disciplined band of Martian fighters. But as he is in no personal danger from him, the narrator simply departs in disgust and continues his war-story pursuit. Soon, now, it comes to its end, and the narrator finally has no choice but to return home to his wife — and to a sense of emptiness and life unfulfilled.

and a day, but to me it seemed—it seems now—an interminable length of time.

And so our widened incompatibility ended at last in open conflict. For two vast days we struggled in undertones and wrestling contests. There were times when I beat and kicked him madly, times when I cajoled and persuaded him, and once I tried to bribe him with the last bottle of burgundy, for there was a rain-water pump from which I could get water. But neither force nor kindness availed: he was indeed beyond reason. He would neither desist from his attacks on the food nor from his noisy babbling to himself. The rudimentary precautions to keep our imprisonment endurable he would not observe. Slowly I began to realize the complete overthrow of his intelligence, to perceive that my sole companion in this close and sickly darkness was a man insane.

From certain vague memories I am inclined to think my own mind wandered at times. I had strange and hideous dreams whenever I slept. It sounds strange, but I am inclined to think that the weakness and insanity of the curate warned me, braced me and kept me a sane man.

On the eighth day he began to talk aloud instead of whisper, and nothing I could do would moderate his speech.

"It is just, O God!" he would say over and over again. "It is just. On me and mine be the punishment laid. We have sinned, we have fallen short. There was poverty, sorrow; the poor were trodden in the dust, and I held my peace. I preached acceptable folly—my God, what folly!—when I should have stood up, though I died for it, and called upon them to repent—repent!... Oppressors of the poor and needy.... The winepress of God!"

Then he would suddenly revert to the matter of the food I withheld from him, praying, begging, weeping, at last threatening. He began to raise his voice—I prayed him not to; he perceived a hold on me—he threatened he would shout and bring the Martians upon us. For a time that scared me; but any concession would have shortened our chance of escape beyond estimating. I defied him, although I felt no assurance that he might not do this thing. But that day, at any rate, he did not. He talked with his voice rising slowly, through the greater part of the eighth and ninth days—threats, entreaties, mingled with a torrent of half-sane and always frothy repentance for his vacant sham of God's service, such as made me pity him. Then he slept awhile, and began again with renewed strength, so loudly that I must needs make him desist.

"Be still!" I implored.

He rose to his knees, for he had been sitting in the darkness near the copper.

"I have been still too long,"[150] he said in a tone that must have reached the pit, "and now I must bear my witness. Woe unto this unfaithful city! Woe! woe! Woe! woe! woe! to the inhabitants of the earth by reason of the other voices of the trumpet——"

"Shut up!" I said, rising to my feet, and in a terror lest the Martians hear us. "For God's sake——"

"Nay," shouted the curate at the top of his voice, standing likewise and extending his arms. "Speak! The word of the Lord is upon me."

In three strides he was at the door into the kitchen.

"I must bear my witness. I go. It has already been too long delayed."

I put out my hand and felt the meat-chopper hanging to the wall. In a flash I was after him. I was fierce with fear. Before he was half-way across the kitchen I had overtaken him. With one last touch of humanity I turned the blade back and struck him with the butt. He went headlong forward, and lay stretched on the ground. I stumbled over him, and stood panting. He lay still.

Abruptly I heard a noise without, the run and smash of slipping plaster, and the triangular aperture in the wall was darkened. I looked up and saw the lower surface of a Handling Machine coming slowly across the hole. One of its gripping limbs curled amidst the débris; another limb appeared, feeling its way over the fallen beams. I stood petrified, staring. Then I saw through a sort of glass plate near the edge of the body the face, as we may call it, and the large dark eyes of a Martian peering, and then a long metallic snake of tentacle came feeling slowly through the hole.

I turned by an effort, stumbled over the curate, and stopped at the scullery door. The tentacle was now some way, two yards or more, in the room, and twisting and turning with queer sudden movements, this way and that. For a while I stood fascinated by that slow, fitful advance. Then, with a faint, hoarse cry, I forced myself across the scullery. I trembled violently; I could scarcely stand upright. I opened the door of the coal-cellar, and stood there in the darkness, staring at

---

150. A dim echo of Isaiah 42:14, "I have been still, and refrained myself." The rest of the curate's rantings descend into more biblical-sounding rhetoric. He is now so self-indulgent in his righteousness that he loses control of scripture, once the very basis of his sense of failing. It is a nice comment on the weakness of theological doctrine to cope with truly catastrophic, even apocalyptic events like the Lisbon earthquake (note 71).

the faintly lit doorway into the kitchen, and listening. Had the Martian seen me? What was it doing now?

Something was moving to and fro there, very quietly; every now and then it tapped against the wall, or started on its movements with a faint metallic ringing, like the movement of keys on a split-ring. Then a heavy body—I knew too well what—was dragged across the floor of the kitchen towards the opening. Irresistibly attracted, I crept to the door and peeped into the kitchen. In the triangle of bright outer sunlight I saw the Martian in its Briareus of a Handling Machine,[151] scrutinizing the curate's head. I thought at once that it would infer my presence from the mark of the blow I had given him.

I crept back to the coal-cellar, shut the door, and began to cover myself up as much as I could, and as noiselessly as possible, in the darkness, among the firewood and coal therein. Every now and then I paused rigid, to hear if the Martian had thrust its tentacle through the opening again.

Then the faint metallic jingle returned. I traced it slowly feeling over the kitchen. Presently I heard it nearer—in the scullery, as I judged. I thought that its length might be insufficient to reach me. I prayed copiously. It passed, scraping faintly across the cellar door. An age of almost intolerable suspense intervened; then I heard it fumbling at the latch. It had found the door! The Martian understood doors!

It worried at the catch for a minute, perhaps, and then the door opened.

In the darkness I could just see the thing—like an elephant trunk more than anything else—waving towards me and touching and examining the wall, coals, wood, and ceiling. It was like a black worm swaying its blind head to and fro.

Once, even, it touched the heel of my boot. I was on the verge of screaming; I bit my hand. For a time it was silent. I could have fancied it had been withdrawn. Presently, with an abrupt click, it gripped something—I thought it had me!—and seemed to go out of the cellar again. For a minute I was not sure. Apparently, it had taken a lump of coal to examine.

I seized the opportunity of slightly shifting my position, which had become cramped, and listened. I whispered passionate prayers for safety.

---

151. Briareus, in Greek mythology, is a giant with fifty heads and a hundred hands. The Martians' robotic Handling Machines are the multiplex hands of their guiding heads — one giant in their common purpose.

Then I heard the slow, deliberate sound creeping towards me again. Slowly, slowly it drew near, scratching against walls and tapping furniture.

While I was still doubtful, it rapped smartly against the cellar door and closed it. I heard it go into the pantry, and the biscuit-tins rattled and a bottle smashed, and then came a heavy bump against the cellar door. Then silence, that passed into an infinity of suspense.

Had it gone?

At last I decided that it had.

It came into the scullery no more; but I lay all the tenth day, in the close darkness, buried among coals and firewood, not daring even to crawl out for the drink for which I craved. It was the eleventh day before I ventured so far from my security.

V

THE STILLNESS.

MY first act, before I went into the pantry, was to fasten the door between kitchen and scullery. But the pantry was empty; every scrap of food had gone. Apparently, the Martian had taken it all on the previous day. At that discovery I despaired for the first time. I took no food and no drink either on the eleventh or the twelfth day.

At first my mouth and throat were parched, and my strength ebbed sensibly. I sat about in the darkness of the scullery, in a state of despondent wretchedness. My mind ran on eating. I thought I had become deaf, for the noises of movement I had been accustomed to hear from the pit ceased absolutely. I did not feel strong enough to crawl noiselessly to the peephole, or I would have gone there.

On the twelfth day my throat was so painful that, taking the chance of alarming the Martians, I attacked the creaking rain-water pump that stood by the sink, and got a couple of glassfuls of blackened and tainted rain-water. I was greatly refreshed by this, and emboldened by the fact that no inquiring tentacle followed the noise of my pumping.

During these days I thought much of the curate, and of the manner of his death, in a rambling, inconclusive manner.

On the thirteenth day I drank some more water, and dozed and thought disjointedly of eating and of vague impossible plans of escape. Whenever I dozed I dreamt of horrible phantasms, of the death of the curate, or of sumptuous dinners; but, sleeping or awake, I felt a keen pain that urged me to drink again and again. The light that came into the scullery was no longer grey but red. To my disordered imagination it seemed the colour of blood.

On the fourteenth day I went into the kitchen, and I was surprised to find that the fronds of the Red Weed had grown right across the hole in the wall, turning the half-light of the place into a crimson-coloured obscurity.

It was early on the fifteenth day that I heard a curious familiar sequence of sounds in the kitchen, and, listening, identified it as the snuffing and scratching of a dog. Going into the kitchen, I saw a dog's nose peering in through a break among the ruddy fronds. This greatly surprised me. At the scent of me he barked shortly.

I thought if I could induce him to come into the place quietly I should be able, perhaps, to kill and eat him, and in any case it would be advisable to kill him, lest his actions attracted the attention of the Martians.

I crept forward, saying "Good dog!" very softly; but he suddenly withdrew his head and disappeared.

I listened—I was not deaf—but certainly the pit was still. I heard a sound like the flutter of a bird's wings, and a hoarse croaking, but that was all.

For a long while I lay close to the peephole, but not daring to move aside the red plants that obscured it. Once or twice I heard a faint pitter-patter like the feet of the dog going hither and thither on the sand far below me, and there were more bird-like sounds, but that was all. At length, encouraged by the silence, I looked out.

Except in the corner, where a multitude of crows hopped and fought over the skeletons of the dead the Martians had consumed, there was not a living thing in the pit.

I stared about me, scarcely believing my eyes. All the machinery had gone. Save for the big mound of grayish-blue powder in one corner, certain bars of aluminium in another, the black birds and the skeletons of the killed, the place was merely an empty circular pit in the sand.[152]

Slowly I thrust myself out through the red weed, and stood up on the mound of rubble. I could see in any direction save behind me, to the north, and neither Martian nor sign of Martian was to be seen. The pit dropped sheerly from my feet, but a little way along, the rubbish

---

152. The huge pile of blue dust, plus a few uncollected aluminum ingots, is all that remains of the industrial activity at note 147. Now crows pick over the carrion of skeleton-reduced bodies drained by the Martians for their blood. Such is the cost to common humanity for the march of progress, represented by the metal of the future and with it the statist organization of the future. The Modern State Octopus, after all, is a sucker-out of the lifeblood of local communities into the veins of a higher organism (see Appendix II of the present work)—the collectivist giant Briareus at note 151.

afforded a practicable slope to the summit of the ruins. My chance of escape had come. I began to tremble.

I hesitated for some time, and then, in a gust of desperate resolution and with a heart that throbbed violently, I scrambled to the top of the mound in which I had been buried so long.

I looked about again. To the northward, too, no Martian was visible.

When I had last seen this part of Sheen in the daylight, it had been a straggling street of comfortable white and red houses, interspersed with abundant shady trees. Now I stood on a mound of smashed brickwork, clay and gravel, over which spread a multitude of red cactus-shaped plants, knee-high, without a solitary terrestrial growth to dispute their footing. The trees near me were dead and brown, but further, a network of red threads scaled the still living stems.

The neighbouring houses had all been wrecked, but none had been burned; their walls stood sometimes to the second story, with smashed windows and shattered doors. The Red Weed grew tumultuously in their roofless rooms. Below me was the great pit, with the crows struggling for its refuse. A number of other birds hopped about among the ruins. Far away I saw a gaunt cat slink crouchingly along a wall, but traces of men there were none.

The day seemed, by contrast with my recent confinement, dazzlingly bright, the sky a glowing blue. A gentle breeze kept the Red Weed, that covered every scrap of unoccupied ground, gently swaying. And oh! the sweetness of the air![153]

---

153. After fifteen days of imprisonment, waiting for the Martians to leave the vicinity of his hiding place, the narrator is relieved to be free. But free for what? He now surveys the spooky desolation of the whole area, the Red Weed creeping over everything in the stillness, all humans gone. Ah, "The sweetness of the air!" He alone survives, the only man alive; as the last man on earth, in his fantasy, he is free to be his utterly selfish self. It then comes as a disappointment to him, at the end, to find himself entrapped, as before, in a loveless marriage. The larger meaning of the Martian invasion for the future of humanity is completely lost on him.

VI

THE WORK OF FIFTEEN DAYS.

FOR some time I stood tottering on the mound, regardless of my safety. Within that noisome den from which I had emerged, I had thought with a narrow intensity only of our immediate security. I had not realized what had been happening to the world, had not antici-pated this startling vision of unfamiliar things. I had expected to see Sheen in ruins—I found about me the landscape, weird and lurid, of another planet.

For that moment I touched an emotion beyond the common range of men, yet one that the poor brutes we dominate know only too well. I felt as a rabbit might feel returning to his burrow, and suddenly con-fronted by the work of a dozen busy navvies digging the foundations of a house. I felt the first inkling of a thing that presently grew quite clear in my mind, that oppressed me for many days, a sense of dethronement,[154] a persuasion that I was no longer a master, but an animal among the animals, under the Martian heel. With us it would be as with them, to lurk and watch, to run and hide; the fear and empire of man had passed away.

But so soon as this strangeness had been realized, it passed, and my dominant motive became the hunger of my long and dismal fast. In the direction away from the pit, I saw, beyond a red-covered wall, a patch of garden ground unburied. This gave me a hint, and I went

---

154. The narrator now has second thoughts about his freedom as the last man on earth (note 153). Maybe he is not alone. Maybe he is but a rabbit like all his kind, hiding in the false personal security of their rabbit-burrows, while all the time higher beings are able to dig them out: the "dethronement" of man. The Martians are those beyondist higher beings who are destined to uproot and then elevate low humanity by their example to greater things. The narrator, however, cannot see that far.

knee-deep, and sometimes neck-deep, in the Red Weed. The density of the weed gave me a reassuring sense of hiding. The wall was some six feet high and when I attempted to clamber it I found I could not lift my feet to the crest. So I went along by the side of it, and came to a corner and a rockwork that enabled me to get to the top and tumble into the garden I coveted. Here I found some young onions, a couple of gladiolus bulbs, and a quantity of immature carrots, all of which I secured, and, scrambling over a ruined wall, went on my way through scarlet and crimson trees towards Kew—it was like walking through an avenue of gigantic blood-drops[155]—possessed with two ideas: to get more food, and to limp, as soon and as far as my strength permitted, out of this accursed unearthly region of the pit.

Some way further, in a grassy place, was a group of mushrooms, which I also devoured, and then I came upon a brown sheet of flowing shallow water, where meadows used to be. These fragments of nourishment served only to whet my hunger. At first I was surprised at this flood in a hot, dry summer, but afterwards I discovered that this was caused by the tropical exuberance of the Red Weed. Directly this extraordinary growth encountered water, it straightway became gigantic and of unparalleled fecundity. Its seeds were simply poured down into the water of the Wey and Thames, and its swiftly-growing and Titanic water-fronds speedily choked both these rivers.

At Putney, as I afterwards saw, the bridge was almost lost in a tangle of this weed, and at Richmond, too, the Thames water poured in a broad and shallow stream across the meadows of Hampton and Twickenham. As the waters spread the weed followed them, until the ruined villas of the Thames Valley were for a time lost in this red swamp, whose margin I explored, and much of the desolation the Martians had caused was concealed.

In the end the Red Weed succumbed almost as quickly as it spread. A cankering disease,[156] due, it is believed, to the action of certain

---

155. A possible echo of Luke 22:44, "...and his sweat was as it were great drops of blood falling to the ground." The narrator is now as scriptural as the curate, and just as garbled in his last days. He really has no faith-founded purpose in theology or anything else, save a self-serving quest to pursue the war to its end. His is a despicable character, so much sweat wasted, contrasting with the auctoral point of view in which the invasion has far greater consequences beyond the narrator's imagination.

156. The dying out of the Red Weed is a classic example of foreshadowing in the Victorian novel, already hinted at note 142. But while it is a "canker-

bacteria, presently seized upon it. Now, by the action of natural selection, all terrestrial plants have acquired a resisting power against bacterial diseases—they never succumb without a severe struggle; but the Red Weed rotted like a thing already dead. The fronds became bleached, and then shrivelled and brittle. They broke off at the least touch, and the waters that had stimulated their early growth carried their last vestiges out to sea....

My first act on coming to this water was, of course, to slake my thirst. I drank a great bulk of water, and, moved by an impulse, gnawed from fronds of Red Weed; but they were watery, and had a sickly metallic taste. I found the water was sufficiently shallow for me to wade securely, although the Red Weed impeded my feet a little; but the flood evidently got deeper towards the river, and I turned back towards Mortlake. I managed to make out the road by means of occasional ruins of its villas and fences and lamps, and so presently I got out of this spate, and made my way to the hill going up towards Roehampton, and came out on Putney Common.

Here the scenery changed from the strange and unfamiliar to the wreckage of the familiar; patches of ground exhibited the devastation of a cyclone, and in a few score yards I would come upon perfectly undisturbed spaces, houses with their blinds trimly drawn and doors closed, as if they had been left for a day by the owners, or as if their inhabitants slept within. The Red Weed was less abundant; the tall trees along the lane were free from the red creeper. I hunted for food among the trees, finding nothing, and I also raided a couple of silent houses, but they had already been broken into and ransacked. I rested for the remainder of the daylight in a shrubbery, being, in my enfeebled condition, too fatigued to push on.

All this time I saw no human beings, and no signs of the Martians. I encountered a couple of hungry-looking dogs, but both hurried circuitously away from the advances I made them. Near Roehampton I had seen two human skeletons—not bodies, but skeletons, picked clean—and in the wood by me I found the crushed and scattered bones of several cats and rabbits, and the skull of a sheep. But though I gnawed parts of these in my mouth, there was nothing to be got from them.

---

ing disease," like the spreading cancerous growth of the Martians themselves, it is a benevolent cancer. The Martian-bearing plants may die, the Martians die, but their example metastasizes. Finally, in *Sleeper*, it *does* take over the world: the Modern State Octopus triumphant.

After sunset, I struggled on along the road towards Putney, where I think the Heat-Ray must have been used for some reason. And in a garden beyond Roehampton I got a quantity of immature potatoes sufficient to stay my hunger. From this garden one saw down upon Putney and the river. The aspect of the place in the dusk was singularly desolate: blackened trees, blackened, desolate ruins, and down the hill the sheets of the flooded river, red-tinged with the weed. And over all—silence. It filled me with indescribable terror to think how swiftly that desolating change had come.

For a time I believed that mankind had been swept out of existence, and that I stood there alone, the last man left alive.[157] Hard by the top of Putney Hill I came upon another skeleton, with the arms dislocated and removed several yards from the rest of the body. As I proceeded I became more and more convinced that the extermination of mankind was, save for such stragglers as myself, already accomplished in this part of the world. The Martians, I thought, had gone on, and left the country desolated, seeking food elsewhere. Perhaps even now they were destroying Berlin or Paris, or it might be they had gone northward....

157. See note 153.

VII

THE MAN ON PUTNEY HILL.[158]

I SPENT that night in the inn that stands at the top of Putney Hill, sleeping in a made bed for the first time since my flight to Leatherhead. I will not tell the needless trouble I had breaking into that

---

158. This is the novel's key chapter, and there is much to say about it. Apart from the significance of the place name (Putney Hill), there is the question of how the chapter came to be in the book version. It does not appear in the magazine version of 1897.

In that year, 1897, there appeared *Auf zwei Planeten* by Kurd Lasswitz, *Two Planets* in the abridged translation of 1971 here cited. Lasswitz wrote books on the ethics of Immanuel Kant, the first modern philosopher to dismiss culture, history and tradition. His novel fictionalizes all that, with his big-headed (yet humanoid) Martians. They land at the North Pole (using some antigravitic device), from which they plan to extend to earth the socialist world-state they enjoy at home. German polar explorers discover their base camp, then go along with them — ostensibly. Having their own plan now for a Germanic world state, the explorers learn enough from Martian military science to drive off the invaders and then to carry on their mission on their own Teutonic terms: "we ... no longer need the Martians! Let us show that we have understood the example of their planet" (Lasswitz:1897:309). Their ethical superiority lies in their living Kant's categorical imperative. "It does not matters much whether we do the right thing, but it is essential whether we do it out of the right motives." What counts is "whether the motive is pure for what you want" (109). By contrast humans are retarded; each one dwells on "what others think and say about him" (197). This is precisely the meaning of "selfish intelligence" at note 145, the same quality of mind Wells attributes to *his* Martians. No wonder he found Lasswitz an agreeable source for rounding off *Worlds*.

As for Putney Hill, it is not a hill but the name of a hilly road in Putney, a London district south of the Thames about seven miles west of the city cen-

house—afterwards I found the front-door was on the latch—nor how I ransacked every room for food, until, just on the verge of despair, in what seemed to me to be a servant's bedroom, I found a rat-gnawed crust and two tinned pineapples. The place had been already searched and emptied. In the bar I afterwards found some biscuits and sandwiches that had been overlooked. The latter I could not eat, but the former not only stayed my hunger, but filled my pockets. I lit no lamps, fearing some Martian might come beating that part of London for food in the night. Before I went to bed I had an interval of restlessness, and prowled from window to window, peering out for some sign of these monsters. I slept little. As I lay in bed I found myself thinking consecutively—a thing I do not remember to have done since my last argument with the curate. During all the intervening time my mental condition had been a hurrying succession of vague emotional states, or a sort of stupid receptivity. But in the night my brain, reinforced, I suppose, by the food I had eaten, grew clear again, and I thought.

Three things struggled for possession of my mind: the killing of the curate, the whereabouts of the Martians, and the possible fate of my wife. The former gave me no sensation of horror or remorse to recall; I saw it simply as a thing done, a memory infinitely disagreeable, but quite without the quality of remorse. I saw myself then as I see myself now, driven step by step towards that hasty blow, the creature of a sequence of accidents leading inevitably to that. I felt no condemnation; yet the memory, static, unprogressive, haunted me. In the silence of the night, with that sense of the nearness of God that sometimes comes into the stillness and the darkness, I stood my trial, my only trial, for that moment of wrath and fear. I retraced every step of our conversation from the moment when I had found him crouching beside me, heedless of my thirst, and pointing to the fire and smoke that

---

ter. Putney Church is famous as the site of the so-called Putney Debates held in October and November 1647 in the midst of the English Civil War, Oliver Cromwell presiding. His parliamentary army fighting the monarch contained a radical egalitarian faction, the Levellers, whom Cromwell at length out-debated (Aylmer 1975:97–130).

When at note 164 the artilleryman says he is "not an ornamental soldier," he means to identify himself with the Puritan roundheads vis-à-vis the lace-cuffed cavaliers on the king's side in that Civil War. But he is not a Leveller either, as his speechifying indicates. His proposals to the narrator smack of Cromwell in the Putney Debates, which align him with Wells's New Republic in *Anticipations.* Its world rulers profess to a "new Cromwellism" (1901:189).

streamed up from the ruins of Weybridge. We had been incapable of co-operation—grim chance had taken no heed of that. Had I foreseen, I should have left him at Halliford. But I did not foresee; and crime is to foresee and do. And I set this down as I have set all this story down, as it was. There were no witnesses—all these things I might have concealed. But I set it down, and the reader must form his judgment as he will.

And when, by an effort, I had set aside that picture of a prostrate body, I faced the problem of the Martians and the fate of my wife. For the former I had no data; I could imagine a hundred things, and so, unhappily, I could for the latter. And suddenly that night became terrible. I found myself sitting up in bed, staring at the dark. I found myself praying that the Heat-Ray may have suddenly and painlessly struck her out of being. Since the night of my return from Leatherhead I had not prayed. I had uttered prayers, fetich prayers, had prayed as heathens mutter charms when I was in extremity; but now I prayed indeed, pleading steadfastly and sanely, face to face with the darkness of God. Strange night! strangest in this, that so soon as dawn had come, I, who had talked with God, crept out of the house like a rat leaving its hiding-place—a creature scarcely larger, an inferior animal, a thing that for any passing whim of our masters might be hunted and killed. Perhaps they also prayed confidently to God. Surely, if we have learnt nothing else, this war has taught us pity—pity for those witless souls that suffer our dominion.[159]

The morning was bright and fine, and the eastern sky glowed pink, and was fretted with little golden clouds. In the road that runs from the top of Putney Hill to Wimbledon was a number of pitiful vestiges of the panic torrent that must have poured Londonward on the Sunday night after the fighting began. There was a little two-wheeled cart inscribed with the name of Thomas Lobb, Greengrocer, New Malden, with a smashed wheel and an abandoned tin trunk; there was a straw hat trampled into the now hardened mud, and at the top of West Hill a lot of blood-stained glass about the overturned water-trough. My movements were languid, my plans of the vaguest. I had an idea of

---

159. As humans are to Martians, the "witless souls" of lower animals are to humans (see note 6). The narrator's "pity" for them is no more than self-pity, now that he has just suffered the indignity of hiding "like a rat." Nor are his prayers for his wife's safety any more sincere. His prayerful mood soon passes once he comes out of hiding and presses on, Londonward, the scene of the gathering action.

going to Leatherwood, though I knew that there I had the poorest chance of finding my wife. Certainly, unless death had overtaken them suddenly, my cousins and she would have fled thence; but it seemed to me I might find or learn there whither the Surrey people had fled. I knew I wanted to find my wife, that my heart ached for her and the world of men, but I had no clear idea how the finding might be done. I was also clearly aware now of my intense loneliness. From the corner I went, under cover of a thicket of trees and bushes, to the edge of Wimbledon Common, stretching wide and far.

That dark expanse was lit in patches by yellow gorse and broom; there was no Red Weed to be seen, and as I prowled, hesitating, on the verge of the open, the sun rose, flooding it all with light and vitality. I came upon a busy swarm of little frogs in a swampy place among the trees. I stopped to look at them, drawing a lesson from their stout resolve to live. And presently, turning suddenly, with an odd feeling of being watched, I beheld something crouching amidst a clump of bushes. I stood regarding this. I made a step towards it, and it rose up, and became a man armed with a cutlass. I approached him slowly. He stood silent and motionless, regarding me.

As I drew nearer, I perceived he was dressed in clothes as dusty and filthy as my own; he looked, indeed, as though he had been dragged through a culvert. Nearer, I distinguished the green slime of ditches mixing with the pale drab of dried clay and shiny coaly patches. His black hair fell over his eyes, and his face was dark and dirty and sunken, so that at first I did not recognise him. There was a red cut across the lower part of his face.

"Stop!" he cried, when I was within ten yards of him, and I stopped. His voice was hoarse. "Where do you come from?" he said.

I thought, surveying him.

"I come from Mortlake," I said. "I was buried near the pit the Martians made about their cylinder. I have worked my way out and escaped."

"There is no food about here," he said. "This is my country. All this hill down to the river, and back to Clapham, and up to the edge of the Common. There is only food for one. Which way are you going?"

I answered slowly.

"I don't know," I said. "I have been buried in the ruins of a house thirteen or fourteen days. I don't know what has happened."

He looked at me doubtfully, then started, and looked with a changed expression.

"I've no wish to stop about here," said I. "I think I shall go to Leatherhead, for my wife was there."

He shot out a pointing finger.

"It is you," said he. "The man from Woking. And you weren't killed at Weybridge?"

I recognised him at the same moment.

"You are the artilleryman who came into my garden."[160]

"Good luck!" he said. "We are lucky ones! Fancy *you*!" He put out a hand, and I took it. "I crawled up a drain," he said. "But they didn't kill everyone. And after they went away I got off towards Walton across the fields. But—— It's not sixteen days altogether—and your hair is gray." He looked over his shoulder suddenly. "Only a rook," he said. "One gets to know that birds have shadows these days. This *is* a bit open. Let us crawl under those bushes and talk."

"Have you seen any Martians?" I said. "Since I crawled out——"

"They've gone away across London," he said. "I guess they've got a bigger camp there. Of a night, all over there, Hampstead way, the sky is alive with their lights. It's like a great city, and in the glare you can just see them moving.[161] By daylight you can't. But nearer—I haven't seen them——" He counted on his fingers. "Five days. Then I saw a couple across Hammersmith way carrying something big. And the night before last"—he stopped, and spoke impressively—"it was just a matter of lights, but it was something up in the air. I believed they've built a flying-machine, and are learning to fly."

I stopped, on hands and knees, for we had come to the bushes.

"Fly!"

"Yes," he said, "fly."

I went on into a little bower, and sat down.

"It is all over with humanity," I said. "If they can do that they will simply go round the world...."[162]

He nodded.

"They will. But—— It will relieve things over here a bit. And besides——" He looked at me. "Aren't you satisfied it *is* up with humanity? I am. We're down; we're beat."

I stared. Strange as it may seem, I had not arrived at this fact—a fact perfectly obvious so soon as he spoke. I had still held a vague hope; rather, I had kept a lifelong habit of mind. He repeated his words, "We're beat." They carried absolute conviction.

---

160. See note 67, whereat the artilleryman is last seen by the narrator.

161. The Martians' progressive development of electrification (note 52) is here matched with their equally progressive aluminum-making (note 147).

162. The first mention of Martian aviation, the surprising revelation promised at note 145. It is possible thanks only to aluminum (note 147).

"It's all over," he said. "They've lost *one*—just *one*.[163] And they've made their footing good, and crippled the greatest power in the world. They've walked over us. The death of that one at Weybridge was an accident. And these are only pioneers. They keep on coming. These green stars—I've seen none these five or six days, but I've no doubt they're falling somewhere every night. Nothing's to be done. We're under! We're beat!"

I made him no answer. I sat staring before me, trying in vain to devise some countervailing thought.

"This isn't a war," said the artilleryman. "It never was a war, any more than there's war between men and ants."[164]

Suddenly I recalled the night in the observatory.

"After the tenth shot they fired no more—at least, until the first cylinder came."

"How do you know?" said the artilleryman. I explained. He thought. "Something wrong with the gun," he said. "But what if there is? They'll get it right again. And even if there's a delay, how can it alter the end? It's just men and ants. There's the ants builds their cities, live their lives, have wars, revolutions, until the men want them out of the way, and then they go out of the way. That's what we are now—just ants. Only——"

"Yes," I said.

"We're eatable ants."

We sat looking at each other.

"And what will they do with us?" I said.

"That's what I've been thinking. After Weybridge I went south—thinking. I saw what was up. Most of the people were hard at it squealing and exciting themselves. But I'm not so fond of squealing. I've been in sight of death once or twice; I'm not an ornamental soldier,[165] and at the best and worst, death—it's just death. And it's the man that keeps on thinking comes through. I saw everyone tracking away south. Says I, "Food won't last this way," and I turned right back. I went for the Martians like a sparrow goes for man. All round"—he waved a hand to the horizon—"they're starving in heaps, bolting, treading on each other...."

---

163. Actually a second Martian tripod has been lost (I:17), although neither the artilleryman or the narrator is aware of this fact.

164. Reiterates the artilleryman's odds given at note 64, when he calculates them as no better than "bows and arrows against the lightning."

165. See note 158 for this indication of the artilleryman's Cromwellian stance.

He saw my face, and halted awkwardly.

"No doubt lots who had money have gone away to France," he said. He seemed to hesitate whether to apologize, met my eyes, and went on: "There's food all about here. Canned things in shops; wines, spirits, mineral waters; and the water mains and drains are empty. Well, I was telling you what I was thinking. 'Here's intelligent things,' I said, 'and it seems they want us for food. First, they'll smash us up—ships, machines, guns, cities, all the order and organization. All that will go. If we were the size of ants we might pull through. But we're not. It's all too bulky to stop. That's the first certainty. Eh?"

I assented.

"It is; I've thought it out. Very well, then, next: at present we're caught as we're wanted. A Martian has only to go a few miles to get a crowd on the run. And I saw one, one day out by Wandsworth, picking houses to pieces and routing among the wreckage. But they won't keep on doing that. So soon as they've settled all our guns and ships, and smashed our railways, and done all the things they are doing over there, they will begin catching us systematic, picking the best and storing us in cages and things. That's what they will start doing in a bit. Lord! they haven't begun on us yet. Don't you see that?"

"Not begun!" I exclaimed.

"Not begun. All that's happened so far is through our not having the sense to keep quiet—worrying them with guns and such foolery. And losing our heads, and rushing off in crowds to where there wasn't any more safety than where we were. They don't want to bother us yet. They're making their things—making all the things they couldn't bring with them, getting things ready for the rest of their people. Very likely that's why the cylinders have stopped for a bit, for fear of hitting those who are here. And instead of our rushing about blind, on the howl, or getting dynamite on the chance of busting them up, we've got to fix ourselves up according to the new state of affairs. That's how I figure it out. It isn't quite according to what a man wants for his species, but it's about what the facts point to. And that's the principle I acted upon. Cities, nations, civilization, progress—it's all over. That game's up. We're beat."

"But if that is so, what is there to live for?"

The artilleryman looked at me for a moment.

"There won't be any more blessed concerts for a million years or so; there won't be any Royal Academy of Arts, and no nice little feeds at restaurants.[166] If it's amusement you're after, I reckon the game is up.

---

166. Resonates with the narrator's "last civilized dinner" at note 39. The

If you've got any drawing-room manners, or a dislike to eating peas
with a knife or dropping aitches, you'd better chuck 'em away. They
ain't no further use."

"You mean——"

"I mean, that men like me are going on living—for the sake of the
breed. I tell you, I'm grim set on living. And, if I'm not mistaken, you'll
show what insides *you've* got, too, before long. We aren't going to be

---

Martian assault on the overly-cultured aspects of modern civilization is all to
the good in the artilleryman's view, which accords with Wells's view of the invasion as a necessary cleansing of bourgeois respectability (note 23). The narrator, however, clings to it and so remains throughout skeptical of the artilleryman's plan to follow through with the Martian initiative, once the invaders are
defeated. At last the narrator parts company with him, after he gives himself to
drink and gluttony like the curate at note 149; under stress, neither of them can
sustain their respective theodicies. On the other hand, the artilleryman was right
to suspect the narrator from the start of being a weakling given to "a lot of complicated thinking."

The artilleryman's relish in reviewing the prospect as he sees it — "Cities,
nations, civilisation, progress — it's all over" — clearly evokes those concerns for
degeneration and moral rot that Spengler in *Decline of the West* (1926, 1928)
brought to spectacular fame. He favored the Nazis as they favored his work,
rooted as it was in a late nineteenth century worry that industrialism threatened
something organic in real life — exactly the artilleryman's view that "Life is real
again, and the useless and cumbersome and mischievous have to die." The history of this reaction in declinist thought is richly documented in Siegfried
Giedion's *Mechanization Takes Command* (1948). Chief among the back-to-
nature movements was the *Wandervögel*, a German youth organization promoting regeneration through fresh air and physical fitness in outdoor activities like
hiking (Speake 1997:471), which fed into Hitler Youth (Bleuel 1974: chapter 4;
see also Herman 1997:126). Its purifying aim had its dress in the short pants,
open-necked short-sleeved shirt, sandals, and hiking stick devised by a Dr.
Arnold Rikli *c.* 1870 (Giedion 1940:675, fig. 466). See fig. 11 in the plates of the
present work.

The artilleryman's proposal to form such a hygienic band of "able-bodied,
clean-minded" men and women (note 171) derives from this romantic, anti-
modernist tradition. His *Wandervögel* looks to Wells's New Puritans, who renew
the world with a vision of what civilization ought to be on a different ethical
basis. That the artilleryman fails, that "the gulf between his dreams and his powers" (note 174) proves too great in his fight against decadence, may be read as
anticipating the fatal contradictions of the Third Reich, at once modern in practice and romantic in ideology (see more in Schoenbaum 1980).

exterminated. And I don't mean to be caught, either, and tamed and fattened and bred like a thundering ox. Ugh! Fancy those brown creepers!"

"You don't mean to say——"

"I do. I'm going on. Under their feet. I've got it planned; I've thought it out. We men are beat. We don't know enough. We've got to learn before we've got a chance. And we've got to live, and keep independent while we learn. See? That's what has to be done."

I stared, astonished, and stirred profoundly by the man's resolution.

"Great God!" cried I. "But you are a man indeed!" And suddenly I gripped his hand.

"Eh?" he said, with his eyes shining. "I've thought it out, eh?"

"Go on," I said.

"Well, those who mean to escape their catching must get ready. I'm getting ready. Mind you, it isn't all of us are made for wild beasts; and that's what it's got to be. That's why I watched you. I had my doubts. You're thin and slender. I didn't know it was you, you see, or just how you'd been buried. All these—the sort of people that lived in these houses, and all those damn little clerks that used to live down *that* way— they'd be no good. They haven't any spirit in them—no proud dreams and no proud lusts; and a man who hasn't one or the other—Lord! what is he but funk and precautions? They just used to skedaddle off to work—I've seen hundreds of 'em, bit of breakfast in hand, running wild and shining to catch their little season-ticket train, for fear they'd get dismissed if they didn't; working at businesses they were afraid to take the trouble to understand; skedaddling back for fear they wouldn't be in time for dinner; keeping indoors after dinner for fear of the back-streets; and sleeping with the wives they married, not because they wanted them, but because they had a bit of money that would make for safety in their one little miserable skedaddle through the world. Lives insured and a bit invested for fear of accidents. And on Sundays—fear of the hereafter. As if hell was built for rabbits!¹⁶⁷ Well, the Martians will

---

167. The human "rabbit," timorous and everydayist, thinks too highly of himself if he believes that transgressions of bourgeois morality are deserving of Dantean hellfire in all its purgative splendor. As if their property-valued insurance policies (a repeated theme from note 44) were a guarantee! The artilleryman is especially harsh on "all those damn little clerks," commuters on the London & Southwestern Railway, who each day worry only to "catch their little season-ticket train." Wells is of the same mind when he says, with contempt, "the attraction and necessity of home increase with the square of the distance,

just be a godsend to these. Nice roomy cages, fattening food, careful breeding, no worry. After a week or so chasing about the fields and lands on empty stomachs, they'll come and be caught cheerful. They'll be quite glad after a bit. They'll wonder what people did before there were Martians to take care of them. And the bar-loafers, and mashers, and singers—I can imagine them. I can imagine them," he said, with a sort of sombre gratification. "There'll be any amount of sentiment and religion loose among them. There's hundreds of things I saw with my eyes, that I've only begun to see clearly these last few days. There's lots will take things as they are, fat and stupid; and lots will be worried by a sort of feeling that it's all wrong, and that they ought to be doing something. Now, whenever things are so that a lot of people feel they ought to be doing something, the weak, and those who go weak with a lot of complicated thinking, always make for a sort of do-nothing religion, very pious and superior, and submit to persecution and the will of the Lord. Very likely you've seen the same thing. It's energy in a gale of funk, and turned clean inside out. These cages will be full of psalms and hymns and piety.[168] And those of a less simple sort will work in a bit of—what is it?—eroticism."

He paused.

---

and not to have a return ticket is for most of us a symbol of disaster" (1928b:180). His proposal, reprinted in Appendix VII of the present work, for the "scientific administration" of the greater London economic area, is for a delocalized-minded elite to direct the mindless, rabbit-burrow mentality of all those commuters who think the security of their private homes is more important than working for the collective good. The Martians tear up the tracks of the London & SWRR with the same object (see plates, fig. 9 in the present work): to disillusion self-reliance and make for a new collectivist order. In *A Modern Utopia*, men are released from the "fetters of localty" (1905:49). "[A]ll the world will be awash with anonymous stranger men" (162). Such is "freedom from tradition" (84). The Wellsian future is populated by "workers of a new dawn. Men of no nation. Men without tradition. Men who look forward and not back" (1930:313). Wells's "War with Tradition" (1931:65) is the story of *The War of the Worlds*. Its Martian victory, forwarded by humans, is the story of *Sleeper*, the sequel in which men at last awake to their forward-looking destiny. The narrator never quite foresees, however, the necessity of that happy outcome.

168. The artilleryman evokes, and relishes, the memory of Christians martyred in the Roman arena. They deserved what they got. The element of "eroticism" in it (*infra*) is a cynical comment on the Christian hope of Heaven, no different, albeit sublimated, than the carnal Islamic Paradise of willing virgins. Doctor Moreau makes the same connection (Stover 1996b:140–141, *n*109).

"Very likely these Martians will make pets of some of them; train them to do tricks—who knows?—get sentimental over the pet boy who grew up and had to be killed. And some, maybe, they will train to hunt us."

"No," I cried, "that's impossible! No human being——"

"What's the good of going on with such lies?" said the artilleryman. "There's men who'd do it cheerful. What nonsense to pretend there isn't!"

And I succumbed to his conviction.

"If they come after me," he said—"Lord! if they come after me!" and subsided into a grim meditation.

I sat contemplating these things. I could find nothing to bring against this man's reasoning. In the days before the invasion no one would have questioned my intellectual superiority to his—I, a professed and recognised writer on philosophical themes, and he, a common soldier—and yet he had already formulated a situation that I had scarcely realized.

"What are you doing?" I said presently. "What plans have you made?"

He hesitated.

"Well, it's like this," he said. "What have we to do? We have to invent a sort of life[169] where men can live and breed, and be sufficiently secure to bring the children up. Yes—wait a bit, and I'll make it clearer what I think ought to be done. The tame ones will go like all tame beasts; in a few generations they'll be big, beautiful, rich-blooded, stupid— rubbish! The risk is that we who keep wild will go savage—degenerate into a sort of big savage rat.... You see, how I mean to live is under-

---

169. A marvelously perceptive phrase, "to invent" a sort of life. It says that society itself may be the object of scientific planning as are advances in technology, a progressive ideal. "We have not *insisted* that scientific methods could be applied to all human relations, to law and government — as well as material things" (1934a:149f). These are the inspiring words of John Cabal, founder and leader of the Air League. His mantra for his Airmen is, "RESEARCH, INVENTION, WORLD PLANNING—AND SCIENTIFIC CONTROL" (150). Cabal's name is highly significant. A *cabal* is a small group of plotters, a private junta of men serving a cause particular to its own purpose. This is what the Airmen, like the New Republicans, are: a "conspiracy of intellectuals and wilful people against existing institutions and existing limitations and boundaries" (1914b:x). They conspire to "carve out a Society of its own from Society" (1928:74). The artilleryman has in mind to organize a cabal against the Martians then, not unlike the Airmen, to rule the world in its name.

ground. I've been thinking about the drains. Of course, those who don't know drains think horrible things; but under this London are miles and miles—hundreds of miles—and a few days' rain and London empty will leave them sweet and clean. The main drains are big enough and airy enough for anyone. Then there's cellars, vaults, stores, from which bolting passages may be made to the drains.[170] And the railway tunnels and subways. Eh? You begin to see? And we form a band—able-bodied, clean-minded men. We're not going to pick up any rubbish that drifts in. Weaklings go out again."

"As you meant me to go?"

"Well—I parleyed, didn't I?"

"We won't quarrel about that. Go on."

"Those who stop, obey orders. Able-bodied, clean-minded women we want also—mothers and teachers. No lackadaisical ladies—no blasted rolling eyes. We can't have any weak or silly.[171] Life is real again, and the useless and cumbersome and mischievous have to die. They ought to die. They ought to be willing to die. It's a sort of disloyalty, after all, to live and taint the race. And they can't be happy. Moreover, dying's none so dreadful;—it's the funking makes it bad.

---

170. The artilleryman's repeated insistence on "drains" (= sewer mains), as at once a place of refuge and a base for counterattacking the Martians, has its echo in Wells's own proposal for "national service in the drains" (1917a:205). Cleaning them up could be the starting point for a labor draft along military lines — a thought suggested by universal conscription during World War I (see note 66). What was done in wartime can be done on the same large scale in peacetime for the purpose of "direct public service" (1916:69). What is wanted in social reconstruction is the same "spirit of the soldier, the spirit of subordination to a common purpose" (1916a:147) in a "general labour conscription" (1912:46).

171. The artilleryman's proposal to recruit "able-bodied, clean-minded" men *and* women to his cause anticipates those makers of the octopus state in *The Shape of Things to Come*, those partymen or Fellows of the Modern State who form "a cult primarily devoted to social and political service, self-appointed, self-trained and self-disciplined" (1933:125). They are the New Puritans who establish the Air Dictatorship that leads on to the accomplished Modern State Octopus. In the derivative film of 1936, *Things to Come*, these Airmen (or should we say Airpersons?) include women dressed in the same black uniforms and jackboots of male fashion (Stover 1987: plate 30). Critics who find the artilleryman a protofascist, and therefore disagreeable in light of twentieth century totalitarianism, are reluctant to see him as a Wellsian spokesman, and so are easily disposed to discredit him without regard for his defense at note 174.

And in all those places we shall gather. Our district will be London. And we may even be able to keep a watch, and run about in the open when the Martians keep away. Play cricket, perhaps. That's how we shall save the race. Eh? It's a possible thing? But saving the race is nothing in itself. As I say, that's only being rats. It's saving our knowledge and adding to it is the thing. There men like you come in. There's books, there's models. We must make great safe places down deep, and get all the books we can; not novels and poetry swipes, but ideas, science books.[172] That's where men like you come in. We must go to the British Museum and pick all those books through. Especially we must keep up our science—learn more. We must watch these Martians. Some of us must go as spies. When it's all working, perhaps I will. Get caught, I mean. And the great thing is, we must leave the Martians alone. We mustn't even steal. If we get in their way, we clear out. We must show them we mean no harm. Yes, I know. But they're intelligent things, and they won't hunt us down if they have all they want, and think we're just harmless vermin."

The artilleryman paused, and laid a brown hand upon my arm.

"After all, it may not be so much we may have to learn before—— Just imagine this: Four or five of their Fighting Machines suddenly starting off—Heat-Rays right and left, and not a Martian in 'em. Not a Martian in 'em, but men—men who have learnt the way how. It may be in my time, even—those men. Fancy having one of them lovely things, with its Heat-Ray wide and free! Fancy having it in control! What would it matter if you smashed to smithereens at the end of the run, after a bust like that? I reckon the Martians 'll open their beautiful eyes! Can't you see them, man? Can't you see them hurrying, hurrying—puffing and blowing and hooting to their other mechanical affairs? Something out of gear in every case. And swish, bang, rattle, swish! just as they are fumbling over it, *swish* comes the Heat-Ray, and, behold! man has come back to his own."[173]

---

172. Like Wells in "A Modern Education" (1917b), the artilleryman argues against liberal education in favor of the natural sciences. His crack about "poetry swipes" is a trope for humanistic studies in general, *swipes* being spoiled beer. The "dear old Humanities" are just that for Wells, "all so much mental thumb-twiddling" (1937a:60). His makers of the Modern State "must be educated in the scientific outlook as the old Puritans were educated in the Bible" (1936a:192). That is why both they and the artilleryman's proposed band of revolutionaries are New Puritans (note 171).

173. Here the artilleryman speaks like the Martian-fighting guerrilla warriors in Lasswitz: "Thus we will no longer need the Martians!" (note 158).

For a while the imaginative daring of the artilleryman, and the tone of assurance and courage he assumed, completely dominated my mind. I believed unhesitatingly both in his forecast of human destiny and in the practicability of his astonishing scheme, and the reader who thinks me susceptible and foolish must contrast his position, reading steadily, with all his thoughts about his subject, and mine, crouching fearfully in the bushes and listening, distracted by apprehension. We talked in this manner throughout the early morning time, and later crept out of the bushes, and, after scanning the sky for Martians, hurried precipitately to the house on Putney Hill where he had made his lair. It was the coal-cellar of the place, and when I saw the work he had spent a week upon—it was a burrow scarcely ten yards long, which he designed to reach the main drain on Putney Hill—I had my first inkling of the gulf between his dreams and his powers.[174] Such a hole I could have dug in a day. But I believed in him sufficiently to work with him all that morning until past mid-day at his digging. We had a garden barrow, and shot the earth we removed against the kitchen range. We refreshed ourselves with a tin of mock-turtle soup and wine from the neighbouring pantry. I found a curious relief from the aching strangeness of the world in this steady labour. As we worked, I turned his project over in my mind, and presently objections and doubts began to arise; but I worked there all the morning, so glad was I to find myself with a purpose again. After working an hour, I began to speculate on the distance one had to go before the cloaca was reached—the chances we had of missing it altogether. My immediate trouble was why we should dig this long tunnel, when it was possible to get into the drain at once down one of the manholes, and work back to the house. It seemed to me, too, that the house was inconveniently chosen, and required a needless length of tunnel. And just as I was beginning to face these things, the artilleryman stopped digging, and looked at me.

"We're working well," he said. He put down his spade. "Let us

---

174. Like the curate (note 149), the artilleryman had lapsed into drink and gluttony. But while the curate has only false dreams of a theological order, the artilleryman has valid dreams of a scientific order. The only problem is "the gulf between his dreams and his powers." His is no more than a failed experiment, the way it is in both experimental science and political revolution. "Revolution ... has to be learned by experiment. Revolution is just like science; it progresses by a succession of experimental failures, each of which brings it nearer to success" (1940b:118).

knock off a bit," he said. "I think it's time we reconnoitred from the roof of the house."

I was for going on, and after a little hesitation he resumed his spade; and then suddenly I was struck by a thought. I stopped, and so did he at once.

"Why were you walking about the Common," I said, "instead of being here?"

"Taking the air," he said. "I was coming back. It's safer by night."

"But the work?"

"Oh, one can't always work," he said, and in a flash I saw the man plain. He hesitated, holding his spade. "We ought to reconnoitre now," he said, "because if any come near they may hear the spades and drop upon us unaware."

I was no longer disposed to object. We went together to the roof and stood on a ladder peeping out of the roof door. No Martians were to be seen, and we ventured out on the tiles, and slipped down under shelter of the parapet.

From this position a shrubbery hid the greater portion of Putney, but we could see the river below, a bubbly mass of Red Weed, and the low parts of Lambeth flooded and red. The red creeper swarmed up the trees about the old palace, and their branches stretched gaunt and dead, and set with shrivelled leaves, from amidst its clusters. It was strange how entirely dependent both these things were upon flowing water for their propagation. About us neither had gained a footing; laburnums, pink mays, snowballs, and trees of arbor vitae, rose out of laurels and hydrangeas, green and brilliant, into the sunlight. Beyond Kensington dense smoke was rising, and that and a blue haze hid the northward hills.

The artilleryman began to tell me of the sort of people who still remained in London.

"One night last week," he said, "some fools got the electric light in order, and there was all Regent's Street and the Circus ablaze, crowded with painted and ragged drunkards, men and women, dancing and shouting till dawn. A man who was there told me. And as the day came they beheld a Fighting Machine standing near by the Langham, and looking down at them. Heaven knows how long he had been there. He came down the road towards them, and picked up nearly a hundred too drunk or frightened to run away."

Grotesque gleam of a time no history will ever fully describe!

From that, in answer to my questions, he came round to his grandiose plans again. He grew enthusiastic. He talked so eloquently of the possibility of capturing a Fighting Machine, that I more than half believed in him again. But now that I was beginning to understand something of his quality, I could divine the stress he laid on doing nothing precipitately. And I noted that now there was no question that he personally was to capture and fight the great machine.

After a time we went down to the cellar. Neither of us seemed disposed to resume digging, and when he suggested a meal, I was nothing loath. He became suddenly very generous, and when we had eaten he went away, and returned with some excellent cigars. We lit these, and his optimism glowed. He was inclined to regard my coming as a great occasion.

"There's some champagne in the cellar," he said.

"We can dig better on this Thames-side burgundy," said I.

"No," said he; "I am host to-day. Champagne! Great God! we've a heavy enough task before us! Let us take a rest, and gather strength while we may. Look at these blistered hands!"

And pursuant to this idea of a holiday, he insisted upon playing cards after we had eaten. He taught me euchre, and after dividing London between us, I taking the northern side, and he the southern, we played for parish points. Grotesque and foolish as this will seem to the sober reader, it is absolutely true, and what is more remarkable, I found the card game and several others we played extremely interesting.

Strange mind of man! that, with our species upon the edge of extermination or appalling degradation, with no clear prospect before us but the chance of a horrible death, we could sit following the chance of this painted pasteboard and playing the "joker" with vivid delight. Afterwards he taught me poker, and I beat him at three tough chess games. When dark came we were so interested that we decided to take the risk and light a lamp.

After an interminable string of games, we supped, and the artilleryman finished the champagne. We continued smoking the cigars. He was no longer the energetic regenerator of his species I had encountered in the morning. He was still optimistic, but it was a less kinetic, a more thoughtful optimism. I remember he wound up with my health, proposed in a speech of small variety and considerable intermittence. I took a cigar, and went upstairs to look at the lights he had spoken of, that blazed so greenly along the Highgate hills.

At first I stared across the London valley, unintelligently. The northern hills were shrouded in darkness; the fires near Kensington glowed redly, and now and then an orange-red tongue of flame flashed up and vanished in the deep blue night. All the rest of London was black. Then, nearer, I perceived a strange light, a pale violet-purple fluorescent glow, quivering under the night breeze. For a space I could not understand it, and then I knew that it must be the Red Weed from which this faint irradiation proceeded. With that realization, my dormant sense of wonder, my sense of the proportion of things, awoke again. I glanced from that to Mars, red and clear, glowing high in the west, and then gazed long and earnestly at the darkness of Hampstead and Highgate.

I remained a very long time upon the roof, wondering at the grotesque changes of the day. I recalled my mental states from the midnight prayer to the foolish card-playing. I had a violent revulsion of feeling. I remember I flung away the cigar with a certain wasteful symbolism. My folly came to me with glaring exaggeration. I seemed a traitor to my wife and to my kind; I was filled with remorse.[175] I resolved to leave this strange undisciplined dreamer of great things to his drink and gluttony, and to go on into London. There, it seemed to me, I had the best chance of learning what the Martians and my fellow-men were doing. I was still upon the roof when the late moon rose.

---

175. At this point, all the narrator can think on is his own "folly," his continuing to play cards with the artilleryman, whose grandiose dreams (note 174) he already has dismissed as a worse folly, all the while the great issue of the "extermination or appalling degradation" of the human species hangs in the balance. "Grotesque gleam of a time no history will ever fully describe!" Yet the narrator passes over that tragic prospect, as he now congratulates himself on feeling "remorse" for neglecting his wife. But his next thought (*infra*) is "to go into London!" He is ever the war correspondent, but less journalist than escapee from married humdrum.

VIII

DEAD LONDON.

AFTER I had parted from the artilleryman, I went down the hill, and by the High Street across the bridge to Lambeth. The Red Weed was tumultuous at that time, and nearly choked the bridge roadway, but its fronds were already whitened in patches by the spreading disease that presently removed it so swiftly.

At the corner of the lane that runs to Putney Bridge Station I found a man lying. He was as black as a sweep with the black dust, alive, but helplessly and speechlessly drunk. I could get nothing from him but curses and furious lunges at my head. I think I should have stayed by him but for the brutal type of his face.

There was black dust along the roadway from the bridge onwards, and it grew thicker in Fulham. The streets were horribly quiet. I got food—sour, hard, and mouldy, but quite eatable—in a baker's shop here. Some way towards Waltham Green the streets became clear of powder, and I passed a white terrace of houses on fire; the noise of the burning was an absolute relief. Going on towards Brompton, the streets were quiet again.

Here I came once more upon the black powder in the streets and upon dead bodies. I saw altogether about a dozen in the length of the Fulham Road. They had been dead many days, so that I hurried quickly past them. The black powder covered them over, and softened their outlines. One or two had been disturbed by dogs.

Where there was no black powder, it was curiously like a Sunday in the City, with the closed shops, the houses locked up and the blinds drawn, the desertion, and the stillness. In some places plunderers had been at work, but rarely at other than the provision and wine-shops. A jeweller's window had been broken open in one place, but apparently the thief had been disturbed, and a number of gold chains and a watch were scattered on the pavement. I did not trouble to touch them. Further on was a tattered woman in a heap on a doorstep; the hand that hung over her knee was gashed and bled down her rusty brown dress, and a smashed magnum of champagne formed a pool across the pavement. She seemed asleep, but she was dead.

The further I penetrated into London, the profounder grew the stillness. But it was not so much the stillness of death—it was the stillness of suspense, of expectation. At any time the destruction that had already singed the north-western borders of the Metropolis, and had annihilated Ealing and Kilburn, might strike among these houses and leave them smoking ruins. It was a city condemned and derelict....

In South Kensington the streets were clear of dead and of black powder. It was near South Kensington that I first heard the howling. It crept almost imperceptibly upon my senses. It was a sobbing alternation of two notes, "Ulla, ulla, ulla, ulla,"[176] keeping on perpetually. When I passed streets that ran northward it grew in volume, and houses and buildings seemed to deaden and cut it off again. It came to a full tide down Exhibition Road. I stopped, staring towards Kensington Gardens, wondering at this strange remote wailing. It was as if that mighty desert of houses had found a voice for its fear and solitude.

"Ulla, ulla, ulla, ulla," wailed that superhuman note—great waves of sound sweeping down the broad, sunlit roadway, between the tall buildings on either side. I turned northward, marvelling, towards the iron gates of Hyde Park. I had half a mind to break into the Natural History Museum and find my way up to the summits of the towers, in order to see across the park. But I decided to keep to the ground, where quick hiding was possible, and so went on up the Exhibition Road. All the large mansions on either side of the road were empty and still, and my footsteps echoed against the sides of the houses. At the top, near the park gate, I came upon a strange sight—a 'bus over-

---

176. The haunting "ulla, ulla, ulla, ulla" heard ever and again is the death wail of the last Martian standing (in its tripod) on Primrose Hill, where the last cylinder has landed. The hill overlooks the London Zoo, where man has captured his planet's wild beasts. The "ulla, ulla" is the last gasp of Martians run free to encapture humans. At last their superior technology is learned from to human advantage (note 180). The "ulla, ulla" of the last of them echoes the Irish Gol, or Ullaloo, a lamentation over the dead. It has classical references in Virgil (*Magnoque ululante tumulta*) and in Ovid (*Ululatibus omne / Implevere nemus*), as in the title of E.A. Poe's ballad "Ulalume."

turned, and the skeleton of a horse picked clean. I puzzled over this for a time, and then went on to the bridge over the Serpentine. The Voice grew stronger and stronger, though I could see nothing above the housetops on the north side of the park, save a haze of smoke to the northwest.

"Ulla, ulla, ulla, ulla," cried the Voice, coming, as it seemed to me, from the district about Regent's Park. The desolating cry worked upon my mind. The mood that had sustained me passed. The wailing took possession of me. I found I was intensely weary, footsore, and now again hungry and thirsty.

It was already past noon. Why was I wandering alone in this city of the dead? Why was I alone when all London was lying in state, and in its black shroud? I felt intolerably lonely. My mind ran on old friends that I had forgotten for years. I thought of the poisons in the chemists' shops, of the liquors the wine-merchants stored; I recalled the two sodden creatures of despair who, so far as I knew, shared the city with myself....

I came into Oxford Street by the Marble Arch, and here again was black powder and several bodies, and an evil, ominous smell from the gratings of the cellars of some of the houses. I grew very thirsty after the heat of my long walk. With infinite trouble I managed to break into a public-house and get food and drink. I was weary after eating, and went into the parlour behind the bar, and slept on a black horsehair sofa I found there.

I awoke to find that dismal howling still in my ears, "Ulla, ulla, ulla, ulla." It was now dusk, and after I had routed out some biscuits and a cheese in the bar—there was a meat-safe, but it contained nothing but maggots—I wandered on through the silent residential squares to Baker Street—Portman Square is the only one I can name—and so came out at last upon Regent's Park. And as I emerged from the top of Baker Street, I saw far away over the trees in the clearness of the sunset the hood of the Martian giant from which this howling proceeded. I was not terrified. I came upon him as if it were a matter of course. I watched him for some time, but he did not move. He appeared to be standing and yelling, for no reason that I could discover.

I tried to formulate a plan of action. That perpetual sound of "Ulla, ulla, ulla, ulla," confused my mind. Perhaps I was too tired to be very fearful. Certainly I was rather curious to know the reason of this monotonous crying than afraid. I turned back away from the park and struck into Park Road, intending to skirt the park, went along under shelter of the terraces, and got a view of this stationary howling Martian from the direction of St. John's Wood. A couple of hundred yards out of Baker Street I heard a yelping chorus, and saw, first a dog with a piece of putrescent red meat in his jaws coming headlong towards me, and then a pack of starving mongrels in pursuit of him. He made a wide curve to avoid me, as though he feared I might prove a fresh competitor. As the yelping died away down the silent road, the wailing sound of "Ulla, ulla, ulla, ulla," reasserted itself.

I came upon the wrecked Handling Machine halfway to St. John's Wood Station. At first I thought a house had fallen across the road. It was only as I clambered along the ruins that I saw, with a start, this mechanical Samson lying, with its tentacles bent and smashed and twisted, among the ruins it had made. The fore-part was shattered. It seemed as if it had driven blindly straight at the house, and had been overwhelmed in its overthrow. It seemed to me that this might have happened by a Handling Machine escaping from the guidance of its Martian. I could not clamber among the ruins to see it, and the twilight was now so far advanced that the blood with which its seat was smeared, and the gnawed gristle of the Martian that the dogs had left, was invisible to me.

Wondering still more at all that I had seen, I pushed on towards Primrose Hill. Far away, through a gap in the trees, I saw a second Martian, motionless as the first, standing in the park towards the Zoological Gardens, and silent. A little beyond the ruins about the smashed Handling Machine I came upon the Red Weed again, and found Regent's Canal a spongy mass of dark-red vegetation.

Abruptly, as I crossed the bridge, the sound of "Ulla, ulla, ulla," ceased. It was, as it were, cut off. The silence came like a thunder-clap.

The dusky houses about me stood faint, and tall and dim; the trees toward the park were growing black. All about me the Red Weed clambered among the ruins, writhing to get above me in the dim. Night, the Mother of Fear and Mystery, was coming upon me. But while that voice sounded, the solitude, the desolation, had been endurable; by virtue of it London had still seemed alive, and the sense of life about me had upheld me. Then suddenly a change, the passing of something—I knew not what—and then a stillness that could be felt. Nothing but this gaunt quiet.

London about me gazed at me spectrally. The windows in the white houses were like the eye-sockets of skulls. About me my imagination found a thousand noiseless enemies moving. Terror seized me, a horror of my temerity. In front of me the road became pitchy black as though it was tarred, and I saw a contorted shape lying across the pathway. I could not bring myself to go on. I turned down St. John's Wood Road, and ran headlong from this unendurable stillness towards Kilburn. I hid from the night and the silence, until long after midnight, in a cabmen's shelter in the Harrow Road. But before the dawn my courage returned, and while the stars were still in the sky, I turned once more towards Regent's Park. I missed my way among the streets, and presently saw, down a long avenue, in the half-light of the early dawn, the curve of Primrose Hill. On the summit, towering up to the fading stars, was a third Martian, erect and motionless like the others.

An insane resolve possessed me. I would die and end it. And I would save myself even the trouble of killing myself. I marched on recklessly towards this Titan, and then, as I drew nearer and the light grew, I saw that a multitude of black birds was circling and clustering about the hood. At that my heart gave a bound, and I began running along the road.

I hurried through the Red Weed that choked St. Edmund's Terrace (I waded breast-high across a torrent of water that was rushing down from the waterworks towards the Albert Road), and emerged upon the grass before the rising of the sun. Great mounds had been heaped about the crest of the hill, making a huge redoubt of it—it was the final and largest place the Martians made—and from behind these heaps there rose a thin smoke against the sky. Against the skyline an eager dog ran and disappeared. The thought that had flashed into my mind grew real, grew credible. I felt no fear, only a wild trembling exultation, as I ran up the hill towards the motionless monster. Out of the hood hung lank shreds of brown at which the hungry birds pecked and tore.

In another moment I had scrambled up the earthen rampart and stood upon its crest, and the interior of the redoubt was below me. A mighty space it was, with gigantic machines here and there within it, huge mounds of material and strange shelter-places. And, scattered about it, some in their over-turned war-machines, some in the now rigid Handling Machines, and a dozen of them stark and silent and laid in a row, were the Martians—*dead!*—slain by the putrefactive and disease bacteria against which their systems were unprepared; slain as the Red Weed was being slain; slain, after all man's devices had failed, by the humblest things that God, in His wisdom, has put upon this earth.[177]

---

177. A profound irony. Martian "sanitary science" (note 140) has cleaned up their home planet to a fault. The sanitary revolution of the nineteenth cen-

For so it had come about, as, indeed, I and many men might have foreseen had not terror and disaster blinded our minds. These germs of disease have taken toll of humanity since the beginning of things—taken toll of our prehuman ancestors since life began here. But by virtue of this natural selection of our kind we have developed resisting-power; to no germs do we succumb without a struggle, and to many—those that cause putrefaction in dead matter, for instance—our living frames are altogether immune. But there are no bacteria in Mars, and directly these invaders arrived, directly they drank and fed, our microscopic allies began to work their overthrow. Already when I watched them they were irrevocably doomed, dying and rotting even as they went to and fro. It was inevitable. By the toll of a billion deaths, man has bought his birthright of the earth, and it is his against all comers; it would still be his were the Martians ten times as mighty as they are. For neither do men live nor die in vain.

Here and there they were scattered, nearly fifty altogether in that great gulf they had made, overtaken by a death that must have seemed to them as incomprehensible as any death could be. To me also at that time this death was incomprehensible. All I knew was that these things that had been alive and so terrible to men were dead. For a moment I believed that the destruction of Sennacherib had been repeated, that God had repented, that the Angel of Death had slain them in the night.

I stood staring into the pit, and my heart lightened gloriously, even as the rising sun struck the world to fire about me with his rays. The pit was still in darkness; the mighty engines, so great and wonderful in their power and complexity, so unearthly in their tortuous forms, rose weird and vague and strange out of the shadows towards the light. A multitude of dogs, I could hear, fought over the bodies that lay darkly in the depth of the pit, far below me. Across the pit on its further lip, flat and vast and strange, lay the great flying-machine with which they had been experimenting upon our denser atmosphere when decay and death arrested them. Death had come not a day too soon. At the sound of a cawing overhead I looked up at the huge Fighting Machine, that would fight no more for ever, at the tattered red

tury was very much a Saint-Simonian initiative (Coleman 1982: chapter 10), and Lowellian Mars can be no cleaner since his own Martians are Saint-Simonists. Wells's Martians, coming from the same place, are so far from germicidal reality they have been Metchnikoffed (see the Introduction to the present work, section 5). The irony is, Metchnikoff himself was a pioneering specialist on immunology (Tauber and Chernyak 1991).

shreds of flesh that dripped down upon the overturned seats on the summit of Primrose Hill.

I turned and looked down the slope of the hill to where, enhaloed now in birds, stood those other two Martians that I had seen overnight, just as death had overtaken them. The one had died, even as it had been crying to its companions; perhaps it was the last to die, and its voice had gone on perpetually until the force of its machinery was exhausted. They glittered now, harmless tripod towers of shining metal, in the brightness of the rising sun....

All about the pit, and saved as by a miracle from everlasting destruction, stretched the great Mother of Cities. Those who have only seen London veiled in her sombre robes of smoke can scarcely imagine the naked clearness and beauty of the silent wilderness of houses.

Eastward, over the blackened ruins of the Albert Terrace and the splintered spire of the church, the sun blazed dazzling in a clear sky, and here and there some facet in the great wilderness of roofs caught the light and glared with a white intensity. It touched even that round store place for wines by the Chalk Farm Station, and the vast railway yards, marked once with a graining of black rails, but redlined now with the quick rusting of a fortnight's disuse, with something of the mystery of beauty.

Northward were Kilburn and Hampstead, blue and crowded with houses; westward the great city was dimmed; and southward, beyond the Martians, the green waves of Regent's Park, the Langham Hotel, the dome of the Albert Hall, the Imperial Institute, and the giant mansions of the Brompton Road, came out clear and little in the sunrise, the jagged ruins of Westminster rising hazily beyond. Far away and blue were the Surrey hills, and the towers of the Crystal Palace glittered like two silver rods. The dome of St. Paul's was dark against the sunrise, and injured, I saw for the first time, by a huge gaping cavity on its western side.

And as I looked at this wide expanse of houses and factories and churches, silent and abandoned; as I thought of the multitudinous hopes and efforts, the innumerable hosts of lives that had gone to build this human reef, and of the swift and ruthless destruction that had hung over it all; when I realized that the shadow had been rolled back, and that men might still live in the streets, and this dear vast city of mine be once more alive and powerful, I felt a wave of emotion that was near akin to tears.

The torment was over. Even that day the healing would begin. The survivors of the people scattered over the country—leaderless, lawless, foodless, like sheep without a shepherd—the thousands who had fled by sea, would begin to return; the pulse of life, growing stronger and stronger, would beat again in the empty streets, and pour across the vacant squares. Whatever destruction was done, the hand of the destroyer was stayed. The hand of the destroyer was stayed. All the gaunt wrecks, the blackened skeletons of houses that stared so dismally at the sunlit grass of the hill, would presently be echoing with the hammers of the restorers and ringing with the tapping of the trowels. At the thought I extended my hands towards the sky and began thanking God. In a year, thought I—in a year....

And then, with overwhelming force, came the thought of myself, of my wife, and the old life of hope and tender helpfulness that had ceased for ever.

IX

WRECKAGE.

AND now comes the strangest thing in my story. And yet, perhaps, it is not altogether strange. I remember, clearly and coldly and vividly, all that I did that day until the time that I stood weeping and praising God upon the summit of Primrose Hill. And then I forget....

Of the next three days I know nothing. I have learnt since that, so far from my being the first discoverer of the Martian overthrow, several such wanderers as myself had already discovered this on the previous night. One man—the first—had gone to St. Martin's-le-Grand, and, while I sheltered in the cabmen's hut, had contrived to telegraph to Paris. Thence the joyful news had flashed all over the world; a thousand cities, chilled by ghastly apprehensions, suddenly flashed into frantic illumination; they knew of it in Dublin, Edinburgh, Manchester, Birmingham, at the time when I stood upon the verge of the pit. Already men, weeping with joy, as I have heard, shouting and staying their work to shake hands and shout, were making up trains, even as near as Crewe, to descend upon London. The church bells that had ceased a fortnight since suddenly caught the news, until all England was bell-ringing. Men on cycles, lean-faced, unkempt, scorched along every country lane, shouting of unhoped deliverance, shouting to gaunt, staring figures of despair. And for the food! Across the Channel, across the Irish Sea, across the Atlantic, corn, bread and meat were tearing to our relief. All the shipping in the world seemed going Londonward in those days. But of all this I have no memory. I drifted—a demented man. I found myself in the house of kindly people who had found me on the third day, wandering, weeping and raving, through the streets of St. John's Wood. They have told me since that I was singing some inane doggerel about "The Last Man Left Alive, Hurrah! The Last Man Left Alive." Troubled as they were with their own affairs,

these people, whose name, much as I would like to express my gratitude to them, I may not even give here, nevertheless cumbered themselves with me, sheltered me and protected me from myself. Apparently they had learnt something of my story from me during the days
of my lapse.

Very gently, when my mind was assured again, did they break to me
what they had learnt of the fate of Leatherhead. Two days after I was
imprisoned it had been destroyed, with every soul in it, by a Martian.
He had swept it out of existence, as it seemed, without any provoca-
tion, as a boy might crush an anthill, in the mere wantonness of power.

I was a lonely man, and they were very kind to me. I was a lonely
man and a sad one, and they bore with me. I remained with them four
days after my recovery. All that time I felt a vague, a growing craving
to look once more on whatever remained of the little life that seemed
so happy and bright in my past. It was a mere hopeless desire to feast
upon my misery. They dissuaded me. They did all they could to divert
me from this morbidity. But at last I could resist the impulse no longer,
and promising faithfully to return to them, and parting, as I will confess, from these four-day friends with tears, I went out again into the
streets that had lately been so dark and strange and empty.

Already they were busy with returning people, in places even there
were shops open, and I saw a drinking fountain running water.

I remember how mockingly bright the day seemed as I went back
on my melancholy pilgrimage to the little house at Woking, how busy
the streets and vivid the moving life about me. So many people were
abroad everywhere, busied in a thousand activities, that it seemed
incredible that any great proportion of the population could have been
slain. But then I noticed how yellow were the skins of the people I met,
how shaggy the hair of the men, how large and bright their eyes, and
that every other man still wore his dirty rags. The faces seemed all with
one of two expressions—a leaping exultation and energy, or a grim resolution. Save for the expression of the faces, London seemed a city of
tramps. The vestries were indiscriminately distributing bread sent us
by the French Government. The ribs of the few horses showed dismally. Haggard special constables with white badges stood at the corners of every street. I saw little of the mischief wrought by the Martians until I reached Wellington Street, and there I saw the Red Weed
clambering over the buttresses of Waterloo Bridge.

At the corner of the bridge, too, I saw one of the common contrasts
of that grotesque time: a sheet of paper flaunting against a thicket of
the Red Weed, transfixed by a stick that kept it in place. It was the

placard of the first newspaper to resume publication—the *Daily Mail*. I bought a copy for a blackened shilling I found in my pocket. Most of it was in blank, but the solitary compositor who did the thing had amused himself by making a grotesque scheme of advertisement stereo on the back page. The matter he printed was emotion; the news organization had not as yet found its way back. I learnt nothing fresh except that already in one week the examination of the Martian mechanisms had yielded astonishing results. Among other things, the article assured me what I did not believe at the time: that the "Secret of Flying" was discovered. At Waterloo I found the free trains that were taking people to their homes. The first rush was already over. There were few people in the train, and I was in no mood for casual conversation. I got a compartment to myself, and sat with folded arms, looking grayly at the sunlit devastation that flowed past the windows. And just outside the terminus the train jolted over temporary rails, and on either side of the railway the houses were blackened ruins. To Clapham Junction the face of London was grimy with powder of the Black Smoke, in spite of two days of thunderstorms and rain, and at Clapham Junction the line had been wrecked again; there were hundreds of out-of-work clerks and shopmen working side by side with the customary navvies, and we were jolted over a hasty relaying.

All down the line from there the aspect of the country was gaunt and unfamiliar; Wimbledon particularly had suffered. Walton, by virtue of its unburnt pine-woods, seemed the least hurt of any place along the line. The Wandle, the Mole, every little stream, was a heaped mass of Red Weed, in appearance between butcher's meat and pickled cabbage. The Surrey pine-woods were too dry, however, for the festoons of the red climber. Beyond Wimbledon, within sight of the line, in certain nursery grounds, were the heaped masses of earth about the sixth cylinder. A number of people were standing about it, and some sappers were busy in the midst of it. Over it flaunted a Union Jack, flapping cheerfully in the morning breeze. The nursery grounds were everywhere crimson with the weed, a wide expanse of livid colour cut with purple shadows, and very painful to the eye. One's gaze went with infinite relief from the scorched grays and sullen reds of the foreground to the blue-green softness of the eastward hills.

The line on the London side of Woking Station was still undergoing repair, so I descended at Byfleet Station and took the road to Maybury, past the place where I and the artilleryman had talked to the hussars, and on by the spot where the Martian had appeared to me in the thunderstorm. Here, moved by curiosity, I turned aside to find, among a tangle of red fronds, the warped and broken dogcart with the whitened bones of the horse, scattered and gnawed. For a time I stood regarding these vestiges....

Then I returned through the pine-wood, neck-high with Red Weed here and there, to find the landlord of the Spotted Dog had already found burial; and so came home past the College Arms. A man standing at an open cottage door greeted me by name as I passed.

I looked at my house with a quick flash of hope that faded immediately. The door had been forced; it was unfastened, and was opening slowly as I approached.

It slammed again. The curtains of my study fluttered out of the open window from which I and the artilleryman had watched the dawn. No one had closed that window since. The smashed bushes were just as I had left them nearly four weeks ago. I stumbled into the hall, and the house felt empty. The stair-carpet was ruffled and discoloured where I had crouched soaked to the skin from the thunderstorm, the night of the catastrophe. Our muddy footsteps I saw still went up the stairs.

I followed them to my study, and found lying on my writing-table still, with the selenite paper-weight upon it, the sheet of work I had left on the afternoon of the opening of the cylinder. For a space I stood reading over my abandoned arguments. It was a paper on the probable development of Moral Ideas with the development of the civilizing process; and the last sentence was the opening of a prophecy: "In about two hundred years," I had written, "we may expect——" The sentence ended abruptly. I remembered my inability to fix my mind that morning, scarcely a month gone by, and how I had broken off to get my *Daily Chronicle* from the newsboy. I remembered how I went down to the garden gate as he came along, and how I had listened to his odd story of the "Men from Mars."

I came down and went into the dining-room. There were the mutton and the bread, both far gone now in decay, and a beer bottle overturned, just as I and the artilleryman had left them. My home was desolate. I perceived the folly of the faint hope I had cherished so long. And then a strange thing occurred. "It is no use," said a voice. "The house is deserted. No one has been here these ten days. Do not stay here to torment yourself. No one escaped but you."

I was startled. Had I spoken my thought aloud? I turned, and the French window was open behind me. I made a step to it, and stood looking out.

And there, amazed and afraid, even as I stood amazed and afraid, were my cousin and my wife—my wife white and tearless. She gave a faint cry.

"I came," she said. "I knew—I knew——"

She put her hand to her throat—swayed. I made a step forward, and caught her in my arms.[178]

---

178. All critics think this a weak ending, and ending it was in the serial version of 1897. The Epilogue is new to the book but it, too, strikes the very same note. To fault it as failing to resolve the story belittles Wells's power of characterization: The narrator is a specimen case of what the invasion actually cured — except to himself. For all his philosophical pretensions, as another Dr. Pangloss, he has not learned the lesson of the "great disillusionment" (note 4). After his war fever is spent, he returns to wife and family, to the embrace of everydayism, to that "cosmic *crambe repetita*" (note 40) of the Normal Social Life. He remains indifferent to the lesson of Darwinian biology taught by the collectivist Martians, which "consists essentially in diminishing the importance of the individual and developing the realisation of the species" (1917:70). He ignores "The Immensity of the Issue and the Triviality of Men" (1922a:1). In the face of great events, war and revolution, trivialty is his name. He is no more than a "human rabbit" (1925a:364) (see note 167).

> For rabbits are rabbits, made to eat and breed, and men are human beings and creatures of habit and custom and prejudice; and what has made them, what will judge them, what will destroy them — they may turn their eyes to at times as the rabbits will glance at the concussion of the guns, but it will never draw them away from eating their lettuce and sniffing after their does [1915:313f].

In a work discussing why he is a scientific atheist, Wells cites the conclusion of Kant's *Critique of Pure Reason.* Its words are his credo, "Two things fill my mind with every renewed wonder and awe the more often and deeper I dwell on them — the starry vault above me, and the moral law within me" (in 1917:85). How like the Martians! It is their credo, too, the basis for their "selfish intelligence" (note 139): a two-word *summa* of Kantian ethics and its categorical imperative.

That is the theology of *Worlds*, in light of the author's cosmic vision; it is meant to contrast with, show up, and indict its rabbitlike opposite in the persona of his cowardly narrator. Filled with war fever, he has heard the concussion of the guns, yet returns to his lettuce and his doe.

For Wells, the auctorial voice behind exposure of the narrator's fallibility, *the* great question that trivializes the everydayism of the human rabbit must be answered or else man is doomed: What is the nature of the cosmos? It is Kantian. When Wells takes to heart the "moral law" within as a mirror of the "starry vault" above, he asserts Darwinian reality, Martian reality, that cosmic reality to be grasped if a new utopian order, correcting the mistakes of humanity's entire historical past, is to be achieved. Such, happily, is realized in the Great

State, which eventuates in *Sleeper* in response to the invasion and in which the individualities of the Normal Social Life are totally subordinated for the collective advancement of mankind. That possible human "commonweal" (note 180) the narrator is able to speculate upon, to be sure, but he is void of the necessary inner "moral law." He no more reflects the "starry vault" above than any other lowly creature habituated to "animal individualism" (1933:334).

X

THE EPILOGUE.

I CANNOT but regret, now that I am concluding my story, how little I am able to contribute to the discussion of the many debatable questions which are still unsettled. In one respect I shall certainly provoke criticism. My particular province is speculative philosophy. My knowledge of comparative physiology is confined to a book or two, but it seems to me that Carver's suggestions as to the reason of the rapid death of the Martians is so probable as to be regarded almost as a proven conclusion. I have assumed that in the body of my narrative.

At any rate, in all the bodies of the Martians that were examined after the war, no bacteria except those already known as terrestrial species were found. That they did not bury any of their dead, and the reckless slaughter they perpetrated, point also to an entire ignorance of the putrefactive process. But probable as this seems, it is by no means a proven conclusion.

Neither is the composition of the Black Smoke known, which the Martians used with such deadly effect, and the generator of the Heat-Ray remains a puzzle. The terrible disasters at the Ealing and South Kensington laboratories have disinclined analysts for further investigations upon the latter. Spectrum analysis of the black powder points unmistakably to the presence of an unknown element with a brilliant group of three lines in the green, and it is possible that it combines with argon to form a compound which acts at once with deadly effect upon some constituent in the blood. But such unproven speculations will scarcely be of interest to the general reader, to whom this story is addressed. None of the brown scum that drifted down the Thames after the destruction of Shepperton was examined at the time, and now none is forthcoming.

The results of an anatomical examination of the Martians, so far as the prowling dogs had left such an examination possible, I have already given. But everyone is familiar with the magnificent and almost complete specimen in spirits at the Natural History Museum, and the countless drawings that have been made from it; and beyond that the interest of the physiology and structure is purely scientific.

A question of graver and universal interest is the possibility of another attack from the Martians. I do not think that nearly enough attention is being given to this aspect of the matter. At present the planet Mars is in conjunction, but with every return to opposition I, for one, anticipate a renewal of their adventure. In any case, we should be prepared. It seems to me that it should be possible to define the position of the gun from which the shots are discharged, to keep a sustained watch upon this part of the planet, and to anticipate the arrival of the next attack.

In that case the cylinder might be destroyed with dynamite or artillery before it was sufficiently cool for the Martians to emerge, or they might be butchered by means of guns so soon as the screw opened. It seems to me that they have lost a vast advantage in the failure of their first surprise. Possibly they see it in the same light.

Lessing[179] had advanced excellent reasons for supposing that the

---

179. More Panglossian name-dropping, as at note 143, in a pretentious, vain, and self-deluded all-knowing familiarity with authorities on any subject, both real and unreal. Lessing is a fictive reference, although the narrator, were he not so ugly, could have named some astronomer of contemporary renown; more than one speculated on interplanetary flight. Instead he cites a made-up Lessing to establish what is now happening in the solar system. The Martians, having given up on earth, now choose to invade Venus. This may or not be so. A planetary opposition is said to be right for it, but then again this never was a factor in the earth–Mars case (note 8). From the auctorial point of view, the narrator's philosophical speculation, as to who shall be Lords of the Universe (see note 182), quite accords with his own, but he (the vainglorious narrator) is not philosophical enough, having learned nothing from the invasion (note 183).

At this point the artistic mystery of *Worlds* comes to a crunch. The narrator, reliable or unreliable, reports the firing of a Martian gun one night, and the next day or so a cylinder lands (helpful opposition or not) in one June–July summer heat wave. Is this hallucinatory or what? Everything else is faultlessly photojournalistic. The author himself grants the Martians great speed and might, but is this, too, a wild imagining in aid of his wiser philosophy, his hortatory warning to learn what the everydayist narrator has not?— the imperative for humanity to unite in a world-state on the Martian model or suffer a self-inflicted war catastrophe not so benevolent. The childish rivalry of "belligerent patriotism"

Martians have actually succeeded in effecting a landing on the planet Venus. Seven months ago now, Venus and Mars were in alignment with the sun; that is to say, Mars was in opposition from the point of view of an observer on Venus. Subsequently a peculiar luminous and sinuous marking appeared on the unillumined half of the inner planet, and almost simultaneously a faint dark mark of a similar sinuous character was detected upon a photograph of the Martian disc. One needs to see the drawings of these appearances in order to appreciate fully their remarkable resemblance in character.

At any rate, whether we expect another invasion or not, our views of the human future must be greatly modified by these events. We have learned now that we cannot regard this planet as being fenced in and a secure abiding-place for Man; we can never anticipate the unseen good or evil that may come upon us suddenly out of space. It may be that in the larger design of the universe this invasion from Mars is not without its ultimate benefit for men; it has robbed us of that serene confidence in the future which is the most fruitful source of decadence, the gifts to human science it has brought are enormous, and it has done much to promote the conception of the commonweal of mankind.[180] It may be that across the immensity of space the Martians have watched the fate of these pioneers of theirs and learned their lesson, and that on the planet Venus they have found a securer

---

(1927:18), characteristic of "competitive nationalism" (1930a:26), must grow into something more mature, bringing primitive mankind to its childhood's end. It's "unity or smash" (1938b:33), utopia or oblivion.

180. The narrator ticks off three items of "benefit" of the invasion, which is why it is a "Benevolent Catastrophe" (see the Introduction to the present work, section 3: heading). First, it came as a "great disillusionment" (note 4), shattering man's false "belief in some underlying benevolence in uncontrolled events" (1933:30), as if the future will providentially take care of itself without human direction. This is the fundamental error leading to *fin de globe* in *The Time Machine*. Second, the "gifts" of Martian science, which make possible the advanced technology of A.D. 2100 in *Sleeper*. Thirdly, and most important, the shock of the invasion did "much to promote the conception of the commonweal of mankind." This is the principal legacy of the Martians, fulfilled in the world state of 2100: a future willed into being by wilful intellectuals who won their own war of the worlds — progressives vs. reactionaries — in the Wellsian "War with Tradition" (1931:65). The narrator himself, however, is not one of those who help to make that future. The Great State to come will swallow him and his kind, all who still live the Normal Social Life (1912) deluded by everydayism.

settlement. Be that as it may, for many years yet there will certainly be no relaxation of the eager scrutiny of the Martian disc, and those fiery darts of the sky, the shooting stars, will bring with them as they fall an unavoidable apprehension to all the sons of men.

The broadening of men's views that has resulted can scarcely be exaggerated. Before the cylinder fell there was a general persuasion that through all the deep of space no life existed beyond the petty surface of our minute sphere. Now we see further. If the Martians can reach Venus, there is no reason to suppose that the thing is impossible for men, and when the slow cooling of the sun makes this earth uninhabitable, as at last it must do, it may be that the thread of life that has begun here will have streamed out and caught our sister planet within its toils. Should we conquer?[181]

Dim and wonderful is the vision I have conjured up in my mind of life spreading slowly from this little seed-bed of the solar system throughout the inanimate vastness of sidereal space. But that is a remote dream. It may be, on the other hand, that the destruction of the Martians is only a reprieve. To them, and not to us, perhaps, is the future ordained.[182]

I must confess the stress and danger of the time have left an abiding

---

181. In *The Undying Fire*, Wells argues the case for yes to "should we conquer?"

> Not for ever shall life be marooned upon this planet, imprisoned by the cold and incredible emptiness of space. Is it not plain to you all, from what man in spite of everything has achieved, that he is but at the beginning of achievement? [1919:210f].

"Man is immortal, but not men" (1932:135). But it is the responsibility of individual men to keep alive that "undying fire" that is the immortal life of the species, and to see that its collective achievements go on forever into outer space, once our own little planet, like Mars, has cooled beyond its hospitality to life. Such is the cosmic significance of Oswald Cabal's ambitious space program in *Things to Come*: his experimental Space Gun (see fig. 8 of the plates in the present work) being a twin of Martian space cannon.

182. The quotation from Kepler on the title page of *Worlds* (see note 1) is here brought to bear with compelling force: are we or *they* to be Lords of the Universe? For humans are in a Darwinian struggle with other intelligent life-forms out there; to know that fact is to prevail, if only men will wake up to it. They do in *Sleeper*, first conquering a world state, then planning for the conquest of space (Stover 2000). Not that the narrator ever conceives of such a development, much less participate in it, however much he may philosophize the "benefits" of the invasion (note 180).

sense of doubt and insecurity in my mind. I sit in my study writing by lamplight, and suddenly I see again the healing valley below set with writhing flames, and feel the house behind and about me empty and desolate. I go out into the Byfleet Road, and vehicles pass me, a butcher-boy in a cart, a cabful of visitors, a workman on a bicycle, children going to school, and suddenly they become vague and unreal, and I hurry again with the artilleryman through the hot, brooding silence. Of a night I see the black powder darkening the silent streets, and the contorted bodies shrouded in that layer; they rise upon me tattered and dog-bitten. They gibber and grow fiercer, paler, uglier, mad distortions of humanity at last, and I wake, cold and wretched, in the darkness of the night.

I go to London and see the busy multitudes in Fleet Street and the Strand, and it comes across my mind that they are but the ghosts of the past, haunting the streets that I have seen silent and wretched, going to and fro, phantasms in a dead city, the mockery of life in a galvanized body. And strange, too, it is to stand on Primrose Hill, as I did but a day before writing this last chapter, to see the great province of houses, dim and blue through the haze of the smoke and mist, vanishing at last into the vague lower sky, to see the people walking to and fro among the flower-beds on the hill, to see the sightseers about the Martian machine that stands there still, to hear the tumult of playing children, and to recall the time when I saw it all bright and clear-cut, hard and silent, under the dawn of that last great day....

And strangest of all is it to hold my wife's hand again, and to think that I have counted her, and that she has counted me, among the dead.[183]

THE END.

---

183. It is breathtaking to find the narrator so observantly detached from the mean little examples of everydayism all about him, only to steadfastly continue living it — as if his war experience had no meaning save in theory (see note 178). His one personal gain reduces to gratitude that both he and his wife have survived the rabbit-alarming concussions of the guns. He reverts to those odious habits of personal security that his whole account, from the opening paragraph, targets as the proper object of "the great disillusionment" (note 4).

BILLING AND SONS, PRINTERS, GUILDFORD.

Critics who nonetheless find the narrator a flat, personally undeveloped spokesman for the author himself perhaps overlook Wells's cosmic theory of characterization. "But the truth is the individuality of a man is not his complete expression. A man is a specimen of a species of social animal — plus a specimen of some sort of culture, plus a slight personal difference" (1897d; in Parrinder and Philmus 1980:127). These three levels plainly manifest themselves in the narrator's persona. (1) First of all he is a specimen of *Homo sapiens* contrasting conspicuously with an alien species. Most of humanity reacts *en masse* in terror and flight, with only the artilleryman being a second exception. (2) He surely is a specimen of bourgeois culture, and remains unreconstructed to the end. (3) As for "a slight personal difference," like the artilleryman he does not run from the Martians, but rather at personal risk pursues them in a quest of a good war story. At the same time, he is motivated to leave home to escape the boring routine and *crambe repetita* of family life — to which he returns when the excitement is over. Not so slight, however, is the narrator's differentiation from the author who portrays him. Far from being his mouthpiece, for all his sharing Wells's speculative turn of mind, he fails to learn the lesson of the invasion: the doom of bourgeois culture. That is for a later generation of men to apply, which they do in *Sleeper* the sequel. From the author's point of view, the narrator, at bottom, is just another human rabbit whose complacent way of life is destined for radical change: come the socialist world-state.

Contrary to critical opinion, the ending is not tired and feeble, it is punchy. Wells is at all times in complete control of the narrative. He remains always on point in designing to tell a philosophical tale, or ideological fable. Nor, by his lights, is it lacking in characterization.

Appendix I
"The Man of the Year Million,"
by H.G. Wells (1893)

This is the essay alluded to by the narrator at textual note 137, published in the 6 November 1893 issue of *Pall Mall Gazette*, in which he had "forecast for man a final structure not unlike the actual Martian condition." He then mentions a caricature of it in the humor magazine *Punch*.

The *Punch* item, a piece of doggerel titled "1,000,000 A.D.," is done anonymously. It goes as follows:

1,000,000 A.D.

["The descendants of man will nourish themselves by immersion in nutritive fluid. They will have enormous brains, liquid, soulful eyes, and large hands, on which they will hop. No craggy nose will they have, no vestigial ears; their mouths will be a small, perfectly round aperture, unanimal, like the evening star. Their whole musculature system will be shrivelled to nothing, a dangling pendant to their minds."—*Pall Mall Gazette, abridged*]

What, a million years hence will become of the *Genus
   Humanum*, is truly a question vexed;
At that epoch, however, *one* prophet has seen us
   Resemble the sketch annexed.

For as Man undergoes Evolution ruthless,
   His skull will grow "domelike, bald, terete";
And his mouth will be jawless, gumless, toothless —
   No more will he drink or eat!

He will soak in a crystalline bath of pepsine,
   (No ROBERT* will then have survived, to wait,)
And he'll hop on his hands as his food he steps in —
   A quasi-cherubic gait!

---

*Type-name for a personal servant or valet.

> No longer the land or the sea he'll furrow;
>   The world will be withered, ice-cold, dead.
> As the chill of Eternity grows, he'll burrow
>   Far down underground instead.
>
> If the *Pall Mall Gazette* has thus been giving
>   A forecast correct of this change immense,
> Our stars we may thank, then, that *we* shan't be living
>   A million years from hence.

The poem was illustrated with drawings, one of which is reproduced in the plates for the present work, fig. 4. It perfectly captures Wells's evolutionary perspective on man's past and future. The shadow behind the man of the year million has to the right the silhouetted prognathous profile of his ape-like ancestor, to the left his present-day silhouette.

Wells later claimed that his essay was just as facetious as the *Punch* caricature. But this is rather belied by his not-too subtle imitation of Thomas Carlyle, his model prophet. The essay reports the speculations of a Professor Holzkopt at the University of Weissnictwo (=Nobody-knows-where). He is the same imaginary figure Carlyle draws upon for the reportage of his *Sartor Resartus* (1838, popularized from 1871 onward). No doubt this essay is what caused contemporary critics to tag Wells as "a second Carlyle," as he himself notes in his autobiography (1934:427).

In *Worlds*, the narrator with typical unreliability, cites the Wells essay as having appeared not in *Pall Mall Gazette* but in its sister publication, the *Pall Mall Budget*. This calculated mistake on the author's part also serves to distance the narrator from Wells himself, whose ideas he closely identifies with but cannot fathom. It characterizes him as a pseudo-intellectual lacking in philosophical gravitas.

THE MAN OF THE YEAR MILLION
A Scientific Forecast

ACCOMPLISHED literature is all very well in its way, no doubt, but much more fascinating to the contemplative man are the books that have not been written. These latter are no trouble to hold; there are no pages to turn over. One can read them in bed on sleepless nights without a candle. Turning to another topic, primitive man, in the works of the descriptive anthropologist, is certainly a very entertaining and quaint person; but the man of the future, if we only had the facts, would appeal to us more strongly. Yet where are the books? As Ruskin has said somewhere, apropos of Darwin, it is not what man has been, but what he will be, that should interest us.

The contemplative man in his easy chair, pondering this saying, suddenly beholds in the fire, through the blue haze of his pipe, one of these great unwritten volumes. It is large in size, heavy in lettering, seemingly by one Professor Holzkopf, presumably Professor at Weissnichtwo. "The Necessary Characters of the Man of the Remote Future Deduced from Existing Stream of Tendency," is the title. The worthy Professor is severely scientific in his method, and deliberate and cautious in his deductions, the contemplative man discovers as he pursues his theme, and yet the conclusions are, to say the least, remarkable. We must figure the excellent Professor expounding the matter at great length, voluminously technical, but the contemplative man—since he has access to the only copy—is clearly at liberty to make such extracts and abstracts as he chooses for the unscientific reader. Here, for instance, is something of practicable lucidity that he considers admits of quotation.

"The theory of evolution," writes the Professor, "is now universally accepted by zoologists and botanists, and it is applied unreservedly to man. Some question, indeed, whether it fits his soul, but all agree it accounts for his body. Man, we are assured, is descended from ape-like ancestors, molded by circumstances into men, and these apes again were derived from ancestral forms of a lower order, and so up from the primordial protoplasmic jelly. Clearly, then, man, unless the order of the universe has come to an end, will undergo further modification in the future, and at last cease to be man, giving rise to some other type of animated being. At once the fascinating question arises, What will this being be? Let us consider for a little the plastic influences at work upon our species.

"Just as the bird is the creature of the wing, and is all molded and modified to flying, and just as the fish is the creature that swims, and has had to meet the inflexible conditions of a problem in hydrodynamics, so man is the creature of the brain; he will live by intelligence, and not by physical strength, if he lives at all. So that much that is purely 'animal' about him is being, and must be, beyond all question, suppressed in his ultimate development. Evolution is no mechanical tendency making for perfection according to the ideas current in the year of grace 1892; it is simply the continual adaptation of plastic life for good or evil, to the circumstances that surround it.... We notice this decay of the animal part around us now, in the loss of teeth and hair, in the dwindling hands and feet of men, in their smaller jaws, and slighter mouths and ears. Man now does by wit and machinery and verbal agreement what he once did by toil; for once he had to catch his dinner, capture his wife, run away from his enemies, and continually exercise himself, for love of himself, to perform these duties well. But now all this is changed. Cabs, trains, trams, render speed unnecessary, the pursuit of food becomes easier; his wife is no longer hunted, but rather, in view of the crowded matrimonial market, seeks him out. One needs wits now to live, and physical activity is a drug, a snare even; it seeks artificial outlets and overflows in games. Athleticism takes up time and cripples a man in his competitive examinations and in business. So is your fleshy man handicapped against his subtler brother. He is unsuccessful in life, does not marry. The better adapted survive."

The coming man, then, will clearly have a larger brain, and a slighter body than the present. But the Professor makes one exception to this. "The human hand, since it is the teacher and interpreter of the brain, will become constantly more powerful and subtle as the rest of the musculature dwindles."

When in the physiology of these children of men, with their expanding brains, their great sensitive hands, and diminishing bodies, great changes were necessarily worked. "We see now," says the Professor, "in the more intellectual sections of humanity an increasing sensitiveness to stimulants, a growing inability to grapple with such a matter as alcohol, for instance. No longer can men drink a bottle full of port; some cannot drink tea; it is too exciting for their highly-wrought nervous systems. The process will go on, and the Sir Wilfrid Lawson of some near generation may find it his duty and pleasure to make the silvery spray of his wisdom tintinnabulate against the tea-tray. These facts lead naturally to the comprehension of others. Fresh raw meat was once a dish for a king. Now refined persons scarcely touch meat unless it is cunningly disguised. Again, consider the case of turnips; the raw root is now a thing almost uneatable, but once upon a time a turnip must have been a rare and fortunate find, to be torn up with delirious eagerness and devoured in ecstasy. The time will come when the change will affect all the other fruits of the earth. Even now only the young of mankind eat apples raw—the young always preserving ancestral characteristics after their disappearance in the adult. Someday, boys even will regard apples without emotion. The boy of the future, one must believe, will gaze on an apple with the same unspeculative languor with which he now regards a flint in the absence of a cat.

"Furthermore, fresh chemical discoveries came into action as modifying influences upon men. In the prehistoric period even, man's mouth had ceased to be an instrument for grasping food; it is still growing continually less prehensile, his front teeth are smaller, his lips thinner and less muscular; he has a new organ, a mandible not of irreparable tissue, but of bone and steel—a knife and fork. There is no reason why things should stop at the partial artificial division thus afforded; there is every reason, on the contrary, to believe my statement that some cunning exterior mechanism will presently masticate and insalivate his dinner, relieve his diminishing salivary glands and teeth, and at last altogether abolish them."

Then what is not needed disappears. What use is there for external ears, nose, and brow ridges now? The two latter once protected the eye from injury in conflict and in falls, but in these days we keep on our legs, and at peace. Directing his thoughts in this way, the reader may presently conjure up a dim, strange vision of the latter-day face: "Eyes large, lustrous, beautiful, soulful; above them, no longer separated by rugged brow ridges, is the top of the head, a glistening, hairless dome, terete and beautiful; no craggy nose rises to disturb by its unmeaning shadows the symmetry of that calm face, no vestigial ears project; the mouth is a small, perfectly round aperture toothless and gumless, jawless, unanimal, no futile emotions disturbing its roundness as it lies, like the harvest moon or the evening star, in the wide firmament of face." Such is the face the Professor beholds in the future.

Of course parallel modifications will also affect the body and limbs. "Every day so many hours and so much energy are required for digestion; a gross torpidity, a carnal lethargy, seizes on mortal men after dinner. This may and can be avoided. Man's knowledge of organic chemistry widens daily. Already he can supplement the gastric glands by artificial devices. Every doctor who administers physic implies that the bodily functions may be artificially superseded. We have persine, pancreatine artificial gastric acid—I know not what like mixtures. Why, then, should not the stomach be ultimately superannuated altogether? A man who could not only leave his dinner to be cooked, but also leave it to be masticated and digested, would have vast social advantages over his food-digesting fellow. This is, let me remind you here, the calmest, most passionless, and scientific working out of the future forms of things from the data of the present. At this stage the following facts may perhaps stimulate your imagination. There can be no doubt that many of the arthropods, a division of animals more ancient and even now more prevalent than the vertebrata, have undergone more phylogenetic modification"—a beautiful phrase—"than even the most modified of vertebrate animals. Simple forms like the lobsters display a primitive structure parallel with that of the fishes. However, in such a form as the degraded *Chondracanthus* the structure has diverged far more widely from its original type than in man. Among some of these most highly modified crustaceans the whole of the alimentary canal—that is, all the food-digesting and food-absorbing parts—form a useless solid cord: The animal is nourished—it is a parasite—by absorption of the nutritive fluid in which it swims. Is there any absolute impossibility in supposing man to be destined for a similar change; to imagine him no longer dining, with unwieldy paraphernalia of servants and plates, upon food queerly dyed and distorted, but nourishing himself in elegant simplicity by immersion in a tub of nutritive fluid?

"There grows upon the impatient imagination a building, a dome of crystal, across the translucent surface of which flushes of the most glorious and pure prismatic colors pass and fade and change. In the center of this transparent chameleon-tinted dome is a circular marble basin filled with some clear, mobile, amber liquid, and in this plunge and float strange beings. Are they birds?

"They are the descendants of man—at dinner. Watch them as they hop on their hands—a method of progression advocated already by Björnsen—about the pure white marble floor. Great hands they have, enormous brains, soft, liquid, soulful eyes. Their whole muscular system, their legs, their abdomens, are shriveled to nothing, a dangling degraded pendant to their minds."

The further visions of the Professor are less alluring.

"The animals and plants die away before men, except such as he preserves for his food or delight, or such as maintain a precarious footing about him as commensals and parasites. These vermin and pests must succumb sooner or later to his untiring inventiveness and incessantly growing discipline. When he learns (the chemists are doubtless getting toward the secret now) to do the work of chlorophyll without the plant, then his necessity for other animals and plants upon the earth will disappear. Sooner or later, where there is no power of resistance and no necessity, there comes extinction. In the last days man will be alone on the earth, and his food will be won by the chemist from the dead rocks and the sunlight.

"And—one may learn the full reason in that explicit and painfully right book, the *Data of Ethics*—the irrational fellowship of man will give place to an intellectual co-operation, and emotion fall within the scheme of reason. Undoubtedly it is a long time yet, but a long time is nothing in the face of eternity, and every man who thinks of these things must look eternity in the face."

Then the earth is ever radiating away heat into space, the Professor reminds us. And so at last comes a vision of earthly cherubim, hopping heads, great unemotional intelligences, and little hearts, fighting together perforce and fiercely against the cold that grips them tighter and tighter. For the world is cooling—slowly and inevitably it grows colder as the years roll by. "We must imagine these creatures," says the Professor, "in galleries and laboratories deep down in the bowels of the earth. The whole world will be snow-covered and piled with ice; all animals, all vegetation vanished, except this last branch of the tree of life. The last men have gone even deeper, following the diminishing heat of the planet, and vast steel shafts and ventilators make way for the air they need."

So with a glimpse of these human tadpoles, in their deep close gallery, with their boring machinery ringing away, and artificial lights glaring and casting black shadows, the Professor's horoscope concludes. Humanity in dismal retreat before the cold, changed beyond recognition. Yet the Professor is reasonable enough, his facts are current science, his methods orderly. The contemplative man shivers at the prospect, starts up to poke the fire, and the whole of this remarkable book that is not written vanishes straightway in the smoke of his pipe. This is the great advantage of this unwritten literature: There is no bother in changing the books. Our contemplative man consoles himself for the destiny of the species with the lost portion of Kublai Khan.

Appendix II
"Administrative Areas,"
by H.G. Wells (1903)

Wells joined the Fabian Society in February 1903. The next month he delivered his first paper, "The Question of Scientific Administrative Areas in Relation to Municipal Undertakings." It is here reprinted as the Appendix he offered in *Mankind in the Making* (1904:371–392), a title suggesting the world-state-making task of his New Republicans, first mooted in *Anticipations* (1901).

As it turns out, the Fabian Society, a think-tank for the Labour Party, was not visionary enough for what later evolved as his Modern State Octopus (1933): the mere municipalization of gas, water, transport and other public services within the greater metropolitan London area. That unitary economic area was to be but the beginning and nucleus of global unity in "the coming scientifically organized state" (1938a:134).

Hence the Vampire State (see the Introduction to the present work, section 5), hinted at in this paper, with its metaphor of a higher organism, or state monster, sucking the lifeblood out of local communities: feudalistic, parochial entities no longer relevant to the globalization of a universal industrial civilization. These obsolete localities must inevitably come under the worldwide control of a single delocalized brain center Martian in scope.

A PAPER ON ADMINISTRATIVE AREAS
READ BEFORE THE FABIAN SOCIETY

LET ME begin this paper upon the question of Scientific Administrative areas in relation to municipal undertakings by defining the sort of Socialism I profess. Because, you know, it is quite impossible to conceal that there are very many different sorts of socialism, and your society is, and has long been, a remarkably representative collection of the various types. We have this much in common, however, that we insist upon and hammer home and never lose sight of the fact that Property is a purely provisional and law-made thing, and that the law and the community which has given may also, at its necessity, take away. The work which the Socialist movement has done is to secure the general repudiation of any idea of sacredness about property. But upon the extent to which it is convenient to sanction a certain amount of property, and the ways in which existing excesses of property are to be reduced, Socialists differ enormously. There are certain extreme expressions of Socialism that you will connect with the names of Owen and Fourier, and with Noyes's "History of American Socialism," in which the abolition of monopoly is carried out with logical completeness to the abolition of marriage, and in which the idea seems to be to extend the limits of the Family and of intimate intercourse to include all humanity. With these Socialisms I have nothing in common. There are a large number of such questions concerning the constitution of the family upon which I retain an open and inquiring mind, and to which I find the answers of the established order, if not always absolutely incorrect, at any rate glaringly incomplete and totally inadequate; but I do not find the answers of these Socialistic Communities in any degree more satisfactory.

There are, however, more limited Socialisms, systems which deal mainly with economic organizations, which recognize the rights of individuals to possessions of a personal sort, and which assume without detailed discussion the formation of family groups within the general community. There are limited socialisms whose repudiation of property affects only the common interests of the community, the land it occupies, the services in which all are interested, the necessary minimum of education, and the sanitary and economic interaction of one person or family group upon another; socialisms which, in fact, come into touch with an intelligent individualism, and which are based on the attempt to ensure equality of opportunity and freedom for complete individual development to every citizen. Such socialists look not so much to the abolition of property as to the abolition of inheritance, and to the intelligent taxation of property for the services of the community. It is among such moderate socialists that I would number myself. I would make no hard and fast rule with regard to any portion of the material and apparatus used in the service of a community. With regard to any particular service or concern, I would ask, Is it more convenient, more likely to lead to economy and efficiency, to let this service rest in the hands of some single person or group of persons who may offer to do the service or administer the concern, and whom we will call the owners, or to place it in the hands of some single person or group of persons, elected or chosen by lot, whom we will call the official or group of officials? And if you were to suggest some method of election that would produce officials that, on the whole, were likely to manage worse than private owners, and to waste more than the private owner's probable profits, I should say then by all means leave the service or concern in private hands.

You see upon this principle the whole question of the administration of any affair turns upon the question, Which will give the maximum efficiency? It is very easy to say, and it stirs the heart and produces cheering in crowded meetings to say, "Let everything be owned by all and controlled by all for the good of all," and for the general purposes of a meeting it is quite possible to say that and nothing more. But if you sit down quietly by yourself afterwards and try and imagine things being "owned by all and controlled by all for the good of all," you will presently arrive at the valuable discovery in social and political science that the phrase means nothing whatever. It is also very striking, on such rhetorical occasions, to oppose the private owner to the community or the state or the municipality, and to suppose all the vices of humanity concentrated in private ownership, and all the virtues of humanity concentrated in the community, but indeed that clear and striking contrast will not stand the rough-and-tumble of the workaday world. A little examination of the matter will make it clear that the contrast lies between private owners and public officials— you must have officials, because you can't settle a railway time-table or make a bridge by public acclamation—and even there you will find it is not a simple question of the white against black order. Even in our state to-day there are few private owners who have absolute freedom to do what they like with their possessions, and there are few public officials who have not a certain freedom and a certain sense of proprietorship in their departments, and in fact, as distinguished from rhetoric, there is every possible gradation between the one thing and the other. We have to clear our minds of misleading terms in this affair. A clipped and regulated private ownership—a private company, for example, with completely published accounts, taxed dividends, with a public representative upon its board of directors and parliamentary powers—may be an infinitely more honest, efficient, and controllable public service than a badly elected or badly appointed board of governors or officials. We may—and I for one do—think that a number of public services, an increasing number of public services, can be best administered as public concerns. Most of us here to-night are, I believe, pretty advanced municipalizers. But it does not follow that we believe that any sort of representative or official body pitched into any sort of area is necessarily better than any sort of private control. The more we are disposed to municipalize, the more incumbent it is upon us to search out, study, and invent, and to work to develop the most efficient public bodies possible. And my case to-night is, that the existing local government bodies, your town councils, borough councils, urban district boards, and so forth, are, for the purposes of municipalization, far from being the best possible bodies, and that even your county councils fall short, that by their very nature all these bodies must fall far short of the highest possible efficiency, and that as time goes on they must fail even more than they do now to discharge the duties we Fabians would like to thrust upon them. And the general reason upon which I would have you condemn these bodies and seek for some newer and ampler ones before you press the municipalization of public concerns to its final trial, is this—that their areas of activity are impossibly small.

The areas within which we shape our public activities at present, derive, I hold, from the needs and conditions of a past order of things. They have been patched and repaired enormously, but they still preserve the essential conceptions of a vanished organization. They have been patched and repaired first to meet this urgent specific necessity and then that, and never with any comprehensive anticipation of coming needs, and at last they have become absolutely impossible. They are like fifteenth-century houses which have been continuously occupied by a succession of enterprising but short-sighted and close-fisted owners, and which have now been, with the very slightest use of lath-and-plaster partitions and geyser hot-water apparatus, converted into modern residential flats. These local government areas of to-day represent for the most part what were once distinct, distinctly organized, and individualized communities, complete minor economic systems, and they preserve a tradition of what was once administrative convenience and economy. To-day, I submit, they do not represent communities at all, and they become more wasteful and more inconvenient with every fresh change in economic necessity.

This is a double change. Let me first of all say a word in justification for my first assertion that existing areas do not represent communities, and then pass to a necessary consequence or so of this fact. I submit that before the railways, that is to say in the days in which the current conception of local government areas arose, the villages, and still more the boroughs, and even the counties, were practically complete minor economic systems. The wealth of the locality was, roughly speaking, local; rich people resided in contact with their property, other people lived in contact with their work, and it was a legitimate assumption that a radius of a mile or so, or of a few miles, circumscribed most of the practical interests of all the inhabitants of a locality. You got rich and poor in visible relationships; you got landlord and tenant, you got master and workman all together. But now, through a revolution in the methods of locomotion, and chiefly through the making of railways, this is no longer true. You can still see the villages and towns separated by spaces of fields and physically distinct, but it is no longer the case that all who dwell in these old limits are essentially local inhabitants and mutually interdependent as once they would have been. A large proportion of our population to-day, a large and an increasing proportion, has no localized interests at all as an eighteenth-century person would have understood locality.

Take for example Guildford, or Folkestone, and you will find that possibly even more than half the wealth in the place is non-local wealth—wealth, that is, having no relation to the local production of wealth—and that a large majority of the more educated, intelligent and active inhabitants derive their income, spend their energies, and find their absorbing interests outside the locality. They may rent or own houses, but they have no reality of participation and little illusion of participation in any local life. You will find in both towns a considerable number of hotels, inns, and refreshment places which, although they are regulated by local magistrates upon a basis of one license to so many inhabitants, derive only a small fraction of their profits from the custom of the inhabitants. You find too in Folkestone, as in most seaside places, a great number of secondary schools, drawing scarcely a pupil from the neighbourhood. And on the other hand you will find labour in both towns, coming in by a morning train and going out at night. And neither of these instances is an extreme type. As you come in towards London you will find the proportion of what I would call non-local inhabitants increasing until in Brixton, Hoxton, or West Ham you will find the really localized people a mere thread in the mass of the population. Probably you find the thinnest sham of a community in the London boroughs, where a clerk or a working man will shift his sticks from one borough to another and move on to a third without ever discovering what he has done. It is not that all these people do not belong to a community, but that they belong to a larger community of a new type which your administrators have failed to discover, and which your working theory of local government ignores. This is a question I have already written about with some completeness in a book published a year or so ago, and called "Anticipations," and in that book you will find a more lengthy exposition that I can give here and now of the nature of this expansion. But the gist of the argument is that the distribution of population, the method of aggregation in a community, is determined almost entirely by the available means of locomotion. The maximum size of any community of regular daily intercourse is determined by the length of something that I may best suggest to your mind by the phrase—the average possible suburban journey in an hour. A town, for example, in which the only method of progression is on foot along crowded ways, will be denser in population and smaller in area than one with wide streets and a wheeled traffic, and that again will be denser and compacter than one with numerous tubes, trams, and light railways. Every improvement in locomotion forces the suburban ring of houses outward, and relieves the pressure of the centre. Now, this principle of expanding communities holds not only in regard to towns, but also on the agricultural country side. There, also, facilities for the more rapid collection of produce mean finally the expansion and coalescence of what were previously economic unities.

Now if, while this expansion of the real communities goes on, you keep to the old boundary lines, you will find an increasing proportion of your population straddling those lines. You will find that many people who once slept and worked and reared their children and worshipped and bought all in one area, are now, as it were, *delocalized*; they have overflowed their containing locality, and they live in one area, they work in another, and they go to shop in a third. And the only way in which you can localize them again is to expand your areas to their new scale.

This is a change in human conditions that has been a very distinctive event in the history of the past century, and it is still in progress. But I think there is excellent reason for supposing that for practical purposes this change, made by the railway and the motor, this development of local locomotion, will reach a definite limit in the next hundred years. We are witnessing the completion of a great development that has altered the average possible suburban journey in an hour from one of four or five miles to one of thirty miles, and I doubt very much whether, when every tendency of expansion has been reckoned with, this average hour journey will ever get much beyond sixty or seventy miles an hour. A radius of four or five miles marked the maximum size of the old community. A radius of a hundred miles will certainly mark the maximum of the new community. And so it is no effectual answer to my general argument to say that a revision of administrative areas always has been and always will be a public necessity. To a certain extent that always has been and always will be true, but on a scale in no way comparable to the scale on which it is true to-day, because of these particular inventions. This need in its greatness is a peculiar feature of the present time, and a peculiar problem of the present time. The municipal areas that were convenient in the Babylonian, ancient Egyptian, or Roman empires were no larger and no smaller than those that served the purpose of seventeenth-century Europe, and I believe it is highly probable—I think the odds are in favour of the belief—that the most convenient administrative areas of the year 2000 will be no larger and no smaller than those for many subsequent centuries. We are, in this respect, in the full flow of a great and permanent transition. And the social and political aspect of the change, is this steadily increasing proportion of people—more especially in our suburban areas—who are, so far as our old divisions go, *delocalized*. They represent, in fact, a community of a new sort, the new great modern community, which is seeking to establish itself in the room of the dwindling, little, highly localized communities of the past.

Now what are the practical consequences of this large and increasing non-local element in your old local government areas? First, there is this. The non-local people do not follow, have neither the time, nor the freedom, nor the stimulus of sufficient interests to follow, local politics. They are a sort of Outlanders. Local politics remain therefore more and more in the hands of the dwindling section of people whose interests really are circumscribed by the locality. These are usually the small local tradesmen, the local building trade, sometimes a doctor and always a solicitor; and the most energetic and active and capable of these, and the one with the keenest eye to business, is usually the solicitor. Whatever you put into the hands of a local authority—education, lighting, communications—you necessarily put into the hands of a group of this sort. Here and there, of course, there may be variations; an organized labour vote may send in a representative, or some gentleman of leisure and philanthropic tastes, like Mr. Bernard Shaw, may confer distinction upon local deliberations, but that will not alter the general state of affairs. The state of affairs you must expect as the general rule, is local control by petty local interests, a state of affairs that will certainly intensify in the years to come, unless some revision of areas can be contrived that will overtake the amplifying interests of the delocalized section of the population.

Let me point out what is probably the result of a dim recognition of this fact by the non-local population, and that is the extreme jealousy of rates and municipal trading by the less localized paying classes in the community. That is a question we Socialists, believing as we do all of us at least in the abstract theory of municipalization, must particularly consider. The easy exasperation of the £1000-a-year man at the rates and his extreme patience under Imperial taxation is incomprehensible, unless you recognize this fact of his delocalization. Then at once it becomes clear. He penetrates the pretences of the system to a certain extent; and he is infuriated by the fact of taxation without representation, tempered by a mysteriously ineffective voting paper left at his door. I myself, as one of the delocalized class, will confess he has my sympathy. And those who believe in the idea of the ultimate municipalization of most large industries, will continue to find in this non-localized class, working especially through the medium of Parliament, a persistent and effective obstruction to all such projects, unless such a rectification of areas can be contrived as will overtake the delocalization and the diffusion of interests that has been and is still going on. I will confess that it seems to me that this opposition between the localized and the non-localized classes in the future, or to be more correct, the opposition between the man whose ideas and life lie in a small area, and the man whose ideas and life lie in a great area, is likely to give us that dividing line in politics for which so many people are looking to-day. For this question of areas has its Imperial as well as its local side. You have already seen the Liberal party split upon the Transvaal question; you yourselves have—I am told—experienced some slight parallel tendency to fission, and it is interesting to note that this was, after all, only another aspect of this great question of areas, which I would now discuss in relation to municipal trading. The small communities are fighting for existence and their dear little ways, the synthetic great communities are fighting to come into existence, and to absorb the small communities. And curiously enough at our last meeting you heard Mr. Belloc, with delightful wit and subtlety, expounding the very antithesis of the conceptions I am presenting to-night. Mr. Belloc—who has evidently never read his Malthus—dreams of a beautiful little village community of peasant proprietors, each sticking like a barnacle to his own little bit of property, beautifully healthy and simple and illiterate and Roman Catholic and *local*, local over the ears. I am afraid the stars in their courses fight against such pink and golden dreams. Every tramway, every new twopenny tube, every light railway, every improvement in your omnibus services, in your telephonic services, in your organization of credit, increases the proportion of your delocalized class, and sucks the ebbing life from your old communities into the veins of the new.

Well, you may say, no doubt this is right so far as it goes; existing local government areas do not represent real countries, but still these local government devices are of service for cutting up and distributing administrative work. But that is exactly what they are not. They are worse when you consider them in regard to function, than when you consider them in regard to representation. Since our conceptions of what constitutes a local administrative area were developed there has arisen the problems of water supply and of organized sewage, of railways, tramways, and communications generally, and of lighting and telephonic intercourse; there hangs over us, though the average local authority has no eyes to see it, the necessity of adapting our roads to accommodate an increasing new traffic of soft-tyred vehicles, and it is not improbable that heating by wholesale, either by gas or electricity, will presently be also possible and desirable. For all these things we need wide views, wide minds and wide areas, and still more do we want wide views for the business of education that is now also coming into the sphere of local administration.

It happens that I have had an object-lesson in this matter of local government; and indeed it is my object-lesson that has led to this paper to-night. I live upon the boundary line of the Sandgate Urban District Board, a minute authority with a boundary line that appears to have been determined originally about 1850 by mapping out the wanderings of an intoxicated excursionist, and which—the only word is interdigitates—with the borough of Folkestone, the Urban District of Cheriton, and the borough of Hythe. Each of these bodies is by way of being a tramway authority, each is at liberty to secure powers to set up generating stations and supply electricity, each is a water authority, and each does its own little drainage, and the possibilities of friction and litigation are endless. The four places constitute an urban area greatly in need of organized intercommunication, but the four authorities have never been able to agree upon a scheme; and now Folkestone is concerning itself with the project of a little internal tramway system all of its very own. Sandgate has succumbed to the spell of the South Eastern Railway Company, and has come into line with a project that will necessitate a change of cars at the Folkestone boundary. Folkestone has conceded its electrical supply to a company, but Sandgate, on this issue, stands out gallantly for municipal trading, and proposes to lay down a plant and set up a generating station all by itself to supply a population of sixteen hundred people, mostly indigent. In the meanwhile, Sandgate refuses its inhabitants the elementary convenience of the electric light, and when, quite inadvertently, I connected across the convolutions of the boundary with the Folkestone supply, my life was darkened by the threat of impossible litigation. But if Folkestone repudiates municipal enterprise in the matter of lighting, I gather it does not do so in the matter of telephones; and there has been talk of a neat little Folkestone telephonic system competing against the National Telephone Company, a compact little conversazione of perhaps a hundred people, rate sustained. And how is the non-local inhabitant to come into these things? The intelligent non-local inhabitant can only save his two or three pounds of contribution to this folly or that by putting in twenty or thirty pounds' worth of work in local politics. He has no local connections, no local influence, he hasn't a chance against the plumber. When the house I occupy was built, it was a mere interposition of Providence that the drain did not go southward into a Folkestone sewer instead of northward into Sandgate. Heaven knows what would have happened if it had! I and my neighbours are by a special concession permitted to have water from the Folkestone source. By incessant vigilance we do, I believe, usually succeed in deducting the Folkestone water rate from the Sandgate general rate which covers water, but the wear and tear is enormous. However, these are details, dear to my heart, but the merest marginal comments to my argument. The essential fact is the impracticable silliness of these little divisions, the waste of men, the waste of nervous energy, the waste of administrative energy they involve. I am convinced that in the case of almost any public service in the Folkestone district with our present boundaries, the administrative waste will more than equal the profit of a private company with parliamentary powers overriding our local authorities; that if it is simply a choice between these little bodies and a company (of the common type even), then in lighting, locomotion, and indeed in almost any general public service, I would say, "give me the company." With companies one may hope to deal later; they will not stand in the way of developing saner areas, but an obstinate little authority clutching everything in its hands, and led by a clerk naturally interested in litigation, and who is also something of an expert in political organization, will be an altogether harder thing to supersede.

This difficulty in greater or lesser degree is everywhere. In the case of poor law administration in particular, and also in the case of elementary education, the whole country displays what is another aspect of this same general phenomenon of delocalization; the withdrawal of all the wealthier people from the areas that are specializing as industrial centres, and which have a rising population of poor workers, to areas that are specializing as residential, and which have, if anything, a falling proportion of poor labourers. In a place like West Ham or Tottenham you find starved schools and an abundant delocalized industrial population, and, by way of contrast, at Guildford or Farnham for example, you will find enormously rich delocalized people, belonging to the same great community as these workers, who pay only the most trivial poor rate and school rate for the benefit of their few immediate neighbours, and escape altogether from the burthens of West Ham. By treating these places as separate communities you commit a cruel injustice on the poor. So far as these things go, to claim convenience for the existing areas is absurd. And it is becoming more and more evident that with tramways, with lighting, with electric heating and force supply, and with the supply of water to great populations, there is an enormous advantage in large generating stations and large areas; that these things must be handled in areas of hundreds of square miles to be efficiently done.

In the case of secondary and higher education one discovers an equal stress and incompatibility. At present, I must point out, even the boundaries of the projected educational authority for London are absurdly narrow. For example, in Folkestone, as in every town upon the south coast, there are dozens of secondary schools that are purely London schools, and filled with London boys and girls, and there are endless great schools like Tonbridge and Charterhouse outside the London area that are also London schools. If you get, for example, a vigorous and efficient educational authority for London, and you raise a fine educational system in the London area, you will find it incomplete in an almost vital particular. You will give the prosperous middle class and the upper class of London the alternative of good teaching and bad air, or of what very probably, under tolerant local authorities, will be relatively bad teaching and open air and exercise out of London. You will have to tax this influential class of people for the magnificent schools they in many cases will be unable to use. As a consequence, you will find again all the difficulties of their opposition, practically the same difficulties that arise so naturally in the way of municipal trading. I would suggest that it would be not only logical but politic, for the London Educational Authority, and not the local authority, to control every secondary school wherever it happened to be, which in an average of years drew more than half its attendance from the London area. That, however, by the way. The point more material to my argument here is that the educational organization of the London area, the Thames valley, and the southern counties are inseparable; that the question of local locomotion is rapidly becoming impossible upon any smaller basis than such an area; that roads, light railways, drainage, water, are all clamouring now to be dealt with on the big scale; and that the more you cut this great area up, the more you leave it in the hands of the localized men, the more you sin against efficiency and the light.

I hope that you will consider this first part of my case proved. And now I pass on to the more debatable question—the nature of the new divisions that are to replace the old. I would suggest that this is a matter only to be answered in detail by an exhaustive analysis of the distribution of population in relation to economic standing, but I may perhaps just indicate roughly what at a first glance I imagine would be one suitable local government area. Let me remind you that some years ago the Conservative party, in an outbreak of intelligence, did in a sort of transitory way see something of what I have been trying to express to-night, and created the London County Council—only to quarrel with it and hate it and fear it ever since. Well, my proposal would be to make a much greater area even than the London County, and try to include in it the whole system of what I might call the London-centred population. I believe if you were to take the whole valley of the Thames and its tributaries and draw a line along its boundary watershed, and then include with that Sussex and Surrey, and the east coast counties up to the Wash, you would overtake and anticipate the delocalizing process almost completely. You would have what has become, or is becoming very rapidly, a new urban region, a complete community of the new type, rich and poor and all sorts and aspects of economic life together. I would suggest that watersheds make excellent boundaries. Let me remind you that railways, tramways, drainpipes, water-pipes, and high-roads have this in common—they will not climb over a watershed if they can possibly avoid doing so, and that population and schools and poor tend always to distribute themselves in accordance with these other things. You get the minimum of possible overlap—such overlap as the spreading out of the great midland city to meet London must some day cause—in this way. I would suggest that for the regulation of sanitation, education, communication, industrial control, and poor relief, and for the taxation for these purposes, this area should be one, governed by one body, elected by local constituencies that would make its activities independent of imperial politics. I propose that this body should replace your county councils, boards of guardians, urban and rural district councils, and all the rest of them altogether; that you should elect it, perhaps triennially, once for all. For any purpose of a more local sort, local water-supply systems, local tramway systems—the tramways between Brighton and Shoreham, for example—this body might delegate its powers to subordinate committees, consisting, it has been suggested to me by Mrs. Sidney Webb, of the members for the local constituencies concerned, together with another member or so to safeguard the general interests, or perhaps with an appointed expert or so in addition. These committees would submit their detailed schemes for the approval of committees appointed by the general body, and they would be controllable by that body. However, there is no need for detailed scheming here and now. Let us keep to the main idea.

I submit that such a mammoth municipality as this will be, on the one hand, an enormously more efficient substitute for your present little local government bodies, and on the other hand, will be able to take over a considerable proportion of the detailed work and a considerable proportion of the detailed machinery, of your overworked and too extensive central machinery, your local government board, education department, and board of trade. It will be great enough and fine enough to revive the dying sentiment of local patriotism, and it will be a body that will appeal to the ambition of the most energetic and capable men in the community. They will be picked men, to a much greater extent than are your guardians, your urban district councillors and town councillors and so on, at present, because there will be perhaps a hundred or a couple of hundred of them in the place of many thousands. And I venture to think that in such a body you may confidently hope to find a collective intelligence that may be pitted against any trust or board of directors the world is likely to produce.

I suggest this body as a sort of concrete example of the thing I have in mind. I am quite open to hear and accept the most far-reaching modification of this scheme; it is *the idea of the scale* that I wish particularly to enforce. Municipalize on this scale, I would say, and I am with you altogether. Here is something distinctly and clearly subserving that making of mankind upon which all sane social and political proposals must ultimately base themselves. But to put more power, and still more power in the hands of these petty little administrative bod-

ies that we have to-day, is, I submit, folly and darkness. If the existing areas are to remain the same, then, on the whole, my vote is against
municipal trading, and on the whole, with regard to light, to tramways
and communications, to telephones, and indeed to nearly all such public services, I would prefer to see these things in the hands of companies, and I would stipulate only for the maximum publicity for their
accounts and the fullest provision for detailed regulation through the
Board of Trade.

Appendix III
"The Philosophy of
a Bacteriologist," a Review
by H.G. Wells (1903)

This is a review of Elie Metchnikoff's book, *The Nature of Man*, published the same year. The question is, did Wells know of the man (*d.* 15 July 1916) when he posited his Metchnikoffed Martians? Most likely. His heartfelt obituary (1917: Chapter 4) suggests a long familiarity with his life and work, which he acknowledged as a vital example validating his own stance as a complete Darwinist and scientific atheist (see textual note 178). The book review has its interest in that light.

Indeed, I dare say that Metchnikoff directly inspired the title figure in *The Island of Doctor Moreau* (1896). I have always held a fixed image of Doctor Moreau ever since I read the scientific romances more than sixty years ago, and when I first saw photos of Metchnikoff I was dumbfounded: that's *him*, there he is, that's Moreau! I refer to figs. 6 and 7 in Tauber and Chernyak (1991), showing the bearded man at age 51: the very image of the elderly Moreau and just as radiantly benign.

THE PHILOSOPHY OF A BACTERIOLOGIST.*

DR. CHALMERS MITCHELL has acted as sponsor to the English version of an extremely interesting and typical book, and he is to be unreservedly thanked for his bold abstinence from the interventions and

---

*The Nature of Man, Studies in Optimistic Philosophy. By Elie Metchnikoff, Professor at the Pasteur Institute. The translation edited by Dr. F. Chalmers Mitchell. 12s 6d. net. London: William Heinemann. 1903.

expurgations that might have been its lot in other hands. He furnishes it with an introduction of admirable tone, and, save for one unfortunate substitution of "impossible" for "possible" on p. 252, and the use of "intoxication" for "poisoning," it is hard to find any fault in the translation for which he has assumed responsibility. He tells the English readers—it is a lamentable necessity—something of the greatness of the great man he brings before them. Of the generation of biologists who were students in the splendid prime of Darwin, Huxley, and Pasteur, one would, I suppose, place Metchnikoff among the very foremost; but his work has gone on, high above the tumultuous popular levels of the Marconigram and the teeming laboratory of Edison, and the people know him not. Here, for the first time, he leaves his specialised cytological inquiries, and enters upon questions that bring him into relation with the general body of intelligent men. With a distinguished frankness and simplicity—he avoids technical gibberish as instinctively as an American writer upon these subjects would seek it—he defines his attitude to our universal prepossessions, to the perplexities of sex, and the problems of senility and death, and his conceptions of the practical significance of life and of the work that lies before mankind.

The very titles of the three parts into which he divides his book—indeed the title of the first alone strikes out the form of what one may reasonably call the biological view of life. He calls his first part "Disharmonies in the Nature of Man," and nothing could better express the predominating idea that gives a distinctive quality to the modern biologist's way of thinking. The sense of pervading imperfection in life is, indeed, no modern discovery; countless generations, all generations from the beginning, have had that sense, and have explained it for the most part by a mystery of one or many devils, but it has been left to almost contemporary thinkers to replace this obsession of an active and vigilant malignancy by the perception of a general lack of adjustment, to find in the explanation of the origin of species the qualification almost out of recognition of the problem of the origin of evil. The old method was to declare that in Nature

"Every prospect pleases,
And only man is vile."

The biologist declares roundly that all nature is imperfect, existent through that very instability, and that all that is inharmonious and painful in human life is merely an aspect of a universal loose play and wear of the past against past.

The first portion of Professor Metchnikoff's book is directed against this old superstition of Nature's perfection (a superstition so tenacious and elusive that one may find it, for example, in even so deliberately an advanced mind as that of Mr. Bernard Shaw); and it is a singularly powerful and convincing arrangement of considerations. He discusses one or two of the most striking instances of "disharmony" among the lower animals and plants, and the evidences of the simian still in man, but it is in Chapters IV., V., and VI. that the deeper interest of this demonstration resides. Here, with the straightforward clearness of profound and habitual knowledge, he sets out the incurable imperfections, the inevitable inharmoniousness, first of man's digestive system, then of his reproductive organs and instincts, and then of his instincts of self-preservation. He sweeps aside with all the decision of authority and all the persuasiveness of ordered knowledge any belief in an ideal state of health. There is no health in us, and it is only by effort, by wisdom and continence, by the suppression of instincts that are a part of us, that even a sufferable equilibrium may be maintained.

The question of adjustments then arises. From the biological point of view morality is the attempt to square incompatibilities of motive, as religion attempts the emotional adjustment and philosophy the intellectual difficulties. Professor Metchnikoff makes no pretence of dealing with the former of these three, but he discusses the religious solution and pronounces it a failure, and devotes what is certainly his least engaging chapter to show that the end towards which all philosophy tends is neither reconciliation or remedy but renunciation. Thence he passes to his third part, at once the most original and interesting, and the least complete. His thesis is that in scientific knowledge and methods lies the possibility of at least a sufficient adjustment of physical conditions to the desires and emotions that determine human happiness. It is at once the most interesting of his three parts, for in it he rests most securely upon his own special work, and it is least complete because, for example, he offers not a word to indicate his conception of an effectual reconciliation of those sexual disharmonies he has so fully and so luminously discussed.

He concentrates about his work upon senile decay and discusses age and death as though these were the predominating sorrows of men. One does not know how it may be upon those further slopes, but most certainly for human beings under forty nowadays—and these are the great majority of humanity—death certainly, and probably the decline of health and strength, are by no means prevailing obsessions. To many readers of Dr. Metchnikoff, indeed, and those by no means his least intelligent or appreciative readers, to his readers of the younger generation, the idea that the prospect of living out life in a state of moral and intellectual efficiency, through a long and painless decline to a death as natural and grateful as sleep at a hundred and twenty or more, should seem the most desirable and reconciling of human possibilities, will come with an effect of intellectual shock. It arrests the enterprise of our younger wisdom, and at first the prominent thing is the light of personal experience and personal aspiration that is suddenly reflected from these illuminating passages upon the whole book. The impersonal scientific strain is suffused with individuality. "Here," one says, "is this great senior at the crest of life, and this is the measure of his vision of the descending side—a bleak, dangerous, and painful descent, wasteful of life, and needlessly bleak and painful." At first one is disposed to take it at that, and to underrate what follows on account of this element of personal aspiration. Then as the trend of the writer's thought breaks more fully upon one, this tint of personality fades again, and one finds oneself in the clear and invigorating dawn of a whole world of new ideas.

For Professor Metchnikoff's surprising and suggestive treatment of senility as a universal but curable disease, and for his exposition of the large intestine as a sort of death-organ in man, the reader must go to the book itself. Suffice it here to remark that albeit he draws his evidence from sources of very variable value—he adduces, for example, the Biblical ages of the patriarchs and fails to quote the Biblical limit of "three score and ten"—his case, as the statement of a possibility, is extraordinarily convincing. But one may remark, perhaps, here, how singularly this amplification of the human scope falls in with the unconscious trend of the civilising process, which is certainly not only towards raising the age of the average man, but towards the artificial and deliberate retardation of all the great crises of life. It is a fact altogether too neglected by literary criticism to-day in the comparison of past and present—and yet it is one of the most patent of facts—that our intellectual and moral atmosphere as compared, let us say, with the Tudor atmosphere is, by ten years or so, more adult. A girl of fifteen or a lad of twenty to-day have as yet to come into the world; in Tudor times she might be a courted beauty or a mother and he a father and a master and leader of men. The proportion, not only of old people, but of people we should nowadays call mature, was lower, and in art and thought and enterprise youth sets the key. To that irrecoverable quality of youth it is that the Tudor world owes its warm, inimitable zest and glow. The minority of older men and women lived amid a superabundance of youth and was preserved in the quality of the time. To-day love comes to freedom and enterprise only in the twenties and with an increasing armoury of knowledge, it is the woman of thirty who rules our song, men under forty carry themselves with the seemly respectfulness of youth, and what our life had lost in zest and bloom, I for one, who am no poet or romancer, conceive it to have gained in strength and breadth and intellectual pleasure. One may trace the change of note in all the cardinal aspects of life. Who would be jealous like Othello now—with the murderous intensity of undisciplined twenty-two? Romeo—transfer young Romeo to the full and subtle atmosphere of Mr. Henry James's "Ambassadors"! Young Romeo now dodges proctors in a purified town, and except, maybe, for lapses that have nothing to do with love, a game of tennis with somebody's sister is the limit of his amorous freedoms. Who would make war as they made war then for the sake of glory? And who dreamt then, as we now by the hundred dream and hope, for a peace and order that shall encompass the earth? These changes are part and consequence of a shifting of the average age through a matter of some ten years, due to changes in the material conditions of life that no one foresaw would have psychological consequences at all. Think, then, what it really portends for the emotional and intellectual world if this that Metchnikoff tells us is even to a limited extent true; if a world is to come wherein most children born will live, tranquillised, indeed, but not debilitated, until perhaps a hundred and forty, in which the majority will be over rather than under sixty, and with love and parentage and all these things of the personal life gone past!

In fact, a sort of Front Bench world?

That is just one of those quick inferences that do so damage new speculations. It is essential to Metchnikoff's theory—indeed, it is Metchnikoff's theory—that the infirmities of age are to be overcome. The new possibility is old men, not aged. His initial research in this direction was into the causes of the loss of pigment in grey hairs, and his assumption is clearly an old age without gout, without baldness or white hairs, without obesity, with an unimpaired, if dieted, digestion. I should not dare to feign these things in a story, but here is this man beside whose knowledge of physiology not only my grain of knowledge, but the expert knowledge of a practising doctor, is as the knowledge of a little boy, and he says that things may be so. Are we to believe that his psychology is as trustworthy as his physiology, and that the psychic defects of old age, the growing egotism, the unteachableness, are to be as easily disposed of by serums and tonics and the removal of the large intestine? That at any rate is his implication. If that is so, then without any deliberate breeding (a possibility of the future he curiously ignores) humanity is to be profoundly changed, and what we call all life now will be but the childhood and youth and adolescence of that longer and larger life.

H.G. WELLS.

Appendix IV
Preface to the Atlantic Edition (1924)

At textual note 2, on the dedication of *Worlds*, Wells is happy to acknowledge the help of his elder brother Frank. Here he explains. Frank Wells, an artist, is again credited with help on the 1936 film, *Things to Come*. He then served as Art Director (Stover 1987:xvii–xviii). Destruction of the world, and its reconstruction, is a family franchise as with the Cabal's. So too with Plato's line of king bees (*ibid*.:77).

THE PREFACE

"The War of the Worlds" was suggested to the writer by his elder brother, Frank, to whom the first edition was dedicated. Mr. Frank Wells is a practical philosopher with a disbelief even profounder than that of the writer in the present ability of our race to meet a great crisis either bravely or intelligently. The Great War, the Mean Peace, the Russian Famine, and the present state of the world's affairs have but confirmed that early persuasion. Our present civilisation, it seems, is quite capable of falling to pieces without any aid from the Martians.

Once or twice in reading this book, written a quarter of a century ago, the reader will be reminded of phases and incidents in the Great War: the use of poison-gas, for instance, or the flight before the Martians. These were intelligent anticipations; the story has not been touched up at all. The scene is laid mainly in Surrey in the country round about Woking, where the writer was living when the book was written. He would take his bicycle of an afternoon and note the houses and cottages and typical inhabitants and passers-by, to be destroyed after tea by Heat-Ray or smothered in the red weed. He could sit by the way-side imagining his incidents so vividly that now when he passes through that country these events recur to him as though they were actual memories.

Appendix V
Excerpt from *Philosophical Dialogues*, by Ernest Renan (1883)

Renan (*d.* 1890) was a notable second-generation Saint-Simonist (Chadbourne 1968), whose *The Future of Science* (1891) is the definitive classic of post–Christian rationalism — a work invigorating Wells's outlook and everybody else's looking to a scientific organization of society. In this excerpt, God does not exist, but will be created by the collective self-perfection of the human species. As a God-builder, man himself will embody cosmic truth in a divinized State, the point of *Men Like Gods* (1923). But already this prospect is mooted in Wells's New Republic, that "higher organism, the world-state of the coming years" (1901:190). It realizes Renan's view that just such a "higher organism" must come into being to represent the final evolutionary product of reason; it shall stand to the present order as men now do to the lower animals. Such as the Martians to men, who acquired that godhead in the Modern State Octopus.

Renan's most seminal work, *The Future of Science*, is subtitled *Ideas of 1848*. He reflects on the European Revolutions of that year, which saw a Marxist-driven proletarian insurgency in every capital city, quickly put down. Nowhere was the reaction more ruthless than in Paris, but for a permanent cure to the perverse ills of democratic sentimentality Renan invokes the sweet reasonableness of Saint-Simonian doctrine. It is here that Old Testament socialism regains vitality as a weapon against Marxism: a fundamental source for Wells's attack on the world-destructive forces of New Testament socialism.

THE HIGHER ORGANISM OF REASON TO COME

THEOCTISTES.

DO NOT, however, push me too far, or else I will propound to you a hypothesis that will make my nightmare dream a possibility. I have never said that the future would prove cheerful. Who knows but that truth is of a sad nature? Power has been hitherto maintained over mankind only by the care which those possessed of it have taken to keep the barbarous masses placed in their hands as blind tools of their purposes. The positivist* tyrants that we have been speaking of would hardly hesitate to maintain, in some lost district of Asia, a nucleus of Bashkirs or Kalmuks, obedient machines, unencumbered by moral scruples and prepared for every sort of cruelty. Please to notice, besides, that I am now supposing an immense advancement of the human consciousness, a realisation of the true and of the just, of which we have not yet seen any instance. I am supposing (and I believe I am right in this) this step in advance accomplished, not by the whole race, but by an aristocracy placed at the head of humanity, and which will be the depository of the reason of the mass. It is clear that the absolute reign of one portion of humanity over another is odious, if we suppose the governing body to be swayed only by personal egoism or by class egoism; but the aristocracy of which I dream would be the incarnation of reason; this would be a papacy of real infallibility. Power, in its hands, could not but be beneficial, and there would be no need to haggle with such an aristocracy for it. This would be legitimate power *par excellence*, since it would enforce true opinions on the ground of real terrors. The Church and Bráhmanism were based upon an error. No Bráhman ever blighted any one with his curse; he therefore founded a false doctrine on an unfounded fear. But the being possessed of science would set up unlimited terror in the service of truth. Terrors, however, would soon become superfluous. The inferior portion of humanity, on such a supposition, would soon be checkmated by evidence, and the very idea of revolt would disappear.

Truth will one day be power. That "knowledge is power," is the noblest word that was ever spoken. The ignorant will see the effects and will believe; theory will be verified by its applications. A theory which shall lead to the invention of terrible engines, overpowering and subjugating all, will establish its truth by irrefragable evidence. The forces of humanity will thus be concentrated in a very small

---

*i.e., having an eye to material advantage.—TR.

number of hands, and become the property of a league capable of regulating the life of the planet, and of, by that threat, terrifying the whole world. On the day when a few persons favoured of reason shall really possess the means of destroying the planet, their supremacy will be established; these privileged persons will rule by means of absolute terror, because they shall have in their hands the life of all; we may almost say that they will be gods, and that the theological epoch dreamt of by the poet for primitive humanity will then be a reality. *Primus in orbe deos fecit timor.**

Thus we may imagine a time when power will actually establish the reign of reason without the need of having recourse to imposture, which is only the weapon of the weak, and a substitute for power. The worship of reason will then be a truth; for, whoever shall offer any resistance to it, that is to say, shall not recognise the reign of science, will have to atone for his offence on the spot. What childish folly it was to celebrate the Feast of Reason when its army was composed of an unintelligent people, with exceedingly little reason and no constancy, and armed with pikes and bad muskets! When reason shall be all-powerful, she will indeed be a veritable goddess. Then it will no longer be necessary to speak of authority; that word has now no meaning, except to denote a force of opinion that is ineffective: it is a pure trick of language. Then the power of reason will be effective in the highest degree, since all disregard of that power will be punished with instant death. Preventive measures will be useless. This will be the realisation of what was formerly fabled as the vengeance of the gods; but the reality will be far superior to the myth, inasmuch as the vengeance of the gods was slow, uncertain, imperfect, and as we now know, devoid of truth; while, on the other hand, the sanctions of scientific law will be infallible, instantaneous, and, like Nature herself, without appeal.

EUDOXES.

Among a thousand objections that I might make to your views, I shall mention but one. You suppose an immense improvement in science, and you are right, but you say nothing of the condition of the thinking subject. Now, the advance in science and power that you have just delineated far exceeds the capability of any brain whatever. There is a contradiction between the conquests of reason that you imagine, and the intellectual and physical capacities, which always remain very limited.

*Fear was the first thing to create gods in the world.—TR.

THEOCTISTES.

I have told you that the class of ideas with which I am now dealing, refers but imperfectly to the planet earth, and that such speculations must be understood to aim at what transcends humanity. No doubt the knowing and thinking subject will be always limited, but knowledge and power are unlimited, and, consequently, the thinking nature itself will be capable of being greatly improved without quitting the known domain of biology. A broad application of the discoveries of physiology and of the principle of selection might lead to the creation of a superior race, deriving its right to rule not only from its science, but from the very superiority of its blood, its brain, and its nerves. Thus there might be a race of gods, or *devas*, beings of ten times greater worth than we are, and capable of subsisting in artificial *media*. Nature produces nothing but what is capable of living under general conditions; but science may extend the limits of viability. As yet Nature has produced only what she could; spontaneous forces will not pass beyond the low-water mark which they have reached. It is for science to take up the work where Nature has left it. Botany artificially maintains certain vegetable products, which would disappear unless the hand of man continually sustained them. It is possible to conceive a time when the production of a *deva* might be estimated at a definite capital, representing costly apparatus, slow processes, elaborate selections, a complicated education, and the laborious preservation of such a being in antagonism to Nature. A manufactory of Ases, an *Asgaard*,* may be re-established in the heart of Asia; and, if myths like these are repugnant to any one, let him note carefully the method that ants and bees employ to determine the functions to which each individual is to be devoted; let him reflect, especially, on the means employed by botanists when they create their artificial rarities. It is always the nutrition, or rather the development, of one organ by the atrophy of another which is the secret of these anomalies. Call to mind the *Vedic* doctor whose name, according to Burnouf, signified, οὐ τὸ σπέρμα εἰς τὴν κεφάλην ἀνέβη.† As double flowers are obtained by the hypertrophy, or the transformation of the organs of generation, as florescence and fructification exhaust the vital powers of the being that performs these functions, so also it is possible that means may be found one day of

---

*The divine world of the Scandinavians; from *As* = god, and *gaard* = a place. The singular of *Ases* in old Norse is *As*, pl. *Aesir*; and in Gothic, *Ans*; in Saxon, *os* (*es*).—TR.

†He whose semen has gone up unto his head.—TR.

290 H.G. Wells. *The War of the Worlds.* Appendices

concentrating in the brain the entire power of the nervous system, and of transmuting all nerve-energy into brain-energy, by atrophying, if we may say so, the opposite pole. One of these functions is an enfeeblement of the other; what is given to the one is taken away from the other. It is unnecessary to say that we are not speaking of those shameful suppressions* that produce only imperfect beings. We are speaking of an inner transfusion by means of which the forces that Nature has directed towards various operations might be employed for one and the same object.

We may imagine, then, (no doubt, beyond the limits of our planet), the possibility of beings who might be almost as superior to man as man is to the lower animals; a time when science would supersede existing animals by higher organisms, just as we see that by chemistry whole series of natural products have been supplanted by far more perfect ones. As humanity issued from animality, so from humanity would issue divinity. There might exist beings who would employ man as he now employs the lower animals. Man hardly pauses at the thought that a single step, a movement of his, crushes myriads of animalcules. But, I repeat, intellectual superiority carries with it religious superiority; these future masters we must conceive of as incarnations of the good and the true; there would be joy in being subject to them.

The principle most strongly denied by the democratic school is the inequality of races and the legitimacy of the rights derived from superiority of race. Far from seeking to exalt the race, democracy tends to lower it; she would have no great men; and if there were a democrat present, and he heard us dwelling on the improved means of creating masters for other men he would be a little surprised. It is absurd and unjust, in fact, to impose upon men, by a sort of divine right, masters who are in no respect superior to them. The aristocracy of the present day in France is insignificant enough, since the titles of nobility, of which three-fourths are usurped, and of which the remaining fourth, with hardly ten exceptions, is derived from royal grants and not from conquest, no longer correspond, as at their institution, to a superiority of race. But this superiority of race might again become real; and then the fact of nobility would be as scientifically true, and as undeniable, as the pre-eminence of civilised man over the savage, or of man in general over the lower animals.

Thus we can imagine a time when all that formerly held sway in the form of prejudice and groundless opinion may hold sway as genuine

---

*Probably castration is meant.—Tr.

and true: gods, heaven, hell, spiritual power, monarchy, nobility, legitimacy, superiority of race, supernatural powers, may all be revived by virtue of the existence of man and of reason. Should such a solution ever be in any measure realised on the face of the planet earth, it seems as though Germany would fulfil it.

EUDOXES.

Do you mean this as a eulogium or a criticism?

THEOCTISTES.

Take it whichever way you please. France always inclines to liberal and democratic solutions; that is her glory; the happiness of men and liberty is her ideal. If the final upshot of things is that individuals should enjoy in peace their little limited destiny (as it possibly may be, after all), liberal France will have been in the right; but she is not the country that will ever attain great harmony, or rather than great subordination of consciousness of which we speak. On the other hand, the government of the world by reason, should it ever come to pass, seems more suited to the genius of Germany, which shows little anxiety for the equality, or even the dignity, of individuals, and which aims before everything at increasing the intellectual powers of the race.

EUTHYPHRON.

You forget that in the age of the far-off avatars, Frenchmen, Sclavs, and Germans will have long ago ceased to exist, and that history will have altogether ceased to remember these mean provincial varieties.

THEOCTISTES.

My aim was merely to draft from existing humanity some outline of the great battles of the future.

EUDOXES.

But don't you think that the people, when they see their master growing up, will foresee the danger and be on their guard?

THEOCTISTES.

Assuredly. If the order of ideas that we are now tracing ever attain to any reality, there will arise persecutions against science, more particularly against physiology and chemistry, compared with which those of the Inquisition will seem mild. With a profound instinct the crowd of simple beings will detect their enemy. Science will again take refuge in hiding-places. A time may come when a work on chemistry will compromise its owner as much as a work on alchemy did in the Middle Ages. Probably the most dangerous moments in the life of a planet are those in which science begins at length to unmask its hopes. There may then arise fears and reactions destructive to the spirit. Thousands of humanities have perhaps foundered in this strait. But among them there will be one that will clear it; mind will triumph.

Necessity, moreover, is in this case the best of securities. Man cannot any longer do without science. In degraded epochs, as, for example, in the Middle Ages, medicine was the only stay of the rational spirit; because a patient desires at any cost to be cured, and no cure can be wrought without a measure of science. But at the present time, war, machinery, the industrial arts require science, so that even persons most opposed to the scientific spirit are obliged to learn Mathematics, Physics, and Chemistry. The supremacy of science is, on all hands, thrust even upon its enemies.

EUDOXES.

You hypothesis of the oligarchical triumph of the spirit conducts you only to a gloomy picture of things. Why not allow that the advent of a superior humanity may prove a benefit to all, and that this very superiority may consist in the advantages being distributed less than they are in our sad world, all men being then assimilated and deified into a single glorious type? But I wait impatiently to hear what conception you have of the monarchical future of the universe. That will be more comforting, I hope. I feel the need of a Heavenly Father to deliver me from your hell.

THEOCTISTES.

St. Paul has admirably said: ἵνα ἡ ὁ θεὸξ πάντα ἐυ πᾶσιν.* More than six hundred years before, Xenophanes had said still better: οὖλος ὁρᾷ, οὖλος δὲ νοεῖ, οὖλος δε τ' ἀκούει.† At the present time, such a formula is not realised; but the unitarian solution, in which the whole universe should minister to the perceptions, the sensations, and the enjoyments of a single being, cannot, considering the infinitude of time to come, be regarded as an impossibility. France, in the time of Louis

---

*"That God may be all in all."—I Cor. XV. 28.
†"He sees as the whole, thinks as the whole, hears as the whole."—TR. Fragm. Philos. Græc. i, p. 101 (Didot).

XIV. and Louis XV., presented the example of a whole country contributing to the production of a brilliant and complete life, namely, that of the King, all social functions being organised with a view to his glory and pleasures. We may imagine a state of the world in which everything might likewise culminate in a single conscious centre, in which the universe might be reduced to a single existence, in which the conception of personal monotheism might become a truth. An all-knowing and all-powerful being may be the last term of god-developing evolution, whether we conceive him as enjoying (*jouissant*) by all (all also enjoying by him), according to the dream of Christian mysticism, whether we conceive him as an individuality attaining paramount power; or whether we conceive him as the resultant of a thousand million of beings, as the harmony, the sum-total of the universe.

Thus the universe might be consummated in a single organised being, in whose infinity would be summed up at once myriads of myriads* of lives, those that are dead and those that are living. All animate nature would produce a central life, a grand hymn issuing from thousands of millions of voices, just as the animal springs from millions of organic cells, and the tree from millions of buds. A single consciousness would be the work of all, and all would participate in it; the universe would be an infinite polype, of which all the beings that have ever existed would be soldered together at their base, each living at once after its own life and the life of the whole.

Already we participate in the life of the universe (a life as yet very imperfect) through morality, science, and art. Religions are the epitomised and popular forms of this participation; in this their sacredness consists. But Nature aspires to a far closer and more intense communion, a communion which will attain its final term only when there shall arise a really perfect being. Such a being does not yet exist, since we have only three ways of verifying the existence of a being, namely, by seeing him, by hearing others speak of him, and by beholding his acts, and since by none of these three means is such a being as we are speaking of known; but we can conceive the possibility of a state in which, in the infinity of space, everything lives. At present, only a small quantity of matter is organised, and even that feebly organised; but we may conceive of an age in which all matter might be organised, in which thousands of suns united together might go to form a single being, feeling, enjoying, and imbibing, through its burning

---

*Literally, "*Decillion,*" according to the French notation, means a thousand, raised to the eleventh power.—Tʀ.

throat, a river of delights which might flow out of him in a stream of life. Such a living universe would present the two poles that every nervous structure presents, the pole, namely, which thinks, and the pole which enjoys. At present the universe thinks and enjoys through millions of individuals. Some day a gigantic mouth may taste with some relish the infinite; an ocean of intoxicating delight may flow into it; an inexhaustible discharge of life, conscious of neither rest nor fatigue, may gush forth into eternity. To coagulate this divine mass, the earth will, perhaps, have been taken and tempered like a clod, which we knead without thought of the ant or the worm that is concealed in it. What would you have?* We do the very same thing. It is Nature's sole care, at every step, to gain a superior end at the expense of inferior individualities. Does a general, the chief of a State, take account of the poor people whose lives he sacrifices?

A single being summing up the fruition (*jouissance*) of the universe, an infinite number of individuals joyful in contributing to it, no contradiction is involved here, save to our superficial individualism. The world is but a series of human sacrifices; their sting might be removed by joy and by resignation. Alexander's companions lived on Alexander, and enjoyed Alexander. There are certain states of society in which the lower classes enjoy the pleasures of their nobles, take delight in their princes, call them "our princes," and make their glory their own. The animals that contribute to the maintenance of the man of genius, or of the good man, would feel they ought to be satisfied, if they knew what service they are rendering. Everything depends on the aim and object; and if some day vivisection on a large scale became necessary in order to discover the profound secrets of animate Nature, I can imagine creatures coming crowned with flowers to offer themselves up in the ecstasy of voluntary martyrdom. The useless slaughter of a fly is a censurable act; he who is sacrificed for ideal purposes has no right to complain, and his fate with regard to the infinite (τῷ θεῷ), is an enviable one. So many others die without leaving a trace in the construction of the tower of infinity! The sacrifice of one living being to the egoism of another is monstrous; but the sacrifice of a living creature to an end desired by Nature is justifiable. Strictly speaking, the man of purely selfish aims commits an act of cannibalism in eating flesh; only the man that works, to the best of his might, for the good and the true, has the right to do this. The sacrifice in that case is made

---

*It is difficult to give an exact equivalent in English of the French phrase, "Que voulez-vous?" The nearest approach to it is "it is so."—TR.

to the ideal, and the victim has that which so many others have not, his small share in the work of eternity. In good old times, the immolation of an animal intended to be eaten was justly regarded as a religious action. Such slaughter committed under pressure of an absolute necessity should be disguised, it was thought, by garlands and some religious ceremony.

The majority have to think and live by proxy. The idea, which prevailed in the Middle Ages, of people praying for those who have no time to pray, is a very just one. The mass is devoted to labour; a few perform for them the high functions of life; this is humanity. The result of the obscure work of a thousand peasants, serfs of an abbey, was a Gothic chapel in the midst of a beautiful valley, shaded by tall poplars, to which pious people used to resort six or eight times a day to chant psalms to the Eternal. This constituted a rather noble way of doing worship, particularly when, among the ascetics, there were a St. Bernard, a Rupert de Tuy, and an abbot Joachim. That valley, those rivers, those trees, those rocks would fain call upon God, but they were voiceless; the abbey gave them a tongue. Among the Greeks, a nobler race, this was done better by means of the flute and the sports of shepherds. Some day this will be done better still when a laboratory of chemistry or of physics shall supersede the abbey. But in our days the thousand rustics that were formerly serfs, being now emancipated, give themselves up, as is like, to a coarse merrymaking, without any ideal result whatever, on the lands of the aforesaid abbey. The tax imposed on these lands alone purifies them a little by making them contribute to a higher purpose.

There are some who live for all. Were this rule changed, nobody would live. The Egyptian, a subject of Chéphrem, who died building the pyramids, spent a better life than he that spends his useless days under his palm trees. Herein consists the dignity of the people; they desire no other; they will never be satisfied with egoism. Their wish is that, if they themselves do not reap enjoyment, there should be others who do. They are ready to die for the glory of a chief, that is to say, for something from which they themselves do not derive any direct advantage. I am speaking of the true people, the unreflective mass given up to the instincts of race, whom reflection has not yet taught that the greatest folly that can be committed is to submit to be slain for anything whatever.

Thus, I sometimes conceive of God as the great inner festival of the universe, as the vast consciousness in which everything is reflected and echoed back. Each class of society forms, as it were, a system of wheels, an arm of the lever, in this vast machine. This is why each class has its own virtues. We are all functions of the universe; duty consists in each one of us acting his part well. The virtues of the plebeian ought not to be those of the noble; that which constitutes a perfect nobleman would be a blemish in a humble commoner. The virtues of each are determined by the requirements of Nature; the State in which there are no social classes is in the teeth of Providence. It signifies little that St. Vincent de Paul was not a great genius. Raphaël would have gained nothing by being well-ordered in his manners. The divine energy, which is in all, is brought forth by upright men, scholars, and artists. Each one has his part to play. The duty of Goethe was to be an egoist with reference to his work. The transcendent immorality of the artist is in its own way a supreme morality, if it helps towards the accomplishment of the particular divine mission with which each one is entrusted here below.

For myself I enjoy a taste of the whole universe by that kind of general sentiment which makes us feel sad in a sad town and merry in a merry one. I thus share the pleasures of the voluptuous, the debaucheries of the debauchee, the worldly-mindedness of the worldly, the sanctity of the virtuous man, the meditations of the scholar, and the austerity of the ascetic. By a sort of sweet sympathy I imagine myself as their consciousness. The discoveries of the scholar are my property; the triumphs of the ambitious are a festive season to me. I should feel grieved if the world were to suffer any want; for I have the consciousness of all that is in it. My only grief is that the present age is so debased that it no longer knows how to enjoy. I therefore take refuge in the past, in the sixteenth and seventeenth centuries, and in antiquity; all that has been of beautiful, of courteous, of true, and of noble, is like a paradise to me. With this idea I defy any misfortune to reach me; I carry with me the enchanting garden of my varied thoughts.

Appendix VI
Excerpt from *Mars,*
by Percival Lowell (1896)

What could be more basic to *Worlds* than Lowellian Mars? The conclusion (pages 201–212) to his bestseller is here reprinted as a reminder that contemporary readers of *Worlds* had to have had that sensational work in mind. They were prepared to see not "men in trousers" but something else, if Martians were to take up missionary work as Christians then did in darkest Africa.

CONCLUSION

To REVIEW, now, the chain of reasoning by which we have been led to regard it probable that upon the surface of Mars we see the effects of local intelligence. We find, in the first place, that the broad physical conditions of the planet are not antagonistic to some form of life; secondly, that there is an apparent dearth of water upon the planet's surface, and therefore, if beings of sufficient intelligence inhabited it, they would have to resort to irrigation to support life; thirdly, that there turns out to be a network of markings covering the disk precisely counterparting what a system of irrigation would look like; and, lastly, that there is a set of spots placed where we should expect to find the lands thus artificially fertilized, and behaving as such constructed oases should. All this, of course, may be a set of coincidences, signifying nothing; but the probability points the other way. As to details of explanation, any we may adopt will undoubtedly be found, on closer acquaintance, to vary from the actual Martian state of things; for any Martian life must differ markedly from our own.

The fundamental fact in the matter is the dearth of water. If we keep this in mind, we shall see that many of the objections that spontaneously arise answer themselves. The supposed herculean task of constructing such canals disappears at once; for, if the canals be dug for irrigation purposes, it is evident that what we see, and call by ellipsis the canal, is not really the canal at all, but the strip of fertilized land bordering it,—the thread of water in the midst of it, the canal itself, being far too small to be perceptible. In the case of an irrigation canal seen at a distance, it is always the strip of verdure, not the canal, that is visible, as we see in looking from afar upon irrigated country on the Earth.

We may, perhaps, in conclusion, consider for a moment how different in its details existence on Mars must be from existence on the Earth. One point out of many bearing on the subject, the simplest and most certain of all, is the effect of mere size of habitat upon the size of the inhabitant; for geometrical conditions alone are most potent factors in the problem of life. Volume and mass determine the force of gravity upon the surface of a planet, and this is more far-reaching in its effects than might at first be thought. Gravity on the surface of Mars is only a little more than one third what it is on the surface of the Earth. This would work in two ways to very different conditions of existence from those to which we are accustomed. To begin with, three times as much work, as for example, in digging a canal, could be done by the same expenditure of muscular force. If we were transported to Mars, we should be pleasingly surprised to find all our manual labor suddenly lightened threefold. But, indirectly, there might result a yet greater gain to our capabilities; for if Nature chose she could afford there to build her inhabitants on three times the scale she does on Earth without their ever finding it out except by interplanetary comparison. Let us see how.

As we all know, a large man is more unwieldly than a small one. An elephant refuses to hop like a flea; not because he considers the act undignified, but simply because he cannot bring it about. If we could, we should all jump straight across the street, instead of painfully paddling through the mud. Our inability to do so depends upon the size of the Earth, not upon what it at first seems to depend, on the size of the street.

To see this, let us consider the very simplest case, that of standing erect. To this every-day feat opposes itself the weight of the body simply, a thing of three dimensions, height, breadth, and thickness, while the ability to accomplish it resides in the cross-section of the muscles of the knee, a thing of only two dimensions, breadth and thickness. Consequently, a person half as large again as another has bout twice the supporting capacity of that other, but about three times as much to support. Standing therefore tires him out more quickly. If his size were to go on increasing, he would at last reach a stature at which he would no longer be able to stand at all, but would have to lie down. You shall see the same effect in quite inanimate objects. Take two cylinders of paraffine wax, one made into an ordinary candle, the other into a gigantic facsimile of one, and then stand both upon their bases. To the small one nothing happens. The big one, however, begins to settle, the base actually made viscous by the pressure of the weight above.

Now apply this principle to a possible inhabitant of Mars, and suppose him to be constructed three times as large as a human being in every dimension. If he were on Earth, he would weigh twenty-seven times as much, but on the surface of Mars, since gravity there is only about one third of what it is here, he would weigh but nine times as much. The cross-section of his muscles would be nine times as great. Therefore the ratio of his supporting power to the weight he must support would be the same as ours. Consequently, he would be able to stand with as little fatigue as we. Now consider the work he might be able to do. His muscles, having length, breadth, and thickness, would all be twenty-seven times as effective as ours. He would prove twenty-seven times as strong as we, and could accomplish twenty-seven times as much. But he would further work upon what required, owing to decreased gravity, but one third the effort to overcome. His effective force, therefore, would be eighty-one times as great as man's, whether in digging canals or in other bodily occupation. As gravity on the surface of Mars is really a little more than one third that at the surface of the Earth, the true ratio is not eighty-one, but about fifty; that is, a Martian would be, physically, fifty-fold more efficient than man.

As the reader will observe, there is nothing problematical about this deduction whatever. It expresses an abstract ratio of physical capabilities which must exist between the two planets, quite irrespective of whether there be denizens on either, or how other conditions may further affect their forms. As the reader must also note, the deduction refers to the possibility, not to the probability, of such giants; the calculation being introduced simply to show how different from us any Martians may be, not how different they are.

It must also be remembered that the question of their size has nothing to do with the question of their existence. The arguments for their presence are quite apart from any consideration of avoirdupois. No

Herculean labors need to be accounted for; and, if they did, brain is far more potent to the task than brawn. Something more we may deduce about the characteristics of possible Martians, dependent upon Mars itself, a result of the age of the world they would live in.

A planet may in a very real sense be said to have life of its own, of which what we call life may or may not be a subsequent detail. It is born, has its fiery youth, sobers into middle age, and just before this happens brings forth, if it be going to do so at all, the creatures on its surface which are, in a sense, its offspring. The speed with which it runs through its gamut of change prior to production depends upon its size; for the smaller the body the quicker it cools, and with it loss of heat means beginning of life for its offspring. It cools quicker because, as we saw in a previous chapter, it has relatively less inside for its outside, and it is through its outside that its inside cools. After it has thus become capable of bearing life, the Sun quickens that life and supports it for we know not how long. But its duration is measured at the most by the Sun's life. Now, inasmuch as time and space are not, as some philosophers have from their too mundane standpoint supposed, forms of our intellect, but essential attributes of the universe, the time taken by any process affects the character of the process itself, as does also the size of the body undergoing it. The changes brought about in a large planet by its cooling are not, therefore, the same as those brought about in a small one. Physically, chemically, and, to our present end, organically, the two results are quite diverse. So different, indeed, are they that unless the planet have at least a certain size it will never produce what we call life, meaning our particular chain of changes or closely allied forms of it, at all. As we saw in the case of atmosphere, it will lack even the premise to such conclusion.

Whatever the particular planet's line of development, however, in its own line, it proceeds to greater and greater degrees of evolution, till the process stops, dependent, probably, upon the Sun. The point of development attained is, as regards its capabilities, measured by the planet's own age, since the one follows upon the other.

Now, in the special case of Mars, we have before us the spectacle of a world relatively well on in years, a world much older than the Earth. To so much about his age Mars bears evidence on his face. He shows unmistakable signs of being old. Advancing planetary years have left their mark legible there. His continents are all smoothed down; his oceans have all dried up. *Teres atque rotundus,* he is a steady-going body now. If once he had a chaotic youth, it has long since passed away. Although called after the most turbulent of the gods, he is at the present time, whatever he may have been once, one of the most peaceable of the heavenly host. His name is a sad misnomer; indeed, the ancients seem to have been singularly unfortunate in their choice of planetary cognomens. With Mars so peaceful, Jupiter so young, and Venus bashfully draped in cloud, the planet's names accord but ill with their temperaments.

Mars being thus old himself, we know that evolution on his surface must be similarly advanced. This only informs us of its condition relative to the planet's capabilities. Of its actual state our data are not definite enough to furnish much deduction. But from the fact that our own development has been comparatively a recent thing, and that a long time would be needed to bring even Mars to his present geological condition, we may judge any life he may support to be not only relatively, but really older than our own.

From the little we can see, such appears to be the case. The evidence of handicraft, if such it be, points to a highly intelligent mind behind it. Irrigation, unscientifically conducted, would not give us such truly wonderful mathematical fitness in the several parts to the whole as we there behold. A mind of no mean order would seem to have presided over the system we see,—a mind certainly of considerably more comprehensiveness than that which presides over the various departments of our own public works. Party politics, at all events, have had no part in them; for the system is planet wide. Quite possibly, such Martian folk are possessed of inventions of which we have not dreamed, and with them electrophones and kinetoscopes are things of a bygone past, preserved with veneration in museums as relics of the clumsy contrivances of the simple childhood of the race. Certainly what we see hints at the existence of beings who are in advance of, not behind us, in the journey of life.

Startling as the outcome of these observations may appear at first, in truth there is nothing startling about it whatever. Such possibility has been quite on the cards ever since the existence of Mars itself was recognized by the Chaldean shepherds, or whoever the still more primeval astronomers may have been. Its strangeness is a purely subjective phenomenon, arising from the instinctive reluctance of man to admit the possibility of peers. Such would be comic were it not the inevitable consequence of the constitution of the universe. To be shy of anything resembling himself is part and parcel of man's own individuality. Like the savage who fears nothing so much as a strange man, like Crusoe who grows pale at the sight of footprints not his own, the civilized thinker instinctively turns from the thought of mind other than the one he himself knows. To admit into his conception of the cosmos other finite minds as factors has in it something of the weird. Any hypothesis to explain the facts, no matter how improbable or even palpably absurd it be, is better than this. Snow-caps of solid carbonic acid gas, a planet cracked in a positively mono-maniacal manner, meteors ploughing tracks across its surface with such mathematical precision that they must have been educated to the performance, and so forth and so on, in hypotheses each more astounding than its predecessor, commend themselves to man, if only by such means he may escape the admission of anything approaching his kind. Surely all this is puerile, and should as speedily as possible be outgrown. It is simply an instinct like any other, the projection of the instinct of self-preservation. We ought, therefore, to rise above it, and, where probability points to other things, boldly accept the fact provisionally, as we should the presence of oxygen, or iron, or anything else. Let us not cheat ourselves with words. Conservatism sounds finely, and covers any amount of ignorance and fear.

We must be just as careful not to run to the other extreme, and draw deductions of purely local outgrowth. To talk of Martian beings is not to mean Martian men. Just as the probabilities point to the one, so do they point away from the other. Even on this Earth man is of the nature of an accident. He is the survival of by no means the highest physical organism. He is not even a high form of mammal. Mind has been his making. For aught we can see, some lizard or batrachian might just as well have popped into his place early in the race, and been now the dominant creature of this Earth. Under different physical conditions, he would have been certain to do so. Amid the surroundings that exist on Mars, surroundings so different from our own, we may be practically sure other organisms have been evolved of which we have no cognizance. What manner of beings they may be we lack the data even to conceive.

For answers to such problems we must look to the future. That Mars seems to be inhabited is not the last, but the first word on the subject. More important than the mere fact of the existence of living beings there, is the question of what they may be like. Whether we ourselves shall live to learn this cannot, of course, be foretold. One thing, however, we can do, and that speedily: look at things from a standpoint raised above our local point of view; free our minds at least from the shackles that of necessity tether our bodies; recognize the possibility of others in the same light that we do the certainty of ourselves. That

we are the sum and substance of the capabilities of the cosmos is something so preposterous as to be exquisitely comic. We pride ourselves
upon being men of the world, forgetting that this is but objectionable
singularity, unless we are, in some wise, men of more worlds than one.
For, after all, we are but a link in a chain. Man is merely this earth's
highest production up to date. That he in any sense gauges the possibilities of the universe is humorous. He does not, as we can easily foresee, even gauge those of this planet. He has been steadily bettering
from an immemorial past, and will apparently continue to improve
through an incalculable future. Still less does he gauge the universe
about him. He merely typifies in an imperfect way what is going on
elsewhere, and what, to a mathematical certainty, is in some corners
of the cosmos indefinitely excelled.

If astronomy teaches anything, it teaches that man is but a detail in
the evolution of the universe, and that resemblant though diverse
details are inevitably to be expected in the host of orbs around him.
He learns that, though he will probably never find his double anywhere, he is destined to discover any number of cousins scattered
through space.

Bibliography

Adams, Frank Dawson
    1938   *The Birth and Development of the Geological Sciences.* Baltimore: William & Wilkins.

Akin, William E.
    1977   *Technocracy and the American Dream: The Technocratic Movement, 1900–1941.* Berkeley: University of California Press.

Amis, Kingsley
    1961   *New Maps of Hell: A Survey of Science Fiction.* London: Victor Gollancz.

Arno Press
    1974   *Utopian Literature.* 12 page brochure describing 41 titles under Arthur Orentt Lewis, Jr., Advisory Editor. New York: Arno Press, a New York Times company.

Asimov, Isaac, ed.
    1972   *Asimov's Biographical Encyclopedia of Science and Technology,* revised edition. New York: Equinox Books.

Aylmer, G.E., ed.
    1975   *The Levellers in the English Revolution.* Ithaca, N.Y.: Cornell University Press.

Barry, Iris.
    1965   *D.W. Griffith: American Film Master.* Garden City, N.Y.: Doubleday. Reissue of the original 1940 edition for the Museum of Modern Art.

Beard, Charles
    1929   *Whither Mankind.* New York: Longmans, Green.

Beckson, Karl
    1992   *London in the 1890s: A Cultural History.* New York: W.W. Norton.

Bergonzi, Bernard
    1961   *The Early H.G. Wells: A Study of the Scientific Romances.* Manchester: Manchester University Press.
    1971   "H.G. Wells." In George A. Panichas, ed., *The Politics of Twentieth-Century Novelists.* New York: Hawthorn Books, 1971, pp. 3–14.

Bethell, Tom
    1998   *The Noblest Triumph: Property and Prosperity Through the Ages.* New York:
              St. Martins.

Bleuel, James Peter
    1974   *Sex and Society in Nazi Germany.* Translated by Maxwell Brownjohn. New
              York: Bantam Books.
              Strength Through Joy in the London edition, Secker & Warburg, 1973.

Brewer, E. Cobham
    1894   *The Dictionary of Phrase and Fable.* London: W.H. Smith.

Buchanan, Robert
    1891   *The Coming Terror.* London: William Heinemann.

Butler, E.M.
    1926   *The Saint-Simonian Religion in Germany: A Study of the Young German
              Movement.* Cambridge, England: Cambridge University Press.

Carlyle, Thomas
    1838   *Sartor Resartus.* People's edition. London: Chapman & Hall, 1871.

Carson, Clarence B.
    1990   *Basic Communism: Its Rise, Spread and Debacle in the 20th Century.*
              Wadley, Ala.: American Textbook Committee.

Chadbourne, Richard M.
    1968   *Ernest Renan.* New York: Twayne.

Chamberlin, William Henry
    1936   *Collectivism: A False Utopia.* New York: Macmillan.

Cheyette, Brian
    1991   "Beyond Rationality: H.G. Wells and the Jewish Question." *The Wellsian,*
              n.s. 14 (Summer):41–64.

Clarke, I.F.
    1992   *Voices Prophesying War.* Second edition. Oxford: Oxford University Press.

Clarke, I.F., ed.
    1995   *The Tale of the Next Great War, 1871–1914: Fictions of Future Warfare and
              of Battles Still-to-Come.* Syracuse, N.Y.: Syracuse University Press.

Clute, John, and Peter Nicholls, eds.
    1995   *The Encyclopedia of Science Fiction.* New York: St. Martin's.

Cole, Margaret
    1961   *The Story of Fabian Socialism.* Stanford, Calif.: Stanford University Press.

Coleman, William
    1982   *Death Is a Social Disease: Public Health and Political Economy in Early
              Industrial France.* Madison: University of Wisconsin.

Comte, Auguste
  1877   *System of Positive Polity, or, Treatise on Sociology, Instituting the Religion of Humanity*. Translated from the French. 4 vols. London: Chapman.

Corso, Philip J., with William J. Birnes
  1997   *The Day After Roswell*. New York: Pocket Books.

Dark, Sidney
  1922   *The Outline of H.G. Wells*. London: Leonard Parsons.

Darwin, Sir George Howard
  1911   *The Tides and Kindred Phenomena in the Solar System*, 3rd edition. London: John Murray.

Djilas, Milovan
  1957   *The New Class: An Analysis of the Communist System*. New York: Praeger.

Dunkling, Leslie, and Gordon Wright
  1987   *A Dictionary of Pub Names*. London: Routledge & Kegan Paul.

Durkheim, Emile
  1958   *Socialism and Saint-Simon*. Translated by Charlotte Sattler from an unfinished book of 1895. Yellow Springs, Ohio: Antioch Press.

Eshleman, Lloyd
  1940   *A Victorian Rebel: The Life of William Morris*. New York: Scribner's.

Evans, Ivor H.
  1994   *The Wordsworth Dictionary of Phrase and Fable*. Based on Brewer 1894. Ware, England: Wordsworth Reference.

Faulkner, Peter, ed.
  1973   *William Morris: The Critical Heritage*. London: Routledge & Kegan Paul.

Flammarion, Camille
  1894   *Popular Astronomy: A General Description of the Heavens*. Translated by J. Ellard Gore. New York: D. Appleton.

Frakes, Jonathan, narrator
  1995   *Alien Autopsy: Fact or Fiction?* Vidmark Productions, Ltd.

Frayling, Christopher, ed.
  1991   *Vampyres: Lord Byron to Count Dracula*. London: Faber & Faber.

Funderbuck, Charles, and Robert G. Thobaben
  1994   *Political Ideologies*. Second edition. New York: HarperCollins.

Galton, Francis
  1896   "Intelligible Signals Between Neighboring Stars." *The Fortnightly Review* 60:657–664.

Gascoigne, Bamber
  1993   *Encyclopedia of Britain*. New York: Macmillan.

Gibbons, Tom
    1984   "H.G. Wells's Fire Sermon: *The War of the Worlds* and the Book of Reve-
             lation." *Science Fiction: A Review of Speculative Literature* 6:5–14.

Gleason, Abbott
    1995   *Totalitarianism: The Inner History of the Cold War.* New York: Oxford
             University Press.

Goldsmith, Donald
    1998   *The Hunt for Life on Mars.* New York: Plume Books.

Goodman, Elliot R.
    1960   *The Soviet Design for a World State.* New York: Columbia University
             Press.

Gray, Alexander
    1946   *The Socialist Tradition.* London: Longmans, Green.

Greg, Percy
    1880   *Across the Zodiac: The Story of a Wrecked Record.* Two volumes. London:
             Trübner.

Gregg, Pauline
    1967   *Modern Britain: A Social and Economic History.* Fifth edition, revised.
             New York: Pegasus.

Grun, Bernard, ed.
    1982   *The Timetables of History.* New York: Simon and Schuster.

Hammond, J.R.
    1977   *Herbert George Wells: An Annotated Bibliography of His Works.* New York
             & London: Garland Publishing Co.

Hardach, Gerd, Dieter Karras, and Ben Fine
    1979   *A Short History of Socialist Economic Thought.* Translated by James Wick-
             ham. New York: St. Martin's Press.

Harrison, Fraser, ed.
    1983   *The Yellow Book: An Anthology.* Woodbridge, Suffolk, England: Boydell
             Press. Reprint of the original 1914 edition.

Hayek, F.A.
    1979   *The Counter-Revolution of Science: Studies on the Abuse of Reason.* Second
             edition. Indianapolis: Liberty Press.

Hayek, F.A., ed.
    1935   *Collectivist Economic Planning: Critical Studies on the Possibilities of Social-
             ism.* London: George Routledge & Sons.

Heffernan, William C.
    1981   "Percival Lowell and the Debate Over Extraterrestrial Life." *Journal of the
             History of Ideas* XLII (July–September):527–530.

Heller, Mikhail
    1988   *Cogs in the Wheel: The Formation of Soviet Man.* New York: Knopf.

Herman, Arthur
1997 *The Idea of Decline in Western History*. New York: Free Press.

Hetherington, Norriss S.
1981 "Percival Lowell: Professional Scientist or Interloper?" *Journal of the History of Ideas* XLII (January–March):159–161.

Horn, Charles F., ed.
1911 *Works of Jules Verne*. Fifteen volumes. New York: F. Tyler Daniels.

Howard, Michael
1961 *The Franco-Prussian War*. London: Routledge.

Hoyt, W.
1976 *Lowell and Mars*. Tucson: University of Arizona Press.

Hughes, David Yerkes
1962 *An Edition and a Survey of H.G. Wells's "The War of the Worlds."* Unpublished doctoral dissertation, University of Illinois, Urbana.

Hughes, David Y., and Harry M. Geduld, eds.
1993 *A Critical Edition of "The War of the Worlds": H.G. Wells's Scientific Romance*. Bloomington & Indianapolis: Indiana University Press.

Hughes, Thomas P.
1983 *Networks of Power: Electrification in Western Society, 1880–1930*. Baltimore: Johns Hopkins University Press.

Iggers, Georg G.
1958 *The Cult of Authority: The Political Philosophy of the Saint-Simonians: A Chapter in the Intellectual History of Totalitarianism*. The Hague: Martinus Nijhoff.

Iggers, Georg G., tr. & ed.
1958 *The Doctrine of Saint-Simon: "An Exposition," First Year, 1828–1829*. Boston: Beacon Hill.

Ionescu, Ghita, ed.
1976 *The Political Thought of Saint-Simon*. London: Oxford University Press.

Johnson, Paul
1983 *Modern Times: The World from the Twenties to the Eighties*. New York: Harper & Row.
1988 *Intellectuals*. New York: Harper & Row.

Jones, Carol
1989 "Coal, Gas, and Electricity." In Pope 1989:68–95.

Jordan, John M.
1994 *Machine-Age Ideology: Social Engineering and American Liberalism, 1911–1939*. Chapel Hill: University of North Carolina Press.

Koch, Howard, ed.
    1970   *The Panic Broadcast: Portrait of an Event*. Boston: Little, Brown.

Kornai, Janos
    1992   *The Socialist System: The Political Economy of Communism*. Princeton, N.J.:
            Princeton University Press.

Kornhauser, William
    1960   *The Politics of Mass Society*. London: Routledge and Kegan Paul.

Lake, David
    1988   "The Current Texts of Wells's Early SF Novels: Situation Unsatisfactory
            (Part I)." *The Wellsian*, n.s. 11 (summer):3–12.

Lankester, Sir Ray, ed.
    1918   *Natural Science and the Classical System in Education*. London: William
            Heinemann.

Lasswitz, Kurd
    1897   *Auf zwei Planeten*. Leipzig: Verlag B. Elischer Nachfolger. 1971: *Two Plan-*
    [1971]   *ets*, abridged translation by Hans H. Rudnick. Carbondale: Southern
            Illinois University Press.

Lenin, V.I.
    1917   *State and Revolution*, second revised edition. Moscow: Progress Publish-
            ers, 1965.

Levine, George
    1988   *Darwin and the Novelists: Patterns of Science in Victorian Fiction*. Chicago:
            University of Chicago Press.

Lewis, C.S.
    1945   *That Hideous Strength*. London: Bodley Head.
    1947   *The Abolition of Man*. New York: Macmillan.

Ley, Willy
    1945   *Rockets: The Future of Travel Beyond the Stratosphere*. New York: Viking.

Lipow, Arthur
    1982   *Authoritarian Socialism in America; Edward Bellamy and the Nationalist
            Movement*. Berkeley: University of California Press.

Lowell, Percival
    1895   *Mars*. London: Longmans, Green.
    1896   *Mars*. Boston: Houghton, Mifflin. American edition of Lowell 1895.
    1896a   *Mars and Its Canals*. New York: Macmillan.
    1908   *Mars as the Abode of Life*. New York: Macmillan.
    1909   *The Evolution of Worlds*. New York: Macmillan.

MacDonogh, Giles
    1994   *Prussia: The Perversion of an Idea*. London: Sinclair-Stevenson.

Manuel, Frank E.
1956   *The New World of Henri Saint-Simon.* Cambridge: Harvard University Press.

Mayne, Alan, ed.
1994   *"World Brain": H.G. Wells on the Future of World Education.* London: Adamantine Press. A partial reprint of Wells 1938 with critical apparatus.

Metchnikoff, Élie
1905   *The Nature of Man: Studies in Optimistic Philosophy.* Translated by Sir P. Chalmers Mitchell. London: Heinemann.

Morris, William
1890   *News from Nowhere: or an Epoch of Rest.* Serialized in *Commonweal*, London, 11 January–4 October. For a good reprint see Asa Briggs, ed., Penguin Classics, London, 1986.

Morton, Peter
1984   *The Vital Science: Biology and the Literary Imagination, 1860–1900.* London: George Allen & Unwin.

Morwood, James
1998   *A Dictionary of Latin Words and Phrases.* New York: Oxford University Press.

Myagkov, Aleksei
1976   *Inside the KGB.* New York: Ballantine Books.

Owen, Robert
1894   *The Book of the New Moral World.* London: The Home Colonization Society. Reprint, New York: Augustus M. Kelley, 1970.

Parrinder, Patrick
1977   *H.G. Wells.* New York: Putnam's.
1981   *H.G. Wells: "The War of the Worlds."* York Notes. London: Longman.
1988   "Stoverism Once More." Review of Stover 1998a and 1998b. *The Wellsian*, n.s. 21 (winter):56–59.

Parrinder, Patrick, and Robert Philmus, eds.
1980   *H.G. Wells's Literary Criticism.* Brighton, England: Harvester Press.

Philmus, Robert M., and David Y. Hughes, eds.
1975   *H.G. Wells: Early Writings in Science and Science Fiction.* Berkeley: University of California Press.

Pipes, Richard, ed.
1996   *The Unknown Lenin: From the Secret Archives.* New Haven, Conn.: Yale University Press.

Pope, Rey, ed.
1989   *Atlas of British Social and Economic History Since c. 1700.* New York: Macmillan.

Radel, J.-Lucien
  1975   *Roots of Totalitarianism: The Ideological Sources of Fascism, National Social-ism, and Communism.* New York: Crane, Russak.

Reed, John R.
  1979   "The Literary Piracy of H.G. Wells." *Journal of Modern Literature* 7:537–542.
  1982   *The Natural History of H.G. Wells.* Athens: Ohio University Press.

Renan, Ernest
  1883   *Philosophical Dialogues and Fragments.* Translated by Râs Bihâri Mukharjî. London: Trübner.
  1891   *The Future of Science: Ideas of 1848.* Translated by Albert D. Vandam and C.B. Pitman. London: Chapman and Hall.

Rossi, Jacques, tr.
  1989   *The Gulag Handbook: An Encyclopedic Dictionary of Soviet Penitentiary Institutions and Terms Related to Forced Labor Camps.* New York: Paragon House.

Russell, Alan K., ed.
  1978   *The Collector's Book of Science Fiction by H.G. Wells: From Rare, Original, Illustrated Magazines.* Secaucus, N.J.: Castle Books.

Salvadori, Massimo
  1975   *The Rise of Modern Communism.* Hinsdale, Ill: Dryden.

Schivelbusch, Wolfgang
  1988   *Disenchanted Night; The Industrialization of Light in the Nineteenth Cen-tury.* Translated by Angela Davies. Berkeley: University of California Press.

Schoenbaum, David
  1980   *Hitler's Social Revolution: Class and Status in Nazi Germany, 1933–1939.* New York: Norton.
Scott, Phil
  1995   *The Shoulders of Giants: A History of Human Flight to 1919.* Reading, Mass.: Addison-Wesley.

Sherborne, Michael
  1996   "Two Cheers for Stoverism." Reivew of Stover 1996a and 1996b. *The Wellsian,* n.s. 19 (winter):50–53.

Skidelsky, Robert
  1995   *The Road from Serfdom: The Economic and Political Consequences of the End of Communism.* London: Allen Lane.

Smith, David
  1986   *H.G. Wells: Desperately Mortal: A Biography.* New Haven, Conn.: Yale University Press.

Smith, David C., ed.
　　1998　　*The Correspondence of H.G. Wells.* 4 volumes. London: Pickering & Chatto.

Solzhenitsyn, Aleksandr I.
　　1974　　*The Gulag Archipelago*, volume 1. New York: Harper and Row.

Speake, Jennifer, ed.
　　1997　　*The Oxford Dictionary of Foreign Words and Phrases.* New York: Oxford University Press.

Spengler, Oswald
　　1926–1928　　*Decline of the West*, 2 volumes. Translated by Charles Francis Atkinson. New York: Knopf.

Stover, Leon
　　1987　　*The Prophetic Soul: A Reading of H.G. Wells's "Things to Come."* Jefferson, N.C.: McFarland.
　　1987a　　"H.G. Wells." *Contemporary Authors*, volume 121. Detroit: Gale Research, 432–445.
　　1992　　"Wells's Communist Revision, *Perestroika*, and the New World Order." *The Wellsian*, n.s. 15 (summer):25–34.
　　1996a　　*The Annotated H.G. Wells, 1: The Time Machine.* Jefferson, N.C.: McFarland.
　　1996b　　*The Annotated H.G. Wells, 2: The Island of Doctor Moreau.* Jefferson, N.C.: McFarland.
　　1996c　　"Jules Verne." In Jay P. Pederson, ed., *St. James Guide to Science Fiction Writers*, fourth edition. Detroit: 960–963.
　　1998a　　*The Annotated H.G. Wells, 3: The Invisible Man.* Jefferson, N.C.: McFarland.
　　1996b　　*The Annotated H.G. Wells, 6: The First Men in the Moon.* Jefferson, N.C.: McFarland.
　　2000　　*The Annotated H.G. Wells, 5: When the Sleeper Wakes.* Jefferson, N.C.: McFarland.

Talmon, J.L.
　　1960　　*Political Messianism.* New York: Praeger.
　　1967　　*Romanticism and Revolt: Europe 1815–1848.* New York: W.W. Norton.
　　1980　　*The Myth of the Nation and the Vision of Revolution.* London: Secker & Warburg.

Tauber, Alfred I., and Leon Chernyak
　　1991　　*Metchnikoff and the Origins of Immunology.* New York: Oxford University Press.

Taylor, Keith, ed.
　　1975　　*Henri Saint-Simon: Selected Writings on Science, Industry and Social Organisation.* New York: Homes and Meier.

Tucker, Robert C., ed.
　　1975　　*The Lenin Anthology.* New York: Norton.

United States Geological Survey
    1976   *Topographic Map of Mars*. Map I-961. Washington, D.C.: Department of
            the Interior.

Verne, Jules
    1865   *Trip to the Moon* [*De la Terre à la Lune*]. [*Autour de la Lune*, 1870]. Both
            in Horne 1911: volume 3. Combined in Verne 1873, from which fig. 7
            is taken.
    1872   *Twenty Thousand Leagues Under the Sea*. London: Sampson Low. Standard
            English translation by Lewis Mercier (very badly done) of *Vingt Mille
            Lieues sous les Mers*, 1870.
    1873   *From the Earth to the Moon and a Journey Around It*. London: Sampson
            Low.
    1896   *The Floating Island*. London: Sampson Low. Translated by W.J. Gordon
            from *L'Ile à helice*, 1895.

Welles, Orson, ed.
    1949   *Invasion from Mars: Interplanetary Stories*. New York: Dell.

West, Geoffry
    1930   *H.G. Wells*. New York: W.W. Norton.

West, Shearer
    1994   *Fin de Siècle: Art and Society in an Age of Uncertainty*. Woodstock, N.Y.:
            Overlook Press.

Williams, Raymond
    1983   *Key Words: A Vocabulary of Culture and Society*. Revised edition. New
            York: Oxford University Press.

H.G. Wells

1886   "Democratic Socialism." Abstract of the Proceedings of the Normal School of
        Science & Royal School of Mines Debating Society (8 October). *Science
        Schools Journal* 1 (December):23–25.
1891   "Zoological Retrogression." *Gentleman's Magazine* 271 (September):246–253.
1892   "Ancient Experiments in Co-Operation." *Gentleman's Magazine* 273 (October):
        418–422.
1893   "The Man of the Year Million." *Pall Mall Gazette* 57 (6 November):3. Reprinted
        as "Of a Book Unwritten" in 1898b:161–171.
1894   "In the Avu Observatory." *Pall Mall Budget*, 9 August.
1894a   "Another Basis of Life." *Saturday Review* 78 (22 December):676–677.
1894b   "The 'Cyclic' Delusion." *Saturday Review* (10 November): 505–506.
1895   *The Time Machine*. London: William Heinemann.
1895a   "The Newly Discovered Element." *Saturday Review* (9 February):183–184.
1896   *The Island of Doctor Moreau*. London: William Heinemann.
1896a   "Intelligence on Mars." *Saturday Review* (4 April):345–346.
1896b   "Human Evolution, an Artificial Process." *Fortnightly Review*, n.s. 60 (Octo-
        ber): 590–595.
1896c   "The Sea Raiders." *Weekly Sun Literary Supplement* (6 December). In 1927a:
        471–482.

1897   *The Invisible Man.* New York and London: Edward Arnold.

1897a   "The Star." *Graphic,* Christmas number.

1897b   "Morals and Civilisation." *Fortnightly Review,* n.s.61 (February): 263–268. Reprinted in Stover 1996b as Appendix V:252–264.

1897c   "The War of the Worlds." *Cosmopolitan* XXII:6 (April)–XXIV:2 (December).

1897d   "The Last Quest." Review of Richard Le Gallienne, *The Quest of the Golden Girl. Saturday Review* 83 (6 March):244–50. In Parrinder and Philmus 1980: 124–127.

1898   *The War of the Worlds.* London: William Heinemann.

1898a   *The War of the Worlds.* New York: Harper & Brothers.

1898b   *Certain Personal Matters.* London: Lawrence & Bullen.

1899   *When the Sleeper Wakes.* New York and London: Harper & Brothers.

1899a   "What I Believe: A Chat with Mr. H.G. Wells." Interview by George Lynch. *The Puritan: An Illustrated Magazine for Free Churchmen,* volumes I & II (February–December):218–220.

1901 [1902]   *Anticipations of the Reaction of Mechanical and Scientific Progress Upon Human Life and Thought.* New York: Harper & Brothers. The date is actually 1902, but in deference to Wells who backdated the book to its 1901 serialization, the better to gain a year on his foresightedness, the earlier year has been accepted by nearly all critics and biographers. Were I to break with this hallowed precedent, I would be accused of getting the date wrong!

1901a   *The First Men in the Moon.* London: George Newnes.

1903   "The Philosophy of a Bacteriologist," Review of Metchnikoff 1903. *The Speaker,* n.s. 9 (1 October 1903–March 1904):112–114.

1903a   "The Land Ironclads." *Strand Magazine* (December). In 1927a:131–157.

1904   *Mankind in the Making.* New York: Scribner's.

1904a   "An Age of Specialisation," in *The Daily Mail,* 20 April.

1905   *A Modern Utopia.* London: Chapman & Hall.

1906   *The Future in America: A Search After Realities.* London: Chapman & Hall.

1906a   *In the Days of the Comet.* London: Macmillan.

1908   *New Worlds for Old.* London: Archibald Constable.

1908a   "The Things That Live on Mars." *Cosmopolitan Magazine* XLIV 14 (March). Reprinted in Hughes and Geduld 1993 as Appendix V.

1908b .   *The War in the Air.* London: George Bell.

1908c   *First and Last Things.* New York: Putnam's.

1909   *Tono-Bungay.* London: Macmillan.

1909a   "Of a Cross Channel Passage." *Daily Mail* 27 July. Reprinted as "The Coming of Blériot" in 1914:1–8.

1909b   *Ann Veronica: A Modern Love Story.* London: T. Fisher Unqin.

1910   *The History of Mr. Polly.* London: Thomas Nelson.

1911   *The New Machiavelli.* London: John Lane.

1912   *Socialism and the Great State.* New York: Harper & Brothers.

1912a   "The Past and the Great State." In 1912:3–44.

1912b   *The Labour Unrest.* London: *Daily Mail.* Reprinted without crossheadings in 1914:50–93.

1913   *Little Wars: A Game for Boys from Twelve Years of Age to One Hundred and Fifty and for That More Intelligent Sort of Girls Who Like Boys' Games.* London: Frank Palmer.

1914   *Social Forces in England and America.* New York: Harper & Brothers.

1914a   *The World Set Free.* London: Macmillan.

(H.G. Wells, *continued*)

1914b   Introduction to *Anticipations* (1901), second edition. London: Chapman & Hall, pp. vii–xiii.
1914c   *The War That Will End War.* New York: Duffield.
1915   *Boon, the Mind of the Race.* London: T. Fisher Unwin.
1916   *The Elements of Reconstruction.* London: Nisbet.
1916a   *What Is Coming? A European Forecast.* New York: Macmillan. Subtitle of the London edition (Cassell) is *A Forecast of Things After the War.*
1917   *God the Invisible King.* New York: Macmillan.
1917a   *War in the Future: Italy, France and Britain at War.* London: Cassell.
1917b   "A Modern Education." In Lankester 1918:196–268.
1918   *Joan and Peter: The Story of an Education.* New York: Macmillan.
1919   *The Undying Fire.* London: Cassell.
1920   *The Outline of History.* London: Cassell.
1920a   "An Experiment in Illustration." *Strand* magazine.
1921   *The Salvaging of Civilization.* New York: Macmillan.
1922   *A Short History of the World.* New York: Macmillan.
1922a   *Washington and the Hope of Peace.* London: W. Collins Sons.
1922b   *Secret Places of the Heart.* New York: Macmillan.
1923   *Men Like Gods.* New York: Macmillan.
1924–1927   *The Atlantic Edition of the Works of H.G. Wells.* 28 volumes. London: Unwin/New York: Scribner's.
1925   *A Year of Prophesying.* New York: Macmillan.
1925a   *Christina Alberta's Father.* London: Jonathan Cape.
1926   *The World of William Clissold.* 2 volumes. New York: George H. Doran. Three volumes in the London edition published by Ernest Benn.
1926a   *Mr. Belloc Objects to "The Outline of History."* New York: George H. Doran.
1926–1927   *The Essex Collected Thin Paper Edition of the Works of H.G. Wells.* 24 volumes. London: Ernest Benn.
1927   *Democracy Under Revision.* New York: George H. Doran.
1927a   *The Short Stories of H.G. Wells.* London: Ernest Benn.
1928   *The Open Conspiracy: Blue Prints for a World Revolution.* London: Victor Gollancz.
1928a   "Has the Money-Credit System a Mind?" *The Banker* 6:221–233.
1928b   *Mr. Blettsworthy on Rampole Island.* Garden City, N.Y.: Doubleday, Doran
1928c   *The Way the World Is Going: Guesses & Forecasts of the Years Ahead.* London: Ernest Benn.
1929   *The King Who Was a King: An Unconventional Novel.* Garden City, N.Y.: Doubleday, Doran.
1930   *The Autocracy of Mr. Parham: His Remarkable Adventures in the Changing World.* Garden City, N.Y.: Doubleday, Doran.
1930a   *The Way to World Peace.* London: Ernest Benn.
1931   *What Are We to Do with Our Lives?* Garden City, N.Y.: Doubleday, Doran.
1931a   *The Work, Wealth, and Happiness of Mankind.* 2 volumes. Garden City, N.Y.: Doubleday, Doran
1931b   *The Science of Life: A Summary of Contemporary Knowledge About Life and Its Possibilities.* With Julian Huxley and G.P. Wells, 4 volumes. Garden City, N.Y.: Doubleday, Doran.
1932   *After Democracy: Forecasts of the World State.* London: Watts.
1932a   *The Bulpington of Blup.* London: Hutchinson.

(H.G. Wells, *continued*)

1933 *The Shape of Things to Come.* New York: Macmillan.

1933a *The Scientific Romances of H.G. Wells.* London: Victor Gollancz.

1933b *The Shape of Things to Come; The Ultimate Revolution.* London: Hutchinson.

1934 *Experiment in Autobiography.* New York: Macmillan.

1934a *Whither Mankind?* Film treatment of *Things to Come.* In Stover 1987a, Appendix I, pp. 121–179.

1935 *Things to Come: A Film Story Based on the Material Contained in His History of the Future "The Shape of Things to Come."* London: Cresset. Novelized version of Wells 1936 in advance of the film's release.

1936 *Things to Come.* Release script of the London Films Production in Stover 1987a, Appendix II.

1936a *The Anatomy of Frustration.* London: Cresset Press.

1937 *Star-Begotten.* New York: Viking.

1937a *The Camford Visitation.* London: Methuen.

1938 *World Brain.* Garden City, N.Y.: Doubleday, Doran.

1938a *The Brothers.* New York: Viking.

1938b *Apropos of Dolores.* New York: Scribners.

1939 *The Holy Terror.* New York: Simon & Schuster.

1939a "The World of Tomorrow." *New York Times*, World's Fair edition, 5 March: 5.

1939b *The Fate of Man.* New York: Alliance.

1940 *The Common Sense of War and Peace: World Revolution or War Unending?* London: Penguin Books.

1940a *The New World Order.* New York: Alfred A. Knopf.

1940b *Babes in the Darkling Wood.* New York: Alliance.

1941 *All Aboard for Ararat.* New York: Alliance.

1942 *The Conquest of Time.* London: Watts.

1942a *Phoenix: A Summary of the Inescapable Conditions of World Reorganization.* London: Secker & Warburg.

1944 *'42 to '44: A Contemporary Memoir Upon Human Behavior During the Crisis of the World Revolution.* London: Secker & Warburg.

1984 *H.G. Wells in Love: Postscript to "An Experiment in Autobiography,"* edited by G.P. Wells. London: Faber & Faber.

Index